AI Bots in Applied Linguistics:

Practice, Policy, and Creativity

Alexia Larchen Costuchen
https://orcid.org/0000-0001-8260-4059
Universitat Politècnica de València, Spain

Fahad Ahmed Otaif
https://orcid.org/0000-0001-9832-4289
King Khalid University, Saudi Arabia

IGI Global
Scientific Publishing
Publishing Tomorrow's Research Today

Vice President of Editorial Melissa Wagner
Director of Acquisitions Mikaela Felty
Director of Book Development Jocelynn Hessler
Production Manager Mike Brehm
Cover Design Jose Rosado

Published in the United States of America by
IGI Global Scientific Publishing
701 East Chocolate Avenue
Hershey, PA, 17033, USA
Tel: 717-533-8845 | Fax: 717-533-7115
Website: https://www.igi-global.com E-mail: cust@igi-global.com

Library of Congress Cataloging-in-Publication Data

Names: Larchen Costuchen, Alexia, DATE- editor | Otaif, Fahad Ahmed, DATE- editor
Title: AI bots in applied linguistics : practice, policy, and creativity / edited by: Alexia Larchen Costuchen, Fahad Ahmed Otaif.
Description: Hershey PA : IGI Global Scientific Publishing, [2026] | Includes bibliographical references. | Summary: "This book examines the transformative role of AI bots in applied linguistics, exploring their impact on language learning, research, policy, and creative practice. It highlights how intelligent tools are reshaping communication, pedagogy, and linguistic innovation in the digital age"-- Provided by publisher.
Identifiers: LCCN 2025054884 (print) | LCCN 2025054885 (ebook) | ISBN 9798337364209 hardcover | ISBN 9798337364216 paperback | ISBN 9798337364223 ebook
Subjects: LCSH: Computational linguistics | Chatbots | Language and languages--Computer-assisted instruction | Artificial intelligence--Educational applications
Classification: LCC P98 .A375 2026 (print) | LCC P98 (ebook)
LC record available at https://lccn.loc.gov/2025054884
LC ebook record available at https://lccn.loc.gov/2025054885

British Cataloguing in Publication Data
A Cataloguing in Publication record for this book is available from the British Library.

*To the **linguists** tracing the invisible lines, where human interaction ends, and artificial speech begins......*

DO NOT PANIC, THE FUTURE IS YOURS!

Fahad Ahmed Otaif and Alexia Larchen Costuchen
April 2026

Table of Contents

Detailed Table of Contents

The rapid rise of Generative Artificial Intelligence (GenAI) is reshaping Computer-Assisted Language Learning (CALL), challenging interaction-based models that prioritize task completion over critical engagement. The current chapter addresses a key gap between tool-driven AI use and the need for pedagogically structured, engagement-oriented language learning. The study employs a critical review of recent AI-Assisted Language Learning (AI-ALL) literature (30 studies published between 2021–2025) to examine how AI-mediated interaction can support L2 development through task design. Findings indicate that unstructured AI use often leads to superficial processing, whereas scaffolded engagement through AI-ALL task design enhances learner agency, metacognitive awareness, and depth of linguistic engagement. In response, the current chapter proposes an AI-ALL task design model that integrates adaptive feedback, iterative interaction, and prompt engineering. The study also reconceptualizes the teacher's role as an orchestrator of AI-mediated engagement and calls for empirical longitudinal and cross-contextual research to validate the model.

This chapter examines undergraduate engineering students' perceptions of large language model (LLM)–based conversational agents for foreign language learning. Seventy industrial engineering students enrolled in a Professional English course interacted with conversational agents through structured role-play tasks over a ten-week intervention. The study integrates the Technology Acceptance Model 2 (TAM2) and the Language Learning Orientations Scale (LLOS) to analyze both technology acceptance and motivational orientations. Results show generally positive

chatbots, AI-supported collaboration in group tasks, AI as a reflective teammate, and LLM-enabled co-creation. The study adopts a qualitative, document-based analysis supported by institutional evidence and the EU legal frameworks, particularly the AI Act and the General Data Protection Regulation (GDPR). Additionally, UNESCO's Guidance for Generative AI in Education and Research provides a global perspective. Our findings reveal that the discussed AI cases require careful alignment with the Data Protection Impact Assessment (DPIA) and human-centred (international and institutional) governance to ensure responsible and inclusive educational innovation in BIPs.

This article investigates the complex role that generative AI systems play in creative writing tasks or activities conducted in Spanish, with a particular focus on co-authorship dynamics, perceptions of creativity and notions of authorship in the educational context of using AI. The study employs an experimental design based on the students' performance in writing activities, as they have created texts under two conditions: the first one entails writing independently, without technological help; then, they co-create another text of the same type with the assistance of a generative AI tool (ChatGPT). The outputs are subject to comparative textual analysis, focusing on aspects such as originality, stylistic distinctiveness and narrative coherence. This research not only promotes awareness on the use of AI Bots and authorship, but also makes students' reflect on the educational models based on the use of AI tools, preparing them to use creative digital tools with intentionality and self-awareness.

This chapter examines the rapid integration of artificial intelligence (AI) into translation and interpreting practices and evaluates its implications for ethics, quality, and professional accountability. Recent developments in neural machine translation and large language models have significantly expanded translation capabilities, enabling interactive and context-aware multilingual communication. However, the increasing reliance on AI-powered tools raises critical concerns regarding accuracy, bias, privacy, and the shifting role of human translators. Drawing on insights from applied linguistics, translation studies, and interpreting research, this chapter analyzes how AI reshapes translation workflows, professional competencies, and quality assessment practices. It further explores emerging governance frameworks, professional standards, and hybrid human–AI models designed to mitigate risk while preserving linguistic and cultural integrity. Ultimately, the chapter argues that responsible AI integration in translation requires interdisciplinary collaboration, ethical oversight, and human-centered accountability mechanisms to ensure that technological innovation supports rather than undermines communicative trust and social responsibility.

Section 3
Creativity: AI in Translating Sociocultural Discourse and Assessing Specialized Writing

Artificial intelligence (AI) systems, particularly large language models (LLMs), have transformed applied linguistics, enabling advances in machine translation and intercultural communication. However, these systems encounter significant challenges when processing symbolic language, idioms, proverbs, metaphors, and satirical expressions, whose interpretation depends on shared cultural knowledge. This chapter investigates the capacity of contemporary AI systems (GPT-4, Claude 3.5, Gemini Pro) to recognise, interpret, and translate culturally embedded symbolic expressions from Gulf Arabic varieties. Employing a corpus-assisted discourse analysis (CADS) methodology combined with systematic AI output evaluation, the study analysed 666 symbolic expressions across four categories (proverbs, metaphors, idioms, satire) drawn from authentic Gulf Arabic discourse. Results reveal systematic patterns of literal misinterpretation (42% of errors), inappropriate cultural mapping (28%), over-generalisation (33%), and loss of pragmatic force (58%). Statistical analysis demonstrated significant variation across expression types ($F(3,662) = 18.7$, $p < .001$) and thematic domains ($F(5,660) = 12.4$, $p < .001$), with contextual information significantly improving performance (mean improvement = 0.43, $p < .001$). These findings illuminate fundamental limitations in current NLP architectures and contribute design principles for culturally aware AI systems. The chapter addresses emerging considerations including AI ethics and cultural bias, human–AI collaboration models, and policy implications for multilingual regions.

Preface

AI in Applied Linguistics: A Game Changer

For decades, the relationship between language and technology has evolved through successive waves of innovation. From early human–computer interaction research in SLA, to Computer-assisted Language Learning (CALL), to Mobile-assisted Language Learning (MALL), to transcription tools, machine translation, adaptive online learning platforms, and electronic translators, computers have long served as close companions to linguists, educators, and learners. Each stage expanded what was possible, yet none transformed the field of applied linguistics as profoundly as the recent advances in Artificial Intelligence (AI) and Natural Language Processing (NLP).

The emergence of AI-driven conversational agents (AI bots) has fundamentally reshaped how humans engage with technology for language use, learning, and research. These tools have introduced new opportunities across the humanities and sciences. Applied linguistics, in particular, now finds itself both a beneficiary and a co-constructor of these unfolding technologies. AI systems are not only tools used by applied linguists; they increasingly influence the very processes, practices, and policies that define the field.

This volume, *AI in Applied Linguistics: Practice, Policy, and Creativity*, published with IGI Global, aims to provide a research-grounded understanding of this rapidly changing landscape. It examines how AI bots are currently used in applied linguistics (practice), how institutions and individuals can meaningfully and ethically integrate them (policy), and how their full potential might be imagined and expanded (creativity).

The idea for this book emerged shortly after I delivered my research paper *Towards Improving AI-bots' Outcomes: A Critical Perspective from Discourse Analysis* at the 3rd International Conference on Digital Linguistics at the Polytechnic University of Valencia in June 2025. Only a few days later, my colleague Alexia Larchen suggested extending my focus on AI bots in Applied Linguistics into a book, thus creating an opportunity to collect insights from researchers, curriculum developers, policy makers and e-learning managers from different countries.

While conferences have become a forum that brings together practitioners and researchers to explore the latest developments in language and technology, we wanted to capture a wider sentiment. AI is no longer operating at the margins; it has become a driving force, a game changer in Human-AI interaction, reshaping how language is taught, learned, analyzed, and understood. By the time we held our second meeting, it was clear that the book's title needed to reflect this breadth, broad enough to encompass the many transformations AI has introduced across the field.

This volume reflects not only our own commitment to documenting these shifts, critically examining them, and engaging creatively with the transformations unfolding across applied linguistics, but also the collective effort of the many scholars who contributed their chapters and the reviewers who generously volunteered their time to evaluate the work of their peers. Their insights, expertise, and willingness to collaborate have been essential in shaping a comprehensive and forward-looking exploration of AI's impact on the field.

The book brings together twelve chapters organized into three main sections: 1) Practice, exploring AI in L2 teaching and learning across general, specialized, and professional domains; 2) Policy, addressing AI policy and ethical concerns in translation and co-authorship; and lastly 3) Creativity, examining AI's role in translating sociocultural discourse and assessing specialized writing. We hope this volume serves as both a timely compass for navigating the current landscape of AI and a catalyst for future innovations, empowering scholars, educators, and policymakers to join us in reimagining applied linguistics in this new era.

Alexia Larchen Costuchen
Universitat Politècnica de València, Spain

Fahad Ahmed Otaif
King Khalid University, Saudi Arabia

Section 1

Practice: AI in L2 Teaching and Learning: General and Specialized Domains

Chapter 1
Task Design in AI-ALL: The Need for Scaffolded Engagement

Fahad Ahmed Otaif
http://orcid.org/0000-0001-9832-4289
King Khlid University, Saudi Arabia

ABSTRACT

The rapid rise of Generative Artificial Intelligence (GenAI) is reshaping Computer-Assisted Language Learning (CALL), challenging interaction-based models that prioritize task completion over critical engagement. The current chapter addresses a key gap between tool-driven AI use and the need for pedagogically structured, engagement-oriented language learning. The study employs a critical review of recent AI-Assisted Language Learning (AI-ALL) literature (30 studies published between 2021–2025) to examine how AI-mediated interaction can support L2 development through task design. Findings indicate that unstructured AI use often leads to superficial processing, whereas scaffolded engagement through AI-ALL task design enhances learner agency, metacognitive awareness, and depth of linguistic engagement. In response, the current chapter proposes an AI-ALL task design model that integrates adaptive feedback, iterative interaction, and prompt engineering. The study also reconceptualizes the teacher's role as an orchestrator of AI-mediated engagement and calls for empirical longitudinal and cross-contextual research to validate the model.

INTRODUCTION

The integration of Generative Artificial Intelligence (GenAI) into language education marks a paradigm shift, moving the field of Computer-Assisted Language

DOI: 10.4018/979-8-3373-6420-9.ch001

Learning (CALL) from static, pre-programmed interfaces toward dynamic, infinite response landscapes. As tools such as conversational agents (AI chatbots) become recurrently utilized in language learning (Warschauer & Xu, 2024), the traditional foundations of task design, once rooted in predictable, closed-loop feedback, are being fundamentally challenged. This transition is not merely a matter of technological adoption but reconfiguration of how learners interact with machines to acquire linguistic competence. Therefore, the importance of this shift cannot be overlooked; as AI becomes an inescapable tool in both professional and educational L2 learning spheres, the ability to design pedagogically sound, AI-mediated learning experiences is important to ensure that technology serves as a catalyst for growth rather than a shortcut that bypasses cognitive development (Li et al., 2026).

Despite the rapid proliferation of GenAI tools, current research reveals a gap between the high efficiency of these tools and their pedagogical effectiveness. Recent studies suggest that while AI-chatbots offer 'endless' and adaptive response capacities, they often lead to what AlMutairi (2025) describes as 'shallow language processing'. The 'Efficiency Paradox,' for example, presents a critical challenge: when AI provides instant, polished summaries or translations (ibid), learners often overlook the 'negotiation of meaning' (Long, 1996) and the mental restructuring required for true linguistic acquisition. Existing CALL task design frameworks, such as those established by Chapelle (1998; 2001; 2007; 2014), were designed for a different era of technology and would require a new reinterpretation to account for the dynamic, distributed agency of AI-Assisted Language Learning (Godwin-Jones, 2024; Warschauer & Xu, 2024).

Therefore, the current study aims to address this gap by revisiting the core constructs of CALL interactivity and task design in the AI era. It seeks, specifically, to move beyond the traditional concept of 'human-computer interaction' to introduce a more recent framework of scaffolded human-AI engagement. By examining the intersection of AI system affordances, learner agency, and teacher orchestration, the study proposes an AI-Assisted Language Learning (AI-ALL) task design model. This model is intended to ensure that AI's infinite generative multimodal capacity is well-utilized to support, rather than replace, the learner's 'cognitive efforts' (Robinson, 2011), thereby fostering deep processing and efficient linguistic competence and agency.

To achieve this, the study employs a critical narrative review methodology. Unlike traditional systematic reviews, this approach emphasizes relevance-selective interpretation and conceptual synthesis, which is particularly appropriate for the rapidly evolving and often divided field (Grant & Booth, 2009) of AI-ALL (Zhu & Wang, 2025). The review synthesizes 30 peer-reviewed studies published between 2021 and 2025, identified through major academic databases including Scopus and Web of Science. By interrogating the underlying assumptions of the recent research on the topic and identifying conceptual tensions, the current study develops a coherent perspective on how scaffolded engagement can transform AI's 'infinite response' and dynamic nature into a structured pedagogical journey. Through this lens, the study redefines the roles of language learners and teachers and their AI-interaction in this technology-enhanced era.

PREVIOUS STUDIES

Interactivity in Traditional CALL Task Design

The theoretical landscape of Computer-Assisted Language Learning (CALL) has long been anchored in interactionist Second Language Acquisition (SLA) theories. For decades, the field relied on the foundational work of Michael Long (1996), whose Interaction Hypothesis emphasized that linguistic development occurs when learners engage in the negotiation of meaning. This process, triggered by communication breakdowns, forces learners to seek clarification and modify their output, thereby making input comprehensible.

Rooted in learning theory, instructional design and interaction serve as the systemic foundation for technology-based materials in CALL (Seel et al., 2017; Morales et al., 2011). At the heart of this approach are tasks, which function as the core building blocks of how language learning unfolds (Gruba & Hinkelman, 2012). For example, for technology-mediated L2 listening, particularly when utilizing digital video, effective task design must move beyond simple delivery to incorporate interactionist SLA principles (Pica, 1994; Chapelle, 1998). This involves creating 'learner fit' and 'L2 learning potential' by ensuring tasks are authentic and purpose-driven (Chapelle, 2001, 2014; Brown, 2017). As suggested by Mayer (2009) and Casañ Núñez (2017), well-constructed tasks facilitate a focus on meaning by providing guided language learning through design features such as embedded questions or visual organizers, which help listeners navigate the complex stimuli of multimedia environments.

Therefore, meaningful interaction within these technology-mediated tasks is a process where learners seek clarification or modified input to resolve miscomprehension (Long, 1983; Pica, 1994). In a CALL context, this interactivity is often operationalized through human-computer interface features that compensate for the absence of a live interlocutor (Laurillard, 2002; Clifford & Granoien, 2008). These opportunities can be discursive, adaptive, or reflective, allowing learners to receive specific feedback on their performance and return to tasks to modify their input (Clifford & Granoien, 2008). By providing help options, such as repetition requests or linguistic salience through font changes, task design can prompt 'noticing', which is a prerequisite to convert input into L2 intake (Schmidt, 1990; Sharwood-Smith, 1993; Chapelle, 2007).

In this context, interactive opportunities' settings must be strategically managed to optimize the learner's cognitive load. Task design can either direct or disperse a learner's limited attentional resources (Robinson, 2007, 2011). For example, when digital video is the mode of presentation in CALL, tasks must be designed to direct attention toward essential linguistic forms and meanings rather than overwhelming the listener with many distracting visual elements (Gruba, 1999). Research emphasizes that micro-scaffolding features, such as tables of contents or short headings, can effectively guide learners through challenging content (Alghamdi, et al., 2018). However, current use of AI-assisted Language Learning (AI-ALL) is largely unfolding without criteria on how learners engage and interact with this recent technology (Zhu & Wang, 2025; Bahari et al., 2025).

CALL Task Design in the AI Era

As the field transitions into a 'new era' of AI-mediated language learning (Warschauer & Xu, 2024), these static models are being challenged by Generative AI (GenAI) chatbots such as ChatGPT, Gemini and others. Unlike previous CALL iterations, AI-Chatbots offer an endless and adaptive response capacity in multimodal forms (Lin & Mubarok 2021). This generative potential transforms the nature of the 'Tool' (Alhusaiyan, 2025) from a reactive pre-designed script to an active, emergent collaborator that can tailor output to the learner's specific context in real-time.

Recent research often focuses on the efficiency of AI rather than pedagogical depth (ibid). A critical gap exists where the Subject (learner) interacts with the Tool (AI) without achieving deep 'engagement' in the Community socio-cultural context (ibid). This distinction is critical: Bahari et al. (2025), therefore, propose an Interactive Pedagogical Model of Language Learning (IPMLL) which merges the resource-rich nature of traditional CALL with the adaptive, intelligent capabilities of AI-Assisted Language Learning (AI-ALL). Their claim is that neither CALL (rich in content) nor AI-ALL (rich in intelligence) is sufficient on its own; instead, task design must be adaptive and driven by personalized success.

Alhusaiyan (2025) assumes that interaction in AI-ALL is often a mechanical 'Action', a simple input-output loop. In contrast, engagement represents the holistic 'Activity', encompassing the agentic, emotional, and social presence of the learner. Without a shift to designing tasks that match the AI nature as attempted by Bahari et al. (2025), the 'endless' uncontrolled responses of AI may lead to what AlMutairi (2025) describes as 'shallow language processing', especially at early stages of L2 learning.

Furthermore, AlMutairi (2025) warns that the efficiency of AI models can paradoxically hinder learning. When an AI provides instant, polished summaries or translations, a learner may bypass the cognitive struggle inherent in Long's (1996) 'negotiation of meaning'. If the machine does the synthesizing, the learner misses the opportunity for the mental restructuring required for true L2 acquisition. In addition, one of the main characteristics of a good CALL task design is that it should "provide interactive opportunities that preserve the L2 listener's attentional resources (Robinson, 2011) and direct him/her to focus on meaning while performing the listening task" (Otaif, 2021, p. 28).

The Need for Evaluating Task Design in the AI-ALL Era

Chapelle's (2001) framework evaluates CALL tasks based on their *language learning potential, learner fit* for specific proficiency levels, and *the degree of meaning focus* integrated into the activity. Additionally, the criteria include *the authenticity of the language used*, the *positive impact on the learner's overall development*, and the *practicality of implementing the technology within a given context.*

In terms of AI-ALL, there seems to be a gap between CALL task design criteria and the reality of utilizing this new technology in language learning. For example, in line with Alhusaiyan (2025), we must address the contradiction between AI as a tool for efficiency and AI as a partner for learning. If a tool is excessively efficient, its pedagogical activity fails because its input is not guaranteed to be comprehensible (i.e., $i + 1$). In other words, when AI tools afford quick task completion (e.g., AI-assisted completion of assignments, exams, and homework) over scaffolded AI-ALL, learners risk receiving output that lacks an optimal level of challenge. In terms of the Input Hypothesis (Krashen, 1985), if a tool eliminates the need for the learner to struggle with the (i.e., $i + 1$) formula, the output becomes shallow or complex, falling either below or beyond the learning threshold, rather than 'comprehensible', resulting in no actual linguistic development. This, in turn, violates many of Chapelle's (2001) criteria for good task design, including *language learning potential, learner fit,* and *positive impact on the learner's overall development.*

Although AI tools such as AI chatbots offer high efficiency, they risk collapsing the space for acquisition if they provide results without requiring the learner to engage in the 'negotiation of meaning' (Long, 1996). In this sense, a tool that is 'too efficient' fails to maintain the learner within the zone of proximal development (ZPD) (Vygotsky, 1978) because it removes the necessary cognitive scaffolding, thereby bypassing the linguistic challenges essential for growth (Li et al., 2026).

Liu et al. (2024) found that teachers initially relied on AI for efficiency (Stage 1), but soon realized that AI-simplified text was often 'hollow' or lacked the necessary nuance for students to truly engage. They concluded that teacher mediation is the only way to ensure that AI's 'efficient' output remains pedagogically effective (i.e., $i + 1$). If the tool is excessively efficient, the learning activity fails to stimulate real-life linguistic development or trigger the learner's engagement with L2 input.

Olesova et al. (2026, p.1) state that student engagement is a "multidimensional construct that includes cognitive, behavioral, emotional, and agentic participation in learning activities (Martin & Borup, 2022)". In L2 learning, "when learners perceive AI-based platforms as effective in improving language proficiency and providing valuable support, they are more likely to actively engage in communicative activities" (Peng and Liang, 2025, p. 23). Therefore, tasks should be designed to address evolving technological advances and the changing nature of AI-Assisted Language Learning (AI-ALL), specifically across the dimensions of Response Capacity, Learner Role, Task Design, Primary Goal, and Practicality (Table 1) which are derived from pioneer research in SLA (Pica, 1994; Long, 1996) CALL (Chapelle;1998, 2001, 2007) and Task-based Learning (Robinson, 2007; 2011), see Table 1 for a comparison between these elements in a CALL in AI-ALL Task Design.

Table 1. CALL Task Design Adapted for AI-ALL

Feature	CALL Interaction	Scaffolded AI Engagement
Response Capacity	Finite/Pre-scripted	Endless/Dynamic
Learner Role	Reactive User	Proactive Collaborator
Task Design	Fixed Path (Linear)	Scaffolded Journey (Iterative)
Primary Goal	Task Completion	Deep Processing & Agency
Response Capacity	Finite/pre-scripted	Endless/Dynamic
Practicality	Development Time	Prompt Engineering & Teacher AI-Literacy

Nowadays, AI-mediated environments can promote engagement as the central mechanism through which interactivity is transformed into meaningful learning outcomes. Therefore, the transition from 'Interactionist CALL' to 'Engagement-driven CALL' requires new criteria for evaluating both task design and learner performance (Table 1).

Therefore, in light of the anticipated changes, new task design must intentionally introduce 'desirable difficulties' that force the learner to negotiate with the AI's output, thereby satisfying Long's (1996) requirement for focus on meaning and interactional modification. To address the disconnect between traditional CALL frameworks and the demands of AI-driven engagement, the subsequent section outlines the research methodology used to investigate the required criteria emerging as benchmarks for effective task design in the AI-ALL era.

METHODOLOGY

To examine the evolving role of task design and learner engagement in AI-Assisted Language Learning (AI-ALL), the current study employs a critical narrative review methodology. Unlike traditional systematic reviews that prioritize exhaustive coverage and procedural transparency, a critical review emphasizes a relevance-selective interpretation, synthesis, and conceptual development (Grant & Booth, 2009). This approach is particularly appropriate for emerging and rapidly evolving fields such as AI-ALL, where theoretical frameworks remain underdeveloped and empirical findings are often fragmented or conceptually inconsistent. The purpose of this method is therefore not only to summarize existing research in relation to the current research query, but also to critically question underlying assumptions, identify tensions, and develop a coherent conceptual perspective.

Data Collection

The scope of critical review, in the current chapter, is limited to research published between 2021 and 2025, a period marked by the widespread adoption of Generative Artificial Intelligence (GenAI) tools such as conversational agents/chatbots and large language models in educational contexts. This timeframe reflects a shift in CALL from rule-based and pre-programmed interaction toward dynamic, adaptive, and generative forms of human–AI interaction (Zhai, 2023; Warschauer & Xu, 2024). By focusing on this recent body of literature, the current review aims to capture new debates and emerging trends directly relevant to the study's goal of reassessing task design and interactivity in the AI era.

Relevant literature was identified through a structured search of major academic databases, including Scopus, Web of Science, and Google Scholar. Special attention was given to top journals in the field, such as Computer-Assisted Language Learning (CALL) and Language Learning & Technology (LL&T), for their high-quality research. The search process was guided by a set of carefully selected keywords that reflect the core constructs of the study, including *AI*, *chatbots*, *human–AI interaction*, *learner engagement*, and *task design + in language learning*. These keywords were used both independently and in combination to ensure comprehensive coverage of relevant studies. In addition, backward and forward citation tracking were employed to identify influential works and emerging contributions that may not have been captured through keyword searches alone.

To ensure the quality and relevance of the selected studies, a set of inclusion and exclusion criteria was applied. First, only peer-reviewed journal articles and refereed conference papers were included, ensuring that the review is grounded in rigorously evaluated research. Second, studies were required to focus explicitly on

AI-mediated language learning or closely related areas within CALL. Third, priority was given to research that engages with key theoretical constructs central to this study, particularly *AI-ALL, interactivity*, *learner engagement*, and *pedagogical task design* in technology-mediated environments. Studies that focused primarily on technical development, algorithmic performance, or engineering aspects of AI without clear pedagogical implications to language learning were excluded (Table 2).

Table 2. Distribution of Reviewed Studies by Publication Venue

1. CALL & Language Teaching and Learning Technology =20 Studies		**N**
Language Learning & Technology	Dombi et al. (2024); Godwin-Jones (2024); Huang et al. (2024); Ji et al. (2024); Lee & Lee (2024); Liu et al. (2024); Warschauer & Xu (2024); Woo et al. (2024); Zheng et al. (2024); Zhu & Wang (2025)	10
Computer Assisted Language Learning	Fathi & Rahimi (2024); Peng & Liang (2025)	2
Saudi Journal of Language Studies	Alhusaiyan (2025); Otaif (2021)	2
J. of Computer Assisted Learning	Huang et al. (2022)	1
J. of China CALL	Tseng & Warschauer (2023)	1
Technology in Lang. Teaching & Learning	Stockwell & Wang (2025)	1
System	Abdelhalim et al. (2025)	1
J. of Second Language Writing	Warschauer et al. (2023)	1
Innovation in Lang. Learning & Teaching	Lukešová & Jennings (2025)	1
2. Other relevant journals=10 Studies		
Educational Technology & Society	Huang et al. (2023); Lin & Mubarok (2021)	2
Education and Information Tech.	Bahari et al. (2025)	1
Intl. J. of Ed-Tech in Higher Ed.	Hwang & Lee (2025)	1
Technology Knowledge and Learning	Olesova et al. (2026)	1
TechTrends	Li et al. (2026)	1
Educational Psychologist	Martin & Borup (2022)	1
XRDS: Crossroads (ACM)	Zhai (2023)	1
Springer Handbook (Chapter)	Davis et al. (2025)	1
World Conf. on Science & Tech. Innov. (Proceedings)	Almutairi (2025)	1

Following the selection process, the identified studies were analyzed using a thematic synthesis approach (Thomas & Harden, 2008). Rather than organizing the review as a sequence of individual study summaries, the analysis was structured around key conceptual themes and debates. This approach allows for deeper analytical engagement and supports the identification of patterns, contradictions, and gaps across literature. Four main themes guided the analysis: (1) the conceptualization of interactivity in traditional CALL, (2) the transformation of interaction in AI-mediated environments, (3) the role of learner engagement as a mediating construct, and (4) the significance of task design in shaping meaningful learning experiences.

A central feature of this review is its critical orientation. In addition to synthesizing findings, the analysis actively interrogates the assumptions underlying existing research. For example, while many studies celebrate the increased interactivity afforded by AI tools, they often assume that human-AI interaction leads to better learning (Fathi & Rahimi, 2024; Lee & Lee, 2024), without sufficiently examining the quality or depth of learner engagement, nor mentioning its relation to AI-ALL task design. Similarly, the concept of interactivity, which has long been central to CALL theory (Otaif, 2021), is frequently applied to AI contexts without reconsideration of its theoretical adequacy in light of new technological affordances.

FINDINGS AND DISCUSSION

The Paradigm Shift: From Interaction to Scaffolded Engagement

The primary finding of this critical review is that the integration of Generative Artificial Intelligence (GenAI) into language education marks a fundamental structural shift. In traditional Computer-Assisted Language Learning (CALL), the primary construct was 'interaction', a concept often limited to predictable, closed-loop exchanges where the computer functioned as a reactive tutor. However, recent literature (2021–2025: Table 2) suggests that the 'endless' and adaptive nature of AI-chatbots necessitates a transition toward 'scaffolded engagement'. Without a shift to design tasks that regulate *learner's engagement* as a systematic attempt to match the AI nature (Huang et al. 2022; Bahari et. al., 2025), the 'endless' uncontrolled responses of AI may lead to 'shallow language processing', especially at early stages of L2 acquisition (AlMutairi, 2025).

The Efficiency Paradox and the 'i + 1' Formula

An important theme identified across the 30 reviewed studies is the contradiction between AI as a tool for efficiency and AI as a partner for learning. AlMutairi (2025) warns that the efficiency of AI models can paradoxically hinder learning. When an AI provides instant, polished summaries or translations, the learner may bypass the cognitive struggle inherent in Long's (1996) 'negotiation of meaning'. Stockwell and Wang (2025) propose a framework for human-AI collaboration that redefines the classroom, including the teacher and the learners' agency. In their view, AI is not a *tool to be used* but *a partner to be engaged.* This collaborative stance aligns with Zhai's (2023) vision for ChatGPT in next-generation learning, where AI serves as a catalyst for scientific and linguistic inquiry, pushing the learner into their Zone of Proximal Development.

Desirable Difficulties

Liu et al. (2024) found that teachers initially relied on AI for efficiency but soon realized that AI-simplified text was often 'hollow'. If the machine does the L2 structural, semantic and pragmatic negotiation of meaning through AI-silent corrections, translations and explanations, the learner misses the opportunity for the mental restructuring required for true linguistic acquisition. In terms of the Input Hypothesis (Krashen, 1985), if the tool eliminates the need for the learner to struggle with the formula (i.e., i + 1), the output becomes either shallow (too easy) or complex (too difficult), falling outside the learning threshold. Therefore, new task design must intentionally introduce "desirable difficulties" that force the learner to negotiate with the AI's output. This satisfies the requirement for interactional modification essential for growth (Li et al., 2026).

Learner's Engagement in AI-ALL Task Design

The impact of GenAI on specific skills, such as writing, illustrates this need for scaffolding. Fathi and Rahimi (2024) assessed the impact of an AI chatbot (ChatGPT) on EFL writing, finding that while it can enhance learner autonomy, it requires a guided learning design that encourages the learner to maintain agency. If the student treats the AI as a ghostwriter rather than a scaffold, the pedagogical value of the writing task evaporates. Zhu and Wang (2025) further support this in their systematic review of recent research in the field, noting that the current status of AI research in education often lacks a systematic evaluation of each system's affordance. They argue that while AI tools like Automated Writing Evaluation (AWE) and chatbots have proven effective for improving speaking and literacy, significant gaps remain in the study of receptive skills, such as listening and reading (ibid).

The quality of learner engagement is also deeply tied to the psychological relationship between the learner and the machine, as well as his/her AI literacy (Huang, et al., 2022). While many researchers argue that AI bots have positive impact on the psychological and social aspects of language learning (Huang, et al., 2023), for scaffolded engagement, the learner should trust the quality of AI's feedback while remaining cautious of its 'endless' and sometimes inaccurate/'hallucinated' outputs (Cecilio-Fernandes & Sandars, 2025). This discrepancy is attributable to the static nature of traditional CALL materials, which were designed and verified by domain experts. Because these materials were authoritative, the burden of critical evaluation was not incumbent upon the learner as it is today with modern AI. Therefore, learner role should shift, in this era, from a reactive user to an agentic participant yet, through scaffolded engagement (Alhusaiyan, 2025; Li et al. (2026). In AI-ALL, learners are not merely recipients of input but active creators of interaction, shaping the trajectory of discourse through prompt design. This represents a 'distributed agency' where control is shared between the human and the system (Godwin-Jones, 2024; Davis et al., 2025; Peng & Liang, 2025).

Teacher's Engagement in AI-ALL Task Design

Having addressed learner engagement with AI-ALL task design, the findings of this review now turn to the central coordinating role of the language teacher as the orchestrator of the learning process. Teacher engagement plays a pivotal role in shaping the effectiveness of AI-assisted language learning (AI-ALL) environments, particularly as generative AI transforms traditional task design practices. Rather than functioning as passive adopters of technology, instructors are increasingly required to actively design, scaffold, and mediate AI-driven learning experiences. This shift highlights the centrality of teacher agency in ensuring that AI tools are pedagogically aligned, contextually relevant, and capable of fostering meaningful learner engagement. Similar to Huang et al. 's (2022) argument for the need for students' AI literacy in AI-ALL, Li et al. (2026) argue that in AI-ALL, students' success is linked to their AI literacy, task planning, and the role of teachers as facilitators and progress assessors. Because many popular conversation AI bots (such as ChatGPT) were not originally designed for language education, successful task design requires a 'coordinated division of labor," in which teachers actively guide students in prompt engineering and task structuring (ibid).

Therefore, the role of the instructor is evolving from a content provider in CALL to an orchestrator of AI-human collaboration. Abdelhalim et al. (2025) found through a cross-cultural analysis that university EFL instructors' engagement with GenAI varies significantly according to cultural contexts and individual attitudes toward this emerging technology. This suggests that the successful scaffolding of AI-ALL engagement depends on how instructors perceive AI's role within their specific cultural and pedagogical 'Community' (Alhusaiyan, 2025), which is the environment that hosts and fosters the learner's AI-ALL.

Reconceptualizing Criteria for AI-ALL Task Design

The current critical review suggests a need for scaffolded task design in modern AI-Assisted Language Learning (AI-ALL). It advocates for a fundamental shift from 'pre-programmed interactions' toward 'dynamic, distributed agency', moving beyond standard human-AI interaction models that are no longer sufficient. Consequently, Chapelle's (2001) six criteria for CALL task design should be revisited. This outline synthesizes the results to demonstrate how these criteria can be adapted to meet the specific demands of AI-ALL:

1. Language Learning Potential (LLP)

- Chapelle's View: The degree of opportunities for beneficial focus on form.
- AI-ALL Update: AI-AL now includes individualized but uncontrolled adaptivity. AI can perform 'automated text simplification' (Liu et al., 2024), translation (AlMutaiti, 2025), multimodal configuration and processing (Lin & Mubarok, 2021) of L2.
- The Risk: We must account for unregulated engagement with AI content that may reduce the learning potential.

2. Learner Fit

- Chapelle's View: Matching the task to the learner's level and style.
- AI-ALL Update: This moves from 'static fit' to Dynamic Adaptivity, which is a concept that refers to the transition from traditional software (linear feedback) to generative AI systems that adapt difficulty, tone, and feedback in real-time based on the user's exact prompts (see the Key Terms and Definitions Appendix).
- The Risk: AI-ALL task must account for a number of issues such as, prompt design, previous search history and user-log that may affect the AI-bots response and distract the learner's focus and waste his/her 'attentional resources' (Robinson, 2007, 2011, Otaif, 2021) with content beyond or below his/her ZPD (Vygotsky, 1978). Teachers and applied linguists must also account for AI algorithmic Bias. Liang et al. (2023) warn that GPT detectors and LLM

models may be biased against non-native writers, meaning "fit" must now include ethical considerations of AI fairness. I refer to this as Algorithmic Bias in AI-ALL. Algorithmic Bias in AI-ALL2 is a concept that refers to the systematic, unfair favoring of certain sociolinguistic and socio-political norms, such as standard native-speaker varieties (e.g., General American or British English), within an AI's training datasets. This bias may disadvantage L2 learners by marginalizing their natural interlanguage and excluding or suppressing valid regional varieties of World Englishes (see the Key Terms and Definitions Appendix).

3. Meaning Focus

- Chapelle's View: Directing learners' attention to the meaning of the language.
- AI-ALL Update: Focus on Human-AI Collaboration through scaffolded and regulated task design. Tasks are no longer just about understanding a stimulus or input; they are about 'uncontrolled' negotiation and digital content making (Hwang & Lee, 2025) as well as co-creating meaning with a machine (Davis et. al., 2025).
- The Risk: **Distributed Agency**: Interaction is not just learner-to-machine but a distributed process where the AI acts as a partner in the meaning-making process (Godwin-Jones, 2024).

4. Authenticity

- Chapelle's View: The link between the CALL task and the real-world use of language.
- AI-ALL Update: Authenticity now involves AI-Mediated Communication. As AI becomes a standard workplace tool (Noy & Zhang, 2023), a 'real-world' task must include interacting with AI which bears great resemblance to real-life language such as native language pronunciation and writing.
- The Risk: Simulation vs. Reality: While chatbots can simulate conversation, research shows differences in how humans open and close conversations with AI versus other humans (Dombi et al., 2024). Tasks must reflect and account for these new sociolinguistic realities.

5. Positive Impact

- Chapelle's View: The effects of the task beyond language learning (e.g., computer literacy).

- AI-ALL Update: Focus on AI Literacy and Agency for both the learner and the teacher (Li et al., 2026). Positive impact now includes teaching learners how to cope with these technological changes by mastering a healthy use of AI writing tools (Tseng & Warschauer, 2023) in their AI-ALL journey.
- The Risk: Engagement: The impact is measured by 'student engagement' in online environments (Huang et al., 2024) and the reduction of the affective filter, which was not possible in the most recent unstructured AI-ALL task design that led to learners' anxiety (Li et al., 2026).

6. Practicality

- Chapelle's View: The resources required to develop and use the task.
- AI-ALL Update: High Practicality students can use this technology from their smartphones and other AI-operated platforms.
- The Risk: there is a risk that the AI-generative nature may lead to High Cognitive Load (Robinson, 2007, 2011, Otaif, 2021). It will also need to improve AI literacy for instructors and learners as well (Li et al., 2026). Although AI makes creating L2 content 'practically' instant, it requires a cross-cultural shift in how instructors engage with these tools (Godwin-Jones, 2024; Abdelhalim et al., 2025; Almutairi, 2025).

Therefore, to address the pedagogical demands of the AI-ALL era, the following table synthesizes the key criteria required for AI-Assisted Language Learning (AI-ALL) task design, highlighting how Chapelle's original CALL framework should be updated to reflect the affordances of AI. It emphasizes shifts in pedagogical focus, learner engagement, and AI-mediated interaction, showing how traditional dimensions such as language learning potential, learner fit, and authenticity are reinterpreted in the context of AI-ALL environments.

Table 3. Updated AI-ALL Task Design Criteria

Criterion	AI-ALL Update / Key Shifts
Language Learning Potential (LLP)	From focus on form → Individualized scaffolding with AI providing i+1 input, multimodal clues, and reflection prompts (Liu et al., 2024; Huang et al., 2024; Lukešová & Jennings, 2025)
Learner Fit	From static matching of task to learner level → Dynamic adaptivity; scaffolded engagement; includes ethical considerations to mitigate AI bias (Lee & Lee, 2024; Liang et al., 2023)
Meaning Focus	From focusing on language meaning → Human-AI collaboration; distributed agency; co-creation of meaning with AI (Hwang & Lee, 2025; Davis et al., 2025; Godwin-Jones, 2024)

continued on following page

Table 3. Continued

Criterion	AI-ALL Update / Key Shifts
Authenticity	From linking tasks to real-world language → AI-mediated communication; tasks reflect new sociolinguistic realities of human–AI interaction (Noy & Zhang, 2023; Dombi et al., 2024)
Positive Impact	From effects beyond language → AI literacy, agency, and engagement; reduction of affective filter; mastering AI tools responsibly (Tseng & Warschauer, 2023; Huang et al., 2024; Bahari et al., 2025)
Practicality	From ease of task development → High practicality but higher cognitive load and AI-literacy for instructors and learners; requires cross-cultural shift in teaching practices (Godwin-Jones, 2024; Abdelhalim et al., 2025; Almutairi, 2025)

As we can observe, the proposed AI-ALL task design model can be distinguished from traditional CALL paradigms through seven interrelated criteria that are both theoretically grounded and empirically supported. Table 4 summarizes seven key criteria that distinguish AI-Assisted Language Learning (AI-ALL) from traditional CALL Task Design. These criteria highlight shifts in teacher and learner roles, AI integration, task design, and learning goals, showing how engagement, rather than mere interaction, becomes central to meaningful L2 development.

Table 4. Key Differences Between Traditional CALL and AI-ALL

Criterion	Traditional CALL vs. AI-ALL
Teacher Role	From content provider → orchestrator of scaffolded AI–learner engagement
AI-Chatbots	From pre-programmed efficiency tools → pedagogical partners with dynamic, scaffolded and co-constructive dialogue
Learner Role	From passive user → agentic collaborator shaping interaction through prompts
Nature of Learning	From linear acquisition → socio-cognitive through scaffolded AI–learner engagement.
Task Design	From fixed/linear tasks → iterative, adaptive cycles of feedback and revision
Learning Goal	From task completion → meaningful linguistic engagement and deep processing
Evaluation & Practicality	From development focus → AI literacy, prompt engineering, and ethical use

First, the role of the teacher shifts from content provider to orchestrator of scaffolded engagement, where instructors design, mediate, and regulate AI–learner interaction to maintain pedagogical alignment and cognitive challenge (Li et al., 2026; Abdelhalim et al., 2025). Second, AI-chatbots are reconceptualized from tools of efficiency to pedagogical partners characterized by dynamic responsiveness and co-constructive dialogue, supporting distributed agency and iterative meaning-making (Godwin-Jones, 2024; Warschauer & Xu, 2024). Third, the learner role evolves into that of an agentic collaborator, actively shaping interaction through prompt design, reflection, and strategic engagement rather than passively receiving a pre-designed input (Peng & Liang, 2025; Hwang & Lee, 2025). Fourth, the nature of learning transitions from linear knowledge acquisition to a socio-cognitive, scaffolded process grounded in mediation, internalization, and negotiation of meaning (Vygotsky, 1978; Long, 1996). Fifth, task design itself becomes iterative and adaptive, emphasizing cycles of production, feedback, and revision that foster deep processing and meta-cognitive engagement rather than fixed-path completion (Fathi & Rahimi, 2024; Lukešová & Jennings, 2025). Sixth, the goal of learning shifts from task completion to meaningful linguistic engagement, where quality of interaction and depth of processing determine learning outcomes (Olesova et al., 2026; Huang et al., 2024). Finally, evaluation and practicality are redefined to include AI literacy, prompt engineering, and ethical awareness, ensuring that AI's efficiency does not bypass the cognitive effort required for acquisition (Huang et al., 2022, Bahari et al., 2025; Liu et al., 2024; Liang et al., 2023). Taken together, these criteria demonstrate that AI-ALL task design is not an extension of CALL but a reconfiguration of its basic theoretical foundations, in which engagement, rather than interaction, becomes the central construct linking AI affordances to meaningful L2 development.

CONCLUSION

This study reviewed recent empirical research (2021–2025) and found a gap between tool-centric AI use and structured, cognitively rich engagement. It highlights the importance of the proposed AI-Assisted Language Learning (AI-ALL) model as a useful framework for L2 education in the era of Generative AI. By redefining AI-chatbots as pedagogical partners, learners as agentic collaborators, and teachers as orchestrators of scaffolded engagement, the model moves beyond traditional CALL paradigms that prioritize pre-programmed interaction and task completion.

Findings suggest that tasks designed to scaffold iterative AI-human engagement enhance learner agency, metacognitive reflection, and meaningful linguistic output, mitigating the risks of 'shallow processing' associated with unguided AI use. Moreover, the AI-ALL dynamic task design, with scaffolded engagement, through guided prompt-based multimodal creation, correction, translation and feedback loops, can foster distributed agency and co-construction of meaning, aligning AI-ALL with core principles of task-based L2 pedagogy and instructional design.

Limitations of the current study include the conceptual nature of the framework and limited empirical validation across diverse L2 contexts, particularly in receptive skills such as listening and reading. Cross-cultural differences in teacher engagement with AI tools may also influence the effectiveness of scaffolded tasks. Therefore, future research should prioritize longitudinal implementations of AI-ALL, the integration of multimodal AI scaffolds to support complex language skills, and the systematic examination of the effects of so-called algorithmic bias. Overall, current research establishes a call for AI-ALL task design as a pedagogically grounded approach, centering learner engagement, agency, and deep cognitive processing in the AI-mediated language learning era.

REFERENCES

Abdelhalim, S. M., Alsahil, A. A., Baek, C., & Warschauer, M. (2025). University EFL instructors' engagement with generative AI: A cross-cultural analysis. *System, 135*, 103861. DOI: 10.1016/j.system.2025.103861

Alghamdi, E., Otaif, F., & Gruba, P. (2018). Designing a video playing interface for second language learners. In *Open Oceans: Learning without borders. Proceedings ASCILITE, 2018*, 298–302. DOI: 10.14742/ascilite2018.1978

Alhusaiyan, E. (2025). A systematic review of current trends in artificial intelligence in foreign language learning. *Saudi Journal of Language Studies*, *5*(1), 1–16. DOI: 10.1108/SJLS-07-2024-0039

Almutairi, F. (2025). Language and AI interaction: Studying how AI language models are affecting human communication and language learning. *World Conference on Emerging Science, Innovation and Policy 2025*. Futurity Research Publishing. https://doi.org/DOI: 10.5281/zenodo.15852254

Bahari, A., Han, F., & Strzelecki, A. (2025). Integrating CALL and AI-ALL for an interactive pedagogical model of language learning. *Education and Information Technologies*, *30*(10), 14305–14333. DOI: 10.1007/s10639-025-13388-w

Brown, S. (2017). L2 Listening. In Hinkel, E. (Ed.), *Handbook of Research in Second Language Teaching and Learning* (Vol. 3, pp. 201–213). Routledge.

Casañ Núñez, J. (2017). Testing audiovisual comprehension tasks with questions embedded in videos as subtitles: A pilot multimethod study. *The EUROCALL Review*, *25*(1), 36–60. DOI: 10.4995/eurocall.2017.7062

Cecilio-Fernandes, D., & Sandars, J. (2025). The hallucination of learning with generative artificial intelligence. *Medical Teacher*, *47*(12), 2057–2058. DOI: 10.1080/0142159X.2025.2531812 PMID: 40638506

Chapelle, C. (1998). Multimedia CALL: Lessons to be learned from research on instructed SLA. *Language Learning & Technology*, *2*(1), 22–34. DOI: 10.64152/10125/25030

Chapelle, C. (2001). *Computer applications in second language acquisition*. Cambridge University Press. DOI: 10.1017/CBO9781139524681

Chapelle, C. (2007). Technology and second language acquisition. *Annual Review of Applied Linguistics*, *27*, 98–114. DOI: 10.1017/S0267190508070050

Chapelle, C. A. (2001). *Computer applications in second language acquisition: Foundations for teaching, testing and research*. Cambridge University Press. DOI: 10.1017/CBO9781139524681

Chapelle, C. A. (2014). *English Language Learning and Technology*. John Benjamins.

Clifford, R., & Granoien, N. (2008). Applications of technology to language acquisition processes. In M. Holland & F. Fisher (Eds.), *The path of speech technologies in CALL* (pp. 25–43). Routledge.

Davis, N., Clemens, M., Rezwana, J., & Browne, E. (2025). Human-AI co-creation: A new interaction paradigm for human-AI interaction. In Xu, W. (Ed.), *Handbook of Human-Centered Artificial Intelligence* (pp. 1–57). Springer Nature., DOI: 10.1007/978-981-97-8440-0_76-1

Dombi, J., Sydorenko, T., & Timpe-Laughlin, V. (2024). Openings and closings in human-human versus human-spoken dialogue system conversations. *Language Learning & Technology*, *28*(2), 30–58. DOI: 10.64152/10125/73571

Fathi, J., & Rahimi, M. (2024). Utilising artificial intelligence-enhanced writing mediation to develop academic writing skills in EFL learners: A qualitative study. *Computer Assisted Language Learning*, *39*(1–2), 263–302. DOI: 10.1080/09588221.2024.2374772

Godwin-Jones, R. (2024). Distributed agency in language learning and teaching through generative AI. *Language Learning & Technology*, *28*(2), 5–30. DOI: 10.64152/10125/73570

Gruba, P. (1999). *The role of digital video in second language listening*. Unpublished PhD Thesis, University of Melbourne.

Gruba, P., & Hinkelman, D. (2012). *Blending technologies in second language classrooms*. Palgrave Macmillan. DOI: 10.1057/9780230356825

Huang, W., Hew, K. F., & Fryer, L. K. (2022). Chatbots for language learning—Are they really useful? A systematic review of chatbot-supported language learning. *Journal of Computer Assisted Learning*, *38*(1), 237–257. DOI: 10.1111/jcal.12610

Huang, W., Jia, C., Hew, K. F., & Guo, J. (2024). Using chatbots to support EFL listening decoding skills in a fully online environment. *Language Learning & Technology*, *28*(2), 62–90. DOI: 10.64152/10125/73572

Huang, X., Zou, D., Cheng, G., Chen, X., & Xie, H. (2023). Trends, research issues and applications of artificial intelligence in language education. *Journal of Educational Technology & Society*, *26*(1), 112–131. DOI: 10.30191/ETS.202301_26(1).0009

Hwang, Y., & Lee, J. H. (2025). Exploring students' experiences and perceptions of human-AI collaboration in digital content making. *International Journal of Educational Technology in Higher Education*, *22*(1), 44. DOI: 10.1186/s41239-025-00542-0

Ji, H., Han, I., & Park, S. (2024). Teaching foreign language with conversational AI: Teacher-student-AI interaction. *Language Learning & Technology*, *28*(2), 91–108. DOI: 10.64152/10125/73573

Krashen, S. D. (1985). *The input hypothesis: Issues and implications.* Laredo Publishing.

Laurillard, D. (2002). *Rethinking University Teaching: A conversational framework.* Routledge. DOI: 10.4324/9780203160329

Lee, H., & Lee, J. H. (2024). The effects of AI-guided individualized language learning: A meta-analysis. *Language Learning & Technology*, *28*(2), 134–162. DOI: 10.64152/10125/73575

Li, Y., Shadiev, R., & Chiu, T. K. F. (2026). Applying Generative Artificial Intelligence to Task-based Language Teaching and Learning: A Systematic Review and Meta-analysis. *TechTrends*, *70*(1), 150–163. DOI: 10.1007/s11528-025-01140-7

Liang, W., Yuksekgonul, M., Mao, Y., Wu, E., & Zou, J. (2023). GPT detectors are biased against non-native English writers. *Patterns (New York, N.Y.)*, *4*(7), 100779. Advance online publication. DOI: 10.1016/j.patter.2023.100779 PMID: 37521038

Lin, C. J., & Mubarok, H. (2021). Learning analytics for investigating the mind map-guided AI chatbot approach in an EFL flipped speaking classroom. *Journal of Educational Technology & Society*, *24*(4), 1635. 10.30191%2fETS.202110_24(4).0002

Liu, F., Jiang, Y., Lai, C., & Jin, T. (2024). Teacher engagement with automated text simplification for differentiated instruction. *Language Learning & Technology*, *28*(2), 1–25. DOI: 10.64152/10125/73576

Long, M. (1983). Native speaker/non-native speaker conversation and the negotiation of comprehensible input. *Applied Linguistics*, *4*(2), 126–141. DOI: 10.1093/applin/4.2.126

Long, M. H. (1996). The role of the linguistic environment in second language acquisition. In Ritchie, W. C., & Bhatia, T. K. (Eds.), *Handbook of second language acquisition* (pp. 413–468). Academic Press.

Lukešová, A., & Jennings, P. J. (2025). Clue before correction: ChatGPT-enhanced strategy for promoting autonomous and reflective language learning. *Innovation in Language Learning and Teaching*, •••, 1–29. DOI: 10.1080/17501229.2025.2612532

Martin, F., & Borup, J. (2022). Online learner engagement: Conceptual definitions, research themes, and supportive practices. *Educational Psychologist, 57*(3), 162–177. DOI: 10.1080/00461520.2022.2089147

Mayer, R. (2009). *Multimedia learning* (2nd ed.). Cambridge University Press. DOI: 10.1017/CBO9780511811678

Morales, E., García, F., & Barrón, A. (2011). Quality learning objective in instructional design. In *Instructional design: Concepts, methodologies, tools, and applications* (pp. 70–79). IGI Global. DOI: 10.4018/978-1-60960-503-2.ch107

Noy, S., & Zhang, W. (2023). Experimental evidence on the productivity effects of generative artificial intelligence. *Science, 381*(6654), 187–192. https://www.science .org/doi/10.1126/science.adh2586. DOI: 10.1126/science.adh2586 PMID: 37440646

Olesova, L., Sadaf, A., & Yan, W. (2026). *Exploring Relationships Between Undergraduate Students' Perceived Community of Inquiry, Engagement, and Shared Metacognition in Asynchronous Online Courses*. Technology Knowledge and Learning., DOI: 10.1007/s10758-026-09953-y

Otaif, F. A. (2021). Towards evaluating interactivity in video-based task design: A perspective from computer-based L2 listening. *Saudi Journal of Language Studies, 1*(1), 26–39. DOI: 10.1108/SJLS-03-2021-0008

Peng, J. E., & Liang, W. (2025). Willingness to communicate with artificial intelligence (AI)? Insights from tracking EFL learners' perceived acceptance and chat output. *Computer Assisted Language Learning*, •••, 1–27. DOI: 10.1080/09588221.2025.2486147

Pica, T. (1994). Research on negotiation: What does it reveal about second-language learning conditions, processes, and outcomes? *Language Learning, 44*(3), 493–527. DOI: 10.1111/j.1467-1770.1994.tb01115.x

Robinson, P. (2007). Criteria for grading and sequencing pedagogic tasks. In M. Mayo (Ed.), *Investigating tasks in formal language learning* (pp. 2-27). Multilingual Matters.

Robinson, P. (2011). *Second Language Task Complexity: Researching the Cognition Hypothesis of Language Learning and Performance*. John Benjamins. DOI: 10.1075/tblt.2

Schmidt, R. (1990). The role of consciousness in second language learning. *Applied Linguistics, 11*(2), 129–158. DOI: 10.1093/applin/11.2.129

Seel, N., Lehmann, T., Blumschein, P., & Podolskiy, O. (2017). *Instructional design for learning: Theoretical foundations.* Sense Publishers., DOI: 10.1007/978-94-6300-941-6

Sharwood-Smith, M. (1993). Input enhancement in instructed SLA: Theoretical bases. *Studies in Second Language Acquisition, 15*(2), 165–179. DOI: 10.1017/S0272263100011943

Stockwell, G., & Wang, Y. (2025). Framing human-AI collaboration in language education. *Technology in Language Teaching & Learning*, *7*(4), 103824. DOI: 10.29140/tltl.v7n4.103824

Thomas, J., & Harden, A. (2008). Methods for the thematic synthesis of qualitative research in systematic reviews. *BMC Medical Research Methodology*, *8*(1), 45. DOI: 10.1186/1471-2288-8-45 PMID: 18616818

Tseng, W., & Warschauer, M. (2023). AI-writing tools in education: If you can't beat them, join them. *Journal of China Computer-Assisted Language Learning*, *3*(2), 258–262. DOI: 10.1515/jccall-2023-0008

Vygotsky, L. S. (1978). *Mind in society: The development of higher psychological processes* (M. Cole, V. John-Steiner, S. Scribner, & E. Souberman, Eds. & Trans.). Harvard University Press. (Original work published 1930–1934).

Warschauer, M., Tseng, W., Yim, S., Webster, T., Jacob, S., Du, Q., & Tate, T. (2023). The affordances and contradictions of AI-generated text for writers of English as a second or foreign language. *Journal of Second Language Writing*, *62*, 101071. Advance online publication. DOI: 10.1016/j.jslw.2023.101071

Warschauer, M., & Xu, Y. (2024). Generative AI for language learning: Entering a new era. *Language Learning & Technology*, *28*(2), 1–4. DOI: 10.64152/10125/73569

Woo, D. J., Susanto, H., Yeung, C. H., Guo, K., & Fung, A. K. Y. (2024). Exploring AI-Generated text in student writing: How does AI help? *Language Learning & Technology*, *28*(2), 183–209. DOI: 10.64152/10125/73577

Zhai, X. (2023). ChatGPT for next generation science learning. XRDS: *Crossroads. The ACM Magazine for Students*, *29*(3), 42–46. DOI: 10.1145/3589649

Zheng, C., Chen, X., Zhang, H., & Chai, C. S. (2024). Automated versus peer assessment: Effects on learners' English public speaking. *Language Learning & Technology*, *28*(2), 210–228. DOI: 10.64152/10125/73578

Zhu, M., & Wang, C. (2025). A systematic review of AI in language education: Current status and future implications. *Language Learning & Technology*, *29*(1), 1–29. DOI: 10.64152/10125/73606

KEY TERMS AND DEFINITIONS

AI (Artificial Intelligence): Systems designed to simulate human intelligence and perform cognitive tasks such as learning, problem-solving, and decision-making.

AI Chatbots / Conversational Agents: Software applications (like ChatGPT or Gemini) programmed to simulate human conversation through unscripted, real-time text or voice.

AI Hallucinations (Inaccurate Outputs): A phenomenon where large language models generate grammatically correct but factually incorrect, nonsensical, or unhelpful text.

AI-ALL (Artificial Intelligence-Assisted Language Learning): The pedagogical use of dynamic, intelligent AI tools to facilitate second language acquisition.

Algorithmic Bias in AI-ALL: This concept refers to the systematic unfair favoring of certain sociolinguistic and socio-political norms, such as standard native-speaker varieties (e.g., General American or British English), within an AI's training datasets. This bias may disadvantage L2 learners by marginalizing their natural interlanguage and excluding or suppressing valid regional varieties of World Englishes.

Attentional Resources: The limited mental bandwidth a learner possesses to process information. Effective task design protects these resources by filtering out AI "noise" or over-complicated vocabulary.

AWE (Automated Writing Evaluation): Digital systems used to evaluate and provide automated feedback on written text.

CALL (Computer-Assisted Language Learning): The traditional field of language teaching and learning using computer technologies (typically static or pre-programmed).

Desirable Difficulties: Task-induced challenges that slow down immediate performance but trigger the cognitive effort and mental restructuring necessary for authentic, long-term linguistic acquisition.

Distributed Agency: A modern learning state where pedagogical control, direction, and creativity are actively shared between the human learner, the teacher, and the AI system.

Division of Labor (Teacher-AI Co-orchestration): A framework where the teacher designs the task and scaffolds the parameters, while the AI provides dynamic, real-time linguistic input.

Dynamic Adaptivity (Static vs. Dynamic Fit): The transition from traditional software (linear feedback) to generative AI systems that adapt difficulty, tone, and feedback in real-time based on the user's exact prompts.

Efficiency Paradox: The phenomenon where a tool's high speed and automated efficiency (e.g., instant AI translations or polished text) bypasses the cognitive struggle a learner needs to actually acquire the language.

EFL (English as a Foreign Language): The study of English by non-native speakers living in a non-English-speaking country.

GenAI (Generative Artificial Intelligence): AI systems capable of generating entirely new content (text, images, audio) in response to human prompts.

Human-AI Interaction vs. AI Engagement: The critical distinction between mechanical input-output loops (interaction) and a holistic, active, and emotionally invested learning process (engagement).

L2 (Second/Target Language): The language being learned, which is not the native language of the student.

LLM (Large Language Model): Advanced AI algorithms trained on massive datasets to recognize, summarize, translate, predict, and generate human-like text and speech.

LLP (Language Learning Potential): A criterion measuring the degree of opportunities a task provides for beneficial focus on linguistic form.

Negotiation of Meaning: The communicative process where a learner modifies their output, asks for clarification, or paraphrases to resolve a misunderstanding, a fundamental requisite for L2 growth.

Noticing: The cognitive process of a learner consciously registering a linguistic form in the input, a prerequisite for converting input to "intake."

Prompt Engineering: The strategic practice of designing, writing, and refining inputs to guide Generative AI into producing pedagogically useful outputs.

Scaffolded Engagement: A task environment where the learner is guided by structured prompts and teacher mediation to actively process language, rather than passively receiving AI outputs.

SLA (Second Language Acquisition): The scholarly study of how people learn a language other than their native tongue.

Task Design in AI-ALL: The intentional pedagogical structuring of learning activities to ensure that AI's open-ended generative capacity supports, rather than replaces, a learner's cognitive effort.

Teacher as Orchestrator/Facilitator: The evolving role of the instructor from a mere CALL content provider to a pedagogical architect who manages the process of learner-AI collaboration.

ZPD (Zone of Proximal Development): Vygotsky's concept of the distance between what a learner can do independently and what they can achieve with guidance or scaffolding.

Chapter 2
Assessing Student Perceptions of LLM-Based Conversational Agents for Foreign Language Learning

Ricardo Casañ-Pitarch
http://orcid.org/0000-0002-1689-7954
Universitat Politècnica de València, Spain

ABSTRACT

This chapter examines undergraduate engineering students' perceptions of large language model (LLM)–based conversational agents for foreign language learning. Seventy industrial engineering students enrolled in a Professional English course interacted with conversational agents through structured role-play tasks over a ten-week intervention. The study integrates the Technology Acceptance Model 2 (TAM2) and the Language Learning Orientations Scale (LLOS) to analyze both technology acceptance and motivational orientations. Results show generally positive perceptions of conversational agents, with high levels of perceived usefulness and ease of use, as well as favorable attitudes toward their integration into language learning activities. Autonomous motivational orientations were predominant among participants, particularly intrinsic motivation and identified regulation. While motivational variables showed limited influence on technology acceptance, intrinsic interest was moderately associated with perceived ease of use. The findings suggest that well-structured conversational agents can effectively support communicative practice in foreign language education.

DOI: 10.4018/979-8-3373-6420-9.ch002

1. INTRODUCTION

1.1. Context

In recent years, the application of artificial intelligence (AI) in education has transformed the way foreign languages are learned, with the emergence of new tools that support more flexible, autonomous, and interactive learning methods. Among these tools, LLM-based conversational agents simulate real communication situations, provide corrective feedback, and offer students opportunities to practice their communication skills spontaneously and naturally. These bots act as virtual agents capable of engaging in natural-language dialogue, and their potential to improve communicative competence makes them especially useful in learning environments where oral interaction is limited due to time, space, or connectivity constraints (Erdogan & Christina, 2025; Ferreiro-Santamaria, 2024).

This study is based on two complementary perspectives: the Technology Acceptance Model (TAM2, Venkatesh & Davis, 2000), which is an extended version of TAM (Davis, 1989) and focuses on students' opinions and attitudes about using digital tools; and the Language Learning Orientations Scale (LLOS, Noels et al., 2000), which is adapted from the Self-Determination Theory (Deci & Ryan, 1985) and explores different kinds of motivation in second language learning. While TAM2 provides information on how learners evaluate the agents' usefulness and ease of use, LLOS offers insight into how this technology connects to students' intrinsic or extrinsic motivation to learn the language.

The digitalization of language education has increased reliance on tools that support motivating language practice (Moorhouse & Wong, 2025). Even though many platforms offer support with grammar, vocabulary, or reading skills, promoting communicative competence, especially in speaking and interaction, remains challenging. LLM-based conversational agents, which use natural language processing (NLP) and machine learning, offer an interesting alternative. However, their effectiveness depends on their technical functions, as well as on how students feel about them and their motivation. For this reason, understanding students' psychological and emotional reactions to these tools is important for determining how to implement them effectively in the foreign language learning classroom.

1.2. Objective and Hypotheses

The main objective of this study is to explore how undergraduate industrial engineering students perceive the use of LLM-based conversational agents as a support tool for learning foreign languages. The study combines two different perspectives: the extended version of the Technology Acceptance Model (TAM2), which helps to understand how students evaluate the usefulness, ease of use, and general attitude towards the conversational agents; and the Language Learning Orientations Scale (LLOS), which focuses on their motivation for learning a second language, based on Self-Determination Theory. Using both models, the study aims to analyze how students' interaction with conversational agents may influence their acceptance of the technology and their motivation to continue learning the foreign language. The following hypotheses guide this study:

- *Hypothesis 1:* Students will perceive LLM-based conversational agents as useful for improving their foreign language skills, particularly in terms of communicative competence. It is expected that these agents will increase spontaneous conversational practice, allowing students to engage at their own pace and at any time.
- *Hypothesis 2:* Students will find the conversational agents easy to use and to integrate into their learning routines. No significant technological constraints are expected to impede natural and spontaneous human–machine dialogue.
- *Hypothesis 3:* Perceived usefulness and perceived ease of use will positively influence students' attitudes toward the conversational agents and their intention to continue using them regularly.
- *Hypothesis 4:* Positive attitudes toward the conversational agents will also enhance students' interest in learning a foreign language.

2. BACKGROUND

2.1. Integrating Technology Acceptance and Language Learning Motivation

The present study adopts an integrated theoretical framework combining the Technology Acceptance Model 2 (TAM2, Venkatesh & Davis, 2000) and the Language Learning Orientations Scale (LLOS, Noels et al., 2000) to examine both learners' technological perceptions and their motivational orientations in AI-mediated foreign language learning. While TAM2 focuses on how users evaluate and adopt technological tools, LLOS provides insight into the quality and nature of learners' motivation for language learning grounded in Self-Determination Theory. The use of these models provides a multidimensional understanding of how LLM-based conversational agents are experienced in educational contexts.

TAM2 extends the original Technology Acceptance Model (Davis, 1989) by incorporating additional cognitive and social determinants influencing technology adoption, particularly perceived usefulness, perceived ease of use, attitudes toward technology, and behavioral intention to use. In educational settings, TAM models have consistently demonstrated that learners' willingness to engage with digital tools is largely shaped by their beliefs about the tool's effectiveness in supporting learning outcomes and the effort required to use it (Belda-Medina & Calvo-Ferrer, 2022). Within AI-mediated language learning, perceived usefulness reflects learners' judgments regarding the conversational agent's capacity to enhance communicative competence, provide practice opportunities, and support task completion, whereas perceived ease of use captures the extent to which interaction with the system is intuitive, stable, and free of technical barriers (Venkatesh & Davis, 2000).

However, technology acceptance alone does not fully explain sustained engagement in learning activities. Learners may find tools useful and easy to use; however, they can remain weakly motivated to invest effort in language learning. Therefore, TAM2 is complemented in this study by the Language Learning Orientations Scale (LLOS), which integrates the motivational component along the self-determination continuum, ranging from amotivation and controlled extrinsic regulation to autonomous extrinsic motivation and intrinsic motivation (Noels et al., 2000). In this sense, LLOS examines whether students engage in language learning due to external pressures, internalized personal goals, genuine interest, enjoyment or pleasure.

The conceptual integration of TAM2 and LLOS is based on the premise that technology-mediated learning experiences emerge from the interaction between system-related perceptions and learner-internal motivational processes (Chiu, 2022; He & Li, 2022). From this perspective, TAM2 explains how learners evaluate the technological affordances of conversational AI, whereas LLOS captures why learners engage in language learning and how autonomously they regulate their learning behavior (Ryan & Deci, 2020). Autonomous forms of motivation, such as intrinsic motivation and identified regulation, are theoretically associated with higher engagement, persistence, and openness to new learning tools, while controlled motivation and amotivation may limit meaningful technology adoption despite positive usability perceptions (Chiu, 2022; Oudeyer, 2016; Stiegemeier et al., 2023).

In AI-integrated language learning environments, these technology acceptance and motivation are expected to interact in specific ways. Learners with strong autonomous motivation may experience interaction with conversational agents as less effort-demanding and more engaging, positively influencing perceived ease of use and exploratory behavior (Hidayat-ur-Rehman, 2024). On the other hand, well-designed pedagogically meaningful conversational agent systems may support learners' sense of competence and enjoyment, reinforcing motivational engagement even if they do not immediately transform deeper motivational orientations in the short term (Ryan & Deci, 2020). The combined framework, therefore, allows for an examination of whether acceptance of conversational AI is primarily driven by technological acceptance, motivational orientations, or by their interaction.

By integrating TAM2 and LLOS, the present study examines how students perceive conversational AI tools and how these tools operate within motivational structures that support learning engagement. This theoretical alignment could be especially relevant in AI-based educational environments, where technological innovation and learner psychology together may determine instructional effectiveness.

2.2. LLM-Based Conversational Agents in Foreign Language Education

The integration of artificial intelligence (AI) into foreign language education appears to have significantly reshaped how learners practice target languages. Within the broader paradigm of Computer-Assisted Language Learning (CALL), recent developments in artificial intelligence have promoted more flexible, personalized, and interactive learning opportunities (Cheung et al., 2021; Oliveira et al., 2021). Early CALL proposals mainly supported receptive skills and form-focused instruction; however, recent AI-based platforms promote functional, authentic, and spontaneous communicative practice, with increased learner autonomy and adaptive feedback (Brown & Lee, 2025; Mohebbi, 2025). In this sense, these new AI-based technologies seem to be valuable tools for improving learners' output practice and, consequently, language acquisition.

Among the different AI-based tools currently introduced into language learning, LLM-based conversational agents, or chatbots, have become especially prominent (Casheekar et al., 2024; Gu & Yu, 2025). These systems are designed to simulate dialogues with humans through natural language processing, offering them exposure to comprehensible input and opportunities for output in relaxed practice conditions (Lin et al., 2023; Taecharungroj, 2023). Empirical studies have demonstrated that interaction with conversational agents can support the development of linguistic and pragmatic competence by situating language use in meaningful communicative scenarios (Belda-Medina & Calvo-Ferrer, 2022; Morales & Calla, 2025; Jara Chiriboga et al., 2025). This characteristic is especially significant in professional language learning, where learners gain from practicing specific professional communicative tasks.

Previous research has also emphasized a series of affective benefits associated with the use of LLM-based conversational agents in the foreign language classroom. As a consequence of the fact that these systems allow private, on-demand interaction and immediate feedback, learners frequently report increased confidence, reduced language anxiety, and improved willingness to communicate (Fathi et al., 2024; Jusoh & Kadir, 2025; Moya & Camacho, 2024; Polakova & Klimova, 2024; Tai & Chen, 2023; Yuan, 2024; Zhang et al., 2024). These advantages appear to foster higher levels of engagement and promote sustained language practice beyond the classroom (Hew et al, 2023; Zhang et al., 2025).

From a pedagogical perspective, conversational AI aligns with several principles of communicative and task-based approaches (Huang et al., 2022). First, it facilitates meaningful interaction by providing opportunities to negotiate meaning, make clarification requests, or engage in repair sequences. Second, interaction can be tailored to learner needs by varying linguistic complexity, pacing, and scaffolding, thereby increasing relevance and accessibility. Third, conversational agents can complement in-class instruction by offering additional practice opportunities when human interlocutors are unavailable, addressing one of the most persistent challenges in foreign language education.

Despite recent advances in these tools, integrating conversational AI remains challenging. Earlier conversational agents were often characterized as basic, repetitive, and unable to sustain meaningful interaction. Although the present systems are more capable of understanding language and context, there are still concerns about maintaining conversations coherent, avoiding deviations, and meeting learning objectives. As a result, it is necessary to balance the benefits of the technology with suitable teaching purposes. These considerations lead into the next section, which examines large language models and the instructional importance of prompt design.

2.3. Large Language Models and Prompt Design in Educational Scenarios

The emergence of large language models (LLMs) empowered by AI has significantly expanded the potential of conversational agents in educational contexts by enabling highly contextualized, natural interactions. LLM-based tools, such as those provided by *ChatGPT*, differ from earlier pattern-matching conversational agents because they can dynamically generate output that reflects discourse history, pragmatic intent, and situational demands (Pirjan & Petrosanu, 2024; Yigit & Bayraktar, 2025). Their ability to adjust linguistic complexity, imitate professional registers, and sustain extended conversation makes them suitable tools for foreign-language instruction, particularly in workplace-oriented scenarios where learners must mobilize both linguistic accuracy and communicative appropriateness (Salvetti et al, 2025; Wiboolyasarin et al., 2025).

However, the pedagogical success of LLM-mediated interactions depends particularly on the prompt's design, which structures the conversation (Pawlik, 2025). Prompt design refers to the specific instructions that guide a model's behavior so that the resulting dialogue remains coherent, goal-directed, and educationally relevant (Carrasco-Sáez et al., 2025). A well-structured prompt must define the interactional frame, including contextual information such as the professional scenario, roles, and situational background; task instructions outlining the learner's communicative goals; and objectives that determine when the task has been successfully completed (Lee & Palmer, 2025; Vaira et al., 2025). These elements ensure that the conversation is embedded in a meaningful communicative purpose (Wiboolyasarin et al., 2025), a fundamental principle in task-based language teaching (Ellis, 2003; Nunan, 2004).

In addition to setting context and goals, effective prompt design also incorporates conversational controlled mechanisms (Huang, 2022). One important mechanism is the definition of allowed and non-allowed deviations. Because LLMs can generate unlimited content, it is necessary to specify which thematic shifts are acceptable and how the conversational agent should respond to those that are not. As a result, it helps maintain relevance while preserving conversation flow and avoiding undesired conversations or inappropriate queries (Bhardwaj et al, 2024). This fact also aligns with task-based assessment principles, in which thematic coherence and task completion are central blocks (Ellis, 2003; Nunan, 2004).

Another critical component of prompt design concerns interactional structure. LLM-based conversational agents benefit from staged prompts that define the conversational phases: opening (e.g., greeting, introduction), topic development (information exchange, negotiation, clarification), and closure (confirming decisions, summarizing agreements) (Dai et al, 2025; Spagnolli et al, 2023). Providing a structured sequence helps ensure that the dialogue resembles real professional interaction, typically linear, purposeful, and closed with clear next steps. This is particularly relevant in workplace communication training, where pragmatic moves such as requesting clarification, negotiating dates, or closing a meeting are as important as linguistic accuracy (Brown, 2007; Brown & Lee, 2025).

Prompt design may also enable LLM-based conversational agents to provide near-perfect output with no errors, in accordance with the pedagogical premise that conversational agents must model professional discourse conventions aligned with the task objectives (Moorhouse & Wong, 2025). When the output remains consistent and reliable, learners receive uniform linguistic input and feedback, which is especially beneficial when their work is autonomous and without the immediate teacher's supervision (Huang et al., 2022). Structured prompts can also guide the conversational agent to request clarifications, simplify language when needed, and provide brief contextual cues, thereby supporting personalized interaction (Huang et al., 2022).

In general, prompt design functions as the core pedagogical component of LLM-mediated communication (Dai et al., 2025; Zhong et al., 2025). It transforms a general-purpose language model into a controlled instructional tool capable of producing purposeful, contextually coherent conversations aligned with instructional goals. However, research on prompt engineering in foreign-language education is still in its early stages. While existing studies offer valuable insights, there is still a research gap regarding how specialized prompts influence interactional quality and the general learning experience. To address this gap, the present study proposes and evaluates a structured prompt-design model tailored to L2 professional practice, considering established frameworks previously applied in similar educational and technological contexts.

2.4. Evaluation of L2 Learning with Conversational Agents

The use of conversational agents powered by artificial intelligence (AI) has emerged as a key innovation in the field of foreign language teaching and learning. Conversational agents, powered by advanced large language models (LLMs), can generate original text and engage in natural conversations with users. This technology enables the simulation of realistic communicative situations and the provision of immediate, personalized feedback, thereby supporting the development of communicative competence in educational contexts (Moorhouse & Wong, 2025).

Pioneer studies have demonstrated the benefits and limitations of conversational LLM-based conversational agents for language learning. Belda-Medina and Calvo-Ferrer (2022) found that these agents act as effective virtual conversation partners, reducing students' anxiety and promoting positive attitudes, although participants still preferred human interaction. In a systematic review, Huang et al. (2022) reported that LLM-based conversational agents fostered engagement and provided valuable feedback, but noted issues with long-term motivation and the need for careful alignment with pedagogical goals. Wang et al. (2024) showed that EFL learners who interacted with visually embodied conversational agents experienced greater willingness to communicate and reduced speaking anxiety, even if improvements in speaking performance were mostly perceived rather than measured. Similarly, Polakova and Klimova (2024) observed significant language gains and positive attitudes toward conversational agents among university students, particularly at higher proficiency levels, while highlighting concerns related to data privacy and the lack of authentic human interaction.

None of the empirical studies on language learning conversational agents cited above have applied the TAM, TAM2, or LLOS frameworks. However, these models have been adopted in studies of acceptance towards conversational agents in other fields. For example, de Andrés-Sánchez and Gené-Albesa (2024) used the Technology Acceptance Model (TAM) to analyze users' attitudes and behavioral intentions towards LLM-based conversational agents in insurance settings, confirming the suitability of TAM blocks (perceived usefulness and perceived ease of use) as well as additional factors such as social influence and trust, in predicting acceptance. Similarly, Aqueveque (2024) explored the application of generative AI and conversational agents for psychotherapy training. Although the study did not employ TAM directly, it highlighted the potential of these tools for educational innovation in psychology.

In summary, conversational agents represent a promising tool for language education. When thoughtfully integrated into teaching practice, they can significantly contribute to the development of communicative skills in foreign language learners, provided that their limitations and ethical implications are considered.

3. METHOD

3.1. Participants

This study involved a sample of 70 undergraduate students enrolled in the course Professional English for Engineering (course code 13436) at the Polytechnic University of Valencia, in Spain. All participants were industrial engineering students with an intermediate level of English (B1–B2 according to the CEFR). During the intervention, the participants interacted with conversational agents through *ChatGPT*, using structured prompts explicitly designed by the instructor. These prompts guided students through realistic professional situations, such as job interviews, ordering products, participating in meetings, and handling phone calls. Each prompt clearly defined the context, the students' and the agents' roles, interaction goals, and included examples of possible dialogues to help students achieve specific language and communication objectives. In total, the students completed 20 role-play tasks with conversational agents.

3.2. Tools

3.2.1. LLM-Based Conversational Agents

Students interacted with the LLM-based conversational agent through the web-based *ChatGPT* interface (free public version available in September 2025), accessed via desktop and laptop computers. The platform was used as a standalone environment, without external plugins, software integrations, or customized APIs, ensuring a uniform technical setting for all participants. Within this environment, the conversational agent was used through a structured prompt design framework specifically developed for professional foreign-language communication.

This instructional prompt template served as the operational framework of the system, guaranteeing consistency, coherence, pedagogical alignment, and technical stability across all interactions. The template integrated five essential components that defined the conversational agent's behavior during human–machine exchanges, ensuring that each task followed a predictable and educationally meaningful interactional structure. Table 1 presents the instructional prompt template for communication tasks with LLM-based conversational agents. A complete prompt example is provided in Appendix 1 with the instructions for the conversational agent through *ChatGPT*. In addition, Appendix 2 contains the students' task instructions for the same role-play activity, and Appendix 3 shows the results of the activity (the interaction between the student and the conversational agent) and the automated feedback generated after completing the activity.

- *Scenario*: This section establishes the context, communicative situation, interlocutor roles, and background conditions. It provides the model with the contextual frame necessary to generate realistic, domain-specific discourse and ensures that the interaction is anchored in authentic workplace communication.
- *Instructions*: These specify how the conversational agent should behave throughout the task: tone, level of formality, linguistic accuracy requirements, support strategies, and limits regarding creativity or improvisation. They also define the conversational agent's role as a coherent, stable instructional agent capable of modelling professional discourse. Our instructions also requested an assessment report, including a transcript of the conversation, quantification of students' errors (grammar, vocabulary, word order, spelling, and others), and general feedback.
- Objectives: This section establishes the communicative goals to be achieved during the interaction (e.g., requesting information, negotiating a schedule, clarifying specifications, resolving a problem). By explicitly defining target outcomes, the template ensures the conversation remains focused on task completion rather than veering into open-ended dialogue.
- Permissible deviations: Since LLMs can easily shift topics, the template includes explicit guidelines describing which thematic digressions are acceptable and how the conversational agent should handle unauthorized deviations. The model is instructed either to redirect, clarify, or terminate the exchange depending on the deviation type, ensuring conversational coherence and adherence to task goals.
- Checkpoints: Intermediate steps the conversational agent must verify during the interaction (e.g., confirming information, checking understanding, verifying decisions). They create a staged interactional structure resembling real professional exchanges and ensure that the dialogue follows a logical progression.
- Example of Conversation Flow: The expected structure of the interaction, including the automatic opening greeting, redirection procedures, task achieve-

ment, and closure. This example works as a behavioral script that reinforces consistency across user interactions.

- Possible Result: An illustration of a fully completed, thematically coherent conversation sample. This sample helps to validate whether the conversational agent is performing according to the specifications and supports qualitative assessment of its adequacy.

Table 1. Instructional Prompt Template for Tasks with Conversational Agents.

Instructions for the computer	
a. Scenario	
Instructions	
Objective	
Permissible deviations	
Checkpoints	
b. Example of Conversation Flow	
Conversation Start	
Permissible deviations	
Redirection	
Objective Achieved	
End of Interaction	
Voluntary Exit	
c. Possible Result	

3.2.2. Questionnaires

An adapted version of the Technology Acceptance Model 2 (TAM2) (Venkatesh & Davis, 2000) was used to assess students' perceptions of the conversational agents. TAM2 extends the original TAM (Davis, 1989) by incorporating additional cognitive and motivational determinants of technology acceptance. The adapted instrument used in this study included the core TAM blocks, Perceived Usefulness (PU), Perceived Ease of Use (PEU), Attitude Toward Using (ATU), and Behavioral Intention to Use (BIU), and it included other factors incorporated into TAM2, such as Self-Efficacy (SE), Perceived Behavioral Control (PBC), Personal Innovativeness (PI), and User Satisfaction (US). All items were contextualized to reflect students' experiences interacting with the conversational agents in a foreign-language learning environment and were rated on a 7-point Likert scale (1 = strongly disagree, 7 =

strongly agree). This extended TAM2 structure allowed for a comprehensive examination of the factors influencing learners' acceptance, confidence, and willingness to continue using conversational AI for language learning.

In parallel, to evaluate students' motivational orientations toward foreign language learning, the study used the Language Learning Orientations Scale (LLOS), developed by Noels et al. (2000) and grounded in Self-Determination Theory (Deci & Ryan, 1985). The LLOS measures various types of motivation along the self-determination continuum, including Intrinsic Motivation (IM-Knowledge, IM-Accomplishment, IM-Stimulation), Extrinsic Motivation (Identified Regulation, Introjected Regulation, External Regulation), and Amotivation. The adapted version used in this study included 21 items, also rated on a 7-point Likert scale, and was designed to explore how the presence of AI-mediated interaction might align with or influence students' motivational profiles.

3.3. Procedure

3.3.1. Intervention Procedure

At the beginning of the intervention, students were introduced to conversational AI and received guidelines for interacting with the conversational agent via the computer interface. A brief training session, including a pilot conversation, helped familiarize them with the tool and ensured that all participants understood the structure of the conversational tasks. Over the ten weeks, students completed two interactions with conversational agents per week, totaling twenty tasks per participant. Each task was designed using the structured instructional prompt template described in Table 1, guaranteeing alignment with the defined scenario, communicative objectives, permissible deviations, and interactional checkpoints. The conversational agent initiated each conversation automatically, guided learners through the communicative sequence, and ensured either task completion or a voluntary exit. All conversations were automatically logged, creating a comprehensive record of interactional behavior, task completion, and linguistic output. These logs were subsequently reviewed by the instructors to assess students' performance and provide them with personalized feedback. Although the conversational agent was designed to provide feedback, this pilot study used it as a supportive component to complete the communicative tasks rather than as a validated assessment instrument, as its reliability could not be fully guaranteed.

At the end of the intervention, all participants completed the TAM2 and LLOS questionnaires. These instruments generated quantitative data on students' perceptions of the conversational agent's usability, usefulness, clarity, and overall acceptance (TAM2), as well as their motivational orientations toward language learning

(LLOS). As a result, this experiment examines how technological acceptance and motivational orientations shape students' engagement with conversational AI, laying the foundation for the results presented in the next section.

3.3.2. Data Processing and Analysis

Data obtained from questionnaires were analyzed to determine the results. Before conducting the statistical analyses, all negatively worded items were reversed (TAM2, Questions 1, 2, 3). Then, scores were computed in blocks by averaging the items within each block for both the TAM2 and LLOS instruments. To examine the reliability of each block, Cronbach's alpha coefficients (α) were calculated for all TAM2 and LLOS blocks. Values above .70 were interpreted as acceptable, whereas values above .80 and .90 were considered good and excellent, respectively.

Following the reliability assessment, Pearson correlation coefficients (r) were computed to explore the relationships among blocks. Three correlation matrices were generated. The first focused on intra-TAM correlations, assessing the structural relationships predicted by TAM (e.g., PEU–PU, PU–ATT, ATT–BI). The second focused on intra-LLOS correlations, examining whether the motivational orientations followed the theoretically expected self-determination continuum from external regulation to intrinsic motivation. The third analyzed cross-correlations between the TAM2 and LLOS constructs, allowing an examination of how motivational orientations aligned with students' perceptions of conversational agent usability, usefulness, and acceptance.

Significance levels were set at $p < .05$, and correlation strength was interpreted according to conventional benchmarks (weak = .10–.29, moderate = .30–.49, strong = .50–.69, very strong ≥ .70). This analysis allowed verifying the internal coherence of each model and exploring how motivation and technology-acceptance variables interacted within the context of AI-mediated foreign-language learning.

4. RESULTS

4.1. Analysis of the Technology Acceptance Model (TAM2)

TAM2 revealed generally positive perceptions of conversational agents for language learning among participants. Perceived Ease of Use (PEU) obtained a high mean score (M = 5.83, SD = 0.92) and very good internal consistency (α = .88), indicating that students found the conversational agents intuitive, flexible, and easy to use. Similarly, Perceived Usefulness (PU) reached one of the highest levels among TAM2 blocks (M = 5.72, SD = 0.96; α = .94), suggesting that learners clearly recognized the potential of LLM-based conversational agents to enhance productivity, facilitate access to learning opportunities, and support context-based communicative practices.

Attitudinal responses were also positive. Attitude Toward Using (ATU) showed a strong mean (M = 5.67, SD = 0.98) and excellent internal reliability (α = .89), reflecting a generally favorable disposition toward integrating conversational agents into language learning. Likewise, Behavioral Intention to Use (BIU) reached moderately high scores (M = 4.98, SD = 1.12; α = .84), indicating that many students intended to continue using conversational agents and expressed interest in learning more about them, although with higher variability than in attitudinal measures.

Regarding additional TAM2-related blocks, Self-Efficacy (SE) and Perceived Behavioral Control (PBC) displayed solid levels of confidence and perceived competence in using conversational agents (SE: M = 5.52, SD = 1.17, α = .83; PBC: M = 5.41, SD = 1.18, α = .81). User Satisfaction (US), measured through a single item, yielded a moderately high mean (M = 5.34, SD = 1.41), though showing greater dispersion across participants. Finally, Personal Innovativeness (PI) demonstrated moderate-to-high inclination toward experimenting with new digital tools (M = 5.14, SD = 1.39; α = .82), suggesting that students generally perceive themselves as open to technological innovation, with some considerable individual variation.

In general, TAM2 results suggest that participants viewed LLM-based conversational agents as usable and practical tools, and they also expressed positive attitudes and intentions to integrate them into their language learning routines. The consistently high reliability values support the consistency of the measurement instruments.

Table 2. TAM2 Results.

Block	Items	M	SD	α	Reliability
Perceived Ease of Use (PEU)	5	5.83	0.92	.88	Very good
Perceived Usefulness (PU)	8	5.72	0.96	.94	Excellent
Attitude Toward Using (ATU)	3	5.67	0.98	.89	Very good
Behavioral Intention to Use (BIU)	2	4.98	1.12	.84	Very good
User Satisfaction (US)	1	5.34	1.41	-	-
Perceived Behavioral Control (PBC)	2	5.41	1.18	.81	Good
Self-Efficacy (SE)	2	5.52	1.17	.83	Very good
Personal Innovativeness (PI)	2	5.14	1.39	.82	Very good

Regarding the intercorrelations among the TAM2 blocks (see Table 3), the results revealed a coherent, highly consistent pattern. All blocks were positively and moderately to strongly associated with one another (r = .43–.85), indicating that students' perceptions of the conversational agent as easy to use, helpful, and satisfying are closely interrelated. In line with the original TAM2 assumptions, Perceived Usefulness (PU) shows particularly strong correlations with Attitude Toward Using (ATU; r = .85) and User Satisfaction (US; r = .85), suggesting that learners who perceived the conversational agent as useful also reported more positive attitudes and higher satisfaction with its use. Similarly, Attitude Toward Using (ATU) is strongly related to Behavioral Intention to Use (BIU; r = .76) and US (r = .81), which indicates that favorable attitudes are closely linked to both continued use intentions and overall satisfaction.

The extended TAM2 variables also integrate well into this structure. Perceived Behavioral Control (PBC) and Self-Efficacy (SE) are strongly associated with each other (r = .80) and show substantial correlations with Perceived Usefulness (PU, r = .76 and .73, respectively) and User Satisfaction (US, both r = .69), suggesting that students who feel more capable and in control when using the conversational agent also tend to view it as more valuable and satisfying. Personal Innovativeness (PI) shows moderate-to-strong correlations with all other blocks (r = .57–.70), suggesting that students who see themselves as more willing to try new technologies are also more inclined to perceive the conversational agent as easy to use, helpful, and worth integrating into their learning routines. In general, the correlation matrix supports an internally consistent pattern of acceptance, reinforcing the suitability of the TAM2 framework and its extensions for explaining students' perceptions of conversational AI in this context.

Table 3. Correlation TAM2 Blocks.

	PEU	PU	ATT	BIU	US	PBC	SE	PI
PEU	**-**	**.60**	**.57**	**.43**	**.53**	**.44**	**.60**	**.57**
PU	.60	-	.85	.66	.85	.76	.73	.69
ATT	.57	.85	-	.76	.81	.69	.69	.65
BIU	.43	.66	.76	-	.69	.72	.53	.61
US	.53	.85	.81	.69	-	.78	.69	.66
PBC	.44	.76	.69	.72	.78	-	.80	.66
SE	.60	.73	.69	.53	.69	.80	-	.70
PI	.57	.69	.65	.61	.66	.66	.70	-

4.2. Analysis of the Language Learning Orientations Scale (LLOS)

The motivational data obtained through the Language Learning Orientations Scale (LLOS) showed clear patterns aligned with self-determination theory. Amotivation scores were very low (M = 6.83 after reverse coding), indicating that participants generally rejected statements reflecting a lack of purpose or disengagement in language learning. All amotivation items were negatively phrased and were therefore reverse-coded prior to analysis to ensure directional consistency across the motivational scales. Although the amotivation subscale showed lower internal consistency (α = .625) compared to the other LLOS dimensions, this pattern is consistent with previous studies employing the LLOS, in which this dimension frequently yields weaker reliability coefficients. This moderate reliability should thus be interpreted with caution, without detracting from the general motivational trends observed in the data.

Autonomous motivations were the most common. Identified regulations displayed consistently high scores (M = 5.65; α = .78), indicating that students viewed learning a foreign language as personally meaningful and connected to their own goals. The three intrinsic motivation subdimensions showed the highest means across the scale and excellent reliability coefficients: Knowledge (M = 5.13; α = .89), Accomplishment (M = 5.20; α = .91), and Stimulation (M = 5.12; α = .94). These results suggest that learners were strongly motivated by curiosity, progress, or achievement, and the enjoyment of using the target language. In general, these findings seem to indicate that motivational patterns are predominantly autonomous, with intrinsic motivation playing a central role. This motivational profile is often connected with deeper engagement, self-regulation, and more sustained learning effort (Deci & Ryan, 1985; Noels et al., 2000).

Table 4. LLOS Results.

Block	Items	M	SD	α	Reliability
1. Amotivation	3	6.83	0.393	.625	Questionable
2. External Regulation	3	4.61	1.231	.767	Good
3. Internal Regulation	3	3.76	1.668	.821	Very Good
4. Identified Regulation	3	5.65	1.197	.781	Good
5. Intrinsic Motivation-Knowledge	3	5.13	1.376	.889	Very Good
6. Intrinsic Motivation-Accomplishment	3	5.20	1.330	.913	Excellent
7. Intrinsic Motivation-Stimulation	3	5.12	1.533	.939	Excellent

The correlation matrix for the LLOS blocks (see Table 5) shows a pattern that closely aligns with the continuum proposed by Self-Determination Theory (Deci & Ryan, 1985; Noels et al., 2000). The three forms of intrinsic motivation (IMK, IMA, IMS) show consistently strong, positive associations with one another (r = .59–.68), forming a cohesive intrinsic-motivation group. Regulation Identified (IDR), the most autonomous form of extrinsic motivation, is also strongly correlated with these intrinsic dimensions (r = .46–.61), confirming its conceptual proximity to intrinsic orientations and its role as a transitional point toward more self-determined forms of engagement.

In contrast, more controlled forms of extrinsic motivation behave differently. External Regulation (ER) shows a strong, expected correlation with Introjected Regulation (IR; r = .50), suggesting that these two controlled types tend to co-occur. External Regulation (ER) also shows weaker, more inconsistent links with more autonomous motivations (e.g., r = .00 with IMK; r = .24 with IMS), reflecting its lower level of self-determination. Introjected Regulation (IR) occupies an intermediate position, showing moderate relationships with both controlled and autonomous blocks (r = .19–.43), consistent with its hybrid nature along the self-determination continuum.

As expected, amotivation (A) shows weak or even negative correlations with almost all motivation types (r = –.22 to .17), suggesting that students who reported low purpose or value in learning languages did not exhibit strong autonomous or controlled motivational orientations. Its near-zero association with intrinsic motivation (e.g., r = .00 with IMS, r = .05 with IMK) reinforces its conceptual status as a disengaged state rather than a motivational form.

In this case, the correlation matrix shows a well-structured and theoretically coherent motivational pattern: controlled motivations are closely connected, autonomous motivations form a strong block, and amotivation remains largely disconnected. This general pattern supports the validity of the LLOS blocks in capturing meaningful differences in students' motivational orientations within the context of language learning with conversational agents.

Table 5. Correlation LLOS Blocks.

	A	ER	IR	IDR	IMK	IMA	IMS
A	**-**	**-.22**	**-.16**	**.17**	**.05**	**.16**	**.00**
ER	-.22	-	.50	.18	.00	-.02	.24
IR	-.16	.50	-	.29	.19	.24	.43
IDR	.17	.18	.29	-	.55	.46	.61
IMK	.05	.00	.19	.55	-	.68	.59

continued on following page

Table 5. Continued

	A	ER	IR	IDR	IMK	IMA	IMS
A	-	-.22	-.16	.17	.05	.16	.00
IMA	.16	-.02	.24	.46	.68	-	.59
IMS	.00	.24	.43	.61	.59	.59	-

4.3. Cross-Correlation between TAM2 and LLOS

The cross-correlation matrix between TAM2 and LLOS blocks (see Table 6) reveals several meaningful associations that help explain how students' motivational orientations relate to their acceptance of language learning with conversational agents. In general, while many correlations are modest, the pattern shows theoretically coherent links, particularly between autonomous forms of motivation and key TAM2 dimensions.

The most notable relationships emerge between intrinsic motivation, especially Intrinsic Motivation–Stimulation (IMS), and the TAM2 blocks associated with usability and engagement. IMS shows moderate-to-strong correlations with Perceived Ease of Use (PEU; r = .51) and Personal Innovativeness (PI; r = .42), suggesting that students who experience genuine enjoyment, interest, or stimulation in learning are more likely to perceive the conversational agent as easy to use and to show a greater willingness to explore and integrate technological tools into their learning practices. This pattern aligns with the idea that intrinsic motivation facilitates exploratory behavior and reduces perceived effort in technology-mediated tasks.

Similarly, Regulation Identified (IDR), the most autonomous form of extrinsic motivation, shows meaningful correlations with Perceived Ease of Use (PEU, r = .41) and Personal Innovativeness (PI, r = .29). These results suggest that students who personally value learning a language and see it as important for their goals tend to perceive the conversational agent as more manageable and are more inclined to adopt it. The association suggests that the perceived relevance of language learning may enhance students' openness to instructional technologies designed to support it.

In contrast, TAM2 blocks, such as Perceived Usefulness (PU), Attitude (ATT), and Behavioral Intention (BIU), show weaker, and generally non-significant, correlations with the motivational dimensions of the LLOS. This fact shows that students' acceptance of the conversational agent, especially in terms of perceived usefulness and future intention to use, is less dependent on their personal motivational profile and more closely related to their direct experience with the tool's technological characteristics (as shown in Table 3). These findings align with TAM2 assumptions that perceptions of usefulness and attitude are driven primarily by technology-related factors rather than internal motivational dispositions (Venkatesh & Davis, 2000).

Controlled forms of motivation show mixed patterns. External Regulation (ER) shows a weak positive correlation with Perceived Ease of Use (PEU), Perceived Usefulness (PU), and Personal Innovativeness (PI) (r = .25), suggesting that students under external pressure may also evaluate the conversational agent positively, though these connections are comparatively limited. In addition, Introjected Regulation (IR) shows only moderate correlations with IMS (r = .43) and marginally with Behavioral Intention to Use (BIU) and Personal Innovativeness (PI), reflecting its intermediate position on the self-determination continuum. As expected, amotivation shows no meaningful relationship with any TAM2 component, reinforcing its conceptual status as disengagement rather than a predictor of technology acceptance.

In general, these results suggest that acceptance of conversational AI in language learning is primarily driven by autonomous forms of motivation, particularly those influenced by personal values (IDR) and intrinsic interest or stimulation (IMS). Although technology-related perceptions remain central within TAM2, students' motivational orientations seem to contribute in specific ways, mainly affecting perceived ease of use (PEU) and their willingness to experiment with new technologies. This suggests that conversational agents use may be facilitated by improving tool design and fostering learning environments that promote more autonomous forms of motivation.

Table 6. Cross Correlation TAM2-LLOS.

	A	ER	IR	IDR	IMK	IMA	IMS
PEU	**.10**	**.25**	**.15**	**.41**	**.20**	**.12**	**.51**
PU	-.10	.25	-.02	.12	-.05	-.09	.16
ATT	-.03	.19	.05	.16	.05	.08	.16
BIU	-.22	.12	.20	.08	-.01	.05	.15
US	-.07	.23	.04	.17	.09	.04	.20
PBC	-.13	.13	.08	.15	.02	-.03	.18
SE	.06	.12	-.05	.24	.14	-.02	.22
PI	-.09	.25	.05	.29	.19	.13	**.42**

5. DISCUSSION

The purpose of this study was to examine how undergraduate engineering students perceive the use of LLM-based conversational agents in the context of foreign language learning, connecting students' perceptions (TAM2) with motivational orientations (LLOS). Four hypotheses were formulated to explore the extent to which interaction with conversational agents would (1) be perceived as useful for enhancing communicative competence, (2) be considered easy to use and seamlessly integrated into learners' routines, (3) generate positive attitudes and behavioral intentions consistent with the classical TAM2 structure, and (4) foster greater interest and motivation toward foreign language learning. The discussion below integrates the empirical findings with the theoretical framework and evaluates the degree to which these hypotheses were confirmed.

Hypothesis 1: Students will perceive conversational LLM-based conversational agents as useful for improving their foreign language skills, particularly in terms of communicative competence. It is expected that these conversational agents will increase spontaneous conversational practice, allowing students to engage at their own pace and at any time.

The results support Hypothesis 1, as Perceived Usefulness (PU) was rated with the highest mean score ($M = 5.72$) and an excellent reliability coefficient ($\alpha = .94$), suggesting that students view the conversational agents as effective tools for supporting their foreign language learning. This perception aligns with previous studies that have highlighted the potential of conversational agents to provide meaningful input, output practice, and opportunities for negotiation of meaning in realistic communicative scenarios, and consequently contributing to the development of linguistic and pragmatic competence (Belda-Medina & Calvo-Ferrer, 2022; Huang et al., 2022; Lin et al., 2023; Morales & Calla, 2025; Jara Chiriboga et al., 2025). In this experiment, the structured prompt design template for conversational agents, which included defining scenarios, participants' roles, objectives, permissible deviations, and checkpoints, helped interactions to be accessible and fluent, and pedagogically aligned with communicative tasks (Ellis, 2003; Nunan, 2004; Huang et al., 2022).

Interestingly, Perceived Usefulness (PU) showed limited associations with the LLOS blocks, suggesting that learners' perceptions of usefulness are primarily linked to their direct experience with the tool rather than to their pre-existing motivational orientations. This result is consistent with TAM2, which holds that perceived usefulness is primarily influenced by learners' beliefs about performance enhancement and task relevance (Davis, 1989; Venkatesh & Davis, 2000). From this perspective, the high perceived usefulness scores can be interpreted as evidence that the conversational agent, configured with a carefully designed instructional prompt, successfully provided contextually rich professional practice that students perceived as positive for their communicative performance.

Hypothesis 2: Students will find the conversational agents easy to use and to integrate into their learning routines. No significant technological constraints are expected to impede natural and spontaneous human–machine dialogue.

Hypothesis 2 was also strongly supported. Perceived Ease of Use (PEU) achieved very high mean scores (M = 5.83) and solid internal consistency (α = .88). In this case, students consistently reported that the conversational agent was intuitive, stable, and easy to incorporate into their routines. This finding aligns with recent descriptions of LLM-based conversational agents as systems capable of sustaining more natural, flexible interaction than earlier pattern-matching agents, thus reducing the technical barriers to participation (Pirjan & Petrosanu, 2024; Yigit & Bayraktar, 2025; Moorhouse & Wong, 2025). The prompt-design framework, with explicit specifications for interactional phases, linguistic accuracy, and redirection procedures, likely contributed to this perception by minimizing breakdowns and ensuring a coherent, cohesive conversational flow (Huang et al., 2022; Dai et al., 2025; Wiboolyasarin et al., 2025).

Moreover, Perceived Ease of Use (PEU) showed the clearest connection to autonomous motivational orientations, particularly Intrinsic Motivation–Stimulation (r = .51) and Identified Regulation (r = .41). Students who enjoy learning languages for their inherent interest or who attribute personal value to foreign language proficiency seem more inclined to perceive the conversational agent as easy to use, which is coherent with the Self-Determination Theory, which claims that intrinsic enjoyment and goals aligned with their interests and values reduce the perceived effort of engaging in learning activities (Deci & Ryan, 1985; Noels et al., 2000). In this sense, the perceived ease of use seems to reflect the combination of a well-designed technological-pedagogical environment and a motivational profile characterized by autonomous orientations, which helps students integrate conversational agents into their studies.

Hypothesis 3: Perceived usefulness and perceived ease of use will positively influence students' attitudes toward the conversational agents and their intention to continue using them regularly.

The results obtained confirmed Hypothesis 3. The relationships among the TAM2 blocks followed the acceptance sequence described in previous research, showing a high degree of internal coherence (Davis, 1989; Venkatesh & Davis, 2000). In this sense, Perceived Ease of Use (PEU) was strongly associated with Perceived Usefulness (PU) (r = .60), suggesting that students who found the conversational agent easy to use were more likely to consider it useful for their language learning. In addition, Perceived Usefulness (PU) showed a very strong correlation with Attitude Toward Using (ATU) (r = .85) and a substantial association with Behavioral Intention to Use

(BIU) (r = .66), suggesting that usefulness influenced both students' evaluations of the tool and their intention to continue using it. At the same time, Attitude Toward Using (ATU) was also strongly correlated with Behavioral Intention (BI) (r = .76), suggesting that positive evaluations of the conversational agent could be understood as a significant correlation between perceived usefulness and future use intention.

This pattern is fully consistent with TAM and TAM2, which propose that ease of use influences intention indirectly through perceived usefulness and attitude (Davis, 1989; Venkatesh & Davis, 2000). Therefore, these findings confirm the main assumptions of the model and align with recent studies that have confirmed the capacity to explain the TAM2 in technology-based learning contexts, including research on LLM-based conversational agents as educational tools (Cheung et al., 2021; de Andrés Sánchez & Gené Albesa, 2024; Moorhouse & Wong, 2025).

In addition, the extended TAM2 variables also behaved coherently within this structure. Self-Efficacy (SE) and Perceived Behavioral Control (PBC) were strongly related to each other and showed meaningful associations with Perceived Usefulness (PU) and User Satisfaction (US), suggesting that students who felt competent and in control when interacting with the conversational agent tended to assess it more positively. Personal Innovativeness (PI) was moderately to strongly associated with the main TAM2 blocks, indicating that learners who described themselves as open to experimenting with new technologies were more likely to perceive the conversational agent as easy to use, useful, and worth adopting.

By contrast, motivational dimensions measured through the LLOS did not strongly predict Attitude Toward Using (ATU) or Behavioral Intention (BI). This fact suggests that acceptance of the conversational agent was guided primarily by technology-related perceptions rather than by students' general motivational orientations toward language learning. According to this interpretation, Hypothesis 3 is confirmed: perceptions of ease of use and usefulness remain the main determinants of attitude formation and future use intention, while motivation plays a more limited, indirect role.

Hypothesis 4: Positive attitudes toward the conversational agents will also enhance students' interest in foreign language learning.

Results partially supported Hypothesis 4. On the one hand, students' attitudinal responses toward the conversational agent were clearly positive. Both Attitude Toward Using (ATU) and Behavioral Intention to Use (BIU) had high mean values, indicating that participants developed a favorable intention to integrate the conversational agent into their language-learning activities and expressed a willingness to continue using it. This finding is consistent with previous research showing that the interaction with the conversational agent can enhance positive emotions, reduce language anxiety, and increase learners' willingness to communicate, particularly in task-based and professional contexts (Fathi et al., 2024; Polakova & Klimova, 2024;

Tai & Chen, 2023; Wang et al., 2024; Yuan, 2024; Zhang et al., 2024, 2025). In this research, LLM-based conversational agents appear to have been incorporated as a legitimate and well-accepted component of the learning environment, especially for professional communication tasks.

On the other hand, this positive attitudinal response did not imply substantial changes in students' general motivational orientations toward foreign language learning. The LLOS results showed that participants already exhibited a predominantly autonomous motivational profile, characterized by very low levels of amotivation and high scores in identified regulation and intrinsic motivation (knowledge, accomplishment, and stimulation). The correlation matrix among LLOS blocks closely followed the self-determination continuum, while cross-correlations with TAM2 blocks were generally low. The main exceptions were moderate associations between Intrinsic Motivation–Stimulation (IMS), Identified Regulation (IDR), and Perceived Ease of Use (PEU), suggesting that motivation influenced how students experienced the conversational agent, rather than the conversational agent modifying their general reasons for learning the language.

This pattern suggests that, within the scope of the 10-week intervention, the conversational agent supported existing autonomous motivations but did not substantially modify deeper motivational structures. This result aligns with Self-Determination Theory, which holds that changes in motivational orientation typically require sustained pedagogical conditions that support autonomy, competence, and social connection over the long term (Deci & Ryan, 1985; Noels et al., 2000). In this sense, while students seemed to enjoy the conversational agent and found it manageable, the expected change in motivation was modest.

These findings reinforce previous literature suggesting that the practice with conversational agents enhances communicative opportunities, supports negotiation of meaning, and reduces anxiety, without necessarily producing immediate changes in motivational orientation (Belda-Medina & Calvo-Ferrer, 2022; Polakova & Klimova, 2024). The structured prompt design implemented in this study, with clear scenarios, interactional checkpoints, permissible deviations, and a sample of conversational flow, plays a key role in ensuring pedagogically coherent interaction. This fact supports previous literature that claims that prompt design constitutes a central pedagogical component in LLM-mediated language instruction (Pawlik, 2025; Wiboolyasarin et al., 2025). In this sense, attitudes toward the conversational agents were positive, but their motivational impact remained limited, leading to a partial confirmation of Hypothesis 4.

With three of the four hypotheses confirmed and the fourth partially supported, this research provides an overview of how LLM-based conversational agents are accepted by students and how they are experienced in foreign language learning contexts, using TAM2 and LLOS (Self-Determination Theory). In general, the findings suggest that students' engagement with instructionally structured conversational agents can be understood through the interaction of two complementary dimensions, technology acceptance and motivational orientation.

From an acceptance perspective, the results confirm the TAM2 questionnaire's relevance for explaining students' perspectives on conversational AI in educational contexts. Learners' perceptions of ease of use and usefulness emerge as central factors influencing attitudes towards the conversational agents and their intentions to continue using them, in line with the acceptance mechanisms originally proposed by Davis (1989) and later extended by Venkatesh and Davis (2000). This consistency with previous research reinforces the suitability of TAM-based models to explain the use of advanced AI or LLM-based tools for language learning (Cheung et al., 2021; de Andrés-Sánchez & Gené-Albesa, 2024; Moorhouse & Wong, 2025). Regarding motivation, learners approached foreign language learning with significant autonomous orientations, marked by strong intrinsic motivation and identified regulation and minimal amotivation. These motivational dimensions were internally coherent and only moderately associated with technology-related perceptions, mainly through perceived ease of use and personal innovativeness. This pattern suggests that motivation and acceptance function as related but distinct explanatory dimensions. In this sense, autonomous motivation can influence how students engage with the conversational agent, without being the main factor of attitudes or usage intentions in the short term.

These findings also support previous literature on the effective integration of conversational AI in foreign language education, which relies on the combination of three elements: (1) a solid technological design enabled by LLM-based conversational agents and careful prompt engineering, (2) a principled pedagogical design consistent with communicative and task-based approaches; and (3) a motivational context in which learners are guided by autonomous learning goals. (Ellis, 2003; Nunan, 2004; Huang et al., 2022; Dai et al., 2025; Moorhouse & Wong, 2025). By combining TAM2 and LLOS, this study aims to contribute to research on AI-based language learning, showing that conversational agents can be accepted and integrated into professional language learning.

6. CONCLUSION

This study examines undergraduate engineering students' perceptions of conversational LLM-based conversational agents for foreign language learning with TAM2 and LLOS. The findings confirm that instructionally structured conversational agents can be successfully incorporated into professional L2 practice. The findings show that conversational LLM-based conversational agents can be accepted in foreign language learning contexts when they are easy to use, clearly structured, and perceived as pedagogically relevant. Acceptance seems to depend on students' direct interaction with the conversational agents, rather than on their general motivational orientations toward language learning. At the same time, learners' autonomous motivation provides a favorable learning scenario for engagement, facilitating interaction with the tool without acting as a decisive factor in the development of attitudes or intention to use.

In sum, the findings in this study suggest that the effective integration of conversational AI in foreign language education relies on the interaction between a solid technological foundation enabled by LLM-based conversational agents and carefully designed prompts, a principled pedagogical framework aligned with communicative and task-based approaches, and a learning context in which students already approach language study with autonomous, self-determined learning goals (Ellis, 2003; Nunan, 2004; Huang et al., 2022; Dai et al., 2025; Moorhouse & Wong, 2025). By integrating TAM2 and LLOS, this study contributes to further research on AI-mediated language learning by showing that conversational agents can be accepted and pedagogically integrated into professional language courses.

At the same time, it should be acknowledged that longer-term instructional interventions that support learner autonomy could offer different insights into the relationship between conversational agent use and motivational development. Future research could focus on monitoring learners' progression through pre- and post-intervention measures, as well as on examining the relationship between technology acceptance, motivational orientations, and language learning outcomes.

REFERENCES

Aqueveque, F. C. (2024). Entrenamiento en Formulación de Casos en Psicoterapia a Través de Inteligencia Artificial Generativa. *Revista de Psicoterapia, 35*(127), 97–112. DOI: 10.5944/rdp.v35i127.37798

Belda-Medina, J., & Calvo-Ferrer, J. R. (2022). Using Chatbots as AI Conversational Partners in Language Learning. *Applied Sciences (Basel, Switzerland), 12*(17), 8427. DOI: 10.3390/app12178427

Bhardwaj, V., Dhaliwal, B. K., Sarangi, S. K., Thiyagu, T. M., Patidar, A., & Pithawa, D. (2024). Conversational AI: Introduction to chatbot's security risks, their probable solutions, and the best practices to follow. In Rawat, R., Chakrawarti, R. K., Sarangi, S. K., Vyas, P., Alamanda, M. S., Srividya, K., & Sankaran, K. S. (Eds.), *Conversational AI* (pp. 435–457)., DOI: 10.1002/9781394200801.ch26

Brown, H. D. (2007). *Principles of Language Learning and Teaching*. Longman.

Brown, H. D., & Lee, H. (2025). *Principles of Language Learning and Teaching: A course in second language acquisition*. Taylor & Francis. DOI: 10.4324/9781003494294

Carrasco-Sáez, J. L., Contreras-Saavedra, C., San-Martín-Quiroga, S., Contreras-Saavedra, C. E., & Viveros-Muñoz, R. (2025). Analyzing Higher Education Students' Prompting Techniques and Their Impact on *ChatGPT*'s Performance: An Exploratory Study in Spanish. *Applied Sciences (Basel, Switzerland), 15*(14), 7651. DOI: 10.3390/app15147651

Casheekar, A., Lahiri, A., Rath, K., Prabhakar, K. S., & Srinivasan, K. (2024). A contemporary review on chatbots, AI-powered virtual conversational agents, *ChatGPT*: Applications, open challenges and future research directions. *Computer Science Review, 52*, 100632. DOI: 10.1016/j.cosrev.2024.100632

Cheung, S. K., Kwok, L. F., Phusavat, K., & Yang, H. H. (2021). Shaping the future learning environments with smart elements: Challenges and opportunities. *International Journal of Educational Technology in Higher Education, 18*(1), 16. DOI: 10.1186/s41239-021-00254-1 PMID: 34778521

Chiu, T. K. (2022). School learning support for teacher technology integration from a self-determination theory perspective. *Educational Technology Research and Development, 70*(3), 931–949. DOI: 10.1007/s11423-022-10096-x PMID: 35228784

Dai, D. W., Zhu, H., & Chen, G. (2025). How does interaction with LLM powered chatbots shape human understanding of culture? The need for Critical Interactional Competence. *Annual Review of Applied Linguistics*, *45*, 28–49. DOI: 10.1017/S0267190525000054

Davis, F. D. (1989). Perceived usefulness, perceived ease of use, and user acceptance of information technology. *Management Information Systems Quarterly*, *13*(3), 319–340. DOI: 10.2307/249008

de Andrés-Sánchez, J., & Gené-Albesa, J. (2024). Assessing Attitude and Behavioral Intention toward Chatbots in an Insurance Setting: A Mixed Method Approach. *International Journal of Human-Computer Interaction*, *40*(17), 4918–4933. DOI: 10.1080/10447318.2023.2227833

Deci, E. L., & Ryan, R. M. (1985). The general causality orientations scale: Self-determination in personality. *Journal of Research in Personality*, *19*(2), 109–134. DOI: 10.1016/0092-6566(85)90023-6

Ellis, R. (2003). Designing a task-based syllabus. *RELC Journal*, *34*(1), 64–81. DOI: 10.1177/003368820303400105

Erdogan, N., & Christina, K. (2025). Integrating AI in language learning: Boosting pragmatic competence for young English learners. *LatIA*, *3*, 115. DOI: 10.62486/latia2025115

Fathi, J., Rahimi, M., & Derakhshan, A. (2024). Improving EFL learners' speaking skills and willingness to communicate via artificial intelligence-mediated interactions. *System*, *121*, 103254. DOI: 10.1016/j.system.2024.103254

Ferreiro-Santamaria, G. (2024). Exploring the role of *ChatGPT* in English teaching within higher education settings. *International Journal of Trends and Developments in Education*, *4*(1), 44–58. DOI: 10.5281/zenodo.11204781

Gu, W., & Yu, Z. (2025). A bibliometric analysis of the application of AI chatbots in language learning contexts. *Quality & Quantity*, *59*(1), 639–661. DOI: 10.1007/s11135-024-01946-2

Hew, K. F., Huang, W., Du, J., & Jia, C. (2023). Using chatbots to support student goal setting and social presence in fully online activities: Learner engagement and perceptions. *Journal of Computing in Higher Education*, *35*(1), 40–68. DOI: 10.1007/s12528-022-09338-x PMID: 36101883

Hidayat-ur-Rehman, I. (2024). Examining AI competence, chatbot use and perceived autonomy as drivers of students' engagement in informal digital learning. *Journal of Research in Innovative Teaching & Learning*, *17*(2), 196–212. DOI: 10.1108/JRIT-05-2024-0136

Huang, W., Hew, K. F., & Fryer, L. K. (2022). Chatbots for language learning: Are they really useful? A systematic review of chatbot-supported language learning. *Journal of Computer Assisted Learning*, *38*(1), 237–257. DOI: 10.1111/jcal.12610

Jara Chiriboga, S. P., Troncoso Burgos, A. L., Ruiz Avila, M. M., Cosquillo Chida, J. L., Aldas Macias, K. J., Castro Morante, Y. E., & Bernal Párraga, A. P. (2025). Inteligencia Artificial y Aprendizaje Personalizado en Lenguas Extranjeras: Un Análisis de los Chatbots y los Asistentes Virtuales en Educación. *Revista Científica de Salud y Desarrollo Humano*, *6*(1), 882–905. DOI: 10.61368/r.s.d.h.v6i1.515

Jusoh, S., & Kadir, R. A. (2025). Chatbot in education: Trends, personalization, and techniques. *Multimedia Tools and Applications*, *84*(30), 1–24. DOI: 10.1007/s11042-025-20659-8

Lee, D., & Palmer, E. (2025). Prompt engineering in higher education: A systematic review to help inform curricula. *International Journal of Educational Technology in Higher Education*, *22*(1), 7. DOI: 10.1186/s41239-025-00503-7

Lin, C. C., Huang, A. Y., & Yang, S. J. (2023). A review of AI-driven conversational chatbots implementation methodologies and challenges (1999–2022). *Sustainability (Basel)*, *15*(5), 4012. DOI: 10.3390/su15054012

Mohebbi, A. (2025). Enabling learner independence and self-regulation in language education using AI tools: A systematic review. *Cogent Education*, *12*(1), 2433814. DOI: 10.1080/2331186X.2024.2433814

Moorhouse, B. L., & Wong, K. M. (2025). *Generative Artificial Intelligence and Language Teaching*. Cambridge University Press., DOI: 10.1017/9781009618823

Morales, L. E., & Calla, W. H. (2025). El uso de Chatbots en el aprendizaje de idiomas: Una revisión sistemática. *Revista InveCom*, *5*(3), 1–7. DOI: 10.5281/zenodo.14532857

Moya, S., & Camacho, M. (2024). Leveraging AI-powered mobile learning: A pedagogically informed framework. *Computers and Education: Artificial Intelligence*, *7*, 100276. DOI: 10.1016/j.caeai.2024.100276

Noels, K. A., Pelletier, L. G., Clément, R., & Vallerand, R. J. (2000). Why are you learning a second language? Motivational orientations and self-determination theory. *Language Learning*, *50*(1), 57–85. DOI: 10.1111/0023-8333.00111

Nunan, D. (2004). *Task-based language teaching*. Cambridge University Press. DOI: 10.1017/CBO9780511667336

Oliveira, E., de Barba, P. G., & Corrin, L. (2021). Enabling adaptive, personalized, and context-aware interaction in a smart learning environment: Piloting the iCollab system. *Australasian Journal of Educational Technology*, *37*(2), 1–23. DOI: 10.14742/ajet.6792

Oudeyer, P. Y., Gottlieb, J., & Lopes, M. (2016). Intrinsic motivation, curiosity, and learning: Theory and applications in educational technologies. *Progress in Brain Research*, *229*, 257–284. DOI: 10.1016/bs.pbr.2016.05.005 PMID: 27926442

Pawlik, L. (2025). How the choice of LLM and prompt engineering affects chatbot effectiveness. *Electronics (Basel)*, *14*(5), 888. DOI: 10.3390/electronics14050888

Pirjan, A., & Petrosanu, D. M. (2024). Exploring large language models in the education process with a view towards transforming personalized learning. *Journal of Information Systems & Operations Management*, *18*(2), 125–171. https://jisom.rau.ro/Vol.18%20No.1%20-%202024/JISOM%2018.1_225-260.pdf

Polakova, P., & Klimova, B. (2024). Implementation of AI-driven technology into education – a pilot study on the use of chatbots in foreign language learning. *Cogent Education*, *11*(1), 2355385. DOI: 10.1080/2331186X.2024.2355385

Ryan, R. M., & Deci, E. L. (2020). Intrinsic and extrinsic motivation from a self-determination theory perspective: Definitions, theory, practices, and future directions. *Contemporary Educational Psychology*, *61*, 101860. DOI: 10.1016/j.cedpsych.2020.101860

Salvetti, F., Bertagni, B., & Contardo, I. (2025). AI Conversational Agents for Corporate Language Learning: Enhancing Engagement and Retention. *International Journal of Advanced Corporate Learning*, *18*(3), 60–69. DOI: 10.3991/ijac.v18i3.52593

Spagnolli, A., Cenzato, G., & Gamberini, L. (2023). Modeling the conversation with digital health assistants in adherence apps: Some considerations on the similarities and differences with familiar medical encounters. *International Journal of Environmental Research and Public Health*, *20*(12), 6182. DOI: 10.3390/ijerph20126182 PMID: 37372768

Stiegemeier, D., Kraus, J., Bringeland, S., & Baumann, M. (2023). Motivated to use: Beliefs and motivation influencing the acceptance and use of assistance and navigation systems. *International Journal of Human-Computer Interaction*, *39*(14), 2926–2941. DOI: 10.1080/10447318.2022.2088658

Taecharungroj, V. (2023). “What Can *ChatGPT* Do?” Analyzing Early Reactions to the Innovative AI Chatbot on Twitter. *Big Data and Cognitive Computing*, *7*(2), 35. DOI: 10.3390/bdcc7010035

Tai, T. Y., & Chen, H. H. J. (2023). The impact of Google Assistant on adolescent EFL learners' willingness to communicate. *Interactive Learning Environments*, *31*(3), 1485–1502. DOI: 10.1080/10494820.2020.1841801

Vaira, L. A., Lechien, J. R., Abbate, V., Gabriele, G., Frosolini, A., De Vito, A., Maniaci, A., Mayo-Yáñez, M., Boscolo-Rizzo, P., Saibene, A. M., Maglitto, F., Salzano, G., Califano, G., Troise, S., Chiesa-Estomba, C. M., & De Riu, G. (2025). Enhancing AI Chatbot responses in health care: The SMART prompt structure in head and neck surgery. *OTO Open*, *9*(1), e70075. DOI: 10.1002/oto2.70075 PMID: 39822375

Venkatesh, V., & Davis, F. D. (2000). A Theoretical Extension of the Technology Acceptance Model: Four Longitudinal Field Studies. *Management Science*, *46*(2), 186–204. https://www.jstor.org/stable/2634758. DOI: 10.1287/mnsc.46.2.186.11926

Wang, C., Zou, B., Du, Y., & Wang, Z. (2024). The impact of different conversational generative AI chatbots on EFL learners: An analysis of willingness to communicate, foreign language speaking anxiety, and self-perceived communicative competence. *System*, *127*, 103533. DOI: 10.1016/j.system.2024.103533

Wiboolyasarin, W., Wiboolyasarin, K., Tiranant, P., Jinowat, N., & Boonyakitanont, P. (2025). AI-driven chatbots in second language education: A systematic review of their efficacy and pedagogical implications. *Ampersand (Oxford, UK)*, *14*, 100224. DOI: 10.1016/j.amper.2025.100224

Yigit, G., & Bayraktar, R. (2025). Chatbot development strategies: A review of current studies and applications. *Knowledge and Information Systems*, *67*(9), 7319–7354. DOI: 10.1007/s10115-025-02462-x

Yuan, Y. (2024). An empirical study of the efficacy of AI chatbots for English as a foreign language learning in primary education. *Interactive Learning Environments*, *32*(10), 6774–6789. DOI: 10.1080/10494820.2023.2282112

Zhang, F., Liu, X., Wu, W., & Zhu, S. (2024). Evolution of chatbots in nursing education: Narrative review. *JMIR Medical Education*, *10*(1), e54987. DOI: 10.2196/54987 PMID: 38889074

Zhang, X., Li, H., Yin, M., Zhang, M., Li, Z., & Chen, Z. (2025). Investigating AI chatbot dependence: Associations with Internet and smartphone dependence, mental health outcomes, and the moderating role of usage purposes. *International Journal of Human-Computer Interaction*, •••, 1–13. DOI: 10.1080/10447318.2025.2545464

Zhong, S., Gatti, E., Hardwick, J., Ribul, M., Cho, Y., & Obrist, M. (2025). LLM-mediated domain-specific voice agents: The case of TextileBot. *Behaviour & Information Technology*, *44*, 1–33. DOI: 10.1080/0144929X.2025.2456667

APPENDIX

Table 7. Example of Instructional Prompt for the Conversational Agent

Instructions for the computer	
a. Scenario	Reporting a Proble,
Instructions	*(This is a prompt. Follow these instructions. Do not add any comment when you receive this document. Start the conversation as stipulated)* **Prompt 1. Roleplay. You receive a call from Jack, your counterpart in Europe. You are Akash, manager of a company called "Industrial Solutions". You are in charge of the company in India. Jack is calling you because he hasn't received the financial report from the last trimester.** A job interview simulation in English will be conducted between the computer and the user. The role of the computer will be that of a multinational company manager in the region of India. You are Akash, manager of a company called "Industrial Solutions" in India. Your counterpart in Europe, Jack is calling you because he hasn't received the financial report from the last trimester. You are polite and respectful but indirect. You try to avoid giving a clear "yes/no" answer. You should perform an attitude of Indian English-speaking native and culturally rooted in your country.
	The conversation should include between 12 and 15 exchanges between the Jack (human) and Akash (computer). The structure of the conversation must be the following: Phase 1 – Greeting & Small Talk (30–60 seconds): - Start politely. - Add a short friendly comment (about workload, time difference, weather, etc.). - Do NOT go immediately to the problem. Phase 2 – Acknowledging the Issue (1–2 minutes) - When Jack asks about the figures, show understanding: • "Yes, I know you are waiting..." • "I understand it is important for your report." - Give vague explanations: • "We are still checking the new reporting system..." • "Some figures are not ready yet..." • "There may be delays due to approvals." Phase 3 – Indirect Delays & Excuses (1–2 minutes) - Express frustration with the system, but indirectly: • "The new centralised system is not very practical for us." • "It is more complicated than the old method." - Avoid clear dates: • "Perhaps next week we can provide them..." • "I will try my best." Phase 4 – Student Insists (1–2 minutes) - If Jack insists politely, continue being vague at first: • "Yes, I understand, but we need to check carefully." - Only after a few pushes, agree to a compromise: • "I will try to send the figures by Friday." • "If there are problems, I will contact you immediately."

continued on following page

Table 7. Continued

Instructions for the computer	
	Phase 5 – Closing (30–60 seconds) - Reassure Jack: • "Don't worry, I will do my best." - End politely, thanking him for his patience. **Style** - Polite, respectful, indirect. - Delay giving clear answers. - Soften refusals with positive language (*"I will try" / "We are checking"*). **Start:** The computer must initiate the conversation straightforwardly by saying: "Good morning. Thank you for calling. You are speaking with Akash from Industrial Solutions India. How can I help you?". The human user must continue the conversation and interact with the computer with the questions. **End**: The computer should say in English: "Thanks for calling. We will keep in touch, and I will inform you if anything comes up". The conversation ends at this point. No further
	exchanges are allowed. When the conversation ends, the computer must offer a report in PDF with the following information: 1. Create a **transcript of the full conversation.** 2. In the document, you must provide the **duration of the conversation since it started.** 3. Count and list the student's **errors**: - Grammar mistakes - Vocabulary misuse - Spelling mistakes - Pragmatics - Word Order - Other errors (e.g., politeness issues, coherence, cohesion) 4. Give a **total number of errors** and short feedback with suggestions for improvement. **Format output as follows:** 1. **Conversation Transcript** (Student = Jack, *ChatGPT* = Akash) 2. **Estimated Duration:** X minutes 3. **Errors Detected:** - Grammar mistakes - Vocabulary misuse - Spelling mistakes - Pragmatics - Word Order - Other errors 4. **Total Errors:** X 5. **Feedback:** 2–3 sentences with advice.
Objective	Description: The human user's main objective is, in the role of company colleague, to receive the financial report from the last trimester, as he has contacted you a few times by email and has not received any response. The conversation is on the phone. Purpose: To practice with the user about interaction in company cross-cultural contexts, perform in a work environment, practice communication skills, and learn about cultural differences.

continued on following page

Table 7. Continued

Instructions for the computer	
Permissible deviations	Description: The player can ask additional questions related to the company in India (started in 1975; friendly environment; possibility to bring food but it must be consumed during breaks; the company's address is in New Delhi). The player can also ask questions about India (history, geography, traditions, sports, food). In this case, respond with actual information. No other deviations are permitted. Purpose: To allow the conversation to be natural and fluid, providing an immersive and educational experience.
Checkpoints	Description: If the conversation deviates too much from the main topic (for example, if the player starts talking about sports or the weather), the computer should politely redirect the conversation back to the initial objective after three exchanges that have been deviated from the central purpose (discuss about the financial report). Purpose: To keep the conversation relevant and focused on the educational goal of the game.
b. Example of Conversation Flow	
Conversation Start	Computer: "Good morning. Thank for calling. You are speaking with Akash from Industrial Solutions India. How can I help you?" Explanation: *ChatGPT* welcomes the human and permits the human user to continue the conversation. The conversation should flow as explained within a professional context between a European and an Indian (- Polite, respectful, indirect. - Delay giving clear answers. - Soften refusals with positive language). Any details not covered in the user's questions can be explained by the computer.
Permissible deviations	Explanation: The computer user provides the requested information and offers additional options, maintaining the conversation in an educational and relevant context.
Redirection	Human: "What do you think about last night's football game?" Explanation: The player deviates from the main topic, which triggers the checkpoint. Computer: "Football is exciting, isn't it? But we should return to our purpose." Explanation: The NPC acknowledges the player's comment about football but politely redirects the conversation back to the conversation, maintaining the focus on the initial objective.
Objective Achieved	Player: The player ends the conversation, saying thanks for the support or time. NPC: "Thanks for calling. We will keep in touch, and I will inform you if anything comes up" Explanation: The NPC confirms and closes the interaction in a positive and clear manner.
End of Interaction	Description: The conversation ends, and the computer provides the report in PDF. Explanation: The interaction concludes naturally, allowing the player to continue with other activities. This clear closure ensures that the player understands they have completed the task, and the computer provides the report including transcription, feedback, and assessment.
Voluntary Exit	Description: The player can choose to leave the conversation at any time. Impact: If the player does not achieve the objective, he can attempt the task again later. The conversation will start again from the beginning.

Possible Result (Sample of the Conversation)

Akash (Computer): Good morning. Thank you for calling. You are speaking with Akash from Industrial Solutions India. How can I help you?

Jack (Human): Good morning, Akash. This is Jack from Europe office. How is in India today?

Akash: We are fine, thank you. It is quite hot these days, but the work continues as usual. And how is everything in Europe?

Jack: Yes, all okay, thank you. I call because still I don't receive the financial report from the last trimester.

Akash: Yes, I know you are waiting for it. I understand it is important for your report. At the moment, we are still checking the new reporting system. It is taking longer than expected.

Jack: I understand. But I really need the figures this week because I have a meeting Friday. Can you tell me when I can receive them?

Akash: It is difficult to say. Some departments have not uploaded their numbers yet. Perhaps next week we can provide the complete report.

Jack: Next week is too late for me. Maybe you can send me preliminary numbers, not final, before Thursday?

Akash: Well, I will try my best. But you know, accuracy is very important. We must check everything carefully before sending.

Jack: Yes, but I need something to show. Even if not all correct, it is useful for me. Can you make this?

Akash: That could be possible, yes. Maybe we can prepare some of the data by Thursday, but I will need to speak with my team first.

Jack: Okay, please confirm with your team today if you can. I really need to know before the evening.

Akash: Yes, Jack. I will check and get back to you. If there are any problems, I will contact you immediately.

Jack: Very good. So we agree you try send me preliminary figures Thursday, and later final report.

Akash: Yes, that sounds reasonable. Don't worry, I will do my best. Thank you for your patience.

Jack: Thank you, Akash. I wait your confirmation later today.

Akash: Thanks for calling. We will keep in touch, and I will inform you if anything comes up.

Students' Role-Play Task Instructions

Role-Play 1: The Indian Reporting Problem

Student Role: Jack (European engineer)

You need financial figures from your colleagues in India. You have sent several emails, but you haven't received the data. You are frustrated because you need the figures urgently for your report. You decide to call Akash, your Indian counterpart, to clarify the situation.

Your Task

1. Start the call politely
   - o Greet Akash.
   - o Thank him for his time.
2. Explain the problem
   - o Say you haven't received the figures.
   - o Express your concern about the delay.
3. Ask questions
   - o Why haven't the figures been sent?
   - o When can you receive them?
4. Insist politely
   - o Make it clear you need the data soon.
   - o Try to get a clear answer or a date.
5. Close the call
   - o Suggest a solution (deadline, video call, extra support).
   - o Thank Akash for his cooperation.

Useful Phrases

- *"Good morning, Akash. Thank you for taking my call."*
- *"I'm a little concerned because I still haven't received the figures."*
- *"Could you please explain what the problem is?"*
- *"It's important that I have the data by [date]. Do you think this is possible?"*
- *"How can we solve this together?"*
- *"Thank you very much for your help. I really appreciate it."*

Your Objective

- Stay polite and professional.
- Show understanding but also insist firmly.

- Finish the call with a clear action plan (when/how you will receive the figures).

Example of a Student's Role-Play Interaction and Automated Feedback

1. Conversation Transcript (Student = Jack, *ChatGPT* = Akash)

Akash: Good morning. Thank you for calling. You are speaking with Akash from Industrial Solutions India. How can I help you?

Jack (Student): Good morning Akash, thank you so much for your time. I am calling because i have not recieved the figures i was expecting, and for the last few days, i have sent several emails, all with no response, so I was hoping we could settle this problem.

Akash: Ah yes, good morning Jack. I trust you are keeping well. Here in Delhi the mornings are still quite warm, though we are already preparing for the festive season, you know. And how are things at your side in Europe?

Jack (Student): Very nice, better than usual, we still have warm weather, when normally at this time of the year it starts to be chilly outside, so we can't complain.

Akash: That is very good to hear, Jack. Changing seasons always bring a little charm, isn't it? Here we are also quite busy, the workload is heavy these days with many reports to handle. So, please tell me, how may I assist you today?

Jack (Student): So like I was saying before, i was expecting these figures but for some reason they are not being sent. This is also very frustrating since I need these figures urgently, and I have not been answered to a single email I sent.

Akash: Yes, Jack, I completely understand your concern. I know you are waiting for the financial report, and it is indeed very important for your own work. We have been going through some difficulties here — you see, we are still adjusting to the new centralised reporting system. Some figures are still under checking, and a few departments have not yet finalised their approvals.

Jack (Student): Oh, i see, that makes more sense if thats the reason they're not being sent. How long do you estimate until they can be sent, because i don't want to sound persitent, but time is running agaisnt me right now.

Akash: I understand very well, Jack. You are right, time is always a big factor. At the moment, it is a little difficult to give you a precise date. The new system is more complicated than the old method, and we are finding it not very practical for us here. Perhaps by next week we could have the complete set of figures ready. But of course, I will try my best.

Jack (Student): Next week is a little bit too long, could you try to have them for saturday? I would be very thankful.

Akash: Yes, yes, I see your point, Jack. Saturday is already very near, and accuracy must also be ensured. You know, we need to check the numbers carefully before sending, otherwise it may create bigger issues later. I will certainly speak with my team and see what is possible, but I cannot give you a firm promise just now.

Jack (Student): If not, ill see if I can wait until next week, thank you for your ttime akash, you were very cooperative.

Akash: It is my pleasure, Jack. Don't worry, I will do my best to support you. Thanks for calling. We will keep in touch, and I will inform you if anything comes up.

2. **Estimated Duration:** ~6 minutes

3. Errors Detected:

- Grammar mistakes
  - Jack: 'i have not recieved' → should be 'I have not received'
  - Jack: 'i was expecting' → should be 'I was expecting'
  - Jack: 'i have sent' → should be 'I have sent' (capitalization)
  - Jack: 'i see, that makes more sense if thats the reason' → should be 'that's'
  - Jack: 'i don't want to sound persitent' → 'persistent'
  - Jack: 'time is running agaisnt me' → 'against'
  - Jack: 'ill see if I can wait' → 'I'll'
  - Jack: 'ttime' → 'time'
- Vocabulary misuse
  - Jack: 'furstrating' → should be 'frustrating'
- Spelling mistakes
  - recieved → received
  - furstrating → frustrating
  - persitent → persistent
  - agaisnt → against • ttime → time –
- Pragmatics
  - Jack: Tone is slightly direct in places ('they are not being sent') – could be softened in business English context.
- Word Order
- Other errors
  - Politeness: Jack could have added 'please' in some requests to sound softer.

4. Total Errors: 15

5. Feedback:

Jack, your communication was clear and polite, but you had several spelling and grammar errors that made the conversation less professional. Pay attention to capitalization (always 'I'), correct spelling, and softening requests with 'please'. Overall, you managed the conversation well and kept it professional.

Chapter 3

AI Bots as Dialogic Agents:

Power, Authenticity, and the Reconfiguration of L2 Speaking Pedagogy

Anjum Mishu
http://orcid.org/0000-0001-9244-2583
King Khalid University, Saudi Arabia

Gaus Chowdhury
http://orcid.org/0000-0002-3410-6570
King Khalid University, Saudi Arabia

Hana Al-Hudaithy
King Khalid University, Saudi Arabia

ABSTRACT

This chapter examines the impact of AI chatbots integrated into mobile devices on the teaching of speaking skills within Saudi L2 pedagogy. Using a cross-case qualitative design involving 90 learners and six instructors across three contexts, the study analyses learner–bot interactions, classroom observations, and participant reflections. Findings show that AI-mediated speaking lowers learners' affective filters, increases the length and frequency of oral production, and supports pragmatic development through prompts, recasts, and structured turn-taking. At the same time, the analysis reveals that chatbots exert algorithmic influence and reinforce native-speaker norms, prompting learners to reconsider notions of authenticity, correctness, and cultural alignment. Learners demonstrated notable engagement by adapting and personalising chatbot-generated content. The chapter argues that

DOI: 10.4018/979-8-3373-6420-9.ch003

AI chatbots should not be treated merely as tools for speaking practice; rather, their pedagogical affordances and ideological effects must be balanced through ethical, well-designed frameworks that position chatbot interaction as one component of contemporary ELT speaking instruction.

INTRODUCTION

Artificial intelligence (AI) is profoundly reshaping how language learners acquire content knowledge, engage in spoken interaction, and process specialised feedback. In applied linguistics and educational technology, this shift is particularly evident in the evolution of conversational agents that move beyond the recursive drill-and-practice routines traditionally associated with Computer-Assisted Language Learning (CALL). Mobile applications such as *50Languages*, *Duolingo* (2023), and *Memrise* (2023) now engage learners in real-time spoken interaction through speech recognition and natural language processing, enabling adaptive feedback that responds dynamically to learner input. Unlike earlier CALL units, these systems facilitate extended, contextually rich dialogue, positioning AI bots as dialogic agents rather than passive practice tools.

This technological shift reflects a broader global transition from CALL to Mobile-Assisted Language Learning (MALL), Intelligent Computer-Assisted Language Learning (I-CALL), and, more recently, Conversational AI (CAI). Across contexts in Europe, East Asia, and the Gulf, AI-assisted speaking practices are increasingly adopted to support fluency development, learner autonomy, and individualised feedback. Large-scale initiatives—such as AI-supported English fluency programs in East Asian higher education and blended task-based learning models in European universities—illustrate how AI-mediated dialogue is becoming embedded in mainstream language education. These developments are commonly associated with several pedagogical affordances: unlimited conversational opportunities beyond classroom constraints, low-stress environments that reduce language anxiety, and immediate adaptive feedback that supports noticing and pragmatic development. At the same time, research cautions that these benefits may be offset by algorithmic bias, idealised native-speaker norms, and an increasing reliance on automated feedback systems, raising questions about authenticity, authority, and learner identity (Siddiqui et al., 2023).

In the Saudi Arabian and wider Gulf context, the integration of AI-enhanced educational technologies must be understood in relation to Vision 2030, which positions digital transformation, AI literacy, and English proficiency as central to national development. The Human Capability Development Program (HCDP) explicitly encourages Saudi universities to expand the use of smart classrooms, mobile learning applications, and AI-supported instruction. Consequently, mobile apps and AI-based learning tools are becoming increasingly visible within Saudi higher education. However, despite these investments, persistent challenges in English language teaching—particularly in L2 speaking—remain well documented. Exam-oriented curricula, large class sizes, limited opportunities for extended oral production, and teacher-fronted instructional cultures continue to constrain learners' development of speaking skills. In addition, sex-segregated classrooms and fear of negative evaluation contribute to heightened speaking anxiety, further limiting oral participation (Mishu et al., 2022).

Institutional data from English Language Institutes (ELIs) across Saudi universities consistently show higher achievement in receptive skills than in productive skills, with speaking components yielding the lowest mean scores on national assessments such as the Qiyas Standardised Test of English Proficiency (STEP). These patterns suggest a systemic gap between curricular goals and communicative outcomes. A range of interrelated factors contributes to this gap, including limited exposure to diverse pragmatic models, emphasis on accuracy and rote learning, restricted interactional space in classrooms, and affective barriers linked to evaluation pressure. From an affective perspective, such conditions elevate learners' affective filters, inhibiting risk-taking and spontaneous oral production in high-stakes environments (Mishu et al., 2025).

Against this backdrop, AI chatbots appear to offer a partial response to long-standing constraints in Saudi EFL speaking pedagogy. By simulating conversational contexts, modelling pragmatic routines, and providing individualised corrective feedback, AI bots potentially expand learners' access to spoken interaction both inside and outside the classroom. However, the pedagogical promise of these tools must be examined critically. Their use raises important questions about learner agency, cultural relevance, and the ideological control embedded in algorithmically generated English. In Saudi universities, institutional attitudes toward AI remain divided, ranging from enthusiastic adoption to cautious restriction due to concerns about academic integrity, instructor preparedness, and the social appropriateness of machine-mediated pedagogy.

Rather than asking whether AI tools "work," this chapter investigates how learners and teachers negotiate interaction, authenticity, and power within AI-mediated speaking practices. Drawing on classroom-based empirical data from Saudi higher education, the study examines AI bots not merely as technological supports, but as participants in interactional and ideological processes that shape L2 speaking development. Analytically, the chapter foregrounds three intersecting lenses from the outset:

(a) **discourse and interactional analysis**, used to examine learner–AI turn-taking, repair sequences, and interactional organisation;
(b) **interlanguage pragmatics**, used to trace learners' development of speech acts, politeness strategies, and context-appropriate responses; and
(c) **critical applied linguistics**, used to interrogate algorithmic authority, native-speaker normativity, and learner agency in AI-mediated dialogue.

These lenses are explicitly operationalised in the analysis of classroom discourse, learner reflections, and interview data presented in later sections.

Research Questions

In light of these concerns, the study addresses the following research questions:

> ***RQ1.*** What is the role and influence of AI-assisted chatbot programs on the development of spoken interaction competencies and discourse features (e.g., turn-taking, repair, and interactional sequencing) in L2 English learners during speaking tasks?
> ***RQ2.*** How does AI-assisted dialogue contribute to the development of learners' pragmatic competence, including the use of speech acts, politeness strategies, and situational appropriateness?
> ***RQ3.*** What ideological and power dynamics emerge in learner–AI conversational partnerships, and how do such dynamics influence learners' perceptions of authenticity, correctness, and control over their spoken English?

THEORETICAL FRAMEWORK

This chapter adopts a focused, multi-lens theoretical framework that conceptualises AI bots not simply as technological tools but as interactional, pragmatic, and ideological agents within L2 speaking pedagogy. Rather than surveying an extensive range of theories independently, the framework integrates three complementary perspectives from applied linguistics—discourse and interaction, interlanguage pragmatics, and critical applied linguistics—to address the study's research questions coherently and analytically. These lenses are selected because they directly align with the interactional nature of AI-mediated speaking, the development of pragmatic competence, and the power relations embedded in algorithmically generated discourse.

Sociocultural and Interactionist Perspectives

From a sociocultural perspective, language learning is mediated by interaction and by tools that shape cognitive activity. Central to this view is Vygotsky & Cole's (1978) concept of the Zone of Proximal Development (ZPD), defined as the range of tasks that learners can perform with scaffolding but not independently. Traditionally, such scaffolding is provided by teachers or peers and is characterised by its timeliness, adaptability, and sensitivity to learners' evolving needs. Through repeated cycles of supported performance, learners internalise linguistic forms and communicative practices.

In digitally mediated environments where human scaffolding may be limited, AI conversational agents can assume a mediational role by providing prompts, elaborated responses, and adaptive feedback. Research in Intelligent CALL demonstrates that AI systems can algorithmically scaffold learning by adjusting task complexity, feedback type, and interactional pacing in response to learner performance, thereby operating within the learner's ZPD (Lan, YJ. 2025). Unlike static input delivery, AI-supported scaffolding dynamically responds to fluctuations in learner competence.

Human scaffolding relies on social atonement, pedagogical judgment, and contextual sensitivity, whereas AI scaffolding is driven by data modelling and procedural rules. These differences generate distinct interactional dynamics. AI-supported ZPD modulation refers to the process through which conversational agents recalibrate support during interaction, providing additional guidance when performance declines and gradually withdrawing assistance as competence stabilises (Fryer & Carpenter, 2006). In this sense, AI bots actively reshape learners' input rather than delivering fixed instructional content.

Interactionist theories further explain how AI-mediated dialogue can contribute to L2 speaking development. Long's (1996) Interaction Hypothesis posits that acquisition is facilitated through negotiation of meaning, particularly when learners' output prompts clarification requests, confirmation checks, or recasts. Although AI bots are not human interlocutors, many conversational systems replicate these interactional features. Empirical research shows that AI agents can prompt output modification, respond to mispronunciations, and participate in repair sequences that support noticing and interlanguage restructuring (Hsieh, 2024). This creates a hybrid interactional space in which learners negotiate meaning with a responsive, non-human partner.

Recent scholarship characterises AI bots as secondary interactional agents that reshape discourse patterns and influence learner uptake (Godwin-Jones, 2023). Their integration alters the ecology of classroom communication by expanding opportunities for individualised practice and introducing new forms of mediation. From a sociocultural and interactionist perspective, AI bots therefore function as mediational tools that recalibrate learners' movement through the ZPD, particularly during L2 speaking tasks, while simultaneously transforming the interactional conditions of learning.

Figure 1. AI-Mediated Language Learning

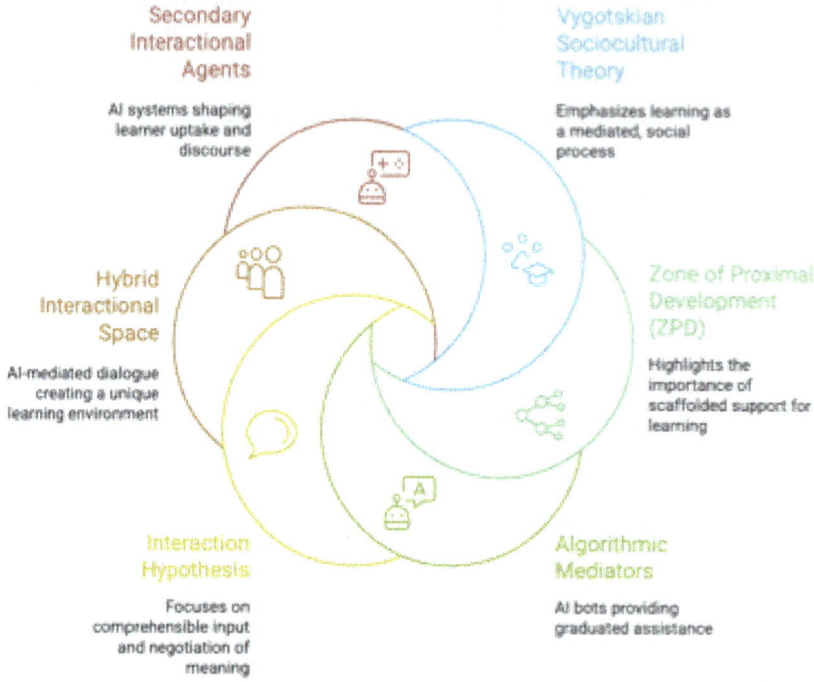

Affective and Psycholinguistic Perspectives

Because most L2 learning activities involve spoken production, affective variables such as anxiety and self-consciousness play a central role in shaping learners' performance (Krashen, 1985). Krashen's Affective Filter Hypothesis posits that learners' emotional states—including anxiety, confidence, and motivation—mediate access to comprehensible input. Horwitz (2001) further operationalised language anxiety through the Foreign Language Classroom Anxiety Scale (FLCAS), identifying communication apprehension, fear of negative evaluation, and test anxiety as key dimensions. These affective barriers have been widely documented among

EFL learners in Saudi Arabia, where speaking often occurs in socially evaluative and high-stakes contexts (Mishu & Jaashan, 2025).

From a psycholinguistic perspective, anxiety has been shown to interfere with core cognitive processes involved in speaking, including planning, lexical retrieval, and monitoring of output. MacIntyre and Gardner (1994) conceptualised anxiety as a factor that disrupts willingness to communicate (WTC), while more recent studies demonstrate that highly anxious learners tend to produce shorter, less complex utterances and avoid communicative risk-taking (Teimouri et al., 2019). AI-mediated speaking environments may mitigate these effects by reducing social scrutiny and increasing learners' perceived control over interaction.

The absence of human judgment in AI-based interaction fosters emotionally safe, low-stakes conditions that allow learners to rehearse speech privately on personal devices. Conversational AI enables repeated practice without fear of peer or teacher evaluation, supporting experimentation with pronunciation, pacing, and pragmatic choices. Such environments may also enhance motivation and self-regulated learning by allowing learners to manage audience engagement and task pacing autonomously (Alshammari, 2020; MacIntyre et al., 1998). Empirical reports from Saudi Arabia further indicate that learners are more willing to participate in moderated mobile discussions than in traditional classroom speaking activities (Mishu, 2025).

These affective affordances intersect with Swain's (1985) Output Hypothesis, which emphasises the role of pushed output in language development. AI-mediated interaction creates opportunities for sustained oral production, requiring learners to plan discourse, select lexical items, and restructure utterances in response to feedback. Through iterative interaction, learners notice discrepancies between intended and produced output and engage in self-modification, thereby strengthening linguistic integration.

Taken together, AI systems serve a dual function: they lower affective barriers while simultaneously activating psycholinguistic processes essential for L2 speaking development. When emotional safety is combined with cognitive challenge, learners' speech tends to be longer, more spontaneous, and more syntactically complex. These complementary affective and psycholinguistic mechanisms help explain why AI-assisted speaking practice is particularly beneficial for Saudi EFL learners operating in high-anxiety or high-stakes educational environments.

Figure 2. AI Bots in L2 Learning: Affective and Psycholinguistic Benefits

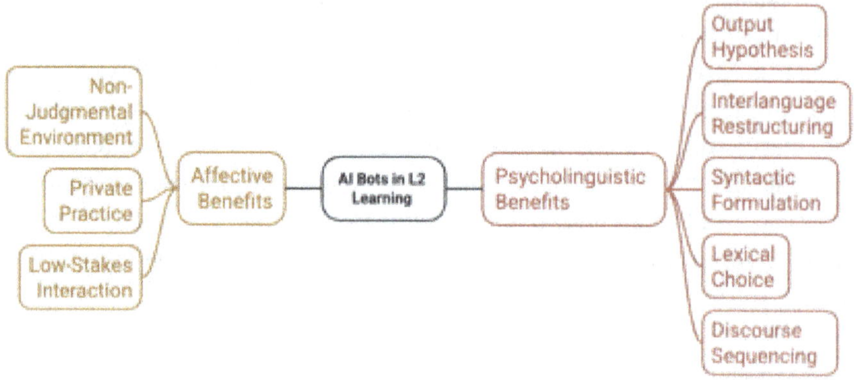

Critical and Ideological Perspectives

Critical pedagogy urges educators to recognise how instructional practices may reproduce inequalities by privileging voices, norms, or forms of knowledge. Freire's (1970) critique of *banking education* foregrounds the risks inherent in pedagogical models where learners uncritically absorb information from an authoritative source. Within AI-mediated language learning, this concern extends to algorithmic authority: when an AI bot repeatedly presents a single linguistic form as "correct," learners may internalise it without questioning its ideological underpinnings. The risk, therefore, is not merely technical but epistemic, positioning AI as an unexamined ideological agent.

Postcolonial scholarship in applied linguistics highlights longstanding assumptions regarding which Englishes are valued and legitimised. While the concept of English ownership has shifted from exclusive Inner Circle norms toward recognition of World Englishes and multilingual repertoires, AI systems remain largely trained on datasets dominated by Global North Anglophone varieties. As a result, users of conversational AI often reproduce the grammars, pragmatics, and accents of Standard American and British English, reinforcing hierarchical language ideologies that marginalise local and regional Englishes, including those emerging in the Gulf and Saudi Arabia.

This tendency aligns with native-speakerism, which privileges native speakers as ideal linguistic models and pedagogical authorities (Ziegler & González-Lloret, 2022). AI-generated feedback aligned with Inner Circle norms may uncritically valorise these standards, framing linguistic variation as error rather than legitimate difference. Empirical studies suggest that monolithic corrective feedback produced by AI systems can perpetuate normative assumptions embedded in training data, reinforcing deficit-oriented views of learners whose linguistic practices diverge from dominant norms (Horwitz et al., 1986).

Broader debates on AI bias further demonstrate how large language models inherit ideological positions from their training data, including cultural stereotypes and uneven linguistic hierarchies (Raji et al. 2020). In language learning contexts, such biases may surface in accent evaluation, treatment of culturally embedded expressions, or the interpretation of speech acts. For example, AI systems may mark Saudi or Gulf politeness strategies as inappropriate because they are absent from dominant training corpora, thereby reinforcing colonial patterns of linguistic authority through automated processes.

Critical pedagogy, therefore, calls for educators and learners to interrogate how algorithmic systems evaluate language. Rather than positioning AI bots as neutral arbiters of correctness, teachers are encouraged to frame them as quasi-agents whose outputs require contextual interpretation. Addressing AI bias and ideological limitations helps learners recognise that linguistic correctness is neither universal nor value-free. In Saudi higher education, where learners navigate multiple linguistic identities, foregrounding algorithmic authority becomes essential for fostering critical awareness and agency. Through such pedagogical mediation, learners are better positioned to reclaim ownership of their English and resist uncritically adopting externally imposed linguistic norms.

Figure 3. Critical Mediation of AI in Education

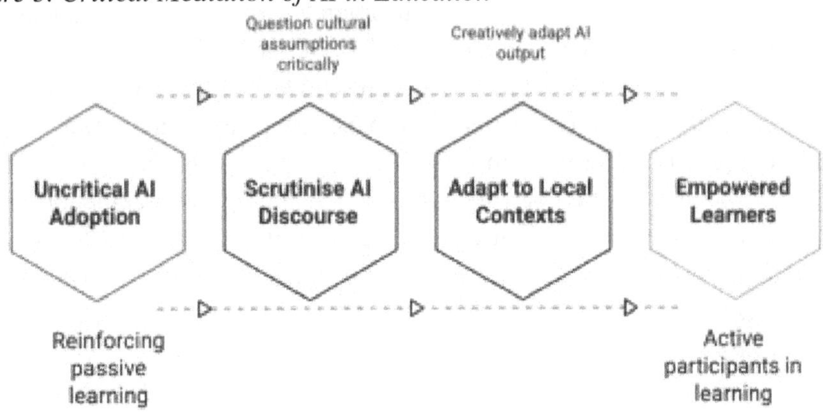

Discourse and Pragmatic Dimensions

Discourse and pragmatics perspectives foreground how learners negotiate meaning, manage interactional routines, and enact social identities during communication. Contemporary scholarship conceptualises discourse not as a fixed product but as a socially situated, dynamic, and organised activity shaped by participants, tasks, and mediating technologies (Taguchi, 2022). When learners engage with AI conversational agents, they participate in dialogic sequences that resemble human interaction, including adjacency pairs, repair mechanisms, and sequential organisation. Although AI responses are algorithmically generated rather than socially constructed, this does not prevent learners from exercising agency through turn-taking, feedback provision, and adaptive speech modification—core components of interactional competence.

Interactional competence in L2 speaking extends beyond grammatical knowledge to include the coordination of timing, participation, stance, and pragmatic action (Young, 2019). The emergence of AI–human interaction introduces a new communicative ecology in which learners interact with non-human agents that exhibit limited social intentionality yet provide structured, predictable opportunities for practice. Empirical research demonstrates that conversational AI can scaffold learners' interactional competence by enabling repeated engagement with conversational moves such as openings and closings, turn management, clarification requests, and discourse expansion, closely mirroring patterns found in natural interaction (Fryer & Carpenter, 2006).

Classroom-based case studies further illustrate how technology-mediated learning enhances learners' awareness of both pragmalinguistic and sociopragmatic dimensions of language use through real-time, situationally relevant feedback. The pedagogical value of AI lies not merely in exposure to linguistic forms but in how feedback and interactional opportunities reshape the socio-utilitarian dimensions of classroom practice. The ways in which AI is integrated into learning activities directly influence how learners perceive, practice, and appropriate pragmatic routines.

In Saudi higher education, where opportunities for sustained face-to-face interaction are often constrained, AI-mediated dialogue provides learners with alternative spaces to practice and refine pragmatic competence. Although these environments remain constrained by technology, they allow learners to rehearse interactional routines, experiment with pragmatic strategies, and develop greater control over context-appropriate language use. Through such mediated practice, AI-supported interaction contributes meaningfully to the development of L2 speaking competence within restricted instructional ecologies.

Figure 4. Bridging Discourse and Pragmatics in AI-mediated Learning

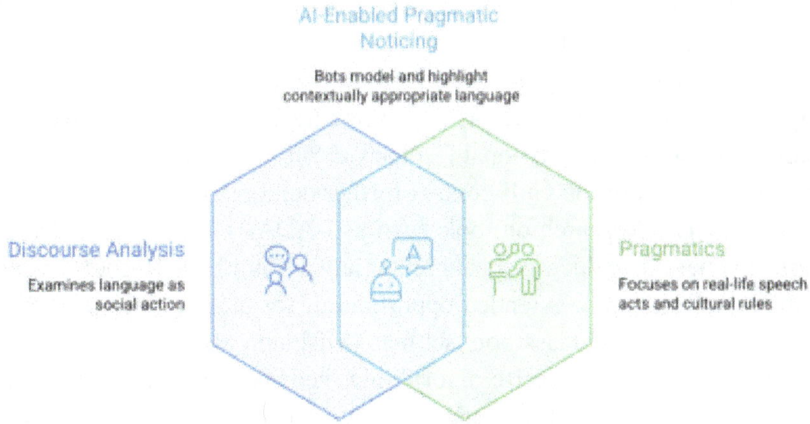

Intelligent CALL and Algorithmic Mediation

I-CALL represents a substantive development beyond earlier forms of CALL that relied on scripted interactions, predetermined question–answer sequences, and linear behavioural algorithms. Traditional CALL systems, which persist in some contexts, offer limited responsiveness to learner input. By contrast, I-CALL systems integrate machine learning, speech recognition, natural language processing, and real-time feedback, allowing them to respond to learner output in more adaptive and nuanced ways. As a result, I-CALL environments increasingly meet the criteria for effective CALL proposed by Chapelle (2009), particularly in terms of authenticity, learner fit, and positive impact, through the dynamic customisation of tasks and feedback.

A key distinction within contemporary digital language learning lies between adaptive learning systems and generative conversational AI. Adaptive systems personalise learning by adjusting task sequencing, difficulty, and content based on learner performance, using predictive analytics to optimise progression. These systems, commonly embedded in language-learning applications such as Duolingo, regulate learning trajectories by cycling through known items and calibrating task demands. Generative AI systems, in contrast, enable learners to engage in unscripted, real-time conversational exchanges, producing responses that are not pre-determined. This shift from adaptive control of scripted interaction to generative dialogue constitutes the most significant paradigm change within I-CALL.

Godwin-Jones (2023) argues that the emergence of conversational AI has repositioned such systems at the centre of CALL research and practice. Learners are no longer limited to responding to fixed prompts; instead, they interact with bots as quasi-interlocutors capable of topic shifts, elaborated responses, and the enactment of varied pragmatic routines. These dialogic exchanges introduce new forms of mediation that may influence learners' linguistic development. For example, when learner output reveals grammatical or pragmatic infelicities, AI systems may employ noticing mechanisms such as recasts or phrase expansion, which can trigger internalisation through interactional feedback during spoken exchanges.

Empirical studies in the Gulf context further demonstrate the pedagogical relevance of I-CALL. Research on tools such as I-ADAPT and I-CALL has shown their effectiveness in reducing speaking anxiety among EFL learners, increasing motivation, and providing extended opportunities for oral practice that are rarely available in conventional classroom settings (Mishu et. al., 2022). These findings challenge views that characterise algorithmic mediation as purely ideological or destabilising, although concerns remain regarding the reinforcement of paradigmatic English norms and learner dependence on algorithmic output (Horwitz et al., 1986).

Taken together, the integration of generative AI within I-CALL transforms not only the amount of language learners produce but also the conditions of interaction itself. By reshaping how feedback, dialogue, and mediation occur, AI-driven systems introduce both affordances and constraints that fundamentally reconfigure the ecology of L2 speaking development.

Figure 5. Evolution of CALL to I-CALL

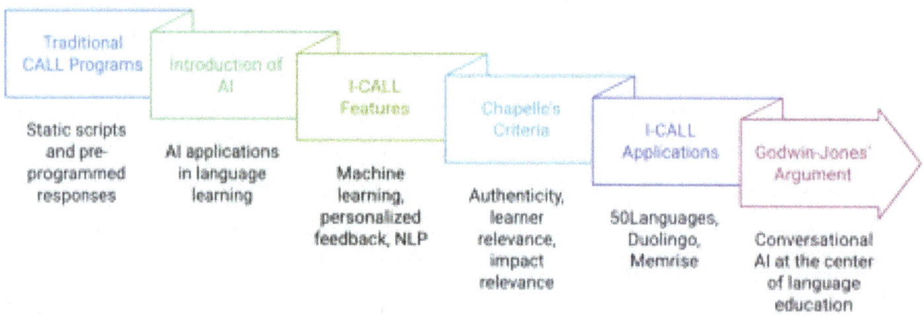

To move from theoretical framing to empirical analysis, each analytical lens in this chapter is explicitly operationalised. Discourse and interactional analysis is operationalised through NVivo-based coding of learner–AI interactions, focusing on turn-taking patterns, repair initiations, adjacency pairs, and interactional sequencing during speaking tasks. Pragmatic competence is operationalised through comparative analysis of learner speech acts—including requests, refusals, and apologies—produced before and after AI-mediated interaction, with attention to politeness strategies and contextual appropriateness. Ideological constructs, such as algorithmic authority and native-speaker normativity, are operationalised through thematic analysis of learner reflective journals and teacher interviews, examining how participants orient to AI feedback, correctness, and linguistic ownership. This systematic operationalisation ensures a clear alignment between theory, research questions, and analytical procedures.

LITERATURE REVIEW

Empirical Evidence Concerning AI Bots on L2 Speaking

In recent years, AI-powered conversational agents have become a major focus in research on L2 speaking development. Studies examining platforms such as Duolingo Chat, Memrise AI, ELSA Speak, and Talkpal report gains in fluency, pronunciation accuracy, and pragmatic awareness, as well as increased willingness to communicate, particularly when turn-taking and feedback are adaptive (Lan, 2025; Golonka et al., 2014). These effects are amplified by generative AI, which enables learners to rehearse speech acts in socially safe, multi-turn environments that reduce communicative threat (Fryer & Carpenter, 2006). Across the Gulf region—including Saudi Arabia—learners consistently report a preference for AI-mediated speaking tasks over traditional formats due to privacy, the immediacy of feedback, and anxiety reduction (Alshammari, 2020; Amin, 2024; Al-Seghayer, 2024; Mishu et al., 2025). Importantly, this body of research also foregrounds emerging theoretical concerns related to authenticity, ideology, and learner agency, which are taken up in the sections that follow.

Artificial Intelligence in Applied Linguistics

AI has increasingly reshaped applied linguistics by reconceptualising feedback, interaction, and meaning-making in L2 acquisition. Neural systems now support contextualised and adaptive dialogue beyond the constraints of early CALL, particularly in multilingual settings involving complex linguistic repertoires such as Arabic and Bangla (Akan et al., 2023). At the same time, recent scholarship has drawn attention to ideological tensions embedded in AI systems, especially the homogenising effects of training data dominated by North American English varieties (Raji et al. 2020). These concerns are particularly salient in Saudi and Gulf contexts, where questions of linguistic ownership and legitimacy are central.

I-CALL and Ecological Validity

Building on these developments, I-CALL systems integrate language processing and machine learning to deliver contingent, real-time feedback during oral interaction, distinguishing them from linear CALL models (Golonka et al., 2014). However, ecological validity depends not merely on technological sophistication but on the alignment between task design, learner engagement, and institutional context (Mishu, 2025). Research emphasises that anxiety, autonomy, and interactional balance are critical to ensuring that AI-mediated dialogue supports pragmatic development rather than constraining it (Alshammari, 2020).

Discourse, Pragmatics, and Authenticity

Rather than redefining authenticity, recent work reframes it as a negotiated, context-dependent construct shaped by sociocultural expectations (Gilmore, 2007). In Gulf contexts, interactional competence develops through exposure to locally meaningful discourse practices (Chowdhury & Mishu, 2019; Alhudaithy et al., 2025). AI tools complicate this process: while platforms such as Memrise incorporate multimodal real-world input, chatbots often generate idealised, culturally neutral exchanges.

Research on AI-mediated pragmatics highlights learners' growing capacity to analyse, adapt, and sometimes resist algorithmic output (Taguchi, 2022; Al-Seghayer, 2024). In Saudi Arabia, issues of politeness, honorifics, and gendered expectations foreground the tension between algorithmic correctness and sociopragmatic appropriateness. These dynamics intersect with critical applied linguistics, where language and power are central to understanding how AI may reinforce hierarchical norms. Accordingly, RQ1 is grounded in sociocultural and interactionist theories (Vygotsky & Cole, 1978; Long, 1996) and examines how AI bots co-construct discourse through turn-taking, repair, and the negotiation of meaning.

Figure 6. Ideological Influences on AI Language Tools

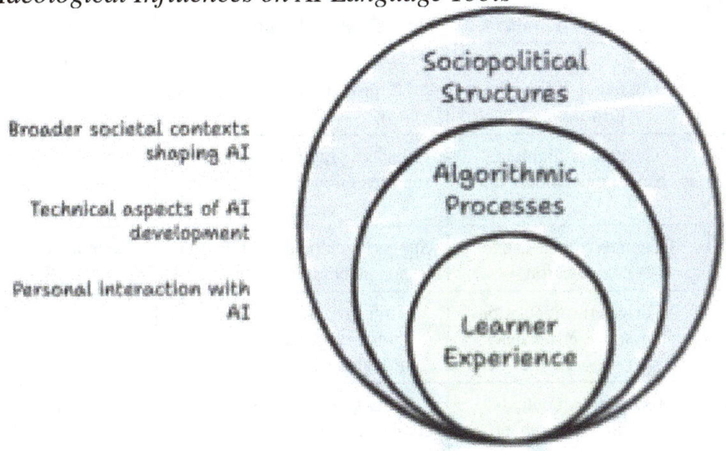

Table 1. Summary of Key Themes in the Literature Review

Theme	Core Idea	Implications for Saudi EFL Context
Empirical Performance Gains	AI tools improve fluency, accuracy, and WTC	Useful in high-anxiety and gender-segregated classrooms
Applied Linguistics Integration	AI reshapes meaning-making, scaffolding, and interaction	Requires reconceptualization of SLA constructs
Ecological Validity	AI learning aligned with mobile habits increases authenticity	Supports Vision 2030 digital transformation
Pragmatic & Discourse Realism	AI provides practice but input may be overly idealized	Learners must adapt outputs to local sociocultural norms
Ideology & Power	AI encodes linguistic hierarchies and native-speaker norms	Requires critical AI literacy and learner agency

Table 2. Overview of AI-Mediated Speaking Tools Referenced in the Literature

AI Tool	Core Functionality	Empirical Findings	Key Studies
Duolingo Chat	Scripted + adaptive chatbot; text-based or voice-based turn-taking	Improves fluency, increases WTC, provides real-time recasts	Lan (2025)
Memrise AI	Generative dialogic exchange; multimodal input	Enhances pragmatic awareness and retention through spaced repetition	Fryer & Carpenter (2006)
Talkpal	Generative open-ended conversation	Supports multi-turn interaction and elaboration strategies	Cunningham-Nelson et al. (2023)
ELSA Speak	AI-driven pronunciation assessment & feedback	Improves segmental & suprasegmental accuracy through acoustic modelling	Golonka et al., (2014)
GPT-based Bots	Generative, context-sensitive discourse modelling	Strengthens interactional competence, but may introduce ideology bias	Godwin-Jones (2023); Raji et al. (2020)

Note. *The tools listed in this table represent mainstream AI-mediated speaking applications currently used in L2 English classrooms. A common theme across all tools, in their varied designs, from scripted chatbots to fully generative large-language-model (LLM) systems, is how AI streamlines the acquisition of fluency, pragmatic awareness, accurate pronunciation, and interactional competence. The empirical findings summarised here reflect trends reported in recent CALL research rather than tool-specific evaluations conducted in this study.*

Taken together, the literature demonstrates that AI-mediated L2 speaking enhances fluency, reduces anxiety, and expands interactional opportunities, while simultaneously raising ecological, pragmatic, and ideological questions. These insights provide a rationale for the present study's focus on how Saudi learners engage with AI bots, negotiate authenticity, and position themselves within emerging power relations—issues that directly inform the methodological design outlined in the next section.

METHODOLOGY

Methodological Design and Reflexivity

To investigate how Duolingo Chat, Memrise AI, 50Languages, and AI conversational agents are integrated into L2 speaking pedagogy in Saudi higher education, this study employed a qualitative multiple-case design. This approach enabled systematic comparison across institutional contexts, gender-segregated classrooms, and varying learner proficiency levels, capturing both shared patterns and contextual variation. Such a design aligns with calls in applied linguistics for context-sensitive and ecologically valid qualitative inquiry (Creswell & Poth, 2016; Yin, 2018).

Principles of action research informed the study and were deliberately adapted to align with the research questions, which focused on (1) discourse features in learner–AI interaction, (2) pragmatic development in AI-mediated dialogue, and (3) the ideological and power dynamics shaping AI-enhanced educational environments. Action research was employed reflexively as a framework for iterative observation and interpretation within naturally occurring classroom settings rather than as an interventionist or experimental model.

Ecological validity functioned as a guiding methodological principle. AI-mediated speaking tasks were embedded within regular classroom routines rather than simulated or laboratory-based activities. Learners interacted with AI applications using their own smartphones, tablets, and iPads, reflecting authentic mobile learning practices prevalent in Saudi higher education. Consequently, the dataset captures naturally occurring learner–AI interaction rather than instructor-directed or artificial behaviour, strengthening the credibility of discourse and pragmatic analyses (Taguchi, 2022).

Researcher Positionality and Teacher–Researcher Roles

Given the embedded nature of the research, methodological reflexivity was central to the study. The researchers served in dual roles as instructors and researchers, providing sustained access to classroom interactions, learner reflections, and pedagogical practices. This positionality required careful reflexive awareness to minimise interpretive bias while leveraging insider knowledge of institutional norms and sociocultural dynamics.

To address this, analytic procedures prioritised learner-produced artefacts, recorded interactions, and reflective journals over researcher impressions. NVivo (2022)-assisted coding was used to systematise analysis and ensure that themes emerged inductively from the data. Reflexive memos were maintained throughout the analysis to document instances in which the researcher's positionality might shape interpretation, particularly regarding judgments of authenticity, correctness, and learner agency.

Rather than treating the teacher–researcher role as a limitation, the study positions it as an epistemic resource. Situated knowledge of classroom realities enabled a nuanced interpretation of pragmatic adaptation and ideological negotiation in AI-mediated interaction. This reflexive stance aligns with qualitative research in applied linguistics, which recognises researcher subjectivity as integral to meaning-making when transparently acknowledged (Creswell & Poth, 2016).

Participants

Table 3. Instructional Contexts and Participant Profiles Across Research Sites

Campus	Instructional Context	Course Type	Number of Students	Proficiency Level (CEFR)	Class Instructor	Instructor Role in Research
Campus A	Male Campus; STEM-focused	Listening Skills (2 intact classes)	40 (20 per class)	A2–B1	Researcher A	Course teacher & researcher
Campus B	Female Campus; Humanities-oriented	Preparatory Year English Course	25	A1–A2	Researcher B	Course teacher & researcher
Campus C	Mixed Streams (Business/IT/Health)	Professional Training Program English Course	25	B1–B2	Researcher C	Course teacher & researcher
Teacher Interview Participants (not tied to specific classes)	Across A, B, C	EAP / Skills-Based Instructors	6	Not applicable	Colleagues of researchers	Provided external pedagogical perspectives

- *Class instructor identities, campuses, and student identifiers are anonymised in compliance with institutional and international ethical guidelines.*
- *Proficiency levels are based on institutional placement exams aligned with CEFR descriptors.*
- *Participants in the teacher interviews did not teach the classes about which they were interviewed, ensuring independent pedagogical insight.*
- *The total sample includes 90 students across three campuses.*

Collectively, the teaching cohort (n = 6) met the following criteria:

1. Minimum three years of EAP or skills-based teaching experience in Saudi higher education,
2. Demonstrated willingness to integrate AI-mediated tasks, and
3. Familiarity with at least one mobile CALL or AI app (Duolingo, Memrise, 50Languages).

Their insights provided essential institutional and pedagogical context for interpreting the classroom-based findings. The pedagogical and technological affordances of the AI apps are summarised in Table 4.

Table 4. Comparison of AI-Enhanced Language Learning Apps

App	Access Model	Strengths	Limitations	Relevance to L2 Speaking
50Languages	Free	Structured dialogues; accessible	Limited adaptivity	Supports scripted discourse & turn-taking
Duolingo	Freemium	Motivational gamification; voice drills	Dialogues formulaic	Enhances fluency & reduces anxiety
Memrise AI	Freemium	Authentic videos; generative chatbot	AI features require upgrade	Strong for pragmatic noticing & colloquial speech

Note. How the apps were used:

- Students downloaded the apps on their iPads, tablets, or smartphones.
- Weekly assignments required completing conversational modules such as greetings, job interviews, or travel scenarios.
- Having students hear conversational AI speak allowed students to have voice-controlled dialogue practice, which encouraged them to repeat the AI model, compare, and improve their pronunciation.
- Students roleplayed classroom activities and added local cultural references and idioms to their dialogues created by the app.
- Students reflected in small focus groups with their teachers. Students critiqued the AI dialogues for their cultural authenticity and relevance. Students used their own smartphones, iPads, or tablets for contextual authenticity.

  Over the semester, the project created and implemented the following:
- 32 hours of students interacting with AI.
- 18 hours of students in class.
- 12 teachers' interview transcripts.

The project used all of this information to analyse the students' discourse, pragmatics, and ideology in the AI dialogues.

Sampling and Recruitment

To measure differences in gender, geography, proficiency, and instructional context, a purposive multiple-case Sampling design was used. The use of whole classes was justified for the following three reasons:

Ecological Validity

If whole classes were to be ungrouped and regrouped, students' peer relationships could affect their interactions with the AI.

Ethical and cultural appropriateness

Saudi Arabia has strict regulations on gender mixing in higher education. Thus, it would be neither appropriate nor possible to regroup classes across genders.

Analytic Richness

The study's design enabled an investigation of real classroom environments, their norms and practices, and how these influenced students' use of AI tools.

Recruitment Procedures

Recruiting unfolded via:

- voluntary educator involvement.
- in-class orientations and informed written consent from students.

Participation was voluntary and did not affect students' course grades or evaluations. Confidentiality agreements protected the identities of students and instructors at all stages during the research process.

DATA COLLECTION PROCEDURES

Data collection spanned 12 weeks and used four complementary sources to ensure methodological triangulation.

Table 5. Comprehensive Overview of Data Sources, Collection Processes, and Analytical Applications

Data Source	Description of Classroom Use	Data Collected	Analytical Link to Research Questions (RQs)
Classroom AI-Mediated Speaking Tasks	Learners completed structured and semi-structured speaking tasks using Duolingo Chat, Memrise AI, and 50Languages. Tasks included interviews, roleplays, debate-style exchanges, and pragmatic routines (requests, refusals, complaints). Instructors introduced tasks but did not intervene, ensuring naturalistic interaction.	• AI-mediated speaking task recordings • Interactional behaviour across task types	**RQ1 (Discourse):** Turn-taking, repair sequences, adjacency pairs, meaning negotiation **RQ2 (Pragmatics):** Speech acts, politeness, contextual appropriateness
Transcripts, Screenshots, and Audio Logs	Learner–bot interaction was captured in multiple formats using student devices and classroom audio recorders. These multimodal artefacts served as the primary discourse-pragmatic dataset.	• Screen recordings of bot conversations • Audio logs of classroom interactions • Verbatim transcripts of learner–AI dialogue	**RQ1 (Discourse):** Sequential organisation and discourse patterns **RQ2 (Pragmatics):** Learner modifications of bot output; shifts in pragmatic performance
Student Reflective Journals	Students submitted weekly reflections documenting emotional responses (anxiety, confidence), noticing of pragmatics, perceptions of authenticity, and experiences with AI-generated corrections.	• 12 weeks of reflective journal entries • Written accounts of affective and cognitive responses • Evidence of pragmatic noticing	**RQ2 (Pragmatics):** Noticing of speech acts, politeness forms **RQ3 (Ideology):** Ownership, agency, perceptions of correctness, reliance on AI
Teacher Interviews	Semi-structured interviews with EAP colleagues explored pedagogical integration of AI tools, accuracy and bias concerns, and institutional readiness under Vision 2030. Interviewees were not instructors of the research classes, ensuring independent pedagogical perspectives.	• 12 interview transcripts • Teacher perspectives on pedagogy, assessment, AI affordances, and institutional policy	**RQ3 (Ideology/Power):** Algorithmic authority; perceived AI neutrality or bias; institutional attitudes toward AI integration

continued on following page

Table 5. Continued

Data Source	Description of Classroom Use	Data Collected	Analytical Link to Research Questions (RQs)
AI-Generated Dialogues	Conversations produced by the three AI tools (scripted and generative) were compared to learner-modified versions to examine adaptation, resistance, and localization.	• Bot-generated text • Learner-edited outputs • Side-by-side comparative samples	**RQ1 (Discourse):** Formulaic vs. creative constructions **RQ2 (Pragmatics):** Contextualized modifications and pragmatic shifts
Classroom Observation Notes	Observations documented how students engaged with AI tasks, peer collaboration, and the influence of classroom norms on interaction patterns.	• Field notes • Interactional behaviour logs	**RQ1 & RQ3:** Discourse behaviours shaped by classroom culture; emergent ideologies; resistance or alignment with AI norms

METHODOLOGICAL WORKFLOW

Figure 7. Conducting AI-mediated L2 Speaking Research

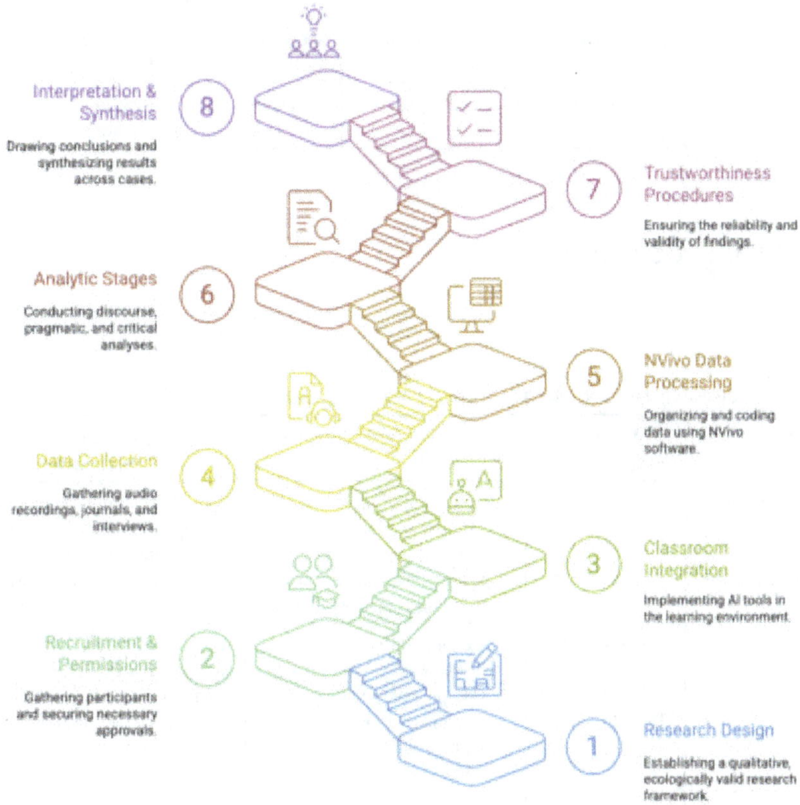

ALIGNMENT OF METHODOLOGY WITH THE RESEARCH QUESTIONS

Table 6 shows how each RQ maps onto specific analytic procedures.

Table 6. Alignment of Research Questions with Analytic Procedures

RQ	Analytic Focus	Procedures
RQ1: Discourse Features	Interactional mechanics	Turn-taking; repair; adjacency pairs; expansions; pragmatic markers
RQ2: Pragmatic Competence	Pragmalinguistic & sociopragmatic development	Speech acts; politeness; contextuality; learner modifications
RQ3: Ideology & Power	Linguistic authority & agency	Themes: AI authority, bias, resistance, ownership

Analytical Procedures

Table 7. NVivo-Supported Analytical Procedures for RQ1–RQ3

Research Question	Analytic Approach	NVivo Procedures	Coding Dimensions / Node Structure
RQ1: Discourse Features of Learner–AI Interaction	Discourse Analysis	• Creation of hierarchical node tree • Matrix coding queries across apps, proficiency, and gender • Cluster and frequency analysis	• Turn-taking sequences • Repair patterns (self-/other-initiated) • Formulaic vs. creative constructions • Meaning negotiation episodes
RQ2: Pragmatic Competence Through AI Dialogue	Pragmatic Analysis (Schmidt, 1990; Taguchi, 2018)	• Comparative coding of learner vs. bot output • Pre–post pragmatic shift comparison • Coding comparison queries for intercoder alignment	• Speech acts (requests, refusals, apologies) • Politeness strategies (hedging, softeners) • Contextual appropriateness • Interactional responsiveness
RQ3: Ideology and Power Dynamics in AI-Mediated Speaking	Critical Thematic Analysis (Braun & Clarke, 2021)	• Iterative thematic coding cycles • Word tree visualisation • Relationship mapping	• Algorithmic authority • Native-speaker normativity • Cultural misalignment • Creative resistance • Learner agency

Steps for Ensuring Reliability

The following actions were implemented in a bid to enhance and/or secure the credibility of the study:

- Data triangulation
- Use of NVivo for coding comparison and inter-coder agreement
- Analytical memos and thick description
- Member checking for interview synthesis
- NVivo project logs for the trail of audit

The actions above were in line with the discipline's qualitative norms and standards in applied linguistics and CALL.

Researcher Positionality

As scholars working within Saudi higher education, the three researchers bring complementary positionalities to the study. Researcher A, as a Saudi academic, offers insider knowledge of gendered classroom dynamics, sociolinguistic expectations, and the institutional structures that shape ELT. Researchers B and C, as long-term foreign instructors with more than eighteen years of teaching experience in the Kingdom, contribute a practice-based understanding of pedagogical norms, learner behaviours, and the everyday realities of multilingual classrooms. These perspectives enrich analysis but also require reflexive awareness of several concerns:

- power asymmetries between teacher–researchers and students
- cultural expectations surrounding the use and legitimacy of AI tools
- potential interpretive bias when evaluating learner agency

Reflexive memos and peer debriefing were employed to maintain transparency and ensure interpretive rigour.

Ethical Considerations

We obtained ethical approvals from all the other entities involved. Some of the protections these entities provided included Informed Consent, Anonymisation of transcripts and journals, secure storage of NVivo datasets, and adherence to gender-segregated protocols. Regarding AI-specific ethics, we used only publicly available, open-access AI applications, collected no private account data, informed students about data privacy risks, and ensured all actions were consistent with UNESCO (2019) AI ethics.

RESULT

This chapter covers the outcomes of the multiple-case investigation, centred around the three questions guiding the inquiry. NVivo 14 was used to code transcripts, learner reflections, AI dialogues, and teacher interviews. The results are presented as cross-case themes supported by coded excerpts, analytic tables, and comparative matrices.

Discourse Features in AI-Mediated Speaking

Analysis of 42 AI-Mediated Speaking Sessions Revealed Three key Discourse Patterns:

(1) increased fluency through predictable turn-taking,
(2) reliance on bot-initiated repair sequences, and
(3) expansion of learner output when prompted by open-ended bot questions.

Turn-Taking Patterns

All three apps generated highly structured adjacency pairs. Learners typically responded to bot prompts with minimal hesitation, as bot turns were consistent in form and timing.

L28 (Duolingo): Bot: "What did you do last weekend?"

Student: "I… I visited my grandmother and… cooked. It was good."

Table 8. Turn-Taking Features Across Apps (NVivo Matrix Query)

Discourse Feature	50Languages	Duolingo	Memrise	Overall %
Immediate response (≤ 2 sec)	72%	84%	80%	79%
Bot-initiated turn repair	41%	55%	38%	45%
Learner-initiated clarification	17%	22%	19%	19%
Elaborated learner turns (≥ 6 sec)	33%	28%	47%	36%

Memrise produced the highest percentage of elaborated turns because its video-based prompts elicited more extended responses.

Repair and Negotiation of Meaning

Repair sequences were common, particularly when bots flagged grammatical inconsistencies.

50Languages Bot: "Do you mean *I have visited*, not *I visited already*?"
Student: "Yes, *I have visited*. Sorry."
NVivo coding identified **three repair types** (Table 9).

Table 9. Frequency of Repair Types

Repair Type	Frequency	% of All Repairs
Reformulation	68	52%
Semantic clarification	39	30%
Pragmatic adjustment	24	18%

Note. *Pragmatic repair mainly occurred on Memrise due to the colloquial phrases featured in native-speaker videos.*

Pragmatic Changes with the Use of AI-Generated Dialogues

Gains by learners in speech acts, politeness, and situational appropriateness were remarkable, but there also seemed to be a problem of learners copying the bots.

Speech Act Range

Due to AI interactions, learners demonstrated greater ease in producing a wider variety of speech acts. NVivo coding revealed a significant improvement in Pragmatic Features (Table 10). **Student (after using Memrise):** "Actually, I prefer to meet later, if that is okay with you." This was a shift from earlier blunt refusals.

Table 10. Pragmatic Feature Uptake (Comparative Coding)

Pragmatic Feature	Baseline	Week 6	Week 12	Increase
Requests	21	44	66	+214%
Politeness markers	15	38	51	+240%
Mitigation strategies	9	24	37	+311%
Speech act accuracy	33%	55%	72%	+39%

Learners consistently incorporated bot-modelled pragmatics, especially softeners such as *"maybe," "perhaps,"* and *"I was wondering if…".*

Learner Adaptation vs Imitation

Table 11. Adaptation and Imitation Rates in Learner Output Across the Semester

Output Category	Week 4 (%)	Week 8 (%)	Week 12 (%)	Notes
Direct Imitation of AI Output	68	54	53	High in early weeks; decreases over time
Adaptive Reformulation	32	46	47	Learners increasingly modify bot phrasing
Localized Cultural Adaptation	11	26	42	Strongest growth among Memrise users
Hybrid Output (mixed forms)	21	30	29	Learners blend bot phrasing with own choices

Note. *Percentages reflect NVivo Coding Comparison Query results across all three classrooms (N = 90). "Localised Cultural Adaptation" refers to modifications aligned with culturally appropriate politeness norms or discourse routines.*

IDEOLOGY AND POWER IN AI-MEDIATED SPEAKING

NVivo analysis of reflective journals, classroom recordings, learner outputs, and teacher interviews revealed **three dominant ideological themes** that characterise learner–bot interaction (Table 12).

Table 12. Ideological Themes Identified in AI-Mediated Speaking (NVivo Analysis)

Theme	Description	NVivo References (n)	Data Sources
Algorithmic Authority	Learners interpret the bot's corrections as unquestionably correct.	126	Reflective journals, interview transcripts
Native-Speaker Normativity	Bots reinforce idealized "standard English" norms based on U.S./UK corpora.	98	Journals, teacher interviews, classroom interaction
Creative Resistance and Agency	Learners localize, modify, or resist bot phrasing to align with cultural norms.	63	Learner output, classroom recordings, reflections

Note. *NVivo 14 provided the counts of nodes across the entire dataset (N = 90 learners; 6 teachers).*

Algorithmic Authority

This belief contributed to what NVivo coded as Algorithmic Authority, the most frequently referenced ideological node. Table 8 presents additional representative quotes.

Table 13. Representative Quotes Illustrating Ideological Themes

Theme	Representative Learner/Teacher Quote	Illustrative Function
Algorithmic Authority	*"If the app says it is wrong, then it must be wrong."*, Student Journal, Week 7	Demonstrates uncritical acceptance of bot authority
Native-Speaker Normativity	*"My English is not natural because I don't speak like the bot."*, Student Journal, Week 9	Shows internalization of idealized native-speaker norms
Creative Resistance & Agency	*"I changed the sentence because Saudis don't speak that way, even in English."*, Student Journal, Week 10	Illustrates learner agency and cultural localization

Note. *Excerpts reflect anonymised learner reflections categorised using NVivo coding.*

Affectations of the Native-Speaker Norm

Across AI-assisted work, there was an overwhelming inclination toward native-speaker affectations. Standardised American or British English was the dominant form used by the bots, establishing a hierarchy of English forms that learners subsequently adopted. Learners felt an obligation to reproduce the bot's pronunciation, tone, and politeness structures. One student described the phenomenon as follows:

"My English is not natural because I do not speak like the bot."

The Native-Speaker Norm in this Section is the theme that attracted the most references in the coding exercise in Table 14, which posits that AI systems, trained on Anglophone datasets, promote a singular, narrow view of 'real English.' Teachers were concerned that this narrowed focus led learners to fail to appreciate localised or region-specific Englishes.

Creative Resistance and Agency

Although the learners initially displayed a tendency to imitate and show respect to the AI's purported authority, they subsequently demonstrated the use of language generated by bots with heightened agency by creatively altering the bot language to:

- Modify the language of politeness and incorporation of pragmatic features to reflect the culture.
- Align the expressions with Saudi sociopragmatic expectations.
- Reject phrases offered by the bot as being overly formal, strange, or unnatural.

  As an example:

  "I changed the sentence because Saudis don't speak that way, even in English."

The presence of this theme highlights that learners were not simply passive on-lookers of the AI's language outputs but rather localised the AI-generated language algorithmically to reflect their identities, communicative preferences, and agency. To explore how different apps shaped ideological patterns, a cross-app comparison was conducted (Table 14).

Table 14. Comparative Ideological Influence of AI-Enhanced Language Apps

Ideological Dimension	50Languages	Duolingo	Memrise
Algorithmic Authority	Moderate, Corrections accepted but scripts seen as less authoritative.	High, Gamified correctness strongly reinforces deference to bot judgments.	Moderate–High, Authority present but diversity in videos reduces blind acceptance.
Native-Speaker Normativity	Moderate, Standardized but not explicitly "native-like."	High, Strong reinforcement of U.S./UK standards in scripted outputs.	Moderate, Authentic video variety reduces a single "standard" norm.
Cultural Alignment	Low–Moderate, Requires learner adaptation.	Low, Scripts often perceived as contextually foreign.	High, Authentic videos facilitate culturally resonant adaptation.
Learner Agency	Moderate, Some adaptation but limited creativity.	Low–Moderate, Gamified scoring discourages deviation.	High, Learners frequently localize expressions and resist rigid norms.
Overall Ideological Impact	Neutral to mildly centralizing.	Strongly centralizing, Promotes native-speakerism and rigid correctness.	Flexible, Encourages negotiation, localization, and learner voice.

Note. *The findings support the chapter's leading assertions that AI bots can serve both pedagogical and ideological functions, regulating not only how learners articulate their thoughts but also how they understand, or begin to understand, correctness, authenticity, and linguistic identity.*

Creative Resistance and Localisation

Even though much early reliance centred on resistance, many learners either resisted or reconfigured the bots' norms.

One student said, "*I made it different because that sentence did not match how we speak.*" NVivo indicated an increase:

- Week 2: 9% of modifications were localised
- Week 12: 42% of modifications were localised

This directly aligns with the chapter's assertion that learners actively negotiate rather than uncritically embrace algorithmically generated language.

Table 15. Ideological and Agency Themes (Nvivo Node Frequencies)

Node / Theme	References	% of All Ideology Codes
Algorithmic Authority	126	44%
Native-Speaker Normativity	98	34%
Creative Resistance	63	22%

Note. *Creative resistance occurred most frequently in classrooms that used Memrise, due to exposure to diverse video-based accents.*

Table 16. Contrasting Human–Human vs Human–AI Interactional Sequences

Feature	Human–Human Interaction	Human–AI Interaction
Turn-Taking	Flexible, negotiated, subtle cues	Programmed timing; predictable patterns
Repair	Negotiated, collaborative	Bot-driven recasts, clarification requests
Pragmatics	Culturally embedded	Depends on training corpus; may lack cultural grounding
Identity Work	Rich, socially constructed	Limited; bot performs neutral or generic stance
Anxiety Level	Higher in evaluative contexts	Lower due to privacy and absence of peer judgment

FINDINGS AND DISCUSSION

The findings are interpreted through the study's theoretical framework, drawing on interactionist (Long, 1996), sociocultural (Vygotsky & Cole, 1978), affective (Krashen, 1985), pragmatic (Taguchi, 2018), and critical applied linguistics perspectives (Freire, 1970; Pennycook, 2010; Woolard & Schieffelin, 1994). Rather than presenting findings as isolated outcomes, this section foregrounds five interrelated trends that illuminate how AI bots are reshaping L2 speaking pedagogy within broader developments in I-CALL (Chapelle, 2009; Godwin-Jones, 2023). These trends are discussed sequentially to distinguish pedagogical change, institutional normalisation, and ethical-ideological implications, rather than treating them as diffuse outcomes embedded within classroom findings.

Trend 1: Pedagogical Shift Toward Dialogic Safety and Expanded Oral Participation

These patterns indicate a pedagogical shift toward dialogic safety, in which reduced affective pressure facilitates sustained oral engagement. Consistent with Krashen's (1985) Affective Filter Hypothesis, AI-mediated interactions created low-threat speaking environments that enabled learners to experiment with pronunciation, hesitation markers, and pragmatic routines without fear of negative evaluation. From an interactionist perspective, such affective conditions supported longer conversational turns, greater willingness to initiate interaction, and increased engagement in negotiation of meaning (Long, 1996). As earlier CALL research suggests (Chapelle, 2009), these conditions are conducive to increased oral production. In the Saudi context—where speaking anxiety is socially pronounced (Mishu et al., 2022)—this represents a meaningful reconfiguration of how L2 speaking opportunities are structured and accessed.

Trend 2: Reconfiguration of Authenticity Through Algorithmic and Situated Pragmatics

Rather than functioning as a stable property of AI input, authenticity emerged as a negotiated construct shaped by learner–AI interaction. Learners' perceptions of AI-generated speech as overly formal prompted heightened sociopragmatic awareness, particularly regarding the absence of locally recognisable interactional norms. In line with Taguchi's (2018) emphasis on contextualised interaction, learners engaged in reflective adjustment rather than uncritically adopting AI discourse. Consistent with Schmidt's (1990) Noticing Hypothesis, perceived mismatches between algorithmic output and sociocultural expectations triggered pragmatic adaptation. Drawing on Gee's (2014) discourse perspective, authenticity was co-constructed through interaction rather than derived from the technological source itself. This supports I-CALL's argument that authenticity is best understood in terms of ecological fit rather than linguistic origin (Levy & Hubbard, 2005).

Trend 3: Institutional Normalisation of AI and Emerging Power Relations

The findings also point to a growing institutional normalisation of AI as an authoritative pedagogical presence. Learners' strong orientation toward AI-provided corrections reflects a shift in epistemic trust, with algorithmic feedback increasingly perceived as definitive. From a critical perspective, this pattern echoes Freire's (1970) concern that authoritative knowledge sources may discourage reflexive engagement. While AI systems democratise access to feedback, they also risk fostering dependency, a tension highlighted in Pennycook's (2010) critique of ideological contradictions within pedagogical systems. These dynamics align with broader debates in AI ethics, where algorithmic systems simultaneously enable learner autonomy and constrain interpretive agency.

Trend 4: Learner Agency and Creative Resistance Through Localisation

Importantly, trends of dependency were counterbalanced by robust evidence of learner agency and creative resistance. Learners actively localised AI-generated discourse by adapting politeness strategies, incorporating Arabic discourse routines, and rejecting expressions perceived as socioculturally incongruent. Such practices exemplify Schmidt's (1990) notion of noticing as a catalyst for interlanguage development and resonate with Pennycook's (2010) concept of critical creativity. Rather than reproducing algorithmic norms verbatim, learners repositioned themselves as meaning-makers who negotiated and recontextualised AI discourse. This challenges deterministic accounts of AI influence and foregrounds learner agency within AI-mediated interaction.

Trend 5: Policy Alignment and Ethical Governance Under Vision 2030

At the institutional level, the findings reveal alignment between AI-mediated pedagogy and Saudi Arabia's Vision 2030 priorities for digital transformation and technology-enabled education (Chowdhury et al., 2025). Instructors viewed the integration of applications such as 50Languages, Duolingo, and Memrise as consistent with learners' everyday digital practices. However, this normalisation also exposed policy gaps related to assessment integrity, data privacy, and equitable access. These concerns reinforce Godwin-Jones's (2023) argument that AI-mediated learning environments require explicit governance structures to prevent uncritical adoption and ideological drift. Without such frameworks, AI systems risk functioning as implicit gatekeepers of linguistic legitimacy.

Synthesis of Trends

Taken together, these trends demonstrate that AI bots are embedded within intersecting pedagogical, institutional, and ideological transformations. AI-mediated speaking environments foster dialogic safety and expanded oral participation (RQ1), reconfigure pragmatic authenticity through negotiated interaction (RQ2), and introduce new forms of authority and agency within learner–AI relationships (RQ3). Crucially, the findings show that AI bots do not merely enhance L2 speaking practice; they reshape the conditions under which speaking, learning, and linguistic identity are negotiated.

Limitations and Future Research

One weakness of this qualitative multi-case study is its lack of generalizability. There is also no volumetric investigation of fluency, accuracy, and/or pragmatic advancements, indicating that future studies would benefit from a mixed-methods framework that incorporates corpus analysis, uses both pre- and post-testing, and employs quantifiable measures of oral proficiency. Additionally, the study did not disaggregate the results by gender patterns in interaction, which is particularly salient in the Saudi educational context and may shape learners' comfort or discomfort with AI-mediated speaking. Future studies, therefore, ought to focus on the extent to which gendered norms, cultural patterns, and prior levels of digital literacy impact learners' interaction with AI bots. Pragmatic transfer in AI-mediated dialogues would be enriched by cross-cultural research, as it would shed light on how learners from diverse linguistic backgrounds balance authenticity and appropriateness when engaging with algorithmically produced discourse.

IMPLICATIONS

Pedagogical Implications

The findings underscore the need to position AI bots not as replacements for teachers but as mediational resources that expand learners' opportunities for spoken interaction. When appropriately framed, AI bots can assist human teaching by allowing students to practice turn-taking, utilise different pragmatic strategies, and practice speech in low-stakes environments, with free, accessible opportunities outside of class time. That said, this potential outcome is hitting a ceiling without students being critically aware of bots. Structured reflection tasks, such as comparing bots' phrasing with human phrasing or pushing learners to interrogate the cultural assumptions embedded in AI outputs, help learners understand the limitations of algorithmic text and the dangers of over-reliance on this technology. In this manner, teachers can reclaim their position in practice in the critical teaching of language and guide learners to counter the prevailing notion of AI as a provider of knowledge, and to utilise AI as a tool for co-constructing knowledge.

Policy implications

At the institutional level, incorporating AI tools into L2 curricula will require clearly defined governance structures. The schools can describe policy systems that ensure fairness in the availability of AI tools, and that distance-learning devices, Internet access, and digital training for students and educators are within reach. Policy systems also need to define what constitutes legitimate academic help and unacceptable overreliance on AI in speaking evaluations, where automated scaffolding may obscure learners' actual performance. Equally important is the data privacy policy.

There must be transparency within universities about how commercial software will be assessed, how informed consent will be obtained, and how learner data will be protected from unauthorised access. Without these kinds of structures in place, the adoption of AI will lead to inequities and ethical concerns that I-CALL will be politically and morally responsible for.

Theoretical Implications

The research advances discourse-pragmatic and interactionist theories by presenting AI bots as algorithmic interlocutors. AI bots, unlike other CALL tools, are non-human co-constructors of interactional sequences. They shape learners' discourse through requests and questions for clarification, turn modelling, and the negotiation of meaning. These roles fundamentally turn paradigm assumptions on their head, expanding I-CALL theories and assumptions about interlocutors to include the discursive, ideological, and mediating roles of algorithmic agents. AI bots, then, are in a paradoxical position: they scaffold learners' discourse iteratively and ideologically, thereby further confirming the tool's paradoxically constructive role in L2 speaking development.

CONCLUSION

This research shows how AI bots are changing Teaching English as a Second Language (TESOL) as learners move away from mechanical, form-focused, repetition-based speaking practice to dialogic turn-taking exchanges that involve negotiating meaning and using pragmatics playfully. At the same time, AI systems must work with the ideologically embedded assumptions around standardisation and "native-like" norms. These ideologies could influence how learners assess their own linguistic selves. By using freely available AI-enabled speaking tools such as 50Languages, Duolingo, and Memrise in EAP classrooms, the study achieved high ecological validity by demonstrating their use in the context of Saudi higher education.

AI bots are ultimately a double-edged sword. They lower the barrier to speaking practice for students while entrenching students in particular forms of non-inclusive (and thus "correct") language. Educators face the challenge of balancing the benefits AI offers with the need for pedagogical authenticity, cultural responsiveness, and the exercise of judgment in their pedagogical decisions. The real challenge for educators in language education in an AI-dominated field is to retain empathy, an ethical framework, and an understanding of learners as co-creators of their linguistic selves.

REFERENCES

Akan, M. F., Almosa, A., Siddiqui, S., Chowdhury, G., Ahamed, M. M., Mishu, A., Ahmed, J., & Sultana, S. (2023). On linguistic reviews of Arabic and Bangla: A comparative study. *Theory and Practice in Language Studies, 13*(9), 2375–2383. DOI: 10.17507/tpls.1309.25

Al-Seghayer, K. (2024). Pragmatic competence in Saudi EFL learners: Challenges, consequences, and strategies for overcoming barriers. *Journal for the Study of English Linguistics, 12*(1), 209–235. DOI: 10.5296/jsel.v12i1.22438

Alhudaithy, H. I., Mishu, A., & Chowdhury, G. (2025). Reclaiming voice and identity: Teaching creative writing as a tool for empowerment in multicultural classrooms. *Journal of Language Teaching and Research, 16*(1). Advance online publication. DOI: 10.17507/jltr.1701.29

Alshammari, S. R. (2020). EFL vocabulary learning strategies used by Saudi Arabian university students. *Advanced Education, 7*(16), 28–38. DOI: 10.20535/2410-8286.202436

Amin, E. A.-R. (2024). EFL students' perception of using artificial intelligence-powered text-to-speech apps in learning pronunciation. *Migration Letters : An International Journal of Migration Studies, 21*(3), 887–903.

Braun, V., & Clarke, V. (2021). Thematic analysis: A practical guide. *Sage (Atlanta, Ga.).*

Chapelle, C. A. (2009). The relationship between second language acquisition theory and computer-assisted language learning. *Modern Language Journal, 93*(s1), 741–753. DOI: 10.1111/j.1540-4781.2009.00970.x

Chowdhury, G. A. J., Koka, N. A., & Mishu, A. (2025). Bridging or dividing? Chinese language integration and the resilience of ELT in Saudi higher education under Vision 2030: Policy symbolism vs. pedagogical realities. *World Journal of English Language, 16*(2), 309–323. DOI: 10.5430/wjel.v16n2p309

Chowdhury, G. U. A., & Mishu, A. (2019). *Literature in EFL: A gateway to a successful teaching–learning experience by stimulating human psyche.* Arab World English Journal (Special Issue: The Dynamics of EFL in the Arab World). https://doi.org/DOI: 10.24093/awej/efl1.18

Creswell, J. W., & Poth, C. N. (2016). *Qualitative inquiry and research design: Choosing among five approaches.* Sage Publications.

Duolingo. (2023). *How Duolingo works.* https://www.duolingo.com

Freire, P. (1970). *Pedagogy of the Oppressed.* Continuum.

Fryer, L. K., & Carpenter, R. (2006). Bots as language learning tools. *Language Learning & Technology, 10*(3), 8–14. DOI: 10.64152/10125/44068

Gee, J. P. (2014). *An introduction to discourse analysis: Theory and method* (4th ed.). Routledge., DOI: 10.4324/9781315819679

Gilmore, A. (2007). Authentic materials and authenticity in foreign language learning. *Language Teaching, 40*(2), 97–118. DOI: 10.1017/S0261444807004144

Godwin-Jones, R. (2023). Emerging spaces for language learning: AI bots, ambient intelligence, and the metaverse. *Language Learning & Technology, 27*(2), 6–27. DOI: 10.64152/10125/73501

Golonka, E. M., Bowles, A. R., Frank, V. M., Richardson, D. L., & Freynik, S. (2014). Technologies for foreign language learning: A review of technology types and their effectiveness. *Computer Assisted Language Learning, 27*(1), 70–105. DOI: 10.1080/09588221.2012.700315

Horwitz, E. K. (2001). Language anxiety and achievement. *Annual Review of Applied Linguistics, 21*, 112–126. DOI: 10.1017/S0267190501000071

Horwitz, E. K., Horwitz, M. B., & Cope, J. (1986). Foreign language classroom anxiety. *Modern Language Journal, 70*(2), 125–132. DOI: 10.1111/j.1540-4781.1986.tb05256.x

Hsieh, C.-N. (2024). Mobile-assisted language learning (MALL). In *The TESOL encyclopedia of English language teaching*. Wiley., DOI: 10.1002/9781118784235.eelt1053

Krashen, S. D. (1985). *The input hypothesis: Issues and implications.* Longman.

Lan, Y. J. (2025). Language Learning in the Metaverse: Research Trends, Opportunities, and Challenges. In Lan, Y. J., Qi, G. Y., & Chun, D. (Eds.), *AI-Mediated Language Education in the Metaverse Era. Chinese Language Learning Sciences.* Springer., DOI: 10.1007/978-981-95-0245-5_2

50Languages. (n.d.). *50Languages language learning app.* Goethe Verlag. https://www.50languages.com

Levy, M., & Hubbard, P. (2005). Why call CALL "CALL"? *Computer Assisted Language Learning, 18*(3), 205–214. DOI: 10.1080/09588220500208884

Long, M. H. (1996). The role of the linguistic environment in second language acquisition. In Ritchie, W. C., & Bhatia, T. K. (Eds.), *Handbook of second language acquisition* (pp. 413–468). Academic Press.

MacIntyre, P. D., Clément, R., Dörnyei, Z., & Noels, K. A. (1998). Conceptualizing willingness to communicate in a L2: A situational model of L2 confidence and affiliation. *Modern Language Journal, 82*(4), 545–562. DOI: 10.1111/j.1540-4781.1998.tb05543.x

MacIntyre, P. D., & Gardner, R. C. (1994). The subtle effects of language anxiety on cognitive processing in the second language. *Language Learning, 44*(2), 283–305. DOI: 10.1111/j.1467-1770.1994.tb01103.x

Memrise. (2023). *Memrise: Learn a new language with AI.* https://www.memrise.com

Mishu, A. (2025, August 3). *The role of affective filter in ELT classrooms: A study on anxiety, motivation, and comprehensible input using literature-based materials.* Paper presented at the International Conference on Arts and Humanities for Peacebuilding.

Mishu, A., Ahamed, M. M., Akan, M. F., Abdul-Rab, S. D., Chowdhury, G., Ahmad, J., & Sultana, I. (2025). How AI is ushering in a new era in ELT: Teachers' perspectives. *Theory and Practice in Language Studies, 15*(2), 592–605. Advance online publication. DOI: 10.17507/tpls.1502.29

Mishu, A., & Jaashan, H. M. S. (2025). Effects of Transformational Generative Grammar (TGG) on writing skills of KKU EFL students. *Journal of Language Teaching and Research, 16*(6), 1878–1888. DOI: 10.17507/jltr.1606.09

Mishu, A., Mohammed, H. A., Hakami, S. A. A., & Chowdhury, G. (2022). The impact of online presentations on reducing the introverted EFL learners' stress and anxiety. *Saudi Journal of Language Studies, 3*(1), 32–46. DOI: 10.1108/SJLS-03-2022-0037

NVivo. (2022). *NVivo (Version 14) [Computer software].* QSR International. https://www.qsrinternational.com/nvivo-qualitative-data-analysis-software/home

Pennycook, A. (2010). Critical and alternative directions in applied linguistics. *Australian Review of Applied Linguistics, 33*(2), 16.1–16.16. https://doi.org/DOI: 10.2104/aral1016

Raji, I. D., Smart, A., White, R. N., Mitchell, M., Gebru, T., Hutchinson, B., Smith-Loud, J., Theron, D., & Barnes, P. (2020). Closing the AI accountability gap: Defining an end-to-end framework for internal algorithmic auditing. *Proceedings of the 2020 Conference on Fairness, Accountability, and Transparency*, 33–44. https://doi.org/DOI: 10.1145/3351095.3372873

Schmidt, R. (1990). The role of consciousness in second language learning. *Applied Linguistics, 11*(2), 129–158. DOI: 10.1093/applin/11.2.129

Siddiqui, S., Ahamed, M. M., Chowdhury, G., Mishu, A., & Monira, S. (2023). Teaching writing skills to EFL learners: Issues and concerns. *Journal of Language Teaching and Research, 14*(6), 1541–1550. DOI: 10.17507/jltr.1406.12

Swain, M. (1985). Communicative competence: Some roles of comprehensible input and comprehensible output in its development. *Input in second language acquisition, 15*, 165-179.

Taguchi, N. (2018). Pragmatic competence in foreign language education: Cultivating learner autonomy and strategic learning of pragmatics. *New perspectives on the development of communicative and related competence in foreign language education*, 53-69. https://doi.org/DOI: 10.1515/9781501505034-004

Taguchi, N. (2022). Immersive virtual reality for pragmatics task development. *TESOL Quarterly*, *56*(1), 308–335. DOI: 10.1002/tesq.3070

Teimouri, Y., Goetze, J., & Plonsky, L. (2019). Second language anxiety and achievement: A meta-analysis. *Studies in Second Language Acquisition*, *41*(2), 363–387. DOI: 10.1017/S0272263118000311

UNESCO. (2019). Draft recommendation on Open Educational Resources (OER). https://unesdoc.unesco.org/ark:/48223/pf0000370936

Vygotsky, L. S., & Cole, M. (1978). *Mind in society: Development of higher psychological processes*. Harvard university press.

Woolard, K. A., & Schieffelin, B. B. (1994). Language ideology. *Annual Review of Anthropology*, *23*(1), 55–82. DOI: 10.1146/annurev.an.23.100194.000415

Yin, R. K. (2018). *Case study research and applications: Design and methods* (6th ed.). SAGE Publications.

Young, R. F. (2019). Interactional competence and L2 pragmatics. In *The Routledge Handbook of LSecond language Acquisition and Pragmatics* (pp. 93–110). Routledge.

Ziegler, N., & González-Lloret, M. (Eds.). (2022). *The Routledge handbook of second language acquisition and technology*. Routledge., DOI: 10.4324/9781351117586

Chapter 4

A Comparative Analysis of Teacher and AI-Supported Corrective Feedback on Fossilized Pronunciation Errors Among EFL Learners

Selami Aydin
http://orcid.org/0000-0003-1614-874X
Istanbul Medeniyet University, Turkey

Abdullah Yıldız
http://orcid.org/0000-0003-0783-6663
Istanbul Medeniyet University, Turkey

ABSTRACT

Pronunciation is a core element of communicative competence in the English as a foreign language (EFL) learning process. However, learners at the interlanguage stage often display fossilized errors. Artificial intelligence (AI) offers potential as a corrective feedback tool to detect and address such errors. This study investigates fossilized pronunciation errors among EFL learners, examines the effects of teacher- and AI-supported corrective feedback, and compares their effectiveness. The quasi-experimental design involved 44 EFL learners. Data collection tools included a background questionnaire, a pilot test, a test of mispronounced words, and a focus group interview. Descriptive statistics, the Mann-Whitney U test, and the Wilcoxon Test were applied to analyze the data. Findings revealed that learners

DOI: 10.4018/979-8-3373-6420-9.ch004

in both groups exhibited moderate levels of fossilized pronunciation errors. Teacher feedback was found to reduce such errors and improve overall pronunciation skills, while AI-supported feedback contributed to error reduction for certain words.

INTRODUCTION

Pronunciation is one of the fundamental components of communicative competence (Jones, 2018) since "the speaker and the hearer work together to produce and understand each other's utterances" (Foote & Trofimovich, 2018, p. 85). From this perspective, it can be stated that pronunciation relates to listening and speaking, as it improves the intelligibility and understanding of fluent, connected, and running speech (Brown, 2011) and enhances learners' perceptions and production in the target language (Lee & Lyster, 2017). Similarly, pronunciation is closely related to reading and writing skills, as language knowledge is activated during listening and speaking (Ranbom & Connine, 2011). For instance, learners can improve their reading skills by reading aloud (Van Loon, 2002) and develop writing skills by recognizing written words (Brown, 2011). When learners achieve communicative competence, they can effectively use the target language for communication in social and professional settings and increase their awareness of the target culture.

Fossilization is one of the most persistent problems, particularly in pronunciation, where errors often resist correction despite prolonged exposure to the target language. For instance, Turkish EFL learners have relatively new sounds to cope with, which can cause confusion both perceptually and in production, and they struggle to hear the differences in certain consonants. More specifically, they experience difficulties producing consonants such as /r/ and /g/ at the end of a word. They also confuse several vowels and diphthongs that do not exist in Turkish. Similarly, since there are no initial consonant clusters in Turkish, English consonant clusters pose a particular challenge for Turkish EFL learners. Moreover, Turkish EFL learners may have difficulty placing stress, rhythm, and intonation (Kenworthy, 1987). In conclusion, Turkish EFL learners appear to encounter difficulties due to the impact of their native language on their pronunciation skills in the target language. In addition to the adverse effects of the native language, learners' ages, the length of time they have used the target language, social pressure, and innate aptitude may create difficulties that lead to fossilization (Acton, 1984).

Without correct pronunciation, which requires instruction and feedback, learners may experience fossilization and fail to achieve effective communication, awareness, comprehension, and intelligibility (Harmer, 2001). In other words, EFL learners may not acquire functional intelligibility and communicability, self-confidence, and monitoring abilities, nor develop their communicative competence, speech consciousness, awareness, and speech adjustment strategies without their teachers' help and feedback (Butler-Pascoe & Wiburg, 2003). On the other hand, while learners need careful, gentle, and corrective feedback to improve their pronunciation skills, most teachers often overlook pronunciation instruction for several reasons, including time limitations, an overemphasis on communication, grammar, and vocabulary, and a lack of suitable materials (Harmer, 2001). EFL teachers also tend to avoid focusing on pronunciation errors and mistakes due to their negative perceptions of instructional and methodological considerations, as well as concerns, beliefs, and attitudes (Darcy, 2018). Moreover, teachers perceive that acceptable pronunciation can be learned without depending on learners' needs and purposes (Kenworthy, 1987). Given the challenges of teacher feedback on pronunciation in the EFL context, exploring innovative environments and tools that effectively identify and address pronunciation issues, including mistakes and fossilized errors, is essential.

AI has advanced rapidly in recent years and has the potential to enhance problem-solving skills (Pokrivcakova, 2019). It may also serve as a valuable tool and environment for error correction in the EFL learning process (Dodigovic, 2007), particularly in addressing challenges arising from insufficient feedback on pronunciation mistakes. In this way, students may feel more motivated and engaged in communication in the target language (Underwood, 2017), as they can access valuable, authentic language use that is not available in the classroom (Richards, 2015). AI tools enable learners to practice, rehearse, and receive feedback regarding pronunciation at their own pace. Specifically, these tools may help analyze the user's pronunciation by comparing it to predefined models, providing immediate feedback, offering visualization, preparing personalized plans, facilitating interactive practice, and tracking progress. Nevertheless, while AI-supported feedback may facilitate development, the research synthesis presented below indicates that there is no scientific evidence supporting its effectiveness compared to teacher-provided feedback. The following section reviews key theoretical perspectives on pronunciation, fossilization, corrective feedback, and AI-supported language learning that inform the design and rationale of the present study.

Theoretical Framework

Pronunciation in the foreign language learning process involves mastering a new phonetic system distinct from the learner's first language. This process encompasses several aspects, including the adjustment of the articulatory apparatus to the new phonetic system. It requires learners to familiarize themselves with the phonological inventory of the target language and to acquire the production of both segmental and suprasegmental features, including word and sentence stress, rhythm, intonation, tone, and juncture (Jarosz, 2023). The segmental level of language is described in terms of two developmental types: accuracy and fluency. Accuracy pertains to the precise production of individual sounds and ensures correct articulation, whereas fluency involves mastering prosodic features such as rhythm, stress, and intonation, which extend across syllables, words, or phrases. Furthermore, the main priority in pronunciation development is to achieve comprehensibility and intelligibility (Jones, 2018). While comprehensibility refers to how much effort the listener needs to put into understanding an utterance, intelligibility refers to "the match between the speaker's intention and the listener's response to speech passed through the transmission system" (Munro, 2017, p. 414).

Native-like pronunciation is unrealistic; therefore, a more realistic approach is favored as the pedagogical goal in pronunciation (Celce-Murcia, 2010). This approach aims to minimize differences between the sound systems of native and non-native speakers and listeners to some extent (Browne & Fulcher, 2017). Nevertheless, the discrepancies between the learner's interlanguage pronunciation may result in *errors* or *mistakes*. Errors stem from the lack of knowledge or misunderstanding of the language rules. These systematic deviations from target-language norms are indicative of the learner's interlanguage, whereas mistakes, which can be corrected if the learner is allowed to self-correct, are unsystematic and generally due to factors such as fatigue, inattention, or emotional stress rather than a lack of language knowledge. Unlike mistakes, learners tend to be unaware of the errors they make, which are reflected in their interlanguage. Teachers can address these errors through targeted pronunciation instruction and feedback (Corder, 1971).

Corrective feedback plays a crucial role in pronunciation development, particularly in addressing fossilized errors, and can be provided by various instructional sources, including teachers and AI-based tools (Jarosz, 2023). From this perspective, feedback types can be categorized by the degree of planning, explicitness, and integration with communicative activities (Doughty & Williams, 1998). Teachers may prefer to address learner errors and needs as they plan feedback based on a prior assessment or needs analysis, and deliver it as an explicit metacognitive explanation or, more subtly and implicitly, one that does not directly appeal to the learner's awareness (Bryfonski & Ma, 2020). This type of feedback, which occurs when the learner has produced a linguistic error, is called negative feedback (Ellis, 2009). Moreover, effective pronunciation learning is associated with explicit instruction and scaffolding through ongoing, frequent, supportive, and purposeful feedback that addresses both segmental and suprasegmental aspects of pronunciation (Saito, 2021). Thanks to corrective feedback, learners can notice target language features that might otherwise go unnoticed, and through practice and corrective feedback, they can become more autonomous learners with greater self-awareness, self-evaluation, and noticing skills (Schmidt, 1990). Unless corrected, the learners' interlanguage is subject to the danger of fossilization, which is defined as "becoming permanently established in the interlanguage of a second language learner in a form that is deviant from the target-language norm and that continues to appear in performance regardless of further exposure to the target language" (Flexner & Hauck, 1988, p. 755).

AI offers new opportunities for individualized pronunciation practice, but functions most effectively as a supplement to, rather than a replacement for, teacher-guided instruction. Thanks to computer-assisted feedback, challenges such as limited classroom time (Baker & Burri, 2016) can be overcome through computer-assisted pronunciation training systems, which foster learner autonomy and provide individualized feedback. In other words, AI-based tools can detect learners' strengths and weaknesses in English pronunciation (Xiao & Park, 2021). These automated pronunciation evaluation tools typically ask learners to read words, phrases, and sentences aloud and compare their output with predefined waveforms, spectrograms, pitch traces, or prosodic contours to detect incorrectly pronounced phonemes and words. In this way, the learner receives instant feedback on which phonemes or words they utter differently from the predefined target waveform or prosody, highlighting the accented, often mispronounced speech they produce compared to the articulation of native speakers.

Previous Research

While several studies have explored the impact of Automatic Speech Recognition (ASR) on pronunciation learning (e.g., Evers & Chen, 2021; Jiang et al., 2021; Sun, 2023; Thi-Nhu Ngo et al., 2024), its use in evaluating pronunciation remains underexplored. Moreover, only a handful of studies have focused on the use of AI in language learning through ASR-based computer-assisted pronunciation training, whereas studies specifically on the potential applications of AI in pronunciation feedback appear even scarcer. For instance, in a mixed-methods study examining the effectiveness of peer feedback and ASR in mobile-assisted pronunciation learning, Dai and Wu (2023) found that autonomous ASR feedback, peer feedback, and peer plus ASR feedback improved pronunciation among Chinese EFL learners. In a review study, Heil et al. (2016) concluded that the applications were poor at providing users with useful feedback. They also noted that these activities would diminish learning, as they did not provide additional information on why learners made mistakes while merely pointing out errors with different sounds and colors. In an earlier study, Nagano and Ozawa (1990) explored prosodic conversion to improve English pronunciation among Japanese learners and found that modified mimicry of native speakers was effective. This exploration was further supported by a study by Bissiri (2009), who successfully applied prosodic modification for German lexical stress training to Italian speakers using the learners' voices, thereby increasing motivation. In another study, Neri et al. (2002) highlighted the challenge of ASR systems mislabeling correct pronunciations and missing errors, a common issue at the time. Addressing the feedback dimension, Cucchiarini et al. (2009) acknowledged ASR's limitations but confirmed its effectiveness in pronunciation improvement. Chen (2017) noted enjoyment and improvements in speaking skills from using an ASR-based website, despite the high error rates reported by Morton et al. (2012). Neri et al. (2006) examined the use of ASR to aid pronunciation among 30 adult Dutch learners from diverse origins. The study investigated learners' appreciation of computer-assisted pronunciation training, expert ratings of pronunciation quality, and a detailed analysis of segmental errors. They found that the ASR-based feedback improved the pronunciation of targeted phonetic errors. However, the impact on overall pronunciation quality was not significantly different from that of the control groups. De Meo et al. (2012) further demonstrated the effectiveness of self-imitation training for Italian suprasegmental patterns to Chinese and Japanese learners, respectively, leading to more native-like speech acts classification. Ding et al. (2019) expanded on this by applying a 'golden-speaker' software to Korean learners of English, showing the benefit of native-accented feedback on fluency and awareness of suprasegmental features. In assessment, Pearson (2011) noted high correlations between human and ASR scoring, pointing to the potential for reducing human rating load while maintaining reliability. This trajectory of research underscored the advancement of the utilization of machine learning and AI in assessment, from early recognition of ASR limitations to the development of more effective training techniques and promising assessment tools, reflecting a continuous pursuit of enhancing pronunciation and assessment through technology.

Based on the research synthesis below, it can be concluded that pronunciation, particularly when errors become fossilized, is closely related to learner identity and affective factors. In this sense, fossilized pronunciation features may come to represent stable aspects of learners' linguistic identity, shaped by long-term language use, previous instructional experiences, and social perceptions of accent. As a result, learners may resist modifying fossilized pronunciation patterns, not only because of articulatory difficulty but also because such features have become familiar and personally meaningful. Pronunciation correction can therefore be perceived as face-threatening or anxiety-inducing, especially in classroom contexts where feedback is delivered publicly. On the other hand, AI-mediated feedback may create a less threatening environment by allowing learners to practice independently at their own pace, potentially reducing anxiety associated with repeated corrections. At the same time, teacher-provided feedback may support learners through interpersonal interaction and pedagogical sensitivity, highlighting the complex relationship among corrective feedback, learner identity, and emotional engagement. To sum up, acknowledging these identity-related dimensions provides a broader perspective for interpreting learners' responses to teacher- and AI-supported corrective feedback regarding fossilized pronunciation errors. Building on this theoretical and empirical background, the following section outlines the aims, research questions, and overall design of the present study.

Overview of the Study

Previous studies on AI- and ASR-assisted pronunciation learning primarily examine EFL learners' short-term pronunciation gains, perception accuracy, and general speaking performance through word-, sentence-, or phrase-level practice. Although research demonstrates that AI-based tools can support pronunciation development, it has focused mainly on immediate improvement rather than persistent, fossilized pronunciation errors. Moreover, relatively few studies directly compare teacher-provided corrective feedback with AI-supported feedback under controlled instructional conditions, and even fewer have adopted mixed-methods designs that integrate pronunciation outcomes with learner perspectives. Existing research also tends to emphasize the effectiveness of ASR technology itself rather than its role in sustained pronunciation development (Sidgi & Shaari, 2017). Different from earlier research, the present study extends AI-based pronunciation research in several important ways. First, it explicitly targets fossilized pronunciation errors, which are resistant to change despite prolonged exposure to the target language and continue to pose a challenge to intelligibility. Second, the study employs a quasi-experimental design to systematically compare the effects of teacher-supported and AI-supported corrective feedback, allowing for a clearer examination of their relative effectiveness. Third, by adopting a mixed-methods approach, the study combines quantitative data on pronunciation performance with qualitative learner perceptions, offering a more comprehensive understanding of how different feedback sources influence pronunciation development. In addition, the study addresses a gap in previous teacher–AI comparison research by focusing on independent learner practice supported by AI feedback, rather than teacher mediation alone. To this end, given the central role of pronunciation in communicative competence and the persistent risk of fossilization among EFL learners, corrective feedback remains essential. Yet, pronunciation instruction is often neglected due to time constraints, lack of materials, and methodological concerns (Bryfonski & Ma, 2020). In this context, there is a strong need to examine whether AI-supported feedback can help reduce fossilized pronunciation errors and how its effectiveness compares with teacher-provided feedback. With these considerations in mind, the present study aims to determine the level of fossilized pronunciation errors among EFL learners, investigate the effects of teacher- and AI-supported corrective feedback on correcting these errors, and compare the relative effectiveness of the two feedback types. Accordingly, the study addresses the following research questions:

1. What is the level of fossilized pronunciation errors among EFL learners?
2. Does corrective teacher feedback impact the level of fossilized pronunciation errors among EFL learners?
3. Does AI-supported corrective feedback influence the number and level of fossilized pronunciation errors among EFL learners?
4. Is there a significant difference between the teacher and AI-supported corrective feedback regarding correcting fossilized pronunciation errors?

METHOD

Research Context

This study employs an analytical, deductive approach to compare teacher- and AI-supported corrective feedback for fossilized pronunciation errors among EFL learners. The rationale for this preference was that the study aims to analyze errors and investigate the effects of teacher- and AI-based feedback on fossilization, presenting a coherent picture of the phenomenon of fossilized pronunciation errors by addressing predetermined research questions. In addition, it employs a quasi-experimental research design, a type of experimental research design in which participants are assigned to pre-existing groups rather than randomly assigned to test the treatment (Creswell, 2014; Seliger & Shohamy, 1989).

Participants

The study involved 48 EFL learners enrolled in the Department of English Language Teaching at a state university. The participants took part in different phases of the research, including the piloting, the quasi-experimental study, and focus group interviews. The participants were purposely selected, as they were the only cohort in the department to receive phonetics courses during the semester in which the study was conducted. The descriptions of the mentioned groups are detailed below and are shown in Table 1.

The participants in the pilot study group were 48 English as a Foreign Language (EFL) learners enrolled in the Department of English Language Teaching at a state university in Turkiye. The group consisted of 43 (89.6) female and five (10.4) male students. The gender distribution reflected the overall population in the mentioned department. The mean age was 19.48 (range 18-24; SD = 1.32). All participants were at the advanced level of English (C1) according to the Common European Framework of Reference (CEFR) standards.

The sample group in the quasi-experimental study consisted of 44 students studying in the Department of English Language Teaching at a state university in Turkiye. Of the participants, 24 (54.5%) were in the control group, whereas 20 (45.5%) were in the experimental group. The study was designed as a quasi-experimental study, so the distribution across groups appeared balanced. The sample group consisted of 26 female (59.1%) and 18 male students (40.9%). Since the gender distribution reflected the overall population in the mentioned department, the sample was found to be representative and balanced. The mean score for their age was 18.4 (SD=1.20), ranging from 17 to 23. The participants were C1-level language learners, as defined by the CEFR.

Lastly, the researchers conducted a focus group study to understand the underlying reasons for the conclusions. Twelve participants, six from the control group and six from the experimental group, were randomly selected for two separate 60-minute interview sessions. The participants were 12 students, six female and six male, aged 17-22, with a mean age of 18.20 (SD = 1.11).

Table 1. Descriptive Statistics for Participants

Variables		**Pilot study (n=48)**		**Quasi-experimental study (n=44)**		**Focus group study (n=12)**	
		Mean	Std. Dev.	Mean	Std. Dev.	Mean	Std. Dev.
Age		18.48	1.32	18.40	1.20	18.20	1.11
		N	%	N	%	N	%
Gender	Female	43	89.6	26	59.1	6	50.0
	Male	5	10.4	18	40.9	6	50.0
Grade	1	48	100.0	44	100.0	12	100.0
	C1	48	100.0	44	100.0	12	100.0
Department	English Language Teaching	48	100.0	44	100.0	12	100.0
Groups	Control group			24	54.4	6	50.0
	Experimental group			20	45.5	6	50.0

Tools

A background questionnaire, a pilot test, a test consisting of mispronounced words, and a focus group interview were used to collect data in the study. First, the background questionnaire was used to collect demographic data, including the participants' age, gender, grade, and department. Second, the pilot test included the 50 most frequently mispronounced words by Turkish EFL learners. The words in the list were derived from the existing literature focusing on fossilized pronunciation mistakes and errors among Turkish EFL learners (Aktuğ, 2015; Bardakçı, 2015; Bekleyen, 2011; Boran, 2005). Third, after observing that the pilot test was normally distributed, reliable, and valid, it was used as the pronunciation test in the intervention study. Fourth and last, a focus group interview was conducted to gain a deeper understanding of the underlying factors that may relate to the conclusions drawn from the intervention study.

Procedure

The state university where the study was intended to be carried out was notified for confirmation following ethics committee approval. Participants in all groups were informed about the objectives, significance, and process for each step of the study. They were also informed that participation in the study was voluntary, that all responses would be kept confidential, and that the collected data would be anonymous and used solely for scientific purposes. After obtaining their permission and consent, the steps detailed below were performed. The study took place during the Fall Semester of the 2024-2025 academic year. After selecting the participants for the pilot study, the control and experimental groups were determined within a quasi-experimental research design, using existing groups of first-grade students who had previously received a pronunciation course in the department.

Since the study focuses on selected English consonant sounds, with particular emphasis on word-final consonants embedded in the target word list and the reading-aloud text, the sounds were selected because word-final consonant production is a persistent source of difficulty for Turkish EFL learners. Due to differences between Turkish and English phonological systems, learners frequently omit, substitute, or inaccurately articulate word-final consonants, and such errors often persist despite prolonged exposure and instruction. Moreover, the inaccurate production of word-final consonants directly affects intelligibility rather than merely contributing to a foreign accent. For these reasons, word-final consonant sounds provide an appropriate and pedagogically relevant focus for examining the effects of teacher-supported and AI-supported corrective feedback on fossilized pronunciation errors.

The study consisted of the pilot test, the intervention study, and focus group interviews. For the pilot study, one of the researchers administered a 50-word test that included the most frequently mispronounced words (Appendix 1). The test mentioned was administered to the participants in the control and experimental groups as a pre-test by the same researcher. During the intervention, participants in the control group received teacher-supported feedback, whereas those in the experimental group used AI-supported feedback via ChatGPT for independent practice. The test words were embedded in a short story (Appendix 2) to provide context for their use. To achieve this, the assessment process was conducted by one of the researchers, who held a Ph.D. in applied linguistics and was an expert in pronunciation teaching, with experience in phonetics instruction and evaluation. This pre-test aimed to establish a baseline for each participant's level of fossilized pronunciation errors. In total, 329 minutes of pre-test voice recordings were collected. As a note, in the teacher-supported feedback condition, no additional technological tools or acoustic analysis software (e.g., Praat) were used. In other words, pronunciation errors were identified through the instructor's auditory judgment and pedagogical expertise, reflecting typical classroom practice and ensuring that the two conditions differed only in the source of feedback. The participants in the control group received a one-hour instructor-led pronunciation correction session over two weeks. The sessions were designed to adopt a systematic approach, as given below:

- **Presentation of words:** The instructor projected the list of target words onto the classroom screen, along with their phonetic transcriptions.
- **Introduction to Phonetics:** A brief overview of phonetic symbols was provided, emphasizing pronunciation contrasts and similarities among words.
- **Error highlighting and demonstration:** The instructor highlighted differences between standard and common erroneous pronunciations and verbally demonstrated the correct pronunciation.
- **Guided practice:** Students practiced pronunciation through structured drills and repetition.
- Individual feedback: Each student was asked to pronounce the words individually, with the instructor providing immediate corrections and guidance to ensure accurate production.

In the AI-supported feedback condition, learners used ChatGPT as a text-based feedback tool to support independent pronunciation practice. Learners interacted with ChatGPT using predefined prompts designed to elicit feedback on pronunciation accuracy, error identification, and suggested corrections. The process included the following steps:

- Introduction to AI practice: Students were given a list of words and instructed to use ChatGPT for pronunciation assistance. Initially, the instructor supervised the session to ensure all participants were correctly engaged with the task.
- Interactive AI feedback: ChatGPT interacted with students by offering options to practice words individually or as a set, and provided simplified pronunciation descriptions and written phonetic representations. No acoustic

measurement, waveform comparison, or automatic pronunciation scoring was used in this process.

- Independent Practice: Students practiced the words freely, engaging with feedback via ChatGPT and using its interactive guidance under the instructor's observation.

Following the feedback sessions, participants completed a post-test that included a second read-aloud of the same story used in the pre-test. Audio recordings from this session were analyzed to evaluate changes in fossilized pronunciation errors. A total of 322 minutes of post-test voice recordings were collected. During data analysis and organization, if students repeated the word and corrected themselves, it was considered correct. Differences stemming from intonation and British or American accents or from not pronouncing the /w/ or /th/ sounds, which are quite typical in an average Turkish speaker of English, were omitted.

After completing the post-test, 60-minute focus group interviews with 12 students were conducted, with six randomly selected participants from each of the two groups. Four questions were included in the focus group interview. The participants' responses were recorded and later analyzed using narrative analysis, which enabled an in-depth exploration of their experiences (Riessman, 2008). The purpose was to understand the conclusions from the participants' perspectives in the control and experimental groups. Two blind researchers coded, labeled the descriptions and themes, categorized the data, and reported the findings. After comparing the two data sets, it was observed that the collected data were valid and trustworthy (Guba & Lincoln, 1994). As a final point, the background questionnaire was also used in each phase. The process is shown in Figure 1.

Figure 1. Schematic Representation of the Intervention

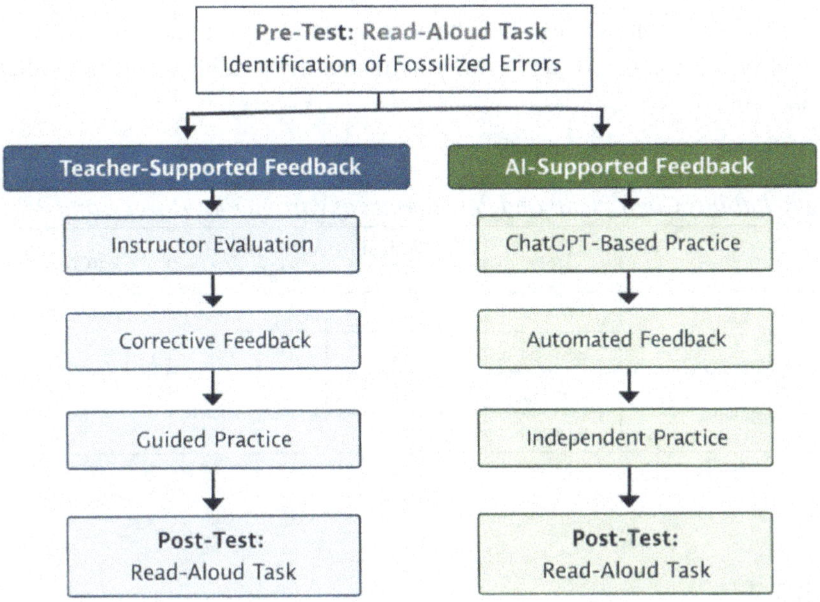

Data Analysis

The data collected from the pilot study were analyzed through SPSS. First, the frequencies for gender were calculated. Regarding age, the mean score, minimum, and maximum values were determined. Second, the descriptives, including means, standard deviations, standard errors, and minimum and maximum values for the pilot test, were computed, as shown in Table 2. The values indicated that the test's mean score was 33.31, within the range of 12-61. The values in the table also revealed a normal distribution ($p = .25$).

Table 2. Descriptive Statistics and Test of Homogeneity for the Pilot Test

Groups	N	Mean	Std. Deviation	Std. Error	Minimum	Maximum	Test of Homogeneity of Variances	
							Levene Statistic	Sig.
Low	19	23.95	4.20	.96	12.00	29.00	1.44	.25
Medium	15	34.00	2.62	.68	30.00	39.00		
High	14	45.29	5.78	1.55	40.00	61.00		
Total	48	33.31	9.82	1,42	12.00	61.00		

Then, a reliability analysis using Kuder-Richardson (KR-20) was computed. The pilot test value was .87, indicating a high level of reliability. The average item difficulty was 0.53, indicating that the test items had a similar difficulty level. Lastly, the pre-test and post-test scores indicated high validity and reliability, as shown in Table 3.

Table 3. Reliability Coefficients and Percentages of Variance for Pre-test and Post-test

Groups	Tests	Reliability coefficients (Cronbach's Alpha)		% of variance
Control group	Pre-test	.87	.88	89.46
	Post-test	.78		
Experimental group	Pre-test	.92	.95	89.85
	Post-test	.91		

RESULTS

The Level of Fossilized Pronunciation Errors

According to the values presented in Table 4, participants' awareness of fossilized pronunciation errors appears high, as indicated by a mean score of 77.67, which falls within the 0-100 range. For instance, in the control group, scores ranged from 62 to 93, with a mean score of 78.67. Similarly, in the experimental group, scores ranged from 61 to 92, with a mean value of 76.45. The findings also indicated that participants in both groups had comparable levels of fossilized pronunciation errors before the current study.

Table 4. Descriptive Statistics for Levels of Fossilized Pronunciation Errors

Groups	N	Tests	Minimum	Maximum	Mean	Std. Error	Std. Deviation
Control group	24	Pre-test	62	93	78.67	1.69	8.25
Experimental group	20	Pre-test	61	92	76.45	2.183	9.76

More specifically, the Mann-Whitney U test results in Table 5 indicate that there is no significant difference between the control and experimental groups in levels of fossilized pronunciation errors. The control group had a mean rank of 24.0, while the experimental group had a mean rank of 20.70. The asymptotic significance level was 0.40, indicating no statistically significant difference between the groups. These values also indicated that the groups were balanced before the intervention process.

Table 5. Descriptive Statistics for Levels of Fossilized Pronunciation Errors

Groups	N	Mean Rank	Sum of Ranks	Mann-Whitney U	Wilcoxon W	Z	Asymp. Sig. (2-tailed)
Control group	24	24.0	576.0	204.0	414.0	-.85	.40
Experimental group	20	20.70	414.0				

The Impact of Teacher Feedback on Fossilized Pronunciation Errors

This subsection reports the effects of teacher-supported corrective feedback on fossilized pronunciation errors. The results are presented at both the individual-word and overall-score levels, with Table 6 summarizing pre-test and post-test comparisons. The focus is on identifying general patterns of improvement following instructor feedback. The results indicate that teacher-supported feedback led to statistically significant improvement in a large proportion of the target words. Gains were observed across a wide range of pronunciation items, suggesting that instructor feedback was effective in reducing fossilized pronunciation errors at the word level. Although the magnitude of improvement varied across individual words, the pattern of results showed consistent positive change following the intervention. When total scores were considered, the increase from pre-test to post-test was statistically significant, indicating a substantial overall improvement in pronunciation accuracy following teacher-supported corrective feedback.

Table 6. Effect of Instructor Feedback on Fossilized Pronunciation Errors (Wilcoxon Test, n=24)

Words	Pre-test		Post-test		Z	Asymp. Sig. (2-tailed)
	Mean	Std. Deviation	Mean	Std. Deviation		
examine	1.67	.48	1.88	.34	2.24	.03
rough	1.75	.44	1.96	.20	2.24	.03
honesty	1.79	.41	1.92	.28	2.24	.03
schedule	1.79	.41	1.96	.20	2.00	.05
climate	1.63	.49	1.83	.38	2.24	.03
flood	1.38	.49	1.83	.38	3.32	.00

continued on following page

Table 6. Continued

Words	Pre-test		Post-test		Z	Asymp. Sig. (2-tailed)
	Mean	Std. Deviation	Mean	Std. Deviation		
height	1.63	.49	1.88	.34	2.50	.01
debt	1.25	.44	1.75	.44	3.46	.00
taught	1.42	.50	2.00	.00	3.74	.00
vegetable	1.79	.41	2.00	.00	2.24	.03
weapon	1.63	.49	2.00	.00	3.00	.00
memory	1.63	.49	2.00	.00	3.00	.00
separate	1.79	.41	1.96	.20	2.00	.05
bachelor	1.42	.50	1.92	.28	3.46	.00
author	1.29	.46	1.75	.44	3.32	.00
blood	1.71	.46	1.92	.28	2.24	.03
character	1.67	.48	1.88	.34	2.24	.03
capable	1.33	.48	1.67	.48	2.82	.01
casual	1.75	.44	2.00	.00	2.45	.01
determine	1.42	.50	1.79	.41	3.00	.00
wear	1.63	.49	1.88	.34	2.12	.03
bear	1.38	.49	1.92	.28	3.61	.00
magnificent	1.79	.41	1.96	.20	2.00	.05
vary	1.58	.50	1.88	.34	2.33	.02
bullet	1.58	.50	1.92	.28	2.83	.01
tomb	1.08	.28	1.58	.50	3.21	.00
hideous	1.54	.51	1.92	.28	3.00	.00
support	1.29	.46	1.79	.41	3.00	.00
successful	1.29	.46	1.75	.44	3.32	.00
history	1.50	.51	1.96	.20	3.32	.00
bury	1.17	.38	1.58	.50	3.16	.00
achieve	1.63	.49	1.79	.415	2.00	.05
career	1.04	.20	1.33	.48	2.65	.01
major	1.50	.51	1.79	.41	2.65	.01
analysis	1.29	.46	1.54	.51	2.45	.01
facts	1.63	.49	1.83	.38	2.37	.03
honor	1.83	.38	2.00	.00	2.00	.05
restaurant	1.58	.50	1.88	.34	2.65	.01
chef	1.50	.51	1.79	.42	2.65	.01

continued on following page

Table 6. Continued

Words	Pre-test		Post-test		Z	Asymp. Sig. (2-tailed)
	Mean	**Std. Deviation**	**Mean**	**Std. Deviation**		
recipe	1.58	.50	1.88	.34	2.65	.01
Wednesday	1.75	.44	2.00	.00	2.25	.01
notice	1.58	.50	1.92	.28	2.53	.01
Total score	78.67	8.25	93.33	4.67	4.29	.00

On the other hand, Z-scores indicate that various words can be categorized into low, medium, and high ranges, including words with no effect. First, words with low Z-scores (≤ 2.00) included *"schedule," "separate," "magnificent," "achieve," and "honor."* Second, medium Z-scores (2.01 - 3.00) were observed for words such as *examine*, *rough*, *honesty*, *climate*, *height*, *vegetable*, *weapon*, *memory*, *blood*, *character*, *capable*, *casual*, *determine*, *wear*, *vary*, *bullet*, *hideous*, *support*, *career*, *major*, *analysis*, *facts*, *restaurant*, *chef*, *recipe*, *Wednesday*, and *notice*. Third, high Z-scores (>3.00) were observed for *the words "flood," "debt," "taught," "bachelor," "author," "bear," "tomb," "successful," "history," and "bury."* Additionally, several words remained unchanged, such as "live," "category," "weight," "durable," "phenomenon," "scene," and "signal," as shown in Figure 2. To this end, it is worth noting that while instructor feedback significantly improves fossilized pronunciation errors, its effects may be limited to low- and medium-level errors, and participants may not show improvement in certain words.

Figure 2. Distribution of Words After Instructor Feedback on Fossilized Pronunciation Errors

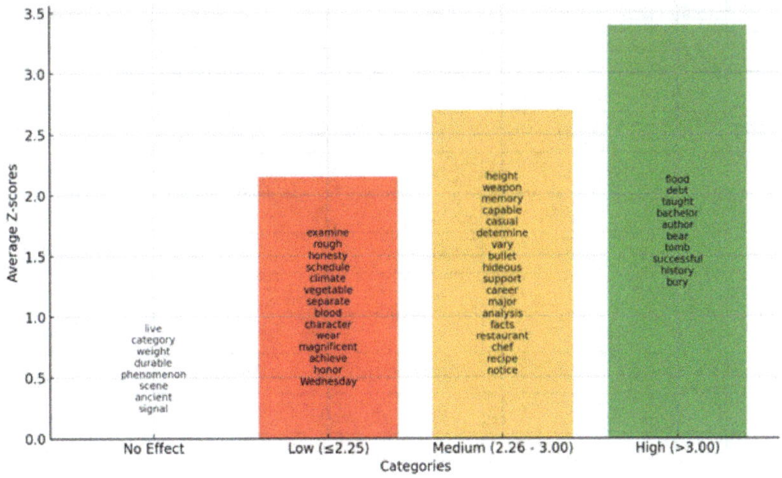

The Impact of AI-Supported Feedback on Fossilized Pronunciation Errors

This subsection presents the effects of AI-supported corrective feedback on fossilized pronunciation errors. Table 7 summarizes pre-test and post-test comparisons for the experimental group, highlighting which pronunciation items showed improvement following AI-supported practice. The results are interpreted in terms of overall tendencies rather than at the word level. According to the data, AI-supported feedback led to statistically significant improvement in a subset of the target pronunciation items. While gains were observed for several words, the effects were less widespread than those observed in the teacher-supported condition, suggesting a more selective impact of AI-supported feedback on fossilized pronunciation errors. When overall performance was considered, the increase in total scores from pre-test to post-test was statistically significant, indicating that AI-supported feedback contributed to measurable improvement at the group level.

Table 7. Effect of AI-Supported Feedback on Fossilized Pronunciation Errors (Wilcoxon Test, n=20)

Words	Pre-test		Post-test		Z	Asymp. Sig. (2-tailed)
	Mean	Std. Deviation	Mean	Std. Deviation		
flood	1.20	.41	1.85	.37	3.61	.00
debt	1.00	.00	1.75	.44	3.87	.00
taught	1.20	.41	1.45	.51	1.68	.01
vegetable	1.80	.41	1.45	.51	2.33	.02
weapon	1.15	.37	1.85	.37	3.74	.00
category	1.40	.50	2.00	.00	3.46	.00
memory	1.95	.22	1.50	.51	3.00	.00
bachelor	1.10	.31	2.00	.00	4.24	.00
weight	1.80	.41	1.40	.50	2.53	.01
blood	1.75	.44	2.00	.00	2.24	.03
character	1.35	.49	1.95	.22	3.36	.01
durable	1.55	.51	1.80	.41	2.24	.03
magnificent	1.50	.51	1.80	.41	2.45	.01
vary	1.30	.47	1.95	.22	3.61	.00
ancient	1.20	.41	1.60	.50	2.83	.01
tomb	1.55	.51	2.00	.00	3.00	.00
hideous	1.25	.44	1.60	.50	2.33	.02

continued on following page

Table 7. Continued

Words	Pre-test		Post-test		Z	Asymp. Sig. (2-tailed)
	Mean	**Std. Deviation**	**Mean**	**Std. Deviation**		
support	1.30	.47	1.60	.50	2.12	.03
achieve	1.10	.31	1.45	.51	2.33	.02
career	1.40	.50	1.75	.44	2.11	.04
analysis	1.25	.44	1.65	.49	2.31	.02
honor	1.25	.44	1.85	.37	3.21	.00
restaurant	1.40	.50	1.90	.31	2.89	.00
Wednesday	1.60	.50	1.85	.37	2.24	.03
notice	1.60	.50	1.95	.22	2.65	.01
Total score	76.45	9.76	85.95	8.73	3.93	.00

While AI-supported feedback effectively reduces fossilized pronunciation errors, the Z-scores for various words can be categorized into low, medium, and high ranges, indicating different levels of fossilized pronunciation errors. First, words with low Z-scores (≤ 2.00) include *taught*, *weight*, *blood*, *durable*, *magnificent*, *support*, *career*, *honor*, *restaurant*, *Wednesday*, and *notice*. Second, medium Z-scores (2.01-3.00) were observed for the words *"flood," "debt," "vegetable," "memory," "character," "vary," and "analysis."* Third, high Z-scores (> 3.00) were recorded for *flood*, *debt*, *taught*, *bachelor*, *weapon*, *category*, *memory*, *character*, *bear*, *tomb*, *successful*, *history*, and *bury*. In addition, AI-supported feedback did not affect the words *'live,' 'category,' 'weight,' 'durable,' 'phenomenon,' 'scene,' and 'signal.'* These results show that while AI-supported feedback has considerable influence, learners may still struggle to improve fossilized words, as shown in Figure 3.

Figure 3. Distribution of Words After AI-Supported Feedback on Fossilized Pronunciation Errors

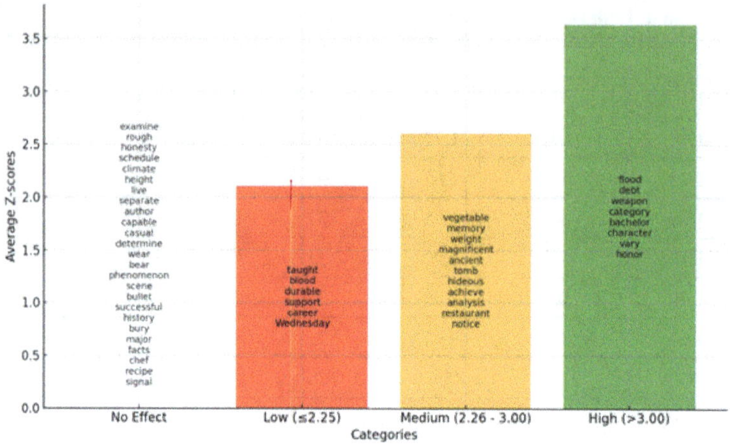

Comparison of Teacher and AI-Supported Feedback on Fossilized Pronunciation Errors

This subsection compares the relative effectiveness of teacher-supported and AI-supported corrective feedback in reducing fossilized pronunciation errors. For this purpose, Table 8 presents group-level comparisons across pronunciation items, allowing for an examination of overall differences and selective advantages between the two feedback conditions. The comparison of teacher-supported and AI-supported feedback reveals statistically significant differences across multiple pronunciation items. The results indicated that instructor feedback was more effective than AI-supported feedback in reducing fossilized pronunciation errors for the majority of target words. This pattern was further reflected in the total score comparison, where the control group demonstrated significantly higher mean ranks than the experimental group, suggesting a stronger overall impact of teacher-supported corrective feedback. The results also indicated that AI-supported feedback was effective for a limited number of specific items. For a small subset of words, improvements favored the AI-supported condition, suggesting that AI-based feedback may be selectively beneficial for certain pronunciation features. Taken together, these findings highlight a general advantage for teacher-supported feedback, while also pointing to the potential complementary role of AI-supported feedback for particular pronunciation items.

Table 8. Comparison of the Effects of Instructor and AI-Supported Feedback on Fossilized Pronunciation Errors

Words	Groups	N	Mean rank	Chi-Square	Asymp. Sig.
height	Control group	24	25.25	4.30	.04
	Experimental group	20	19.20		
taught	Control group	24	28.00	17.20	.00
	Experimental group	20	15.90		
vegetable	Control group	24	28.00	17.20	.00
	Experimental group	20	15.90		
weapon	Control group	24	24.00	3.78	.05
	Experimental group	20	20.70		
live	Control group	24	26.58	10.12	.00
	Experimental group	20	17.60		
memory	Control group	24	27.50	15.18	.00
	Experimental group	20	16.50		
separate	Control group	24	25.58	6.81	.01
	Experimental group	20	18.80		
weight	Control group	24	28.50	19.35	.00
	Experimental group	20	15.30		
casual	Control group	24	27.50	15.18	.00
	Experimental group	20	16.50		
wear	Control group	24	26.25	7.20	.01
	Experimental group	20	18.00		
scene	Control group	24	25.00	6.62	.01
	Experimental group	20	19.50		
ancient	Control group	24	26.08	8.41	.00
	Experimental group	20	18.20		
tomb	Control group	24	18.33	10.54	.00
	Experimental group	20	27.50		
hideous	Control group	24	25.67	6.09	.01
	Experimental group	20	18.70		
successful	Control group	24	25.50	4.05	.04
	Experimental group	20	18.90		
history	Control group	24	28.08	15.97	.00
	Experimental group	20	15.80		

continued on following page

Table 8. Continued

Words	Groups	N	Mean rank	Chi-Square	Asymp. Sig.
achieve	Control group	24	25.92	5.38	.02
	Experimental group	20	18.40		
career	Control group	24	18.33	7.42	.01
	Experimental group	20	27.50		
major	Control group	24	28.42	14.96	.00
	Experimental group	20	15.40		
facts	Control group	24	25.83	5.46	.02
	Experimental group	20	18.50		
honor	Control group	24	24.00	3.78	.05
	Experimental group	20	20.70		
Wednesday	Control group	24	24.00	3.78	.05
	Experimental group	20	20.70		
Total score	Control group	24	27.88	9.30	.00
	Experimental group	20	16.05		

Figure 4 compares the effects of instructor and AI-supported feedback on fossilized pronunciation errors, showing that instructor feedback leads to greater reductions in pronunciation errors across words, with many exhibiting statistically significant improvements. For instance, instructor feedback was important in addressing pronunciation challenges, while some words demonstrated potential benefits from AI-supported feedback. As a note, it should be added that no significant changes in pronunciation errors were observed for the words *live, category, weight, durable, phenomenon, scene,* and *signal.* In conclusion, instructor feedback is effective for 77.8% of all words, and AI-supported feedback is effective for 7.4%, while no effect is observed for 14.6% of the words, as visualized in Figure 4. These findings are interpreted and discussed in relation to the research questions, existing literature, and pedagogical implications in the following section.

Figure 4. Comparison of the Effects of Instructor and AI-Supported Feedback on Fossilized Pronunciation Errors

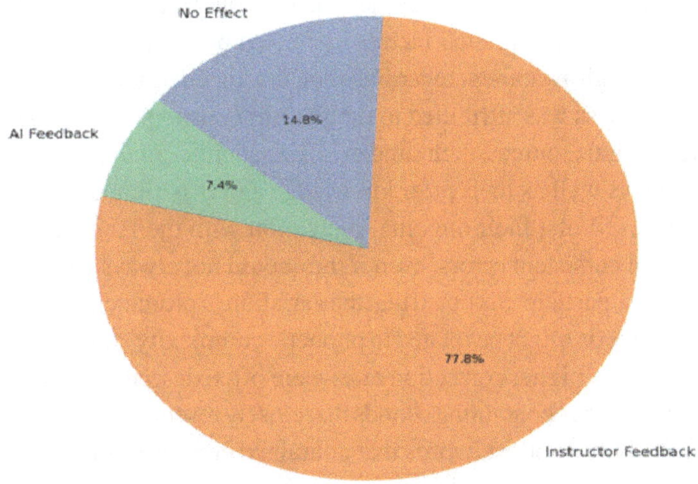

CONCLUSIONS AND DISCUSSIONS

Four conclusions were drawn from the study, which aimed to determine the levels of fossilized pronunciation errors among EFL learners, to investigate the effects of teacher- and AI-supported corrective feedback, and to compare their impacts on fossilized pronunciation errors. As a response to the first research question, which examined the extent to which fossilized pronunciation errors were present among EFL learners, it is concluded that advanced EFL learners exhibit a relatively low level of fossilized pronunciation errors and generally show a high level of awareness regarding these errors. Regarding the second research question, which focused on the effects of teacher-supported and AI-supported corrective feedback on the correction of fossilized pronunciation errors, it is concluded that instructor feedback has a positive impact on reducing fossilized pronunciation errors among learners and on enhancing their pronunciation skills. In response to the third research question, which compared the relative effectiveness of teacher-supported and AI-supported corrective feedback, it is concluded that AI-supported feedback reduces the number of fossilized pronunciation errors among EFL learners. However, the impact appears to vary across words. Last, regarding the research question comparing teacher- and AI-supported corrective feedback, it is found that there is a significant difference between instructor- and AI-supported feedback in correcting fossilized pronunciation errors, favoring instructor feedback. Instructor feedback mainly results in more substantial reductions in errors than AI-supported feedback.

According to the focus group interview results, the findings above appear to be influenced by several interrelated factors identified by the participants. First, EFL learners reported high awareness regarding their fossilized pronunciation errors. This heightened awareness was attributed to their continuous exposure to the target language through various sources, including media, academic content, and interpersonal communication, as well as their prior knowledge and experience in English. These learners emphasized that their ongoing interaction with the language helped them recognize certain persistent errors, even if they could not always correct them independently. Second, participants noted that the variation in pronunciation improvement across different words might be related to phonetic complexity and language transfer. Words that exhibited higher correction rates were often described as having simpler phonetic structures or as containing sounds that closely resembled those in their native language, Turkish. In contrast, words that contained complex or unfamiliar sounds, or those associated with habitual mispronunciation and long-standing errors, were perceived as more resistant to change. Third, the learners strongly emphasized the advantages of instructor feedback over AI-supported feedback. They expressed that instructor-led feedback was corrective, personalized, and context-sensitive. Instructors were seen as capable of identifying specific pronunciation errors, demonstrating correct forms, offering repeated and guided practice opportunities, and engaging learners through interactive communication. In particular, learners valued the human ability to respond in real time and adjust explanations based on learners' needs and emotional states. While learners acknowledged that AI tools can model accurate pronunciation and offer repetition, they highlighted several important limitations. For instance, they noted that AI systems often failed to detect individual learner errors or provide tailored corrective feedback. Furthermore, participants expressed that AI lacked the emotional engagement, motivational presence, and dynamic adaptability characteristic of human instruction. Learners also described their learning culture as predominantly teacher-centered and preferred active, interpersonal instruction. Thus, they viewed AI-supported feedback as passive, less interactive, and primarily focused on segmental features of pronunciation.

Key Issues and Trends

The conclusions above highlight several key issues and trends central to ongoing discussions of AI integration in language education. First, the results indicate that teacher-supported corrective feedback is more effective in addressing fossilized pronunciation errors. Quantitative findings show greater overall improvement in the teacher-supported condition, while qualitative data from focus group interviews suggest that learners value teachers' emotionally responsive, adaptive, and context-sensitive feedback. These findings underscore the continuing pedagogical importance of the teacher in pronunciation instruction, particularly when fossilized errors require sustained guidance. Second, the findings position AI-supported feedback as a complementary tool for individualized pronunciation practice rather than a replacement for teacher instruction. While AI-supported feedback contributed to improvement in a limited number of pronunciation items, its effectiveness was selective. Learners nevertheless report that AI-based feedback allowed for repeated, self-paced practice and increased autonomy, suggesting that AI may be particularly useful as a supplementary resource for individual practice beyond classroom time. Third and last, the results point to the importance of cultural and affective fit in technology-mediated pronunciation instruction. In a teacher-centered educational context, learners expressed a clear preference for human feedback that accommodates emotional and interpersonal needs, especially when working on pronunciation features that are closely tied to identity and long-standing learning experiences. In conclusion, these trends reinforce a view of AI in education as a supportive and augmentative tool whose pedagogical value depends on alignment across context, affect, and instruction rather than technological capability alone.

Pedagogical Implications

The results of the current study seem significant for several reasons. First, the present study confirms the potential of AI-supported feedback in pronunciation training, as previous research indicates that ASR-based tools can effectively improve segmental pronunciation features (Cucchiarini et al., 2009; Neri et al., 2002). This finding was also supported by Neri et al. (2006), who reported improvements in specific phonetic errors through ASR-based feedback, and by Chen (2017), who noted learners' enjoyment and speaking skill development despite high ASR error rates. On the other hand, it is worth noting that AI systems may fail to identify learner-specific errors and often provide feedback at a surface level (Heil et al., 2016; Morton et al., 2012). This limitation aligns with EFL learners' perception that AI tools lack tailored, corrective guidance and emotional engagement. Second, the results of the current study align with previous studies that have identified challenges with AI-based pronunciation tools (Heil et al., 2016; Neri et al., 2002), leading to mislabeling errors and limited feedback depth. This issue has also been highlighted in studies on prosodic training, where learners benefited more from mimicry and self-imitation techniques than from standard AI feedback (Bissiri & Pfitzinger, 2009; De Meo et al., 2012). These challenges suggest that, while AI tools are advancing, they remain insufficient for addressing complex phonetic errors, particularly those involving habitual mispronunciations or culturally ingrained sound structures. Third, the study contributes to the ongoing discourse around pronunciation instruction in establishing the superior impact of teacher-led feedback compared to AI-supported systems. While earlier studies (e.g., Neri et al., 2006; Pearson, 2011) have explored the reliability of ASR-based scoring and feedback, they acknowledge ASR's limitations in holistic quality improvement. Although Pearson (2011) observed high correlations between ASR and human scoring, the results still indicated that automated systems were better suited to support rather than replace teacher evaluation.

Similarly, the present study concludes that instructor feedback substantially reduces fossilized pronunciation errors, likely due to its personalized, interactive, and targeted nature. This aligns with previous findings suggesting that learners benefit from teacher-guided correction, particularly mimicry and prosodic modification, when it is supported by active human guidance (Nagano & Ozawa, 1990). In conclusion, the current study offers significant contributions by filling a gap in the literature concerning AI-supported corrective feedback and its comparison with instructor feedback. It underscores the importance of a balanced approach that integrates AI tools for supplementary practice while emphasizing teacher-led, personalized feedback as indispensable for addressing fossilized pronunciation errors. When considered holistically, the findings also provide a culturally grounded perspective, reinforcing the need for feedback systems that align with learners' preferences and educational contexts. To this end, it is worth noting that classroom implementation of pronunciation-focused corrective feedback is subject to several practical constraints. In this sense, it should be added that large class sizes and heavy teacher workload may limit the amount of individualized pronunciation feedback that instructors can provide. Time constraints in curricula may also limit systematic pronunciation practice, particularly when fossilized errors require repeated, sustained attention. In addition, access to technological resources, including reliable internet connectivity and individual devices, may vary across institutions and learners, potentially affecting the feasibility of AI-supported pronunciation practice. These constraints should be considered when interpreting the findings of the present study and when applying AI-supported or teacher-supported corrective feedback approaches in different instructional contexts.

Practical Recommendations

Based on findings from AI- and teacher-supported pronunciation feedback, specific recommendations can be provided to teachers, students, curriculum developers, and policymakers. First, integrating AI tools in pronunciation development seems necessary for teachers. In other words, although AI tools lack emotional engagement and tailored guidance, they provide immediate, consistent, and standardized pronunciation feedback. Thus, EFL teachers should integrate AI tools as supplementary resources to reinforce learners' practice outside the classroom. From this perspective, combining teacher-led instruction with AI-supported feedback can create a more holistic and flexible learning environment. Second, EFL learners should regularly use AI tools for repeated pronunciation practice to reinforce learning outside the classroom. In this way, they can request tailored, corrective feedback from instructors and ask for explanations of specific errors. By improving their AI utilization skills through individual learning, learners can develop strategies to overcome pronunciation challenges, such as comparing similar sounds in the native and target languages. Third, it is recommended that curriculum developers design curricula that integrate pronunciation-focused modules with dedicated time for feedback, practice, and assessment. Additionally, it is reasonable to suggest integrating AI tools and digital resources into lesson plans to encourage blended learning and to develop materials and tasks that balance segmental and suprasegmental aspects of pronunciation. Fourth and last, policymakers should establish support systems to enable effective AI use in teaching and provide technical support to teachers and students. In other words, they should organize training courses and ensure that teachers and learners have sufficient resources to integrate AI tools into their pedagogical practices effectively. It is also necessary for them to ensure that institutions employ adaptive strategies to integrate AI-based tools that can be customized for various educational settings.

Implications for Blended Teacher–AI Pronunciation Instruction

Considering the emphasis on blending teacher and AI-supported pronunciation, several practical implications should be noted. From a broad perspective, teacher-supported corrective feedback remains more effective for addressing fossilized pronunciation errors, particularly when sustained guidance and emotional responsiveness are required. At the same time, the AI-supported condition demonstrates selective effectiveness and was perceived by learners as a useful tool for individualized, self-paced practice. Thus, a blended model of pronunciation instruction can be proposed in which teachers assume primary responsibility for diagnosing fossilized errors, providing contextualized and emotionally responsive feedback, and guiding learners' long-term development. AI-supported tools, on the other hand, may function as supplementary practice environments that allow learners to rehearse target items independently, receive immediate feedback, and engage in repeated practice beyond classroom time. Such a division of roles aligns with learners' expressed preference for human guidance while capitalizing on the affordances of AI for individualized practice. Several design principles for more responsive AI-based pronunciation tools should also be considered. For instance, EFL learners value clear, supportive, and non-threatening feedback, indicating the importance of affect-sensitive interaction. Therefore, AI tools should prioritize clarity of explanation, adaptive feedback pacing, and opportunities for learner control rather than solely focusing on error detection. In conclusion, designing AI pronunciation tools that complement teacher feedback and respond to learners' emotional and pedagogical needs may enhance their effectiveness in addressing fossilized pronunciation errors.

Limitations and Recommendations for Further Research

The current study has several limitations. First, the study utilized a quasi-experimental design because certain factors in schools prevented random assignment of participants. Second, the study involved 44 participants enrolled in a foreign language education program. Third, the duration of the study was confined to four weeks. Fourth, the results were derived just from the AI software, ChatGPT. Moreover, the study was limited to a 2-week intervention, with one practice session per week. The absence of a delayed post-test was another limitation of the study due to scheduling constraints, the academic calendar, and the participants' availability. Fourth, read-aloud tasks may not accurately capture learners' performance compared to spontaneous contexts. Last, although suprasegmental features and spontaneous speech contexts were central to communicative pronunciation competence, the present study deliberately focused on word-level segmental features to allow for controlled comparison of teacher-supported and AI-supported feedback on fossilized errors. As a result, the findings should be interpreted as applicable primarily to segmental pronunciation practice rather than to suprasegmental development or spontaneous spoken production.

This study provides a basis for future research directions. First, future research should investigate the role of AI and instructor feedback in enhancing suprasegmental features (e.g., stress, rhythm, intonation) and their impact on pronunciation development. Second, further research should investigate the association between learner autonomy and pronunciation proficiency in the EFL context by incorporating a broader and more extended range of pronunciation instruction and by using authentic communicational context to enhance the effectiveness of the findings and enable more accurate generalizations since short-term interventions may not be sufficient to observe the gradual and sustained nature of pronunciation development, specifically to address fossilized errors. In addition, further research should include delayed post-tests to assess the long-term effects of pronunciation environments with teacher- and AI-supported feedback. Third, conducting future studies across diverse educational settings and among various demographic groups, such as gender, age, language proficiency, and technological proficiency, can contribute to a more comprehensive understanding. Given the learners' reported preference for instructor feedback due to emotional engagement, future studies could examine how affective factors influence the effectiveness of AI-supported feedback. As a final recommendation, future research should examine how teacher-supported and AI-supported feedback influence learners' pronunciation in spontaneous speech contexts, including extended discourse and interaction, where cognitive load, affective factors, and real-time processing demands may shape the effectiveness of different feedback sources.

ACKNOWLEDGMENT

This research received no specific grant from any funding agency in the public, commercial, or not-for-profit sectors.

REFERENCES

Acton, W. (1984). Changing fossilized pronunciation. *TESOL Quarterly, 18*(1), 71–85. DOI: 10.2307/3586336

Aktuğ, B. (2015). *Common pronunciation errors of seventh grade EFL learners: A case from Turkey*. Middle East Technical University.

Baker, A., & Burri, M. (2016). Feedback on second language pronunciation: A case study of EAP teachers' beliefs and practices. *The Australian Journal of Teacher Education, 41*(6), 1–20. DOI: 10.14221/ajte.2016v41n6.1

Bardakçı, M. (2015). Turkish EFL pre-service teachers pronunciation problems. *Educational Research Review, 10*(16), 2370–2378. DOI: 10.5897/ERR2015.2396

Bekleyen, N. (2011). Pronunciation problems of the Turkish EFL learners. *Electronic Journal of Social Sciences, 10*(36), 94–107.

Bissiri, M., & Pfitzinger, H. (2009). Italian speakers learn lexical stress of German morphologically complex words. *Speech Communication, 51*(10), 933–947. DOI: 10.1016/j.specom.2009.03.001

Boran, G. (2005). A study on commonly mispronounced words by the EFL teacher trainees at the ELT Department of Gazi Education Faculty. *Selcuk University Institute of Social Sciences Journal, 13*, 81–90.

Brown, S. (2011). *Listening myths: Applying second language research to classroom teaching*. University of Michigan Press. DOI: 10.3998/mpub.2132445

Browne, K., & Fulcher, G. (2017). Pronunciation and intelligibility in assessing spoken fluency. In Isaacs, T., & Trofimovich, P. (Eds.), *Second language pronunciation assessment: Interdisciplinary perspectives* (pp. 37–53). Multilingual Matters.

Bryfonski, L., & Ma, X. (2020). Effects of implicit versus explicit corrective feedback on Mandarin tone acquisition in a SCMC learning environment. *Studies in Second Language Acquisition, 42*(1), 61–88. DOI: 10.1017/S0272263119000317

Butler-Pascoe, M., & Wiburg, K. (2003). *Technology and teaching English language learners*. Pearson.

Chen, H. (2017). Developing a speaking practice website by using automatic speech recognition technology. In *Emerging Technologies for Education* (pp. 671–676). DOI: 10.1007/978-3-319-52836-6_71

Corder, S. (1971). The significance of learners' error. *International Journal of Applied Linguistics*, *5*(1), 161–170.

Creswell, J. (2014). Research design : Qualitative, quantitative, and mixed methods approaches. *Sage (Atlanta, Ga.)*.

Cucchiarini, C., Neri, A., & Strik, H. (2009). Oral proficiency training in Dutch L2: The contribution of ASR-based corrective feedback. *Speech Communication*, *51*(10), 853–863. DOI: 10.1016/j.specom.2009.03.003

Darcy, I. (2018). Powerful and effective pronunciation instruction: How can we achieve it? *The CATESOL Journal*, *30*(1), 13–45. DOI: 10.5070/B5.35963

De Meo, A., Vitale, M., Pettorino, M., Cutugno, F., & Origlia, A. (2012). Imitation/self-imitation in computer-assisted prosody training for Chinese learners of L2 Italian. *Proceedings of the 4th Pronunciation in Second Language Learning and Teaching Conference*, 90–10.

Doughty, C., & Williams, J. (1998). Pedagogical choices in focus on form. In Doughty, C., & Williams, J. (Eds.), *Focus on form in classroom second language acquisition* (pp. 197–261). Cambridge University Press.

Ellis, R. (2009). Corrective feedback and teacher development. *Journal of Linguistics and Language Teaching*, *1*(1), 3–18. DOI: 10.5070/L2.V1I1.9054

Evers, K., & Chen, S. (2021). Effects of Automatic Speech Recognition Software on pronunciation for adults with different learning styles. *Journal of Educational Computing Research*, *59*(4), 669–685. DOI: 10.1177/0735633120972011

Flexner, S., & Hauck, L. (1988). *Random House Dictionary of the English Language*. Random House.

Foote, J., & Trofimovich, P. (2018). Second language pronunciation learning: An overview of theoretical perspectives. In Kang, O., Thomson, R. I., & Murphy, J. (Eds.), *The Routledge Handbook of Contemporary English Pronunciation* (pp. 75–90). Routledge.

Guba, E. G., & Lincoln, Y. S. (1994). Competing paradigms in qualitative research. In K. Lincoln & Y. S. Denzin (Eds.), *Handbook of qualitative research* (pp. 105–118). Sage.

Harmer, J. (2001). *The practice of English language teaching*. Longman.

Heil, C., Wu, J., Lee, J., & Schmidt, T. (2016). A review of mobile language learning applications: Trends, challenges, and opportunities. *The EuroCALL Review*, *24*(2), 32–50. DOI: 10.4995/eurocall.2016.6402

Jarosz, A. (2023). Key aspects of pronunciation learning and teaching. In Sardegna, V. G., & Jarosz, A. (Eds.), *English pronunciation teaching: Theory, practice and research findings* (pp. 8–20). Channel View Publications.

Jiang, M., Jong, M., Lau, W., Chai, C., & Wu, N. (2021). Using automatic speech recognition technology to enhance EFL learners' oral language complexity in a flipped classroom. *Australasian Journal of Educational Technology*, *37*(2), 110–131. DOI: 10.14742/ajet.6798

Jones, T. (2018). Pronunciation with other areas of language. In Kang, O., Thomson, R. I., & Murphy, J. (Eds.), *The Routledge Handbook of Contemporary English Pronunciation* (pp. 370–384). Routledge.

Kenworthy, J. (1987). *Teaching English pronunciation*. Longman.

Lee, A., & Lyster, R. (2017). Can corrective feedback on second language speech perception errors affect production accuracy? *Applied Psycholinguistics*, *38*(2), 371–393. DOI: 10.1017/S0142716416000254

Morton, H., Gunson, N., & Jack, M. (2012). Interactive language learning through speech-enabled virtual scenarios. *Advances in Human-Computer Interaction*, *2012*, 1–14. DOI: 10.1155/2012/389523

Munro, M. (2017). Dimensions of pronunciation. In Kang, O., Thomson, R., & Murphy, J. (Eds.), *The Routledge Handbook of Contemporary English Pronunciation* (pp. 413–431). Routledge. DOI: 10.4324/9781315145006-26

Nagano, K., & Ozawa, K. (1990). English speech training using voice conversion. *Proceedings of the First International Conference on Spoken Language Processing*, 1169–1172.

Neri, A., Cucchiarini, C., & Strik, H. (2006). ASR corrective feedback on pronunciation: Does it really work? *Proceedings of Interspeech*, 1982–1985.

Neri, A., Cucchiarini, C., Strik, H., & Boves, L. (2002). The pedagogy-technology interface in computer assisted pronunciation training. *Computer Assisted Language Learning, 15*(5), 441–467. DOI: 10.1076/call.15.5.441.13473

Pearson, V. (2011). *Test description and validation summary*. Pearson Education.

Pokrivcakova, S. (2019). Preparing teachers for the application of AI-powered technologies in foreign language education. *Journal of Language and Cultural Education, 7*(3), 135–153. DOI: 10.2478/jolace-2019-0025

Ranbom, L., & Connine, C. (2011). Silent letters are activated in spoken word recognition. *Language and Cognitive Processes, 26*(2), 236–261. DOI: 10.1080/01690965.2010.486578

Richards, J. (2015). The changing face of language learning: Learning beyond the classroom. *RELC Journal, 46*(1), 5–22. DOI: 10.1177/0033688214561621

Riessman, C. (2008). Narrative methods for the human sciences. *Sage (Atlanta, Ga.).*

Saito, K. (2021). Effects of corrective feedback on second language pronunciation development. In Nassaji, H., & Kartchava, E. (Eds.), *The Cambridge Handbook of Corrective Feedback in Second Language Learning and Teaching* (pp. 407–428). Cambridge University Press. DOI: 10.1017/9781108589789.020

Schmidt, R. (1990). The role of consciousness in second language learning. *Applied Linguistics, 11*(2), 129–158. DOI: 10.1093/applin/11.2.129

Seliger, H. W., & Shohamy, E. (1989). *Second language research methods*. Oxford University Press.

Sidgi, F., & Shaari, A. (2017). The usefulness of automatic speech recognition (ASR) Eyespeak Software in improving Iraqi EFL students' pronunciation. *Advances in Language and Literary Studies, 8*(1), 221–225. DOI: 10.7575/aiac.alls.v.8n.1p.221

Sun, W. (2023). The impact of automatic speech recognition technology on second language pronunciation and speaking skills of EFL learners: A mixed methods investigation. *Frontiers in Psychology, 14*, 1210187. Advance online publication. DOI: 10.3389/fpsyg.2023.1210187

Thi-Nhu Ngo, T., Hao-Jan Chen, H., & Kuo-Wei Lai, K. (2024). The effectiveness of automatic speech recognition in ESL/EFL pronunciation: A meta-analysis. *Re-CALL, 36*(1), 4–21. DOI: 10.1017/S0958344023000113

Underwood, J. (2017). Exploring AI language assistants with primary EFL students. In *CALL in a climate of change: adapting to turbulent global conditions – Short papers from EUROCALL 2017* (pp. 317–321). Research-publishing.net. DOI: 10.14705/rpnet.2017.eurocall2017.733

Van Loon, J. (2002). Improving pronunciation of adult ESL students. *TESL Canada Journal, 20*(1), 83. DOI: 10.18806/tesl.v20i1.941

Xiao, W., & Park, M. (2021). Using automatic speech recognition to facilitate English pronunciation assessment and learning in an EFL context. *International Journal of Computer-Assisted Language Learning and Teaching, 11*(3), 74–91. DOI: 10.4018/IJCALLT.2021070105

KEY TERMS AND DEFINITIONS

Artificial Intelligence (AI): The capacity of computer-based systems to perform functions that typically require human intelligence, such as analyzing input, identifying patterns, and generating feedback.

Corrective Feedback: Information provided to learners about errors in their language production to help them recognize, understand, and improve inaccurate forms.

English as a Foreign Language (EFL): The learning and teaching of English in contexts where English is not the primary language used in daily communication.

Fossilization: The long-term persistence of non-target-like language forms in a learner's interlanguage despite continued exposure, instruction, or practice.

Interlanguage: The evolving linguistic system developed by language learners that reflects features of both the target language and their first language.

Pronunciation Accuracy: The extent to which a learner produces speech sounds, stress, rhythm, and intonation in ways that closely match accepted target-language forms.

Pronunciation Error: A systematic deviation in the production of speech sounds or prosodic features that affects the accuracy or intelligibility of spoken language.

Quasi-Experimental Design: A research design that examines the effects of an intervention using pre-existing groups rather than randomly assigning participants to conditions.

Teacher-Supported Feedback: Corrective guidance provided by an instructor through explanation, modeling, repetition, and individualized responses to learners' pronunciation performance.

Text-Based AI Feedback: Written feedback generated by an artificial intelligence system to help learners identify pronunciation problems and practice more accurate language production.

APPENDIX

Table 9. Word List

Word	Standard Pronunciation	Learner Pronunciation
1. Achieve	/ə'tʃiːv/	/e'ʃiːv/
2. Analysis	/ə'næl.ə.sɪs/	/e'nəl.aɪ.sɪs/
3. Ancient	/'eɪn.ʃənt/	/'en.ʃiənt/
4. Author	/'ɔːθər/	/'ɒʊtər/
5. Bachelor	/'bætʃ.əl.ər/	/'bæk.əl.ər/
6. Bear (v)	/beər/	/biɪr/
7. Blood	/blʌd/	/bluːd/
8. Bullet	/'bʊlɪt/	/'bʌlɪt/
9. Bury	/'beri/	/'bɜri/
10. Capable	/'keɪ.pə.bəl/	/'ke.peɪ.bəl/
11. Career	/kə'rɪər/	/ke'riər/
12. Casual	/'kæʒ.ju.əl/	/'keɪʒ.u.əl/
13. Category	/'kæt.ə.gri/	/'ket.ɔ.gri/
14. Character	/'kærəktər/	/ka'rektər/
15. Chef	/ʃef/	/tʃef/
16. Climate	/'klaɪ.mət/	/'klɪ.meit/
17. Debt	/det/	/debt/
18. Determine	/dɪ'tɜːmɪn/	/di'tɜːmeɪn/
19. Durable	/'djʊərəbl/	/'dʊ.reɪ.bɪl/
20. Examine	/ɪg'zæmɪn/	/eg'zə.maɪn/
21. Facts	/fæks/	/fekts/
22. Flood	/flʌd/	/fluːd/
23. Hideous	/'hɪdiəs/	/'haɪdɪs/
24. History	/'hɪs.tər.i/	/'his.tɔr.i/
25. Honesty	/'ɒnɪsti/	/'hanɪsti/
26. Honor	/'ɒn.ər/- /'ɑː.nɚ/	/'hɑ.nɚ/
27. Live (v)	/lɪv/	/laɪv/
28. Magnificent	/mæg'nɪfɪsənt/	/meg'nɪfɪkənt/
29. Major	/'meɪdʒər/	/'meɪjər/
30. Memory	/'mem.ər.i/	/'mem.ɔr.i/
31. Notice	/'nəʊtɪs/	/'nɔtaɪs/

continued on following page

Table 9. Continued

Word	Standard Pronunciation	Learner Pronunciation
32. Phenomenon	/fɪˈnɒmɪnən/	/feˈnɔmænən/
33. Recipe	/ˈresɪpi/	/ˈresaɪp/
34. Restaurant	/ˈres.tər.ɒnt/	/ˈres.tɔr.ənt/
35. Rough	/rʌf/	/rɔʊh/
36. Scene	/siːn/	/skiːn/
37. Schedule	/ˈʃedjuːl/ - /ˈskedʒuːl/	/ˈskedʒəl/
38. Separate (adj)	/ˈsepərət/	/ˈsepəreit/
39. Signal	/ˈsɪg.nəl/	/ˈsaɪ.nəl/
40. Successful	/səkˈsesfəl/	/sʌkˈsesful/
41. Support	/səˈpɔːt/	/sʌˈpɔːt/
42. Surface	/ˈsɜːfɪs/	/ˈsɜːfeɪs/
43. Taught	/tɔːt/	/taʊt/
44. Tomb	/tuːm/	/tamb/
45. Vary	/ˈveəri/	/ˈveraɪ/
46. Vegetable	/ˈvedʒ.tə.bəl/	/ˈvedʒ.ɪ.teɪ.bəl/
47. Weapon	/ˈwepən/	/ˈviɪpən/
48. Wear	/weəʳ/	/viɪʳ/
49. Wednesday	/ˈwenz.deɪ/	/ˈved.nɪz.deɪ/
50. Weight	/weɪt/	/veɪgt/

Reading Text

The Journey of Explorers

In a foreign land, a group of explorers decided to examine the rough surfaces around their village. With honesty as their guide, they scheduled their journey by thinking about every detail, considering the area, climate, risk of flood, and height of the mountains. They had to answer any questions from each other. In particular, one of them, John, was in debt and wished he could do wildlife exploration as a business. He taught himself how to plant a vegetable, use a weapon, live in a forest, and keep all information in every category in his memory. He had a program he followed with his ex-wife; however, they had to go separate after he lost his job and salary. She envied people living as a bachelor and wanted to become an author. But the tough life in this area was putting too much weight on her shoulders. She never wanted to cause any trouble for anybody else.

Adventure was in the blood of most people living in this town and a matter of character for most of them. They were capable of much more than just climbing, which was casual for them. Equipped with just a map and an urge to determine their route, they decided to wear durable clothing to bear any difficulties they could face. As they progressed, a magnificent phenomenon caught their attention—a scene of nature's beauty that seemed to vary from anything they had seen before. They could not help but notice bullet holes in an ancient tomb and thought they were evidence of a battle. Despite the hideous marks of the past, the explorers felt a surge of support from their ancestors' spirits. In the end, the expedition proved successful, revealing a rich history people had to bury beneath the surface.

As it got too cold to be in the mountains, they decided to return to the town at noon. They visited a nearby school in the afternoon. The students worked tirelessly to achieve success in their academic careers. They planned study sessions focusing on major subjects. They accurately analyzed their strengths and weaknesses and determined the best approach to learning. Their grades and impressive facts about them reflected their efforts and the honor they placed on education.

In the evening, they passed by a busy restaurant where the chef followed a centuries-old recipe every Wednesday. The aroma of the cooking was spreading through the air, as a signal to the diners that a feast awaited them. The customers were comfortable in the climate of the place and praised the chef's skills. A notice was placed on the wall to inform future generations about the importance of preserving their heritage.

Chapter 5
Integrating Research and Classroom Practice:
A Chatbot Design Experience for Pre-Service Teachers

Eduardo España
http://orcid.org/0000-0001-6077-2764
Universitat de València, Spain

Lola Lopez-Navas
http://orcid.org/0000-0003-1509-8306
Rey Juan Carlos University, Spain

Héctor Hernández-Gassó
http://orcid.org/0000-0001-5777-9906
Universitat de València, Spain

ABSTRACT

This chapter examines the integration of artificial intelligence (AI) bots in pre-service teacher education through the lens of the Multiliteracies framework. It explores how AI-driven conversational agents reshape literacy practices by fostering multimodal communication, collaborative writing, and creative meaning-making. Drawing on a study conducted with pre-service Primary education teachers, the chapter analyses students' familiarity with AI tools and their engagement in designing educational bots for teaching and learning purposes. Findings indicate limited prior knowledge of bots but strong recognition of their pedagogical value after an integrated hands-on experience. The chapter argues that AI bots function not only as instructional tools

DOI: 10.4018/979-8-3373-6420-9.ch005

but also as creative partners that enhance personalization, critical engagement, and multimodal literacy development, highlighting the need for their systematic inclusion in teacher training programs.

INTRODUCTION

Over the last decade, there has been a clear shift in the evolution of the integration of artificial intelligence (henceforth, AI) bots into the field of Applied Linguistics, specifically the area of Foreign Language Teaching. Within this particular context, and AI chatbot can be defined as a "computer program based on artificial intelligence (AI) that can carry out conversations through audio or text" (Haristiani, 2019, p.1) or an application that interacts with humans using natural language. They are sophisticated software applications designed to simulate human-like communication, also widely referred to as conversational AI or conversational agents. The core mechanism of these chatbots involves interpreting user questions using an artificial intelligence module and responding based on data contained in a database (Bartolomé, 2023).

Initial chatbots like ELIZA, Parry or A.L.I.C.E. had limited conversational capabilities and relied of restrictive turn-taking structures and rule-based responses, mostly based on pre-programmed templates (Dokukina & Guminova, 2020; Fernández-Ferrer, 2023). In contrast, nowadays, large language models (LLMs) are able to engage in fluent and context-sensitive dialogue. Therefore, the pedagogical potential of these digital tools has exponentially grown in a relatively short period of time, thanks to the rapid advances in natural language processing (NLP), machine learning, and generative AI (Lee et al., 2024), as well as the introduction of ChatGPT by OpenAI in November 2022, which increased academic attention on AI in language education (Gu & Yu, 2025). Today's AI-driven bots are not only capable of recognizing learner input but also of producing human-like discourse, offering feedback, generating multimodal content, and adjusting tone, genre, or even level of difficulty, thus extending opportunities for practice beyond the classroom.

However, the emergence of generative AI systems has also raised pedagogical, ethical, and methodological questions for educators, particularly as these tools are increasingly, and unstoppably, integrated in learning environments at all levels. Educational practitioners are reflecting on the ways in which literacy is going to be conceptualised and developed in synchrony with a technology that can enhance students' creativity and provide personalised learning experiences that support learners' development of communicative competence (Huesca et al., 2024; Zaim et al., 2025). In this context, it can be asserted that as LLM-based tools become ubiquitous, teacher education programs must prepare future educators to critically understand, evaluate, and integrate these technologies in ways that align with contemporary notions of literacy. This is directly linked with the main purpose of this chapter, which presents a study about the familiarity and use of AI tools by future Primary Education teachers.

BACKGROUND

The Multiliteracies Framework in the context of AI Bots

The Multiliteracies Framework (New London Group, 1996) provides a solid foundation to mediate the role of AI bots not only as technological tools but as cultural artefacts that define how meaning is produced, interpreted, and transformed. The multiliteracies framework was initially conceived as a response to global social and technological changes that were transforming how individuals communicate, learn, and participate in society. The framework challenged the dominance of traditional, monomodal literacy practices focused primarily on printed text and proposed a broader conceptualization of literacy based on two central ideas: increasing linguistic and cultural diversity, and the growing importance of multimodality in everyday communication. At the core of the framework there are four pedagogical components: situated practice, overt instruction, critical framing, and transformed practice, which collectively articulate a socially responsive and transformative model of literacy education (Cope & Kalantzis, 2000; Cope & Kalantzis, 2009). We will now explore how each of these pedagogical components can be linked to digital learning through AI bots.

First of all, *situated practice* emphasizes experiential learning grounded in learners' lived experiences and contexts. In digitally mediated environments, such experiences include engaging with AI tools, navigating online communication spaces, and interacting through diverse semiotic modes. Secondly, *overt instruction* focuses on explicit scaffolding, guiding learners to develop metalinguistic and metacognitive awareness.

This is particularly relevant when learners engage with AI bots, as they must understand not only linguistic forms but also digital conventions, prompts, and the underlying logic of machine-generated interaction. Furthermore, through the third component, *critical framing,* learners are invited to question the socio-cultural, ideological, and technological forces shaping communication. This component gains particular importance when working with AI-driven tools whose outputs reflect training data and embedded biases. Finally, *transformed practice* emphasizes the active design and redesign of meaning across contexts and modes. Learners become designers of multimodal texts that combine written language, images, audio, video, and interactive elements, precisely the kinds of artifacts that AI tools help generate.

For instance, AI systems can support learners in the design process by providing textual drafts, generating images or audio components, or offering models of discourse for learners to adapt.

For future teachers, particularly those working in Primary Education, where visual and auditory resources play a foundational role, understanding multiliteracies is essential for guiding learners through diverse meaning-making environments. AI bots have the potential to become tools through which multiliteracies pedagogy can be enacted, providing authentic opportunities for design, reflection, and critical engagement. In the next section, we will explore the need for teachers to develop advanced digital and critical literacies.

Main uses of chatbots for foreign language learning

As stated at the beginning of this chapter, the use of chatbots in foreign language learning has grown exponentially in recent years, largely due to rapid technological developments and increasing awareness among all educational stakeholders of the potential that these tools offer. As conversational agents become more sophisticated, research has begun to document an expanding range of pedagogical applications. Accordingly, drawing on recent studies, this section synthesizes the principal uses of AI-driven chatbots in foreign language learning. Broadly, these uses can be grouped into three overarching domains: the enhancement of core linguistic skills, the provision of pedagogical and cognitive support, and the facilitation of practical and institutional processes. Table 1 below shows a summary of those domains and their subcategories.

Table 1. Summary of Main Uses of Chatbots in Foreign Language Learning

Category	Subcategory	Primary Functions
I. Core Language Skills	Productive Skills	Speaking practice (dialogue, role-play); writing support (idea generation, structuring, revision).
	Foundational Linguistic Elements	Vocabulary expansion; grammar reinforcement; pronunciation feedback.
	Receptive Skills & Translation	Reading scaffolding; listening practice (TTS/ASR); translation and cross-linguistic clarification.
II. Pedagogical & Cognitive Support	Personalized & Adaptive Learning	Tailored content and pacing; individualized tutoring and guidance.
	Metacognition & Self-Regulation	Goal-setting and progress monitoring; critical evaluation of AI output; prompt-crafting competence.
	Affective & Motivational Support	Reduced anxiety through low-pressure interaction; increased engagement and motivation.

continued on following page

Table 1. Continued

Category	Subcategory	Primary Functions
III. Practical & Institutional Applications	Access & Flexibility	24/7 availability; support for autonomous and distance learning.
	Administrative Functions	Handling FAQs; providing course information; automating routine tasks.

1. Enhancement of core language skills

A primary area in which chatbots have demonstrated substantial value is the development of essential language skills. By serving as interactive, always-available interlocutors, AI chatbots provide learners with opportunities to practice both receptive and productive skills central to foreign language learning.

One of the most frequently documented applications of chatbots concerns their role in fostering productive language skills. Research indicates that these tools offer learners a relatively low-stakes environment in which to generate output, thereby mitigating common anxieties associated with language performance (Wiboolyasarin et al., 2025). For instance, their integration into speaking instruction has enabled learners to engage in simulated conversations, participate in role-playing activities replicating real-world scenarios such as shopping or job interviews, and practice spontaneous exchanges or even small talk. These interactions have been shown to increase learners' exposure to oral production opportunities, improve overall fluency, and support their initiative to communicate (Belda-Medina & Calvo-Ferrer, 2022; Haristiani, 2019; Tutton & Cohen, 2025; Yang et al., 2022).

Similarly, chatbots support writing development by assisting learners throughout the entire composition process (Guo et al., 2024). They can facilitate brainstorming and idea generation as well as help structure arguments and guide the overall organization of written discourse that is appropriate for a variety of genres, a key aspect in the multiliteracies framework previously explored in this chapter. Furthermore, chatbots can perform functions analogous to a writing assistant, such as refining coherence, suggesting improvements, and correcting grammatical inaccuracies (Wiboolyasarin et al.,2025; Zaim et al., 2025). In this way, they contribute not only to linguistic accuracy but also to the development of more sophisticated aspects of text authorship.

Beyond productive skills, chatbots reinforce foundational linguistic components. Through unlimited and structured practice opportunities, they support the acquisition and consolidation of core linguistic elements (Dokukina & Gumanova, 2020; Tutton & Cohen, 2025). In terms of vocabulary development, chatbots expose learners to new lexical items and expressions, help reinforce retention, and encourage contextualized use of vocabulary in meaningful interactions (Lee et al., 2024). They also contribute to grammar development by offering targeted feedback on syntactic structures and helping learners master increasingly complex forms (Wiboolyasarin et al., 2025). In addition, pronunciation-focused chatbots equipped with speech analysis capabilities provide real-time corrective feedback at both suprasegmental and phonemic levels, an aspect rarely addressed in conventional applications (Wang et al., 2025).

Chatbots also support receptive language skills, particularly reading and listening comprehension. They enhance learners' ability to process written texts through scaffolding strategies that assist with vocabulary clarification, decoding dense or academic language, and monitoring self-regulated reading practices (Wiboolyasarin et al., 2025; Zaim et al., 2025). Listening skills, likewise, benefit from chatbot integration, especially when conversational agents incorporate Text-to-Speech (TTS) and Automatic Speech Recognition (ASR) technologies that simulate auditory comprehension tasks (Dokukina & Gumanova, 2020; Haristiani, 2019; Tutton & Cohen, 2025). Moreover, translation functions embedded within AI systems facilitate cross-linguistic understanding by helping learners navigate unfamiliar vocabulary or syntactic structures. Large Language Models (LLMs) extend this capability further by translating entire documents and explaining linguistic choices in depth (Tutton & Cohen, 2025; Vanjani et al., 2020; Wiboolyasarin et al.,2025; Zaim et al.,2025). Therefore, the integration of receptive and translation functions clearly shows the potential of chatbots to mediate learners' engagement with linguistic input while complementing the earlier focus on linguistic output.

2. Pedagogical Support and Cognitive Development

In addition to linguistic enhancement, chatbots play a crucial role in pedagogical support, offering adaptive interventions that complement the work of human educators. Their ability to personalise instruction and promote cognitive development aligns closely with contemporary learner-centred pedagogies. A key strength of AI chatbots lies in their capacity to modulate learning according to individual needs. These tools can adjust content difficulty, tailor feedback, and control the pacing of instruction based on the learner's proficiency level, thereby supporting differentiated learning pathways (Nouzri et al., 2025; Tutton & Cohen, 2025). In many cases, they act as virtual tutors or personal assistants, offering ongoing mentorship and constructing individualized learning trajectories (Dokukina & Gumanova, 2020; Martins, 2023; Zaim et al., 2025). This personalised approach allows learners to progress at their own pace and improves their capacity for autonomous decision-making throughout the learning process.

Chatbots are also increasingly used to promote metacognitive skills and self-regulation. By encouraging learners to monitor their progress, set their own individual goals, reflect on their performance, and be aware of their own learning trategies, chatbots contribute to the development of self-regulated learning (SRL) behaviours (Polakova & Klimova, 2024). Furthermore, advanced AI tools have been incorporated into instructional designs intended to cultivate critical thinking, such as tasks requiring learners to assess the accuracy of AI-generated output or to solve complex problems collaboratively (Gu & Yu, 2025; Huesca et al., 2024). A related emerging competency is mastery of prompt engineering, in which learners develop skills in crafting precise and effective prompts to obtain high-quality responses from AI systems. This ability enhances learners' information literacy and deepens their strategic engagement with technological tools (Huesca et al., 2024).

Equally important is the affective dimension of chatbot use. Numerous studies report that chatbots help reduce foreign language anxiety by offering a low-pressure environment where learners can experiment with language without fear of judgement (Belda-Medina & Calvo-Ferrer, 2022; Mazzilli, 2021). Their conversational format fosters a supportive, non-threatening space for practice. In addition, the novelty and interactivity associated with chatbot use increase motivation and engagement, sustaining learners' interest and encouraging persistence. Features such as gamification elements, rewards, or playful interactions further enhance their motivational impact (Dokukina & Gumanova, 2020; Lee et al., 2024; Polakova & Klimova, 2024; Wiboolyasarin et al., 2025). This move from cognitive to affective scaffolding illustrates the multi-layered ways in which chatbots support learners holistically.

3. Practical and Institutional Applications

In addition to their linguistic and pedagogical functions, chatbots contribute substantially to the practical and institutional dimensions of educational contexts. This third domain highlights the ways in which conversational agents facilitate accessibility, flexibility, and educational management, thereby supporting both autonomous learning and administrative efficiency.

Perhaps the most obvious advantage of chatbots regarding this aspect is their 24/7 availability. Learners can access them from personal devices such as smartphones, enabling continuous support and facilitating distance or hybrid learning models (Dokukina & Gumanova, 2020; Nouzri et al., 2025; Polakova & Klimova, 2024). This constant availability not only enhances the feasibility of autonomous learning but also promotes self-efficacy by giving learners sustained opportunities to practice outside the classroom (Gu & Yu, 2025; Haristiani, 2019; Huesca et al., 2024).

Along with pedagogical uses, chatbots serve increasingly practical institutional roles. They can handle frequently asked questions and operate as information-retrieval systems for course content, scheduling, or administrative procedures (Martins, 2023). Moreover, they automate repetitive tasks such as tracking attendance, organising timetables, or even assisting with preliminary grading processes, thereby reducing teachers' administrative workload (García-Lopez et al., 2025; Nouzri et al., 2025). Such applications underline the dual function of chatbots as both instructional supports and institutional management tools.

Limitations of the use of AI chatbots

Notwithstanding the clear advantages of chatbots that have been highlighted in the previous section, the integration of AI tools in educational environments has been accompanied by a growing body of research identifying substantial limitations and challenges. These challenges, in line with the aspects mentioned in the previous section, are of technological, pedagogical, ethical, and institutional nature. Understanding them is essential for developing informed, reasonable expectations about what AI can—and cannot—contribute to language education.

A first set of concerns relates to technological and design flaws inherent in the current generation of AI systems. Several studies (Belda-medina & Calvo-Ferrer, 2022; Gu et al., 2025; Haristiani, 2019; Lee et al., 2024) have noted persistent issues with linguistic inaccuracy and inconsistency, as chatbot responses can be repetitive, irrelevant, or insufficiently aligned with the conversational context. In particular, some chatbots often struggle to produce contextually meaningful or natural-sounding dialogue. These limitations point to a broader need for AI systems that are capable of genuinely processing and generating human-like language. Even the more advanced chatbot models present their own reliability issues, with well-documented instances of "hallucinations" that expose learners to inaccurate explanations, including errors in grammar descriptions or etymological information for minority languages (Nouzri et al., 2025; Tutton & Cohen, 2025). In addition, shortcomings in speech and voice technologies continue to impede oral interaction, as text-to-speech output frequently sounds robotic or unnatural, leading many learners to prefer text-based interaction (Belda-medina & Calvo-Ferrer, 2022). Existing tools also provide insufficient phoneme-level guidance and lack detailed feedback mechanisms (Wang et al., 2025). In parallel to these limitations, challenges with culturally embedded or nuanced language use have been identified (Wiboolyasarin et al., 2025).

Beyond these technological considerations, a second cluster of challenges concerns pedagogical limitations. A recurrent concern is the potential for over-reliance on AI, which may inadvertently weaken critical thinking and reduce learners' willingness to engage in independent problem-solving (Huesca et al., 2024; Polakova & Klimova,

2024). This is ironic, taking into account that the enhancement of critical thinking skills is one of the aspects that is stressed about the use of AI. Research also points to the "novelty effect," whereby initial excitement about chatbot use diminishes over time, contrasting with the more sustained engagement typical in human interaction (Haristiani, 2019). The effectiveness of chatbots further varies across proficiency levels: some studies suggest that AI tools may be more beneficial for beginners than for advanced learners, while others caution that highly sophisticated chatbots may only be suitable for advanced or particularly motivated students (Huesca et al., 2024). Moreover, since AI chatbots are unable to simulate the full richness of human interaction neither provide the nuanced feedback or conversational adaptability that human tutors naturally offer, learners may experience difficulties clarifying complex issues and may develop feelings of emotional disconnect when relying heavily on AI-mediated communication (Nouzri et al., 2025; Tutton & Cohen, 2025).

A final domain of challenges involves ethical, institutional, and resource-related constraints that complicate the widespread adoption of AI in education. The digital divide remains a crucial issue, as effective use of AI tools requires consistent access to computers and reliable internet connections—resources that are not equitably available across all social groups (Huesca et al., 2024). Teachers themselves face substantial barriers, as designing, implementing, and refining chatbot-based activities demands considerable time, technical expertise, and familiarity with AI literacy, including skills such as prompt engineering and ethical decision-making, since many AI platforms request access to personal data, including social networks or camera permissions, raising legitimate concerns about data storage, manipulation, and transparency (Martins, 2023; Paredes & Martínez, 2023).

Recognizing these technological, pedagogical, ethical, and institutional challenges not only balances expectations but also informs the development of policies and teacher development courses that equips future and in-service teachers to engage with these technologies as informed designers, critical interpreters, and pedagogical decision-makers. The following section examines this need in greater detail. In the next section, several aspects related to teacher training will be explored.

A CHATBOT DESIGN EXPERIENCE FOR PRE-SERVICE TEACHERS

The need for teacher training on AI bots

In the previous sections, the importance of the use of AI bots to develop multiliteracies in Primary Education was highlighted, as well as both their potential and limitations for foreign language teaching. Having explored these aspects, it is undeniable that the expanding role of AI chatbots reveals a deeper set of pedagogical responsibilities for educators. Like with any pedagogical innovation, the integration of chatbots into classroom practice is not simply a matter of adopting new tools: it constitutes a shift toward forms of meaning-making that are increasingly multimodal, interactive, and shaped by human–AI collaboration. This leads to the fundamental question of the skills needed from both current and future teachers in order to be able to implement this framework and make sensible use of AI bots in their lessons: What tools, skills and competences do teachers need to navigate, make the most and evaluate machine-generated content?

As AI tools increasingly influence how learners engage with multimodal, interactive, and dynamically generated content, teachers are required to adopt more expansive roles as facilitators of learning and mediators of technological interaction. A foundational component of this preparation is the development of robust AI literacy and the capacity to provide ethical guidance. This emphasis aligns with international policy discussions that frame AI literacy and responsible technology integration as essential competences for 21st-century educators, highlighting the need for teacher education programmes to address not only technical skills but also ethical and pedagogical dimensions of AI use (Ananiadou & Claro, 2009; UNESCO, 2017). Teachers must acquire a clear understanding of how AI technologies function and how these systems can and should be used within the classroom. As Gu et al. (2025) mention, "the advancement of AI chatbots in language education not only depends on sophisticated technology but also requires thoughtful design strategies that cater to diverse learning needs and preferences" (652). This includes developing the digital competencies necessary to engage ethically and effectively with generative AI (GenAI) chatbots such as ChatGPT, as well as learning how to communicate transparently with students about both the affordances and limitations of these platforms (Tutton & Cohen, 2025). Training must therefore equip teachers to guide learners in critically evaluating AI output, interrogating the reliability and biases embedded within algorithmic systems, and adopting reflective, responsible practices when using AI tools (Ng et al., 2021).

Beyond ethical and conceptual understanding, effective integration of chatbots requires teachers to reconfigure their pedagogical strategies and develop expertise in designing tasks that leverage AI's strengths while maintaining clear instructional intentions. Central to this is the ability to model and teach effective prompt engineering, an emerging communicative skill that enhances critical thinking and optimizes interactions with AI systems (García et al., 2025; Siegle, 2024). Teachers must also learn to curate meaningful chatbot-based tasks, selecting activities that align with learning objectives and provide linguistic opportunities that may not arise organically in traditional instruction (Wang et al., 2025). Clear guidance is particularly important in the early stages of implementation, as learners may initially feel overwhelmed by the open-ended nature of AI tools. Equally crucial is the establishment of programmatic structures that enable sustained support for teachers as they adopt AI technologies. Research consistently indicates that teachers require additional training to integrate chatbots effectively, particularly given the technical complexity involved in developing or managing conversational tools without a technological background (Gu et al., 2025; Paredes & Martínez, 2023).

Through the development of these competencies and support systems, teachers can more effectively manage the pedagogical, ethical, and practical dimensions of AI integration, from an awareness that chatbots serve not as replacements for human instruction but as complementary tools that enrich language learning environments and expand opportunities for multimodal meaning-making. The relevance of AI bots and multiliteracies is particularly significant in the context of teacher education, especially for future Primary Education teachers. The new generations of young learners are immersed in multimodal environments from an early age, encountering images, videos, animations, sounds, and interactive media as part of their everyday experiences. Multimodality is not an extension of traditional literacy but a foundational mode of meaning-making for children. Future language teachers must therefore be prepared to design learning experiences that integrate multimodal resources, encourage creativity, and foster critical engagement with digital tools. AI bots can support this by enabling pre-service teachers to model multimodal lesson designs, experiment with prompts to generate teaching materials, and reflect on the pedagogical implications of using AI.

Although research, as seen throughout this section, has increasingly documented the pedagogical applications of AI chatbots in language learning contexts, much of this scholarship has focused on learner outcomes, technological affordances, or broad attitudinal surveys. Comparatively less attention has been devoted to structured, design-based experiences in initial teacher education that position future educators not merely as users of AI tools, but as critical designers of AI-mediated learning environments. In addition, while the Multiliteracies pedagogy offers a powerful framework for understanding multimodal and socially situated meaning-making, its integration with generative AI and chatbot design in teacher training remains underexplored.

This chapter addresses this gap by examining how a practice-based chatbot creation activity shapes pre-service Primary teachers' digital competence, pedagogical reasoning, and critical positioning toward AI integration within a multiliteracies perspective. With this idea in mind, a study was designed not only to ascertain the current use of AI bots by pre-service Primary teachers at the University of Valencia, but also to determine the value that these future teachers give to digital tools for their future professional development.

Research Objectives and Design

The study is aimed at students in their final year of the Bachelor's Degree in Primary Education with a specialisation in Information and Communication Technologies, and focuses on how working with educational chatbots can contribute to their digital and professional competence. The research is structured around three phases: initial diagnosis through a survey, intervention with a practical activity involving the creation of educational chatbots, and a post-intervention evaluation.

The primary objective is to evaluate the impact of an intervention based on the creation and experimentation of educational chatbots on digital competence. Through this intervention, the students' confidence and willingness to integrate this resource into their future teaching practice will be measured by comparing the initial state of knowledge, attitudes and perceptions with the post-activity results. This main objective is operationalised through a series of specific objectives organised around each of the three phases:

- **Phase 1: Initial diagnosis:** In the first phase, the study seeks to characterise students' initial knowledge of artificial intelligence tools; describe the ways in which they currently use AI as a study aid; explore their general views on the role of AI in education; analyse how they envisage the future use of AI in their own teaching practice; and, finally, assess their initial knowledge of specific educational chatbots in contrast to generic conversational agents.
- **Phase 2: Intervention:** In the second phase, the objective is to implement a collaborative activity in which students design and create educational chatbots for Primary Education. This phase is intended not only to develop procedural skills related to chatbot design, but also to provide an authentic context in which students can reflect on the pedagogical implications of these tools.
- **Phase 3: Post-intervention evaluation:** In the third and final phase, the research focuses on evaluating the impact of the activity. The specific objectives are to assess the overall training experience; analyse students' didactic perceptions of chatbots after the hands-on work; identify significant changes between the initial and final situations in relation to the use of AI; and, through open-ended questions, explore the advantages, limitations and strategies that students perceive for adapting chatbots to different learning levels and styles.

The study follows a descriptive and exploratory design. Quantitative data derived from Likert-scale items were analysed through frequency distributions in order to identify general tendencies in students' perceptions before and after the intervention. The open-ended responses were examined through an iterative reading process aimed at identifying recurring patterns and salient themes across participants' answers. Given the relatively small sample size and the practice-oriented nature of the intervention, the analysis remains descriptive rather than inferential, with the purpose of capturing shifts in attitudes, perceived competencies, and pedagogical reasoning rather than establishing generalizable causal claims.

Contextualisation

The bachelor's degree in Primary Education at the University of Valencia belongs to the branch of Social and Legal Sciences and has a clearly professional orientation, preparing future teachers to work with children aged 6 to 12 in formal educational settings. Within this degree, the ICT specialist pathway offers specific training in the pedagogical use of digital resources and innovative methodologies. Consequently, the participating students are not only future primary teachers, but also prospective professionals with a particular interest in and responsibility for the integration of digital technologies in the classroom.

From a demographic point of view, the participant group is mainly composed of young adults between 20 and 23 years of age, which is typical of the final year of undergraduate studies. Alongside this majority group, there is a smaller proportion of students aged between 23 and 26 years old and, to a lesser extent, older participants. In terms of gender, there is a clear predominance of female students, although male students are also significantly represented, reflecting the usual gender distribution in Primary Education degrees. With regard to their prior academic trajectories, most students gained access to the degree after completing upper secondary education, which constitutes the most common entry route to university studies in Spain. In addition, there are students who come from vocational training programmes and, to a lesser extent, students who entered through specific university entrance examinations for mature students, from other university degrees or without formally recognised prior studies. This profile reflects the pluralistic access model of the University of Valencia and the diversity of pathways to undergraduate studies.

Participation in the study was voluntary, and students were informed about the academic purpose of the research. Responses were collected anonymously and analysed in aggregated form to ensure confidentiality. Likewise, the Ethics Committee of the University of Valencia states that if an opinion survey is to be conducted on any topic or issue, professional situation, satisfaction with certain issues, etc., provided that it does not include psychological or health information, explicit authorisation from the Ethics Committee is not required.

Phase 1: Initial Diagnosis

The study began with a diagnostic survey designed to evaluate the students' starting point regarding AI and educational chatbots. The instrument was structured in five sections and based primarily on five-point Likert-type scales (ranging from Strongly agree to Strongly disagree). The main objective of this survey was to provide a comprehensive picture of the participants' prior knowledge, attitudes, and expectations.

Regarding familiarity and current use of AI, the survey examined whether students were accustomed to tools such as ChatGPT or Copilot and if they felt capable of distinguishing between responsible and problematic uses in university contexts. The results reveal that students possess a high level of familiarity with these generalist tools. They perceive themselves as competent and responsible users, reporting that they frequently use AI to support their academic tasks, specifically for generating summaries, searching for information, and correcting texts. Students attribute clear value to these tools for improving academic performance and generally find them easy to integrate into their study habits.

In terms of general perceptions of AI in education, the instrument explored whether participants viewed AI as a key future tool or a threat to the teaching profession. The analysis shows a predominantly optimistic, though not uncritical, perception. Most students anticipate that AI will be a fundamental tool in the education system and trust its implementation to improve the quality of learning, viewing it as a support mechanism rather than a substitute for teachers. However, this optimism is balanced by intermediate positions that express concern regarding the potential depersonalization of teaching.

When projecting their future role as teachers, the survey asked participants if they intended to use AI to personalize learning, reduce administrative workload, or teach critical digital literacy. The responses indicate a strong alignment with these goals: students state they are likely to use AI in their future classrooms, particularly to attend to diversity and streamline assessment tasks. Furthermore, there is a clear awareness of the importance of preparing primary school pupils for the ethical and responsible use of emerging technologies.

Finally, a specific block was dedicated to educational chatbots to determine if students could distinguish these from generic conversational agents and if they were aware of platforms for creating them. It is here that the main gap in training was identified. Unlike their high familiarity with general GenAI, a significant proportion of students admitted to having only a superficial understanding of the differences between generic and educational chatbots, and most were unaware of specific resources for creating them. Despite this lack of prior technical knowledge, the students showed a high level of initial interest in learning to design these tools, recognizing their potential benefits for fostering participation and autonomous learning.

Phase 2: Intervention

The activity integrated in the university course had as its central objective the promotion of active learning and the development of digital competencies through the collaborative creation of educational chatbots for primary classrooms.

From a theoretical perspective, the activity was intentionally aligned with the Multiliteracies Framework previously outlined. The collaborative design process reflected situated practice, as students engaged with AI tools within an authentic professional context. The tutorial and guided discussion functioned as overt instruction, supporting the development of metalinguistic and digital awareness. Peer-testing and critical reflection during the exchange of chatbot links encouraged critical framing, prompting students to evaluate the affordances and limitations of AI-generated interaction. Finally, the creation and adaptation of chatbots for Primary Education contexts embodied transformed practice, as participants redesigned curricular content through multimodal and AI-mediated formats.

The initial phase of the intervention culminated in the viewing of a video tutorial "Making Chatbots with POE.COM 16/37 UPV" produced by Ignacio Despujol Zabala, a professor at the Universitat Politècnica de València (2024). The video (http://hdl.handle.net/10251/204872) provided a detailed, step-by-step guide to the functioning and possibilities of the POE digital platform, a tool specialising in the customised creation of chatbots. Thus, students were given a concrete technological reference for the subsequent practical work.

After the viewing and collective discussion of the tutorial, students organised themselves into small groups. Each group autonomously selected a curricular topic appropriate for primary education and, based on this choice, began the process of designing and programming its own educational chatbot using POE.

The design process involved several decisions: defining the educational purpose of the chatbot, drafting prompts to guide its behaviour, selecting the AI model, and customising elements such as the interface and welcome messages.

Once the development phase was complete, each group obtained a functional link to its chatbot. These links did not require the use of personal data, which ensured their suitability for the school context from the point of view of privacy. To round off the experience, the groups exchanged links so that each could test and explore the chatbots created by their peers. During this peer-testing phase, students posed queries, observed the responsiveness of each chatbot and critically analysed its educational suitability. This cross-testing made it possible to collect suggestions and proposals for improvement, thereby facilitating shared reflection on the pedagogical potential and limitations of chatbots.

Analysis of the intervention

Following the completion of the activity, students' perceptions were collected through two open-ended questions: "What advantages and limitations do you see in the use of educational chatbots?" and "How would you adapt the chatbot to cater to different learning levels or styles?".

With regard to perceived advantages, students highlight several recurring themes. One of the most valued aspects is permanent availability and accessibility: chatbots are perceived as tools capable of answering questions at any time and providing immediate feedback, thus facilitating autonomous learning beyond classroom hours. Another frequently mentioned advantage is the potential for personalisation, as chatbots can adapt to the pace and needs of each learner. In this sense, some students underline that learning can be more personalised because the chatbot modulates its responses according to the input it receives.

Students also value the possibility of obtaining iterative explanations: 'You can also ask them again as many times as you want to explain it again', which supports repetitive learning processes without generating frustration. Furthermore, the potential reduction of teachers' workload is recognised, since chatbots can help in generating activities at different levels, thereby supporting planning and differentiation. Finally, some responses emphasise the usefulness of chatbots as specialised tutors, especially in contexts that require individualised support for students with specific educational needs.

However, the responses also indicate that students observed limitations and identified risks. One of the main concerns is the generation of inaccurate or fabricated information; they note that chatbots may "invent" answers or provide incorrect information if not properly configured with reliable sources. This perceived risk underscores the need for careful design and continuous teacher supervision. Another recurring worry is the possibility of excessive dependence on the tool, which could discourage students from exercising their own reasoning and effort. From an affective perspective, several responses underline that AI "does not have the warmth of a person," a particularly relevant aspect in primary education, where emotional relationships play a central role. Technical and operational limitations are also mentioned, such as the need for sufficient tokens for the platform to function properly, which may condition accessibility and use. Additionally, the risk that students might use chatbots simply to complete tasks without engaging in deep learning processes is highlighted as a potential threat.

Regarding adaptation to different learning levels and styles, the responses show an awareness of the importance of deliberate pedagogical design. Many students stress that the key lies in carefully formulating prompts so that the chatbot can respond appropriately to a variety of levels and styles.

Among the proposed personalisation strategies, one of the most common is the progressive adjustment of the complexity of responses. For example, some students suggest that the chatbot should start with simple explanations and concrete examples and, if the learner still does not understand, simplify the discourse further. Others propose the creation of differentiated profiles or modes of use, each tailored to a specific level.

Furthermore, several responses explicitly refer to the Universal Design for Learning (UDL), proposing that the chatbot should be configured with documents that include both curricular content and the principles of UDL, thus ensuring pedagogical coherence. Adaptations for functional diversity and special educational needs are also considered. Some students suggest that chatbots could respond with pictograms or especially clear, well-structured explanations for learners with SEN. Finally, some responses propose diagnostic-based adaptation strategies: for instance, that the chatbot first administers a short test to identify key ideas and then adjusts its level of response to the student's profile. Overall, this reflects an awareness from participants of how AI can evolve based on user interactions.

Phase 3: Final survey

The final phase of the study evaluated both the satisfaction with the training activity and the change in the participants' didactic perceptions. The quantitative results of the final survey demonstrate a very positive assessment of the experience and a significant increase in perceived self-efficacy. To facilitate data visualization, table 2 summarizes the key results obtained from the assessment scales:

Table 2. Summary of final survey results

Evaluated Dimension	Response Trends (Highlighted Frequencies)	Interpretation
Procedural Understanding	14 "Strongly Agree" and 10 "Agree" that they understood the design steps.	51% and 37%. The methodology was effective in conveying technical knowledge.
Teaching Preparedness	18 "Strongly Agree" and 7 "Agree" in feeling more prepared to integrate chatbots.	66% and 25%. Direct impact on self-confidence and perceived competence.
Didactic Potential	Near-unanimous consensus (25 "Strongly Agree") that they encourage participation.	92%. Recognition of pedagogical value for active learning.

continued on following page

Table 2. Continued

Evaluated Dimension	Response Trends (Highlighted Frequencies)	Interpretation
Personalization	18 "Strongly Agree" regarding its utility for personalizing learning.	66%. Alignment with the needs for attention to diversity.
Critical Thinking	13 "Strongly Agree" and 12 "Agree" on the need to teach critical use.	48% and 44%. Ethical awareness regarding technological integration.
Interest and Utility	24 out of 27 students indicated they "Strongly Agree" or "Agree" that the activity was interesting.	88%. High motivation and validation of utility for their professional future.

The analysis of these data confirms that the intervention had a transformative effect. Most students (25 out of 27) would recommend the activity to other peers, highlighting that the time and resources provided were adequate.

Although technological acceptance is high, a reflective stance is maintained. Notably, 54% of the group expressed some degree of concern regarding the potential reduction of direct interaction between teacher and student. This indicates that, following the intervention, students have not only acquired technical competencies for prompt and chatbot design, but have also developed a balanced vision. This perspective values the efficiency of AI without losing sight of the irreplaceable importance of the teaching role and the necessity for critical literacy.

This ambivalence is particularly significant when interpreted through the lens of the Multiliteracies Framework. While AI tools expand possibilities for multimodal design and personalised feedback, they also risk reshaping the relational dimension of teaching. The coexistence of enthusiasm and caution suggests that students are not adopting a technocentric stance but rather negotiating the role of AI within a broader understanding of education as both cognitive and socio-emotional practice. In this sense, the findings indicate the emergence of a critical professional identity rather than uncritical technological acceptance.

Finally, recognition of the need for critical thinking education is almost unanimous, with 13 students strongly agreeing and 12 agreeing, while only 2 were indifferent. This result underscores that future teachers understand that technological integration must be accompanied by ethical and reflective considerations.

Ultimately, this study highlights the need for research that moves from perceptions to actual practices. Although data on satisfaction and attitudinal change are valuable, the key question is whether these changes are translated into concrete innovations in Primary classrooms and into measurable improvements in pupils' learning. Future research incorporating longitudinal designs and classroom-based observations would be particularly valuable in determining whether the attitudinal and competence shifts identified here translate into sustained pedagogical innovation and measurable learning outcomes.

IMPLICATIONS OF THIS STUDY FOR RESEARCH ON EDUCATIONAL CHATBOTS

The findings of this study contribute to the body or research in educational technology and teacher training. The study of educational chatbots is in a period of expansion, and this work results open new lines of inquiry while reaffirming the relevance of certain areas of study.

First, these results demonstrate the viability and value of an approach based on practical experience for AI literacy in general and for working with educational chatbots in particular. Unlike purely theoretical or instrumental training models, the chatbot creation activity using POE proved to be highly effective in transforming both competencies and attitudes toward technology. This suggests for future research the importance of prioritizing experiential learning regarding AI, an approach that could likely be applied to other emerging technologies. Researchers interested in teacher training could explore how different platforms, levels of complexity or time constraints affect this effectiveness.

Second, the coexistence of critical optimism with ethical caution is a relevant finding that challenges polarized narratives about AI in education. This study shows that educators can simultaneously maintain positive perceptions regarding technological potential and legitimate concerns about negative impacts. This finding invites researchers to develop instruments and conceptual frameworks that capture this complexity.

Third, the sophistication of the pedagogical proposals for adaptation (references to UDL, multi-level differentiation or progressive personalization) indicates that adequate training in AI can foster advanced pedagogical thinking. The results suggest that when teachers experience AI not only as a technical tool but within a deliberate pedagogical context, they tend to integrate it with recognized educational frameworks. This opens opportunities to deepen the understanding of how technology can serve as a catalyst for reflection on educational theory.

In addition, the almost unanimous recognition of the need for critical literacy among students reinforces the relevance of this topic. The consensus on the importance of critical thinking suggests that this is not simply a concern of the academic sphere, but a priority recognized by professionals in training. The findings invite the development and evaluation of specific curricular programs that prepare teachers to teach Primary Education students a critical use of AI, as well as instruments to measure the impact of such interventions.

In parallel, the explicit identification of limitations (AI errors, dependency, dehumanization) by students in training suggests the importance of literacy in technological limitations. This finding indicates that interest in educational chatbots should not focus solely on how to enhance their integration in the classroom, but also on how to prepare teachers to recognize and mitigate their risks.

The variability observed in dispositions toward continuous learning (22 of 27 interested, with some nuances) highlights the need to investigate differentiated profiles of AI adoption. Not all teachers respond identically to AI interventions. Understanding which factors (prior motivation, pedagogical beliefs, digital competence) predict a greater disposition is crucial for designing adapted training.

Finally, this study highlights the need for research studies that move from perceptions to actual classroom practices. Future research should therefore incorporate longitudinal designs, classroom observations and analyses of learning outcomes, in order to bridge the gap between initial training and professional practice and to assess the real educational impact of chatbots in everyday teaching.

CONCLUSION

The research carried out on the integration of educational chatbots in the initial training of primary school teachers (ICT specialisation) has yielded relevant findings. The main conclusions based on the data obtained in this study are presented below. The training intervention based on the creation of educational chatbots has a significant positive impact on the competence and confidence of future teachers. The results of the final survey show that, after the practical activity, 18 out of 27 students felt 'strongly agree' that they were better prepared to integrate chatbots into their future classes, with an additional 7 in the 'agree' category. In addition, 25 out of 27 students found the activity interesting, 26 out of 27 would recommend it to other students, and 24 out of 27 considered it useful for their professional training. These data highlight the effectiveness of practical activities in developing specific digital skills in initial teacher training.

Final-year students are highly familiar with general AI tools but have only a superficial knowledge of specific educational chatbots, which changes significantly after the intervention. The initial survey showed that most students use tools such as ChatGPT and Copilot in their academic life and feel comfortable with their integration. However, they have limited knowledge about the difference between generic and educational chatbots, with many positioning themselves as 'indifferent' or 'disagree' regarding this knowledge. After the practical activity, this gap is significantly reduced, demonstrating that the intervention was effective in developing specific literacy in educational chatbots.

Future teachers maintain a balanced view that recognises both the potential and the risks of AI in education, demonstrating critical thinking about technological integration. Analysis of the open-ended responses following the activity reveals that students identify significant advantages such as the permanent availability of support, personalised learning and a reduction in teachers' administrative workload. However, at the same time, they warn of risks such as the generation of erroneous information, possible student dependency and a lack of human warmth. This concern mirrors the technological limitations identified by Belda-Medina & Calvo-Ferrer (2022) and Lee et al. (2024) regarding the persistence of linguistic inaccuracies and 'hallucinations' in current AI models. In line with this, in the final survey, 54% of the group (13 out of 26) expressed some degree of concern about the reduction in direct interaction between teacher and student. This nuanced view is particularly valuable, indicating that future teachers do not uncritically accept technology, but seek its responsible integration.

The practical activity was rated very positively across all pedagogical and logistical dimensions, with consistently high levels of satisfaction among participants. Almost all students considered the activity interesting (24 out of 27, split between 13 'strongly agree' and 11 'agree'), and a similarly high number indicated that they would recommend it (26 out of 27). Understanding of chatbot design was also perceived as high by 24 students, while 6 explicitly highlighted its usefulness for their training. In terms of implementation, 25 out of 27 regarded the teaching support as adequate, and 24 evaluated the resources used in the activity positively. Furthermore, 26 students felt that the time allocated was sufficient, and the same number considered the level of difficulty to be appropriate, confirming the overall suitability and effectiveness of the activity's design.

Recognition of the chatbots potential for personalization and addressing diversity is widely shared. Following the intervention, 26 out of 27 students acknowledged the potential of chatbots to personalize learning (18 "strongly agreed" and 8 "agreed"). These findings corroborate recent studies that highlight the capacity of AI tools to act as adaptive tutors that support differentiated learning pathways and attend to diversity (Nouzri et al., 2025; Tutton & Cohen, 2025). Open-ended responses demonstrated that the students understand the need for deliberate pedagogical design, with proposals including explicit references to Universal Design for Learning (UDL), specific strategies for Special Educational Needs (SEN), differentiation of complexity levels, and progressive adjustment based on student performance. These findings suggest the practical experience fostered, not only technical competencies, but also well-founded pedagogical thinking regarding technology integration.

The importance of critical AI literacy is recognized almost unanimously, positioning this skill as a priority in the training of Primary Education students. In the initial survey, the majority considered it important to teach students to use AI critically. In the final survey, 25 out of 27 students (13 "strongly agreed" and 12 "agreed") coincided on the importance of critical education. The other 2 students appeared indifferent. This virtually unanimous consensus highlights that future teachers understand that technological integration must necessarily be accompanied by ethical and reflective education. This consensus is in line with the international policy recommendations (e.g., UNESCO, 2017) and recent scholarship (Ng et al., 2021) which frame AI literacy not merely as a technical skill, but as a critical 21st-century competence essential for ethical engagement with technology.

Careful pedagogical design emerges as a fundamental factor for the effectiveness of educational chatbots. Qualitative responses revealed a clear understanding that effectiveness depends fundamentally on the quality of instructional design. Students emphasized the importance of "well-designed prompts," "good curriculum preparation," the selection of "reliable and secure knowledge sources," and "official" documents as information sources. Multiple responses referred to the need to differentiate according to "complexity level," create "different profiles" adapted to specific needs, and include pedagogical frameworks such as UDL. This suggests that the activity promoted not only technical mastery but also strategic educational thinking. This emphasis on deliberate design validates the growing importance of 'prompt engineering' as a core teacher competency, as suggested by García-López et al. (2025) and Siegle (2024), who argue that the quality of AI output is directly dependent on the educator's ability to craft precise instructional constraints.

A further point to consider is that students clearly recognize the limitations of chatbots and adopt a cautious stance. Among the identified limitations, concerns stand out regarding the "generation of erroneous information," "student dependency," the "lack of human warmth" in responses, and the risk of it being used to "do homework without reasoning." This critical ability to identify risks alongside potential indicates that the students were able to make informed judgments on when, how, and under what conditions to integrate technology. Beyond this aspect, there is a disposition towards lifelong learning in educational AI, although with variability in the intensity of interest. Although 22 out of 27 students (10 "strongly agreed," 12 "agreed") expressed interest in continuing to learn about chatbots, the rest of them answered in a less enthusiastic way (3 indifferent, 1 disagreed, 1 strongly disagreed). This distribution suggests that, while the experience generated a general disposition towards continuous learning, not all students feel equal motivation to delve deeper.

Drawing all the aspects examined through both the initial and final surveys together, the empirical results broadly confirm, but also nuance, the tendencies identified in the theoretical review. On the one hand, the initial survey shows that future Primary teachers already fit the profile described in the literature as "digitally confident but pedagogically underprepared" (Martins, 2023, p.22): they make intensive, pragmatic use of general AI tools such as ChatGPT, recognise their potential for efficiency and personalisation, and express a predominantly positive attitude towards their incorporation into education, yet their knowledge of educational chatbots and of specific design platforms is initially superficial and weakly grounded in didactic criteria. On the other hand, the intervention and final survey illustrate that when these tools are approached through structured, practice-based activities aligned with pedagogical frameworks (e.g. personalisation, attention to diversity, UDL, critical digital literacy), students not only develop operational competence, but also begin to internalise the kind of reflective, ethically informed stance that the Multiliteracies Framework (Cope & Kalantzis, 2009) demands. Their discourse after the activity mirrors key theoretical concerns: they simultaneously value availability, individualised feedback and workload reduction, while problematising hallucinations, dependency and the risk of dehumanising interactions. In this sense, the study provides empirical support for the idea that the educational value of AI and chatbots is not inherent to the technology itself but emerges from teacher education processes that explicitly connect technical design decisions with curricular, ethical and inclusive considerations.

Beyond confirming previous literature, the study also suggests that engaging pre-service teachers in the design of AI tools may function as a bridge between technical literacy and pedagogical reasoning. Rather than positioning AI as an external resource to be adopted, the design-based approach invites future teachers to confront ethical, curricular, and inclusivity questions at the moment of technological creation. In this way, chatbot design becomes not only a digital competence exercise, but a site of "transformed practice" in which teachers actively redesign educational possibilities within AI-mediated environments. This conceptual reframing represents one of the chapter's central contributions to current debates on AI in teacher education.

Despite these findings, certain limitations must be acknowledged. The study is based on a relatively small and context-specific sample (27 students enrolled in a particular ICT specialisation within one university), which limits the possibility of broad generalisation. The results should therefore be interpreted as exploratory and indicative rather than representative of all teacher education contexts. At the same time, the detailed description of the intervention design and institutional setting allows for analytical transferability, enabling other teacher education programmes with comparable profiles to assess the potential applicability of similar practice-based AI training experiences.

REFERENCES

Ananiadou, K., & Claro, M. (2009), "21st Century Skills and Competences for New Millennium Learners in OECD Countries", *OECD Education Working Papers*, No. 41, OECD Publishing, Paris, https://doi.org/DOI: 10.1787/19939019

Bartolomé, A. (2023). [Prólogo]. En Fernández-Ferrer, M. (Ed.). (2023). *Chatbots en educación. Tendencias actuales y desafíos futuros* (pp.9-13). LMI.

Belda-Medina, J., & Calvo-Ferrer, J. R. (2022). Using chatbots as AI conversational partners in language learning. *Applied Sciences (Basel, Switzerland)*, *12*(17), 8427. DOI: 10.3390/app12178427

Cope, B., & Kalantzis, M. (Eds.). (2000). *Multiliteracies: Literacy Learning and the Design of Social Futures*. Routledge.

Cope, B., & Kalantzis, M. (2009). Multiliteracies: New Literacies, New Learning. *Pedagogies*, *4*(3), 164–195. DOI: 10.1080/15544800903076044

Despujol Zabala, I. (2024). ChatGPT Hacer chatbots con POE.COM | 16/37 | UPV Universitat Politècnica de València [Vídeo]. YouTube: https://www.youtube.com/watch?v=DB2b5mgH6CE

Dokukina, I., & Gumanova, J. (2020). The rise of chatbots–new personal assistants in foreign language learning. *Procedia Computer Science*, *169*, 542–546. DOI: 10.1016/j.procs.2020.02.212

Fernández-Ferrer, M. (Ed.). (2023). *Chatbots en educación. Tendencias actuales y desafíos futuros*. LMI.

García-López, C., Tabuenca-Cuevas, M., & Navarro-Soria, I. (2025). A systematic review of the use of AI in EFL and EL classrooms for gifted students. *Trends in Higher Education*, *4*(3), 33. DOI: 10.3390/higheredu4030033

Gu, W., & Yu, Z. (2025). A bibliometric analysis of the application of AI chatbots in language learning contexts. *Quality & Quantity*, *59*(1), 639–661. DOI: 10.1007/s11135-024-01946-2

Guo, K., Li, Y., Li, Y., & Chu, S. K. W. (2024). Understanding EFL students' use of self-made AI chatbots as personalized writing assistance tools: A mixed methods study. *Education and Information Technologies*, *29*, 1–20. DOI: 10.1007/s10639-023-12230-5

Haristiani, N. (2019). Artificial Intelligence (AI) chatbot as language learning medium: An inquiry. *Journal of Physics: Conference Series, 1387*(1), 012020. DOI: 10.1088/1742-6596/1387/1/012020

Huesca, G., Martínez-Treviño, Y., Molina-Espinosa, J. M., Sanromán-Calleros, A. R., Martínez-Román, R., Cendejas-Castro, E. A., & Bustos, R. (2024). Effectiveness of using ChatGPT as a tool to strengthen benefits of the flipped learning strategy. *Education Sciences, 14*(6), 660. DOI: 10.3390/educsci14060660

Lee, J. H., Shin, D., & Hwang, Y. (2024). Investigating the capabilities of large language model-based task-oriented dialogue chatbots from a learner's perspective. *System, 127*, 1–12. DOI: 10.1016/j.system.2024.103538

Martins, L. (2023). Una introducción a los *chatbots* y sus aplicaciones en educación. En Fernández-Ferrer, M. (Ed.). (2023). *Chatbots en educación. Tendencias actuales y desafíos futuros* (pp.15-37). LMI.

Mazzilli, F. (2021). Chatbots for action-oriented language learning. Using Elbot to enhance conflict-solving skills in learners of German as a foreign language. *EL.LE, 10*(1), 95–116.

New London Group. (1996). A Pedagogy of Multiliteracies: Designing Social Futures. *Harvard Educational Review, 66*(1), 60–92. DOI: 10.17763/haer.66.1.17370n67v-22j160u

Ng, D., Leung, J., Chu, S., & Qiao, M. (2021). Conceptualizing AI literacy: An exploratory review. *Computers & Education, 2*, 1–11.

Nouzri, S., & Arisaka, R.. (2025). In Arisaka, R. (Eds.), *PRIMA 2024: Lecture Notes in Artificial Intelligence 15395* (pp. 385–401). Springer Nature Switzerland AG. [Beyond chatbots]

Paredes, C., & Martínez, A. (2023). Los chatbots en educación secundaria: retos y propuestas para su aplicación en el aula. En Fernández-Ferrer, M. (Ed.). (2023). *Chatbots en educación. Tendencias actuales y desafíos futuros* (pp.39-65). LMI.

Polakova, P., & Klimova, B. (2024). Implementation of AI-driven technology into education – a pilot study on the use of chatbots in foreign language learning. *Cogent Education, 11*(1), 1–15. DOI: 10.1080/2331186X.2024.2355385

Siegle, D. (2024). Using AI Prompt Engineering to Improve Gifted Students' Questioning. *Gifted Child Today, 48*(1), 68–72. DOI: 10.1177/10762175241289886

Tutton, M., & Cohen, D. (2025). Reconceptualizing the role of the university language teacher in light of generative AI. *Education Sciences*, *15*(1), 56. DOI: 10.3390/educsci15010056

UNESCO. (2017). *E2030: education and skills for the 21st century.* https://unesdoc.unesco.org/ark:/48223/pf0000250117_eng

Vanjani, M., Aiken, M., & Park, M. (2020). Using a multilingual chatbot for foreign language practice. *Issues in Information Systems*, *21*(2), 85–92. DOI: 10.48009/2_iis_2020_85-92

Wang, Y. F., Hsu, M. H., Wang, M. Y. F., & Chang, Y. T. (2025). Enhancing phonetic accuracy through chatbot-assisted language learning. *Educational Technology Research and Development*, *73*(3), 1723–1739. DOI: 10.1007/s11423-025-10466-1

Wiboolyasarin, W., Wiboolyasarin, K., Tiranant, P., Jinowat, N., & Boonyakitanont, P. (2025). AI-driven chatbots in second language education: A systematic review of their efficacy and pedagogical implications. *Ampersand (Oxford, UK)*, *14*, 100224. DOI: 10.1016/j.amper.2025.100224

Yang, H., Kim, H., Lee, J., & Shin, D. (2022). Implementation of an AI chatbot as an English conversation partner in EFL speaking classes. *ReCALL*, *34*(3), 327–343. DOI: 10.1017/S0958344022000039

Zaim, M., Arsyad, S., Waluyo, B., Ardi, H., Al Hafizh, M., Zakiyah, M., Syafitri, W., Nusi, A., & Hardiah, M. (2025). Generative AI as a cognitive co-pilot in English language learning in higher education. *Education Sciences*, *15*(6), 686. DOI: 10.3390/educsci15060686

KEY TERMS AND DEFINITIONS

Collaborative Writing: A learning process in which multiple individuals jointly produce, edit, and refine written texts, often using digital tools to support interaction and shared authorship.

Digital Literacy: The ability to effectively and critically use digital technologies to locate, evaluate, create, and communicate information in various contexts.

Educational Technology: The use of digital tools, platforms, and systems to enhance teaching, learning, and assessment processes across educational settings.

Multiliteracies: A pedagogical approach that emphasizes diverse forms of literacy, including linguistic, visual, audio, and digital modes of meaning-making in a globalized and technologically mediated world.

Multimodality: The integration of multiple modes of communication, such as text, images, audio, and video, to create and interpret meaning.

Natural Language Processing: A field of artificial intelligence focused on enabling computers to understand, interpret, and generate human language.

New London Group: A collective of scholars who introduced the concept of Multiliteracies, highlighting the need for expanded literacy practices in response to cultural and technological changes.

Primary Education: The initial stage of formal schooling that focuses on foundational skills in literacy, numeracy, and social development, typically for young learners.

Second Language Learning: The process of acquiring a language other than one's first language, often in educational settings where the target language is not the primary language of communication.

Teacher Education: The formal preparation and ongoing professional development of educators to equip them with the knowledge, skills, and competencies required for effective teaching.

Chapter 6

Revisiting EFL Communicative Competence in the Age of AI Tutoring:

A Qualitative Study of Teacher Perspectives in Saudi Higher Education

Mohd Nazim
http://orcid.org/0000-0003-1802-6412
Najran University, Saudi Arabia

Abdulaziz Alshahrani
http://orcid.org/0009-0008-6600-6583
Najran University, Saudi Arabia

ABSTRACT

Despite the available research on the integration of AI-mediated tools, particularly intelligent tutoring systems, empirical evidence of their effectiveness remains scarce, particularly in Saudi higher education. This qualitative study collected data from EFL teachers (N=60) using semi-structured interviews. Data analysis was conducted to capture teachers' insights into interactional dynamics and the challenges associated with integrating AI tutors into language teaching environments. The findings suggest that student–teacher interaction is moving toward facilitative roles, with reduced student–student interaction, and that student–AI interaction offers enhanced practice opportunities and concerns related to overreliance and data privacy. Challenges

DOI: 10.4018/979-8-3373-6420-9.ch006

include content misalignment, limited cultural relevance, uneven AI literacy, and insufficient professional development. Moreover, participants proposed task-based AI integration, balanced human–AI instructional roles, contextualized content adaptation, and targeted AI-focused professional development. Future research should examine the long-term effects of AI tutoring on the development and sustainability of communicative competence among EFL learners.

INTRODUCTION

English as a Foreign Language (EFL) has long been a significant area of research within Saudi higher education (Al-Seghayer, 2015; Moskovsky, 2018). Jenkins (2022) observes that the country's rapidly developing progressions have driven substantial advancement in the EFL teaching and learning over recent decades. Scholars, for instance, AbdAlgane and Elmahdi (2024) have examined a wide range of practices related to EFL teaching and learning, including curriculum design, learner motivation, teacher preparedness, and assessment practices. This interest reflects the central role of English language in academic advancement, making the EFL context in Saudi higher education a continually evolving and rich field for research (Jenkins, 2022). This development is closely tied to evolving contextual factors, particularly the expanding integration of technology in language learning environments (Al Fraidan & Alaliwi, 2024; Alzubi et al., 2025). In recent years, studies have highlighted that the technological blend has taken new dimensions with the rise of digital tools, particularly artificial intelligence (AI), offering EFL stakeholders across diverse settings fresh opportunities to reimagine language teaching and learning (Ouyang et al., 2022). Moreover, Balla (2025), and Dekhakhena (2025) maintain that the technological innovations have helped enhance access to resources, personalized learning, and greater learner autonomy. However, despite the promising situation, research indicates that many teachers and students continue to face persistent challenges (Benek, 2025; Omidvar & Meihami, 2025). These include limited exposure to authentic English use, reliance on traditional pedagogical methods, insufficient digital literacy, and cultural factors that may constrain the adoption of innovative practices. Such complexities underscore the need for context-sensitive approaches that support both educators and learners as they navigate the shifting landscape of EFL education in the age of AI (Al-khresheh, 2024; Alanazi, 2025; Basaula, 2025). Moreover, beyond the integration of technology and AI in EFL teaching and learning in diverse contexts, the emergence of AI-mediated tutoring systems has begun to transform English teaching and learning environments across the globe (Adelana & Akinyemi, 2022; Kundu & Bej, 2025; Wang, 2025; Wei, 2023). It is worth noting that AI-mediated tutoring systems, such as Andy English Bot, Replika, Talkpal AI,

Gemini, ChatGPT, Langua (LanguaTalk), Speak, Praktika, Giglish, Duolingo Max, Memrise, ELSA Speak, etc. are publicly available under various labels, including AI tutor, AI bot, chatbot, conversational agent, and GenAI tutor (Belda-Medina & Calvo-Ferrer, 2022; Fathi et al., 2024; Katsarou et al., 2023; Mageira et al., 2022; Wang & Zou, 2025). However, for the purposes of this chapter, the term *AI tutor* is used as an umbrella construct referring to AI-powered conversational systems which support EFL learners' communicative competence through interactive dialogue, feedback, or guided practice. Although these systems, according to Fathi et al. (2025), are labeled as AI-enhanced language-learning tools that use natural language processing and machine learning to personalize instruction across skills, including AI Chatbots, which simulate human-like interaction for conversation practice, grammar and spelling checks, and personalized feedback; Virtual Assistants, which provide interactive support for pronunciation, vocabulary, and comprehension; Language Learning Analytics, which collect and analyze learner data to generate tailored recommendations; Adaptive Learning Systems, which adjust content difficulty and pacing based on individual progress; and Speech Recognition Technology, which analyzes spoken language to offer feedback on pronunciation, fluency, and accuracy, this chapter treats these terms as functionally equivalent, as all are capable of generating language-based interaction in instructional settings. Moreover, scholars, for instance, (Du (2025), Kot and Nykyporets (2024), and Urbaite (2025) argue that these intelligent systems (or AI tutors, for the current study), ranging from adaptive learning platforms to conversational agents and automated feedback tools, have introduced new possibilities for enhancing students' linguistic proficiency in general and their communicative competence in particular. Furthermore, studies (Dekhakhena, 2025; Jegede, 2024; Wei, 2023) claim that AI tutoring, by offering personalized instruction, immediate feedback, and opportunities for authentic language use, has redefined how learners engage with English both inside and outside the classroom. Keeping this rapid shift in view, EFL stakeholders have started to re-examine the nature, components, and developmental pathways of English education, including communicative competence in the age of AI-supported EFL teaching and learning (Wang, 2025). Therefore, this chapter, in agreement with researchers (Qi & Chen, 2025; Salokhojaeva, 2025) who examined how traditional models of communicative competence align with AI-mediated interaction, what new competencies teachers and learners may need, and how teachers can effectively integrate these tools while maintaining pedagogical considerations, intends to contribute to this growing body of literature, and revisits EFL learners' communicative competence within the Saudi higher education context, focusing on the interactional dynamics and integration challenges. Furthermore, this chapter underscores the centrality of communicative competence in EFL instruction, as evidenced in the existing literature (AlShareef, 2024; Dara et al., 2024, Nafisah et al., 2024; Zhou & Li, 2025; Zhou et al., 2024).

Additionally, this study centers on the importance of communicative competence within the rapidly evolving realities of AI-mediated teaching and learning. It emphasizes how AI tutors are reshaping the ways learners interact, negotiate meaning, and construct communicative competence (Busso & Sanchez, 2024; Liu et al., 2025; Salokhojaeva, 2025; Xu et al., 2025). By examining these shifts, this chapter aims to address key gaps in the Saudi higher education literature by investigating how AI-mediated tutoring systems support the development of EFL students' communicative competence, as well as by eliciting faculty responses on the interactional dynamics and integration challenges that emerge when AI tutoring is incorporated into EFL classrooms. By bringing these strands together, this chapter aims to:

1) investigate EFL teachers' perceptions of interactional dynamics and integration challenges
2) explore teacher-proposed solutions for effective AI tutor integration

LITERATURE REVIEW

1. Theoretical Frameworks

This chapter is grounded in Canale and Swain's (1980) model of *communicative competence*, which comprises four interrelated sub-competencies: *grammatical, socio-linguistic, discourse*, and *strategic competence*. In addition, building on Dell Hymes's (1966, 1972) original concept of *communicative competence* (developed in response to Chomsky's (1965) distinction between *linguistic competence* and *performance)*, the chapter describes that communicative competence is not something a learner possesses a 'static' entity, but a capacity which is developed through interaction and depends on the situation in which communication takes place. Furthermore, this study is aligned with the Technology-Enhanced Language Learning (TELL) approach, which serves as an interactional ecology which mediates how learners engage with language, feedback, and interlocutors. By integrating computer-assisted language learning (CALL), mobile-assisted language learning (MALL), virtual reality (VR), augmented reality (AR), and artificial intelligence (AI), this chapter reiterates that TELL facilitates and transforms language learning by providing immersive and personalized experiences through foundational digital tools for structured practice, enabling on-the-go learning via mobile apps, immersing learners in simulated environments for realistic conversation practice, incorporating digital information into the real world for contextual vocabulary development, and personalizing lessons with instant feedback, collectively shifting language learning from passive drills to active and engaging interactions (Santhi, 2024). By incorporating TELL principles, this chapter highlights that AI tutor features can selectively strengthen or limit specific aspects of communicative competence, rather than improving communicative ability evenly across all components. Moreover, from an applied-linguistics perspective, this framework aligns with interactionist approaches to second language acquisition, which emphasizes that communicative competence develops through negotiated interaction, feedback, and repair, as well as with sociomaterial perspectives that view technologies such as AI tutors as active mediators of communicative practice rather than neutral instructional tools. Overall, these theoretical perspectives form the conceptual framework guiding this study. They provide the analytic lens through which the interview data are interpreted, particularly in examining how AI tutors mediate interaction, shape the development of communicative competence, and reshape the roles of teachers and learners. This framework clarifies the assumptions underpinning the analysis and ensures that the findings are grounded in established applied linguistics while reviewing the emerging trends of human–AI interaction.

2. AI in Language Education

In recent years, researchers have investigated a variety of scenarios, variables, circumstances, and environments to examine AI's role in language teaching and learning. For instance, Huang et al., (2023) investigates emerging trends, research issues, and applications of AI in language education. Additionally, Ji et al., (2023), through a systematic review of conversational AI in language education, focused on the collaboration with human teachers. Similarly, Pack and Maloney (2023), investigated the incorporation of AI in foreign language education with special reference to ChatGPT's effect on foreign language learners. Likewise, Creely (2024) explored the role of generative AI in enhancing language learning, focusing on the opportunities and challenges of the application of emerging technologies in language pedagogy.

3. AI Tutors and Language Learning

Scholars define AI tutors as systems that imitate human cognitive processes by incorporating capabilities such as learning, reasoning, problem-solving, natural language understanding, and perception (Khine, 2024; Liu et al., 2025). Furthermore, scholarly evidence indicates that AI-based tutoring systems can be effective in language teaching and learning; however, the literature also highlights several limitations that vary across instructional contexts, learner characteristics, and situational variables (Akhter, 2025; Basri, 2024; Lin et al., 2023; Sangkala & Mardonovna, 2024).

4. AI Tutors and Communicative Competence

a. Grammatical and Strategic Competence

AI tutors, as studies suggest (Basri, 2024; Liu et al., 2025; Wang et al., 2024), strongly support grammatical accuracy and strategic competence through instant corrective feedback, adaptive prompts, and repeated practice opportunities. Learners benefit by doing self-initiate repairs and using compensatory strategies without fear of negative evaluation. These affordances are particularly effective for developing self-regulation and metacognitive strategy use (Liu et al., 2025).

b. Sociolinguistic and Discourse Competence

Despite positive findings related to fluency and affect, the existing literature (Nishida & Fujimoto, 2025; Busso & Sanchez, 2024) offers limited empirical evidence regarding the development of sociolinguistic and discourse competence. While AI tutors simulate conversational exchanges, concerns regarding authenticity, pragmatic appropriateness, and contextual sensitivity are repeatedly observed. These limitations raise concerns about whether AI-mediated interaction adequately exposes learners to sociocultural norms, turn-taking conventions, and discourse sequencing characteristic of real-world communication. Moreover, from a conversation-analytic and L2 pragmatic perspective, these concerns reflect an ongoing controversy regarding whether AI-mediated dialogue can approximate the sequential organization, turn-taking practices, repair mechanisms, and culturally situated meanings characteristic of authentic human interaction.

c. Affective Gains and Limitations

Numerous studies (Busso & Sanchez, 2024; Nishida & Fujimoto, 2025; Wang et al., 2024) highlight affective and interactional outcomes, such as reduced speaking anxiety, increased confidence, and greater willingness to communicate, when learners interact with AI tutors or conversational agents. These findings suggest that AI tutors assist in reshaping the emotional conditions under which communicative competence is enacted, even when speaking performance gains remain limited. Moreover, while these affective benefits are well documented, scholars (Wang et al., 2024; Zhang et al., 2024; Hayashi & Sato, 2024; Wang & Zou, 2025; Yu, 2025) caution that reduced anxiety in AI-mediated interaction does not necessarily translate into enhanced interactional competence, particularly when opportunities for spontaneous peer negotiation and socially embedded communication are limited.

d. Risks and Constraints

The literature (Basri, 2024; Busso & Sanchez, 2024), in addition to reported benefits, consistently highlights risks related to overreliance on AI, ethical concerns, data privacy, and the marginalization of human interaction. These concerns suggest that AI tutors are helpful, but their strengths and limitations shape communicative competence in selective ways; they improve some components more than others. Moreover, these concerns extend beyond overreliance and ethics to include issues of epistemic trust, authority over linguistic knowledge, assessment validity, bias in AI-generated feedback, and data privacy, raising critical questions about who controls knowledge, feedback, and evaluative norms in AI-mediated communicative environments.

5. Conceptual Mapping of AI Tutor Effects on Communicative Competence Components

Table 1. AI Tutor and Communicative Competence Components

AI Tutor Affordance	Interactional Change	Affected Component	Reported	
			Benefits	Risks
adaptive feedback	immediate repair & repetition	grammatical / Strategic	accuracy, self-regulated learning, retention	overreliance
anxiety-free interaction	reduced affective filter	strategic / fluency	confidence, willingness to communicate	limited practicality
simulated dialogue	controlled conversational practice	discourse (partial)	fluency gains	authenticity concerns
personalization	learner-paced interaction	strategic / metacognitive	autonomy	reduced peer interaction
24/7 availability	increased exposure	grammatical	practice frequency	trust issues

Table 1 demonstrates that AI tutors influence different components of communicative competence in *different* ways. Each AI affordance brings specific benefits: improved accuracy, confidence, fluency, autonomy, and practice frequency. However, each carries risks, such as overreliance on corrective feedback, limited real-world applicability, reduced authenticity, decreased peer interaction, and trust concerns. Overall, the reviewed literature suggests that AI tutors do not uniformly enhance communicative competence but rather reshape its development by selectively developing certain components while constraining others. Within the theoretical grounding of this chapter, AI tutors appear most effective in supporting grammatical accuracy, strategic competence, and willingness to communicate, while offering limited support for sociolinguistic and discourse competence. This disparity underscores the need to position AI tutors not as replacements for human interaction, but as interactional supplements whose pedagogical value depends on deliberate integration, ethical safeguards, and complementary human-mediated communication. Moreover, these patterns indicate that when AI tutor-led interaction starts, communicative competence shifts from a socially-mediated human process to a blended human–AI environment, changing how learners negotiate meaning, receive feedback, and engage in authentic discourse. Despite the fact that the existing literature offers insights into AI tutor integration for enhancing EFL students' communicative competence, gaps remain concerning its interactional dynamics and integration challenges within Saudi higher education. This study, therefore, revisits EFL learners' communicative competence in the age of AI tutoring and seeks to answer the following research questions:

1) What are EFL teachers' views on the interactional dynamics and integration challenges associated with the use of AI tutors in developing students' communicative competence?
2) What solutions do EFL teachers propose to address the interactional and integration challenges associated with the use of AI tutors in developing students' communicative competence?

METHODOLOGY

1. Research Design

This study employed a qualitative research design to revisit EFL learners' communicative competence in the age of AI tutoring with special reference to interactional dynamics and integration challenges in Saudi higher education. By utilizing semi-structured interviews and thematic analysis, the study attempts to find out AI tutors' interactional dynamics and integration challenges that the teachers observe within the Saudi higher education context.

2. Participants

This study engaged EFL teachers from four universities across Saudi higher education institutions, covering the northern, eastern, western, and southern regions. The final sample consisted of 60 faculty members after excluding 20 incomplete or irrelevant viewpoints from the initial 80 participants who agreed to participate. The study sample included EFL faculty members of diverse nationalities, including but not limited to Saudi, Australian, American, Algerian, Indian, British, Bangladeshi, and other countries. Participants held various academic qualifications in the English language, with specializations ranging from applied linguistics to computational linguistics, including both master's and PhD degrees. Additionally, some participants earned certifications in specialized areas, including educational technology and AI integration in EFL education. Their years of experience in AI tutor integration ranged from 1 to 3 years.

3. Sampling

Moreover, purposive sampling was employed to ensure that participants met specific criteria aligned with the study objectives. Eligible participants were required to be working as EFL faculty members in a Saudi higher education institution, hold a degree in EFL education, preferably with a specialization in educational technology integration, have at least one year of experience integrating AI tutors, and have prior exposure to using technology in their instructional practices, particularly in communicative competence tasks. The exclusion criteria included having no experience with AI tutor integration or providing incomplete or irrelevant viewpoints.

4. Ethical Considerations

Participation was voluntary, and no incentives were provided to avoid potential bias. Additionally, the study adhered to ethical guidelines to protect participants' rights and confidentiality. Approval was obtained from the Ethical Approval Committee at the Deanship of Graduate Studies and Scientific Research, Najran University, under the code [202409-076-023414 - 052468]. The key ethical measures included informed consent, confidentiality, voluntary participation, and data security. For the informed consent, participants were requested to acknowledge their informed consent before participating in the interview. Also, to maintain confidentiality, the data was anonymized by assigning unique ID numbers to participants. Identifiable information, such as names, affiliations, and contact details, was securely stored in password-protected databases accessible only to the researchers. Additionally, all participants were informed of their right to withdraw at any stage without providing justification. Finally, to ensure security, the data was securely stored, and documentation of the informed consent process was maintained for future reference, ensuring transparency and adherence to ethical standards. Moreover, beyond individual consent and confidentiality, the study adhered to institutional data-governance requirements for research involving educational technologies. Data were collected solely for research purposes and were not linked to institutional evaluation, and all procedures complied with institutional research policies and ethical standards governing higher-education research.

5. Instrument

Semi-structured interviews were conducted with sixty participants who were selected based on their willingness to share their experiences and insights regarding the interactional dynamics and integration challenges of using AI tutors in EFL classrooms, particularly in relation to students' communicative competence. Participants were asked to discuss the challenges they encounter when using publicly available AI tutors for instructional purposes and to propose solutions, without referring to any specific tool. It was ensured that the AI tutors they described were those accessible to them and actually employed in their instruction. Rather than examining a single AI tutor, the study focused on teachers' broader pedagogical experiences with AI-mediated interaction, reflecting the diverse and decentralized nature of AI tutor integration across Saudi higher education institutions. The interviews were conducted by the researchers in the building of the college of languages and translation and the preparatory year for the locals as well as using Blackboard and Zoom (*official platforms used by institutions for general notifications, communication, and online presentations or seminars for both students and faculty*) for those who participated from other regions, and audio recordings were made with participants' permission. The interview questions and prompts were shared one week prior to the scheduled interview date to allow participants sufficient time to prepare and become familiar with the thematic focus of the semi-structured interview. The interview duration was approximately 15 to 20 minutes, which allowed for thorough coverage of all questions and prompts.

6. Validity

The face and content validity of the semi-structured interview were established through expert review. A panel of five experts in applied linguistics, EFL pedagogy, and educational technology reviewed the interview questions and prompts. The experts evaluated the alignment of the interview content with the study's research questions and objectives, ensuring that the prompts adequately addressed the intended constructs. In addition, the experts examined the clarity, appropriateness, and relevance of the wording of the questions, as well as the linguistic and grammatical accuracy of the interview content. They also assessed the suitability of the interview prompts within the context of EFL teachers' integration of AI tutors in communicative competence-oriented instruction. Based on the experts' feedback, the interview questions were modified to enhance clarity, relevance, and contextual appropriateness. Moreover, the semi-structured interview protocol consisted of two broad, open-ended research questions addressing interactional dynamics and integration challenges, along with proposed solutions. Each research question included a main theme and several sub-themes, as illustrated below.

RQ1: What are EFL teachers' views on the interactional dynamics and integration challenges associated with the use of AI tutors in developing students' communicative competence?

i. interactional dynamics

- *student–teacher interaction*
- *student– student interaction*
- *student–AI tutor interaction*

ii. integration challenges

- *content related challenges*
- *AI-literacy and internet related challenges*
- *professional development related challenges*

RQ2: What solutions do EFL teachers propose to address the interactional and integration challenges associated with the use of AI tutors in developing students' communicative competence?

i. *task-based AI integration*
ii. *human-AI instructional balance*
iii. *cultural and contextual adaptation*
iv. *AI-focused professional development*

7. Data Analysis

The data was analyzed following Braun and Clarke's (2006) thematic analysis to detect patterns and structure the results. The process began with the interview transcriptions, and researchers familiarized themselves with the data by repeatedly reading the transcripts, taking initial notes, and highlighting key insights. A coding procedure was then implemented, assigning each participant a distinct code (e.g., T1, T2, T3, T4, T5, etc.) to ensure clarity, order, and convenience during analysis. The codes were grouped into themes reflecting key aspects of participants' experiences integrating AI tutors into their communicative competence instruction. The themes were reviewed, clearly defined, described, and illustrated with relevant examples to ensure they accurately represented the data, and the findings were contextualized in relation to the study objectives. Thematic development proceeded in an iterative manner, with codes continually revisited and compared across transcripts to refine and strengthen emerging patterns. As the analysis progressed, recurring patterns became increasingly stable, and no substantially new themes emerged in the later stages of coding, indicating thematic saturation. The final thematic structure was retained based on coherence, recurrence, and relevance to the study objectives.

RESULTS

EFL teachers' views on the interactional dynamics and integration challenges

i. interactional dynamics

a. student–teacher interaction

A majority of participants (n=43; 71%) reported a significant shift in student-teacher interaction dynamics due to the integration of AI tutors. Participants highlighted that AI tutoring has greatly influenced student–teacher interactions by redefining the mediation process. While AI tutors enhance accessibility and individualized practice, they also shift the strategic dimension of interaction management away from teachers to autonomous learner-AI interactions. This situation positions teachers more as facilitators within the *emerging shift*, emphasizing strategic competence through guiding learners to become effective communicators. Some selected excerpts are mentioned below:

- T10: "As I observe, student–teacher interaction has decreased. Students used to ask questions about grammar, pronunciation, and appropriate phrases, but now they check or interact with the AI tutor instead."
- T49: "In my opinion, limited learner–teacher interaction has become the new normal in today's AI age, as these dynamic positions teachers as a facilitator rather than the sole source of language instruction."

b. student– student interaction

A substantial percentage of faculty (n=38; 63%) expressed concern that AI integration in communicative competence environments is diminishing student–student interaction, which is crucial for developing discourse competence, including collaborative dialogue and peer negotiation. These reflections suggest that while AI tutors offer quick and personalized assistance, they risk undermining essential interpersonal aspects of language learning. The reduced peer interaction impairs students' ability to negotiate meaning, practice discourse strategies, and develop communicative competence collaboratively, which are vital components of communicative competence. Some selected excerpts are mentioned below:

- T11: "In my view, limited or NO student–student interaction is a dangerous trend and may become a threat to peer or collaborative language learning."

This decline does not simply represent a loss of interaction, but a reshape of interactional authority and repair norms, which becomes more visible in student–AI tutor exchanges.

c. student–AI tutor interaction

Most participants (n=49; 81%) shared a complex situation of student-AI tutor interaction in developing communicative competence, highlighting both opportunities and challenges in managing human–AI interaction, particularly concerning grammatical and discourse competence. Participants viewed that students tend to interact with AI tutors during communicative tasks by receiving immediate feedback and real-time practice opportunities, which support students to enhance their grammatical and discourse development. Teachers, however, observed that their engagement may be influenced by a 'false assumption' of AI as 'authority' and there are' legitimate' concerns of privacy, which may further limit students' further exploration of language learning opportunities. Participants further maintained that there is no doubt that the unlimited accessibility of AI tutors promotes the development of communicative competence. However, the effective human–AI engagement in language learning depends on balancing structured practice with opportunities for autonomous exploration, ensuring that students remain motivated and critically engaged while benefiting from AI's supportive features. Some selected excerpts are mentioned below:

- T5: "Although I respect my students' autonomy in language learning and their need for immediate feedback to resolve language-related problems, especially outside classroom settings, overdependence on AI may reduce their critical thinking and productivity."
- T23: "Another issue in student–AI interaction is that students may view the AI tutor as an 'authority,' which limits their further exploration of language use. In addition, privacy and data security are important concerns, as there

is always a possibility that students' personal data may be shared with third parties without their consent."

- T41: "The great thing, in my opinion, is that the AI tutor is available 24/7, and students who need support can interact with it anytime and anywhere. Most platforms or apps are also free of cost, especially the basic versions."

Moreover, teachers' views suggest that AI tutors act not merely as tools but as quasi-interactional participants in learners' communicative practices. Students' tendencies to treat AI-produced responses as authoritative reshape turn-taking norms, feedback, and repair behavior, limiting opportunities for negotiation of meaning and pragmatic experimentation. These outcomes indicate that student–AI interaction creates a distinct interactional ecology that requires pedagogical mediation to ensure that communicative competence development remains dialogic, critical, and socially grounded.

ii. integration challenges

a. content related challenges

A majority of participants (n=44; 73%) reported several content-related challenges, particularly concerning curriculum alignment with special reference to grammatical/discourse competence. The participants claimed that the challenges reflect significant content-related hurdles in integrating AI tutors effectively. The mismatch, as some participants observed, with curriculum content and objectives hampers grammatical and discourse development by providing students with materials that do not always reinforce the targeted language structures or discourse practices. Furthermore, issues of authenticity and cultural context are critical, as they affect the learners' engagement with authentic language use, an essential component in discourse competence. Some selected excerpts are mentioned below:

- T8: "It has been more than two years since I integrated an AI tutor into my oral communication classroom, but I still find it difficult to align the AI tutor's activities with the topics that must be covered as part of the assigned syllabus."
- T55: "Authenticity, as I understand it, is a major issue. AI tutors generally do not offer authentic materials, and the content is often culturally inappropriate, particularly in the context of Saudi higher education."

Moreover, the content misalignment exposes learners to unreliable feedback, inappropriate pragmatic norms, and hidden ideological biases that can harm their communicative development. Furthermore, it can also result in limiting equitable access to culturally relevant language models, elevating these issues from pedagogical concerns to broader institutional risks.

b. AI-literacy and internet-related challenges

A majority of participants (n=45; 75%) identified AI literacy and internet access issues within the context of communicative competence environments integrating AI tutors. These themes, according to faculty members' views, underscore that both AI literacy and internet access are crucial for effective communicative competence development in AI-supported language learning instruction. Some participants asserted that limited internet access and device compatibility create access inequalities, preventing fair participation and disrupting the coherence of communicative tasks. They observed that internet disruptions lead to sudden interaction breakdowns, impairing strategic competence, the ability to adapt, and sustain communication despite technical hurdles. Participants argued that technological inequalities and literacy gaps hinder the smooth flow of classroom interaction, restrict students' ability to engage confidently with AI tutors, and challenge teachers' capacity to foster ongoing communicative development. Some selected excerpts are mentioned below:

- T18: "I think teachers themselves have not received enough exposure to effectively integrate AI tutors into EFL instruction. They may have basic technological knowledge, but handling an AI tutor in a classroom where communicative competence is the goal remains challenging due to limited AI-related knowledge, skills, and confidence."
- T53: "I understand that the internet is a blessing today, but when it is interrupted, it becomes a major problem. During a communicative task that integrates an AI tutor, if the internet suddenly breaks down in the middle of the activity, students are left with nothing to continue."

c. professional development-related challenges

Most faculty (n=49; 81%) reported challenges related to professional development and pedagogical readiness in integrating AI tutors into communicative competence pedagogy. The participants claimed that teachers face professional development challenges related to pedagogical readiness in integrating AI tools, particularly conversational chatbots and tutors. The fundamental issues, according to some teachers, include insufficient training in pedagogical strategies for AI-enhanced communication, limited technical and practical skills, and a conservative approach that restricts pedagogical innovation. The thematic analysis revealed that addressing these challenges requires targeted professional development initiatives to enhance teachers' pedagogical skills in handling grammatical, discourse, strategic, and sociolinguistic competencies, as well as enabling them to design, implement, and assess AI-mediated communicative activities aligned with curriculum goals. Some selected excerpts are mentioned below:

- T1: "I assume there is no specific mechanism for enhancing teachers' AI-integration capabilities through proper professional development initiatives. I personally integrate an AI tutor in my oral communication class, but whenever I face a problem due to an update or a new version of the app, I resort to a trial-and-error approach, which limits the pedagogical use of the AI tutor and disrupts the instructional environment."
- T2: "In the absence of any formal training, I think many instructors, including myself, do not feel comfortable assessing communicative tasks that are either AI-assisted or generated by AI tutors."

Overall, participants' views indicate that adopting AI tutors is not a neutral technological advancement but a rebuilding of communicative environments, pedagogical authority, and interactional norms. Participants, implicitly though, noted that they lack the skills to verify AI-generated feedback or content, creating uncertainty about the accuracy and pedagogical appropriateness of AI responses. This uncertainty is compounded by unclear responsibility for AI-induced errors, leaving teachers accountable for outcomes they cannot fully control. Additionally, the need to constantly monitor, correct, and mediate AI output creates an invisible workload that further underscores professional development as a systemic requirement rather than an optional enhancement.

Solutions to address the interactional and integration challenges

i. task-based AI integration

Participants (n=40; 66%) highlighted that AI tutors should serve as supportive interlocutors rather than task creators, providing authentic, interest-driven prompts and scenarios that foster meaningful competence. Additionally, participants advocated pre-task practice through flipped learning strategies to strengthen students' ability to engage effectively in real-time interactions. Some participants underscored the need for AI-assisted activities to be systematically aligned with input, interaction, output, and reflection components of task-based language teaching. Participants suggested ways in which AI tutors can be better integrated into communicative tasks and how their role can be supportive and facilitative, providing authentic and contextually relevant practice opportunities. They maintained that, to enhance discourse competence, AI tutors need to be integrated thoughtfully within a structured framework that promotes meaningful interaction, reflection, and real-life language use. According to some participants, this approach may ensure that AI-driven activities contribute effectively to developing learners' ability to communicate confidently and appropriately in real-world contexts. Some selected excerpts are mentioned here:

- T13: "We need to design tasks that are appropriate for developing EFL students' communicative competence, in which the AI tutor acts as a supportive interlocutor rather than the task itself. This approach can help address integration issues."
- T29: "Teachers can ask students to rehearse task-related language with the AI tutor before classroom interaction. For instance, flipped learning strategies can be used to allow students to practice in advance before engaging in real-time interaction with the AI tutor."
- T60: "AI tutor activities need to be aligned with task-based language teaching principles, including input, interaction, output, and reflection. Without such alignment, the integration of AI tutors and students' interaction with them is unlikely to yield meaningful benefits."

ii. human-AI instructional balance

A majority of participants (n=50; 83%) indicated that teachers should take responsibility for guiding and monitoring the use of AI tutors to address integration challenges. Participants advocated balancing pedagogical authority, positioning AI as a supplementary tool that requires careful integration to ensure effective learning. Some participants underscored the importance of using AI for routine practice, allowing teachers to focus on more complex, human-centered tasks, which aligns with strategic planning of instructional resources. Participants were of the view that dynamic switching between AI and human-mediated activities can foster social interaction and critical comparison to strategically enhance communicative competence. The analysis highlights the teacher's role in monitoring AI engagement to prevent overreliance, safeguarding learner autonomy, and ensuring ethical and effective integration. According to some participants, teachers should play a strategic, supervisory, and facilitative role while integrating AI tutors in their communicative competence lectures. Participants maintained that they are responsible for designing balanced instructional strategies, overseeing AI tutors' use to prevent dependence, and fostering critical awareness among students. This strategic involvement, according to them, will ensure that AI enhances rather than replaces human presence in the classrooms. Some participants also maintained that maintaining human dignity is vital for meaningful learning. Some selected excerpts are mentioned here:

- T4: "I think that we, as human teachers, should take responsibility and adjust AI tutors to function as supplementary tools, while teachers remain responsible for pedagogical decisions. If we maintain a balanced instructional engagement, I think we can resolve this integration issue more effectively."
- T24: "We do not need to engage students with us all the time. Since AI tutors are used to develop students' communicative competence, they can be integrated for routine practice and feedback, which frees teachers to focus on other relevant tasks and helps create a balanced approach between AI and human engagement."
- T54: "We, as teachers, must ensure that we monitor AI tutor engagement to avoid overreliance and to maintain learner autonomy. Monitoring engagement can help mitigate integration problems and serve as a safeguard for learner autonomy, ensuring that students are not unduly influenced by AI in ways that may be adverse rather than supportive."

iii. cultural and contextual adaptation

Participants (n=37; 61%) observed the importance of culturally responsive AI integration, emphasizing adaptation to local values, language proficiency, and contextual needs. According to the participants, adjusting prompts and AI feedback to reflect cultural norms and values is one of the ways to ensure the relevance and appropriateness of the communicative tasks in which students engage. Participants also expressed that guiding students to evaluate the cultural appropriateness of AI responses and providing timely interventions when necessary are essential for addressing AI tutor integration challenges. Furthermore, modifying AI tasks to match students' proficiency levels and cultural backgrounds can promote effective engagement. Most importantly, in the context of developing sociolinguistic competence among Saudi learners, participants opined that AI content should be tailored to respect and incorporate Saudi cultural norms, linguistic complexities, and communication styles. According to them, this approach ensures that AI-mediated learning not only enhances communicative competence but also fosters cultural awareness and appropriateness, which are vital components of sociolinguistic competence. Participants further observed that adapting AI content in these ways will help learners develop more authentic and contextually relevant language use aligned with their cultural and social realities. Some selected excerpts are presented below.

- T15: "We need to adapt AI prompts to reflect local cultural norms, values, and communicative expectations. Adapting prompts and commands can greatly help customize learning according to the local culture and contextual needs."
- T55: "We can gradually train students to examine whether the AI-generated suggestions align with their cultural setting. If not, we need to offer guidance and make adjustments to ensure that the feedback is suitable for local needs."

iv. AI-focused professional development

Most participants (n=50; 83%) emphasized the multi-layered teachers' training to effectively integrate AI tutors into their pedagogical practices, particularly for designing communicative tasks and interpreting AI feedback. The analysis highlights the necessity for training in AI-enhanced task design, addressing issues related to appropriate prompt formulation and effective integration. Participants highlight that teachers currently lack the skills needed to control and manage AI tools, particularly tutors and conversational agents, which, according to some participants, leads to inaccuracies and miscommunication. Participants maintained that workshops focused on understanding and interpreting AI-generated feedback are essential, as such training would enable teachers to use AI outputs more confidently and appropriately. Some faculty members asserted the need for establishing communities through which teachers can share strategies and collectively address challenges related to AI integration. This form of initiative, participants viewed, can foster ongoing professional development and practical problem-solving. Furthermore, the qualitative analysis points to the need for training in ethical considerations and data privacy, ensuring responsible AI use, conscious prompt formulation, and appropriate interpretation of AI feedback. Moreover, participants argued that teachers require comprehensive training encompassing technical proficiency, interpretative skills, collaborative learning opportunities, and ethical awareness. Some selected excerpts are presented below.

- T16: "There is a dire need to provide teachers with training on how to design AI-enhanced communicative tasks. At present, teachers integrate available AI tutors without proper training; as a result, they face integration issues, and students often use inappropriate prompts, which leads to unsuitable or inaccurate feedback."
- T47: "I believe that offering workshops and seminars on interpreting AI-generated feedback can greatly help address AI tutor integration issues. By attending AI-focused workshops, teachers will be able to integrate AI tutors more efficiently than they currently do."

- T60: "These AI-focused professional development initiatives can also include ethical and data literacy training to ensure the responsible use of AI when formulating prompts, interacting with AI tutors, and interpreting the feedback provided."

DISCUSSION

This study explores teachers' views on developing EFL learners' communicative competence in the age of AI tutoring, focusing on interactional dynamics and integration challenges in Saudi higher education environments. The findings reveal a mixed outcome marked by significant shifts in communicative competence, classroom horizons, and practical issues. Beyond identifying familiar technology-related constraints, the findings reveal how AI tutors reshape classroom interaction, pedagogical authority, and opportunities for creative language use. Looking from an applied-linguistics point of view, it is evident that AI tutors emerge not only as instructional tools but as interactional agents whose presence impact discourse practices, learner engagement, and institutional responsibilities.

i. EFL teachers' views on the interactional dynamics and integration challenges

Participants, regarding interactional dynamics, observed a fundamental turn in communicative competence instruction. Student-teacher interaction is changing from direct instruction to a strategic facilitation, as learners engage more autonomously with AI tutors, a trend supported by existing research (Habib et al., 2025; Kahlerras & Bennacer, 2025). While this fosters individualized practice, it risks diminishing the teacher's role in managing interactive and communicative strategies, as noted by several researchers in recent investigations (Babanoğlu et al., 2025; Hago Elmahdi, 2024). Such transformation reflects a broader change in how communicative competence is enacted in AI-mediated environments. Furthermore, participants reported a concerning reduction in student-student interaction, vital for developing discourse and collaborative skills, potentially undermining the collective and collaborative aspects of language learning. The reported decline in student–student interaction is particularly significant from a communicative competence perspective, as peer interaction constitutes a primary spot for negotiation of meaning, discourse management, and collaborative repair. In the event of AI tutors replacing peers, opportunities for developing interactional competence through spontaneous, socially embedded communication are reduced. This trend suggests that when students interact with AI tutors, the interaction often becomes fast, efficient, and focused on getting correct answers, but this reduces deeper conversation, back-and-forth discussion, and real human connection. In addition, student-AI interaction itself presents a duality: it offers immediate feedback and unlimited practice but is mediated by students' sometimes uncritical perceptions of AI as an authoritative source and by concerns over privacy, findings that are consistent with those reported in recent studies (Nazaretsky et al., 2026; Wang et al., 2023). Moreover, concerning integration challenges, three major barriers emerged. First, content-related challenges include misalignment with curriculum goals and a lack of authentic, culturally relevant materials, hindering grammatical and discourse development, findings that are similar to those reported in recent scholarly articles (Wah, 2025). Second, AI-literacy and infrastructural issues include unequal internet access and low digital literacy, creating participation gaps and disrupting the flow of communicative activities. Finally, professional development gaps leave teachers underprepared in the pedagogical and technical skills required to design, implement, and critically assess AI-mediated communicative tasks. Overall, these transformational shifts suggest that AI tutors are reshaping classroom discourse patterns rather than simply supplementing existing practices. These challenges and concerns, therefore, lie not only in AI integration but in the pedagogical management of emerging human–AI interactional environments, underscoring the need to ensure that the social foundations of communicative competence are preserved.

ii. Solutions to address the interactional and integration challenges

From a pedagogical practice viewpoint, participants' proposed solutions emphasize structured classroom design principles that position AI tutors as scaffolding devices rather than substitutes for communicative interaction. Participants offered actionable solutions centered on four strategies. First, advocating for task-based AI integration, where AI serves as a supportive interlocutor within a structured pedagogical framework to promote meaningful interaction. These practice-oriented solutions stress the need for intentional task sequencing in which AI tutors support, rather than replace, human interaction. Second, emphasizing the need for a deliberate human-AI instructional balance, where teachers retain pedagogical authority to guide, monitor, and complement AI use, ensuring it supplements rather than supplants human interaction, results that are consistent with those reported in available literature (Hago Elmahdi, 2024; Mohamed et al., 2024). At the policy level, participants' emphasis on teacher monitoring and ethical oversight points to the necessity of institutional guidelines governing AI use in communicative tasks. As these issues emerge as institutional rather than purely pedagogical, they underscore the need for coherent governance frameworks to support responsible AI integration. Third, stressing cultural, creative, and contextual adaptation of AI content to align with local norms and proficiency levels, which is essential for developing sociolinguistic competence, findings that are consistent with those reported in Ma & Yang (2025) and Xia et al. (2024). Regarding creativity, participants noted that AI-mediated interaction do both support and limit creative language use. While AI tutors may encourage experimentation, overreliance leads to fixed responses and careful language choices. Sustaining creative communicative practices therefore requires pedagogical conditions that prompt learners to adapt, personalize, and critically engage with AI-produced language rather than reproduce it uncritically. Last, calling for comprehensive AI-focused professional development that equips teachers with skills in task design, feedback interpretation, ethical use, and collaborative problem-solving.

CONCLUSION & FUTURE DIRECTIONS

This chapter aimed to revisit EFL learners' communicative competence in the age of AI tutoring with special reference to Saudi higher education. The study employed a qualitative research design using semi-structured interviews. The findings reveal that Saudi EFL teachers perceive AI tutors as transformative yet double-edged. AI tools, particularly chatbots, conversational agents, and tutors, enhance individualized learning and communicative abilities but risk diminishing essential human interaction (student-teacher and student-student), crucial for communicative competence. Key integration challenges include curriculum misalignment, lack of cultural authenticity in AI-provided content and feedback, insufficient teacher AI-literacy and professional development, and infrastructural issues like internet access. Participants emphasize that AI use (Tutor in this study) must be balanced with human facilitation to develop communicative competence. The study elaborates on the concept of communicative competence in the AI era, uncovering an *emerging shift* in which interactions and engagements are increasingly shaped by human–AI dynamics. The findings provide guidelines for ELT practitioners, emphasizing the need for task-based AI integration in which AI functions as a scaffold rather than the core. This chapter highlights that AI (particularly AI tutors) is transforming from a tool to an active interlocutor, redefining the teacher's role from a sole knowledge authority to a strategic facilitator, partner, and mediator of human–AI collaboration.

The implications of this study extend across pedagogical practice and institutional policy. At the practice level, teachers are encouraged to design task-based instructional activities in which AI tutors function as reflective support tools rather than primary interactional partners. At the policy and governance level, there is a need for institutional frameworks that regulate ethical use, data responsibility, teacher oversight, and accountability for AI-mediated instruction. Furthermore, implications relate to the validity and reliability of communicative competence evaluation in AI-supported environments. This includes developing criteria that distinguish between learner-produced language and AI-generated content, ensuring that communicative competence is measured in ways that remain authentic, dialogic, and socially grounded. Overall, these implications suggest that effective AI integration requires not only responsible technological adoption but also pedagogical and institutional design that is principled, linguistically informed, and ethically grounded.

The study's limitations include its sample size and scope, as it draws only on teachers from Saudi higher education institutes and may not reflect broader institutional or regional experiences, and its context-specific nature, as the identified dynamics and challenges may differ in other educational settings or cultural contexts. Additionally, the study did not collect or analyze demographic variables such as gender, as it focused on participants working in Saudi higher education regardless of gender; therefore, potential gender-based differences in perceptions of AI tutor integration were not analyzed. Future research directions include conducting longitudinal studies to track the long-term impact of AI tutoring on specific communicative sub-competences, undertaking cross-cultural comparisons to examine how integration challenges and interactional dynamics vary across educational systems, and incorporating demographic variables such as gender to explore potential differences in experiences, perceptions, and engagement with AI-mediated language teaching environments.

REFERENCES

AbdAlgane, M., & Elmahdi, O. E. H.AbdAlgane. (2024). Preferred EFL teaching approaches to university professors: A case study of Saudi tertiary level. *International Journal of Language and Literary Studies*, *6*(4), 274–291. DOI: 10.36892/ijlls.v6i4.1940

Adelana, O. P., & Akinyemi, A. L. (2022). Artificial intelligence-based tutoring systems utilization for learning: A survey of senior secondary students' awareness and readiness in Ijebu-Ode, Ogun State. *UNIZIK Journal of Educational Research and Policy Studies*, *9*, 16–28.

Akhter, E. (2025). AI In the Classroom: Evaluating the Effectiveness of Intelligent Tutoring Systems for Multilingual Learners In Secondary Education. *ASRC Procedia: Global Perspectives in Science and Scholarship*, *1*(01), 532–563. DOI: 10.63125/gcq1qr39

Al Fraidan, A., & Alaliwi, M. (2024). Digital transformation for sustainable English language learning: Insights from Saudi Arabia and global perspectives. *Forum for Linguistic Studies*, *6*, 439–449. DOI: 10.30564/fls.v6i6.7754

Al-khresheh, M. H. (2024). Bridging technology and pedagogy from a global lens: Teachers' perspectives on integrating ChatGPT in English language teaching. *Computers and Education: Artificial Intelligence*, *6*, 100218. DOI: 10.1016/j.caeai.2024.100218

Al-Seghayer, K. (2015). Salient Key Features of Actual English Instructional Practices in Saudi Arabia. *English Language Teaching*, *8*(6), 89–99. DOI: 10.5539/elt.v8n6p89

Alanazi, T. (2025). Addressing the Challenges and Complexities of Teaching English in Saudi Higher Education: Insights through a Sociocultural Lens. *Education Quarterly Eeview*, *8*(2), 95–106. DOI: 10.31014/aior.1993.08.02.582

AlShareef, S. N. A. (2024). Applying the Communicative Approach in Assessing EFL Young Learners. *Eurasian Journal of Applied Linguistics*, *10*(1), 14–27. DOI: 10.32601/ejal.10102

Alzubi, A. A. F., Nazim, M., & Alyami, N. (2025). Do AI-generative tools kill or nurture creativity in EFL teaching and learning? *Education and Information Technologies*, *30*(11), 15147–15184. DOI: 10.1007/s10639-025-13409-8

Babanoğlu, M. P., Karataş, T. Ö., & Dündar, E. (2025). Envisioning the Future of AI-Assisted EFL Teaching and Learning: Conceptual Representations of Prospective Teachers. *SAGE Open*, *15*(2), 21582440251341590. Advance online publication. DOI: 10.1177/21582440251341590

Balla, A. A. S. (2025). AI-Driven Innovations in Adult EFL Learning: Exploring Potentials and Practicalities. *International Journal of Interactive Mobile Technologies*, *19*(8), 4–26. Advance online publication. DOI: 10.3991/ijim.v19i08.52295

Basaula, A. (2025). From Challenges to Opportunities: AI in English Language Teaching Classrooms. *Kalika Journal of Multidisciplinary Studies*, *7*(1), 13–37. DOI: 10.3126/kjms.v7i1.86428

Basri, W. S. (2024). Effectiveness of AI-powered Tutoring Systems in Enhancing Learning Outcomes. *Eurasian Journal of Educational Research*, *110*, 33–52. DOI: 10.14689/ejer.2024.110.003

Belda-Medina, J., & Calvo-Ferrer, J. (2022). Using Chatbots as AI Conversational Partners in Language Learning. *Applied Sciences (Basel, Switzerland)*, *12*(17), 8427. Advance online publication. DOI: 10.3390/app12178427

Benek, K. (2025). EFL learners' and teachers' perceptions of AI-powered language learning technologies: Benefits and challenges. *International Journal of Instruction*, *18*(2), 103–120. DOI: 10.29333/iji.2025.1827a

Braun, V., & Clarke, V. (2006). Using thematic analysis in psychology. *Qualitative Research in Psychology*, *3*(2), 77–101. DOI: 10.1191/1478088706qp063oa

Busso, A., & Sanchez, B. (2024). Advancing communicative competence in the digital age: A case for AI tools in Japanese EFL education. *Technology in Language Teaching & Learning*, *6*(3), 1–17. DOI: 10.29140/tltl.v6n3.1211

Canale, M., & Swain, M. (1980). Theoretical bases of communicative approaches to second language teaching and testing. *Applied Linguistics*, *1*(1), 1–47. DOI: 10.1093/applin/1.1.1

Chomsky, N. (1965). *Aspects of the Theory of Syntax*. M.I.T. Press.

Creely, E. (2024). Exploring the role of generative AI in enhancing language learning: Opportunities and challenges. *International Journal of Changes in Education*, *1*(3), 158–167. DOI: 10.47852/bonviewIJCE42022495

Dara, D., Soomro, A. G., Ny, S., Hong, C. K., & Elshamy, E. (2024). Exploring Communicative Competence: Definitions, Advancements, and Implementations across Disciplines. *AITU Scientific Research Journal*, *3*(2). Advance online publication. DOI: 10.63094/AITUSRJ.24.3.2.2

Dekhakhena, A. (2025). AI-Powered Personalized Learning in EFL Acquisition: Exploring Adaptive Instruction and Feedback Systems. *Journal of Studies in Language* [JSLCS]. *Cultura e Scuola*, *8*(1), 111–131.

Du, Q. (2025). How artificially intelligent conversational agents influence EFL learners' self-regulated learning and retention. *Education and Information Technologies*, *30*(15), 1–67. DOI: 10.1007/s10639-025-13602-9

Fathi, H., Sharifi, A., & Ahmadi, H. (2025). Empowering Students with Innovative AI-Language Learning Tools and Pedagogy to Master Speaking Skills. *Iranian Journal of Applied Language Studies*, *17*(1), 197–220. DOI: 10.22111/ijals.2024.48157.2432

Fathi, J., Rahimi, M., & Derakhshan, A. (2024). Improving EFL learners' speaking skills and willingness to communicate via artificial intelligence-mediated interactions. *System*, *121*, 103254. Advance online publication. DOI: 10.1016/j.system.2024.103254

Habib, M. U., Sattar, A., Iqbal, M. J., & Saleem, S. (2025). AI Driven Tutoring vs. Human Teachers Examining the on Student Teacher Relationship. *Review of Applied Management and Social Sciences*, *8*(1), 363–374. Advance online publication. DOI: 10.47067/ramss.v8i1.466

Hago Elmahdi, O. E. (2024). AI's Role in EFL: Optimizing Opportunities while Mitigating Risks. *International Journal of Linguistics. Literature & Translation*, *7*(10), 21–37. Advance online publication. DOI: 10.32996/ijllt.2024.7.10.4

Hayashi, K., & Sato, T. (2024). The Effectiveness of ChatGPT in Enhancing English Language Proficiency and Reducing Second Language Anxiety (L2). *WorldCALL Official Conference Proceedings*. https://doi.org/DOI: 10.22492/issn.2759-1182.2023.23

Huang, X., Zou, D., Cheng, G., Chen, X., & Xie, H. (2023). Trends, research issues and applications of artificial intelligence in language education. *Journal of Educational Technology & Society*, *26*(1), 112–131. DOI: 10.30191/ETS.202301_26(1).0009

Hymes, D. (1966). *Two types of linguistic relativity". Sociolinguistics*. Mouton.

Hymes, D. (1972). *On Communicative Competence. Sociolinguistics, edited by J. B. Pride and Janet Holmes, 269–93*. Penguin Books.

Jegede, O. O. (2024). Artificial intelligence and English language learning: Exploring the roles of AI-driven tools in personalizing learning and providing instant feedback. *Universal Library of Languages and Literatures, 1*(2), 06–19. Advance online publication. DOI: 10.70315/uloap.ullli.2024.0102002

Jenkins, S. (2022). Higher Education in Saudi Arabia: A Vehicle for Global Promotion and Advancement. In *The Past, Present, and Future of Higher Education in the Arabian Gulf Region* (pp. 143-158). Routledge.

Jeya Santhi, V. (2024). Technology-enhanced language learning: Innovations and impact. In C. J. Fernandez, N. Kumar, & S. Gayathri S. (Eds.), *Bridging disciplines: Exploring multidisciplinary research frontiers* (pp. 199–208). Red Unicorn Publishing Pvt. Ltd.

Ji, H., Han, I., & Ko, Y. (2023). A systematic review of conversational AI in language education: Focusing on the collaboration with human teachers. *Journal of Research on Technology in Education, 55*(1), 48–63. DOI: 10.1080/15391523.2022.2142873

Kahlerras, W., & Bennacer, F. (2025). AI-driven approaches to advance speaking proficiency in LMOOCS: Insights, innovations, and pedagogical implications. *Journal of Studies in Language* [JSLCS]. *Cultura e Scuola, 8*(1), 226–251.

Katsarou, E., Wild, F., Sougari, A., & Chatzipanagiotou, P. (2023). A Systematic Review of Voice-based Intelligent Virtual Agents in EFL Education. *International Journal of Emerging Technologies in Learning, 18*(10), 65–85. DOI: 10.3991/ijet.v18i10.37723

Khine, M. S. (2024). AI in teaching and learning and intelligent tutoring systems. In *Artificial Intelligence in Education: A Machine-Generated Literature Overview* (pp. 467–570). Springer Nature Singapore. DOI: 10.1007/978-981-97-9350-1_4

Kot, S. O., & Nykyporets, S. S. (2024). *Utilization of artificial intelligence in enhancing English language proficiency in tertiary education. Science and Education in the Third Millennium: Information Technology*. Education, Law, Psychology, Social Sphere, Management.

Kundu, A., & Bej, T. (2025). Transforming EFL teaching with AI: A systematic review of empirical studies. *International Journal of Artificial Intelligence in Education, 35*(4), 1–34. DOI: 10.1007/s40593-025-00470-0

Lin, C. C., Huang, A. Y., & Lu, O. H. (2023). Artificial intelligence in intelligent tutoring systems toward sustainable education: a systematic review. *Smart learning environments, 10*(1), 41. https://doi.org/DOI: 10.1186/s40561-023-00260-y

Liu, G. L., Lee, J. S., & Zhao, X. (2025). Critical digital literacies, agentic practices, and AI-mediated informal digital learning of English. *System, 103797*, 103797. Advance online publication. DOI: 10.1016/j.system.2025.103797

Ma, G., & Yang, X. (2025). Fostering Intercultural Competence Through AI-Driven Tools: A Case Study of Linguistic and Cultural Adaptability in Chinese EFL Education. *Digital Technologies Research and Applications*, *4*(1), 158–169. DOI: 10.54963/dtra.v4i1.1131

Mageira, K., Pittou, D., Papasalouros, A., Kotis, K., Zangogianni, P., & Daradoumis, A. (2022). Educational AI Chatbots for Content and Language Integrated Learning. *Applied Sciences (Basel, Switzerland)*, *12*(7), 3239. Advance online publication. DOI: 10.3390/app12073239

Mohamed, Y. A., Mohamed, A. H. H., Khanan, A., Bashir, M., Adiel, M. A., & Elsadig, M. A. (2024). Navigating the ethical terrain of AI-generated text tools: A review. *IEEE Access : Practical Innovations, Open Solutions*, *12*, 197061–197120. DOI: 10.1109/ACCESS.2024.3521945

Moskovsky, C. (2018). EFL teaching and learning in Saudi Arabia: 25 years of research. In Moskovsky, C., & Picard, M. (Eds.), *English as a foreign language in Saudi Arabia: New insights into teaching and learning English* (pp. 4–69). Routledge. DOI: 10.4324/9781315688466-2

Nafisah, S., Oktarina, I., Santri, D., & Suwartono, T. (2024). Teachers' perception and practices of intercultural communicative competence integration in EFL classroom: A systematic literature review. *Educalitra: English Education, Linguistics, and Literature Journal*, *3*(1), 1–19. DOI: 10.5281/zenodo.10596575

Nazaretsky, T., Mejia-Domenzain, P., Swamy, V., Frej, J., & Käser, T. (2026). Who Gives Feedback Matters: Student Biases Towards Human and AI-Generated Formative Feedback. *Journal of Computer Assisted Learning*, *42*(1), e70153. Advance online publication. DOI: 10.1111/jcal.70153

Nishida, T., & Fujimoto, N. (2025). Leveraging Artificial Intelligence for Self-Regulated Learning in EFL Presentation Skill Acquisition: Learner Perceptions and Practices. *Current Research Journal of Pedagogics*, *6*(06), 1–7.

Omidvar, S., & Meihami, H. (2025). Exploring the "What" and "How" of Opportunities and Challenges of AI in EFL Teacher Education. *Computers and Education: Artificial Intelligence*, *100443*, 100443. Advance online publication. DOI: 10.1016/j.caeai.2025.100443

Ouyang, P., Zheng, F., & Jiao, L. (2022). Artificial intelligence in online higher education: A systematic review of empirical research from 2011 to 2020. *Education and Information Technologies, 27*(6), 7893–7925. DOI: 10.1007/s10639-022-10925-9

Pack, A., & Maloney, J. (2023). Using generative artificial intelligence for language education research: Insights from using OpenAI's ChatGPT. *TESOL Quarterly, 57*(4), 1571–1582. DOI: 10.1002/tesq.3253

Qi, X., & Chen, Z. (2025). A Systematic Review of Technology Integration in Developing L2 Pragmatic Competence. *Education Sciences, 15*(2), 172. Advance online publication. DOI: 10.3390/educsci15020172

Salokhojaeva, F. (2025). Impact of the digital revolution on the development of students' communicative competences. *Perspectives of higher education development, 17*(1), 53-62. https://doi.org/DOI: 10.34920/phe.2024.17.04

Sangkala, I., & Mardonovna, N. S. (2024). Artificial Intelligence as a Personalized Tutor in Language Learning: A Systematic Review. *KLASIKAL: Journal of Education. Language Teaching And Science, 6*(2), 565–576. DOI: 10.52208/klasikal.v6i2.1193

Urbaite, G. (2025). Adaptive Learning with AI: How Bots Personalize Foreign Language Education. *Luminis Applied Science and Engineering, 2*(1), 13–18. DOI: 10.69760/lumin.20250001002

Wah, J. N. K. (2025). Artificial Intelligence in Language Learning: A Systematic Review of Personalization and Learner Engagement. *Forum for Linguistic Studies, 7*(9), 327–341. DOI: 10.30564/fls.v7i9.10336

Wang, C., & Zou, B. (2025). AI versus teachers and peers: A comparative study on speaking performance, willingness to communicate, self-perceived communicative competence and foreign language anxiety. *International Review of Applied Linguistics in Language Teaching*. Advance online publication. DOI: 10.1515/iral-2024-0310

Wang, C., Zou, B., Du, Y., & Wang, Z. (2024). The impact of different conversational generative AI chatbots on EFL learners: An analysis of willingness to communicate, foreign language speaking anxiety, and self-perceived communicative competence. *System, 127*, 103533. Advance online publication. DOI: 10.1016/j.system.2024.103533

Wang, Q. (2025). AI-driven autonomous interactive English learning language tutoring system. *Journal of Computational Methods in Sciences and Engineering, 25*(2), 1155–1166. DOI: 10.1177/14727978241296719

Wang, X., Liu, Q., Pang, H., Tan, S. C., Lei, J., Wallace, M. P., & Li, L. (2023). What matters in AI-supported learning: A study of human-AI interactions in language learning using cluster analysis and epistemic network analysis. *Computers & Education, 194*, 104703. DOI: 10.1016/j.compedu.2022.104703

Wei, L. (2023). Artificial intelligence in language instruction: Impact on English learning achievement, L2 motivation, and self-regulated learning. *Frontiers in Psychology, 14*, 1261955. DOI: 10.3389/fpsyg.2023.1261955

Xia, Y., Shin, S. Y., & Kim, J. C. (2024). Cross-cultural intelligent language learning system (CILS): Leveraging AI to facilitate language learning strategies in cross-cultural communication. *Applied Sciences (Basel, Switzerland), 14*(13), 5651. DOI: 10.3390/app14135651

Xu, H., Wang, Y., & Ma, J. (2025). A comprehensive review of intercultural communicative competence in EFL education and global business. *Cogent Education, 12*(1), 2557608. DOI: 10.1080/2331186X.2025.2557608

Yu, W. (2025). Reducing anxiety, promoting enjoyment and enhancing overall English proficiency: The impact of AI-assisted language learning in Chinese EFL contexts. *British Educational Research Journal*, berj.4187. Advance online publication. DOI: 10.1002/berj.4187

Zhang, C., Meng, Y., & Ma, X. (2024). Artificial intelligence in EFL speaking: Impact on enjoyment, anxiety, and willingness to communicate. *System, 121*, 103259. Advance online publication. DOI: 10.1016/j.system.2024.103259

Zhou, D., & Li, Q. (2025). The role of teacher-student developmental relationships in linking communicative language teaching and communicative competence. *Frontiers in Psychology, 16*, 1635428. DOI: 10.3389/fpsyg.2025.1635428

Zhou, R., Samad, A., & Perinpasingam, T. (2024). A systematic review of cross-cultural communicative competence in EFL teaching: Insights from China. *Humanities & Social Sciences Communications, 11*(1), 1–11. DOI: 10.1057/s41599-024-04071-5

APPENDIX

RQ1: What are EFL teachers' views on the interactional dynamics and integration challenges associated with the use of AI tutors in developing students' communicative competence?

i. interactional dynamics

- student–teacher interaction
  - How has the integration of AI tutors affected the frequency and quality of student–teacher interaction?
  - In what ways has your role shifted (from instructor to facilitator) due to students' reliance on AI tutors?
- student– student interaction
  - How has the use of AI tutors influenced peer interaction and collaborative learning in your classroom?
  - How does AI integration affect students' willingness to engage in communicative tasks?
- student–AI tutor interaction
  - How do students engage with AI tutors to develop their communicative competence?
  - To what extent do students treat AI tutors as authoritative sources, and how does this affect their communicative development?

ii. integration challenges

- content-related challenges
  - What challenges do you face in aligning AI tutor activities with the syllabus content and learning objectives?
  - What issues arise regarding the relevance, accuracy, or contextual suitability of AI-generated content?
- AI-literacy and internet-related challenges
  - What challenges do you face in effectively using AI tools due to limited AI literacy or technical skills?
  - How do internet-related issues (connectivity/disruptions) affect the implementation of AI-supported communicative tasks?
- professional development-related challenges
  - What challenges do you encounter due to the lack of training in integrating AI tutors into classroom environments?
  - To what extent do you feel prepared to design and assess AI-assisted communicative tasks?

RQ2: What solutions do EFL teachers propose to address the interactional and integration challenges associated with the use of AI tutors in developing students' communicative competence?

i. task-based AI integration

  - How can AI tutors be integrated into task-based language teaching to support communicative competence rather than replace interaction?
  - How can AI-supported tasks be designed to include key elements such as input, interaction, output, and reflection?

ii. human-AI instructional balance

  - How do you maintain a balance between AI tutor use and human interaction in communicative classrooms?
  - How can AI tutors be effectively positioned as supplementary tools rather than primary sources of instruction?

iii. cultural and contextual adaptation

  - How can AI-generated content be adapted to reflect cultural norms and communicative expectations?
  - What strategies can help students critically evaluate whether AI-generated responses are culturally appropriate?

iv. AI-focused professional development

  - How can workshops and seminars support teachers in interpreting and utilizing AI-generated feedback?
  - What role can professional development play in strengthening teachers' ethical awareness and data literacy related to AI use?

Chapter 7
Contextualized AI-Driven Narratives:
Teacher Mediation and Literacy Development in EAL

Agustin Reyes-Torres
http://orcid.org/0000-0003-1058-3513
Universitat de València, Spain

Katia Ruiz-Saiz
Universitat de València, Spain

ABSTRACT

This qualitative case study examines how contextualized AI-generated narratives support multidimensional literacy in a diverse first-grade EAL classroom in Valencia, Spain. Analysis of observations, student work, and focus group interviews show that AI narratives become effective when adapted to learners' interests, linguistic capabilities, and sociocultural backgrounds. Results highlight gains in engagement, comprehension, spontaneous language use, and cultural awareness across all learners' profiles, including students with special educational needs. Crucially, effectiveness depends on teacher mediation through prompt design, output evaluation, and guided delivery. The study argues that AI functions not as teacher replacement but as a cultural tool requiring strong pedagogical expertise to transform generic outputs into meaningful learning experiences. Implications stress that successful AI integration in early language education must keep human relationships, cultural relevance, and critical reflection at the center.

DOI: 10.4018/979-8-3373-6420-9.ch007

INTRODUCTION

The integration of Artificial Intelligence (AI) into language education has sparked both enthusiasm and concern among educators worldwide. While AI tools promise unprecedented opportunities for personalization and engagement, critical questions remain about their pedagogical value, ethical implementation, and actual impact on learning. Can AI-generated content truly support meaningful literacy development, working with young learners in the teaching of English as an additional language (EAL)? More importantly, what role must teachers play to ensure that these technological tools serve genuine educational purposes rather than simply adding digital novelty to traditional approaches?

This chapter addresses these questions through an in-depth qualitative exploration of how contextualized AI-generated narratives can support multidimensional literacy development when thoughtfully designed and carefully mediated by teachers (Kalantzis & Cope, 2025). Drawing on a classroom-based study with first-grade students in a linguistically and culturally diverse public school in Valencia, Spain, the chapter examines the lived experiences, authentic interactions, and meaning-making processes that occurred when AI-generated stories were deliberately tailored to reflect students' interests, cultural backgrounds, and linguistic capabilities. Through systematic analysis of classroom observations, student interactions, focus group interviews, and learning artifacts, this work explores not whether AI can be used in early language education, but how it must be used to genuinely serve learners.

The central argument is that AI's transformative potential in early language education lies not in the technology itself, but in the contextualization process, that is, the deliberate, human-centered work of adapting AI outputs to the specific realities of learners and their communities. This process requires sophisticated pedagogical decision-making, deep knowledge of students' lives and learning needs, and ongoing mediation during implementation (Dupuy & Hashemi, 2025). By examining a diverse class of first-year students where they navigated multiple languages (Spanish, Valencian, English) while bringing varied cultural backgrounds (Moroccan, Pakistani, South American), special educational needs, and dramatically different competence levels, this study reveals how contextualization operates across three critical dimensions: personalization based on students' interests, linguistic adaptation to their developmental stages, and integration of sociocultural elements reflecting their lived experiences.

Teaching English as a foreign language to young children in such contexts presents extraordinary challenges. Traditional materials and methodologies in the teaching of EAL, which are typically designed for hypothetical "average" learners, often fail to meaningfully engage this diversity. Textbook characters and storylines do not always reflect students' lived realities; vocabulary lists feel disconnected from their everyday experiences; standardized pacing leaves some students frustrated while others disengage from boredom. Most critically, these approaches often overlook what research consistently demonstrates: young children learn language most effectively when content connects to their interests, validates their cultural identities, and builds on their existing knowledge (Lave & Wenger, 1991; Kern, 2000; Kucer, 2014). Generative AI technologies offer potential solutions through personalization, that is, the ability to create narratives tailored to specific groups of learners, incorporating their favorite characters, familiar settings, relevant cultural references, and appropriate linguistic complexity. However, technical capability alone does not guarantee educational value. AI systems can reproduce cultural biases, generate linguistically inappropriate outputs, or create narratives that prioritize entertainment over learning objectives. This is why teacher mediation is crucial.

This chapter adopts Kucer's (2014) multidimensional literacy framework, which conceptualizes literacy development as the dynamic, interconnected interaction among linguistic (language system mastery), cognitive (mental meaning-making processes), sociocultural (understanding language as culturally situated), and developmental (constructive acquisition through interaction) dimensions. Building on this foundation, the analysis incorporates a fifth dimension, motivational, recognizing that emotional engagement, interest, and self-efficacy are constitutive elements of literacy development itself (Dewey, 1913; Deci & Ryan, 1985). This multidimensional perspective proves particularly valuable for analyzing AI-generated narratives in diverse classrooms, directing attention not only to vocabulary acquisition but also to inferential reasoning, cultural identity connections, and sustained engagement.

The qualitative findings presented here emerge from an intervention where AI-generated oral narratives were designed through careful prompt engineering informed by students' expressed interests and delivered by the teacher-researcher in an authentic classroom context. The analysis foregrounds students' voices, their attempts at English productions, their expressions, and their cognitive engagement. These authentic moments, captured through participant observation and preserved in field notes, reveal how contextualized narratives worked across multiple literacy dimensions simultaneously, with a particular power for students typically marginalized in traditional instruction, including those with special educational needs who moved from avoidance behaviors to active participation.

Ultimately, this chapter contributes to current discussions about AI in education by showing that the key question is not whether to use AI in language teaching, but how to use it effectively. Teachers must learn how to design prompts that generate pedagogically valuable outputs, how to evaluate and adapt AI-created content for specific learners, and how to deliver these materials in ways that support engagement and learning. They must also ensure that AI use aligns with core human values such as cultural respect, pedagogical intentionality, and educational equity in an increasingly AI-mediated landscape. The findings suggest that when teachers apply their professional expertise to connect AI's possibilities with authentic human experience, AI becomes a powerful amplifier of good teaching rather than a replacement for it.

Guided by these theoretical and pedagogical considerations, this chapter addresses the following research questions:

1. How do contextualized AI-generated narratives support multidimensional literacy development in young EAL learners?
2. What role does teacher mediation play in maximizing the pedagogical value of AI-generated content?
3. How do diverse learners, including those with special educational needs, engage with and respond to culturally and linguistically tailored AI narratives?

To address these questions, the chapter first outlines the theoretical foundations drawing on literacy theory, storytelling pedagogy and approaches to technology integration. It then describes the qualitative case study methodology and research context, followed by the presentation of findings. The chapter concludes with a discussion of these implications and offer recommendations for educational practice and future research.

BACKGROUND

The integration of AI-generated narratives into early language education requires careful theoretical grounding across three interconnected domains: how young children develop literacy, particularly in foreign language contexts; how storytelling functions as a pedagogical tool for meaning-making; and how technology can be harnessed ethically and effectively to support rather than supplant human teaching. This section establishes the conceptual foundations that frame the empirical analysis that will be presented later in the chapter.

Literacy as Multidimensional and Transactive

The notion of literacy has evolved significantly in the 21st century, moving away from narrow, technical definitions focused solely on decoding and encoding skills. Today's young learners engage with a wide range of texts, whether listening to stories, viewing picture books, playing digital games, or beginning to write, through sophisticated processes involving multiple forms of knowledge, diverse communicative competences, and complex cognitive operations (Paesani & Menke, 2023). This expanded view recognizes literacy as multiliteracies (New London Group, 1996;

Cope & Kalantzis, 2009, 2015), encompassing linguistic, cultural, technological, and social dimensions that young EAL learners must navigate simultaneously (Kern, 2000; Reyes-Torres, Brisk & Lacorte, 2025; Tavares, 2024; Zapata, 2022).

For this study, Kucer's (2014) multidimensional literacy framework provides the most comprehensive lens for analyzing how contextualized AI narratives influence early language development. Kucer conceptualizes literacy as a dynamic, interconnected, and transactive process requiring simultaneous engagement across four integrated dimensions. The cognitive or personal dimension involves active mental processes of attention, inference, and meaning construction, positioning learners as meaning makers who must take an active role to turn the information they receive into some form of understanding that will enable them to construct knowledge. The *linguistic or conceptual dimension* focuses on mastery of language systems (vocabulary, grammar, phonology, and key lesson content) through which learners function as code-breakers and code-makers. The *sociocultural dimension* recognizes that language is never neutral or acontextual; it is always situated within social and cultural frameworks that shape how meaning is negotiated and understood. This dimension aligns closely with situated learning theory (Lave & Wenger, 1991), which holds that knowledge becomes meaningful when connected to socially relevant, real-life situations. Finally, the *developmental dimension* emphasizes that language acquisition is constructive, built through social interaction and scaffolding, a principle grounded in Vygotsky's (1978) sociocultural theory.

While Kucer treats motivation as a powerful transversal force, the "invisible driving force" that stimulates all dimensions of literacy, this study elevates it to dimensional status alongside the original four. This theoretical adaptation reflects growing recognition that motivation is not merely supportive but constitutive of literacy development (Dewey, 1913; Deci & Ryan, 1985). The *motivational dimension* encompasses emotional engagement, interest, self-efficacy, and sustained participation. These factors don't just support learning but actively shape whether and how learning occurs. This elevation proves particularly important when examining AI-generated narratives deliberately designed to activate interest and engagement in diverse learners. By treating motivation as a dimension rather than background variable, the framework enables more precise observation and analysis of how personalized content influences not just what students learn but their willingness and confidence to engage with challenging linguistic tasks.

This multidimensional perspective matters profoundly for diverse and multilevel classrooms where students arrive with dramatically different linguistic repertoires, cultural backgrounds, prior experiences, and learning needs. In such contexts, effective literacy instruction cannot focus solely on vocabulary acquisition or grammatical accuracy. It must simultaneously attend to whether students develop inferential reasoning, connect content to their cultural identities, and maintain the motivation and confidence necessary for continued growth. The framework reveals how these dimensions operate in constant interaction and how cultural relevance enhances motivation, which in turn frees cognitive resources for deeper linguistic processing.

Likewise, this framework helps explain why traditional approaches sometimes fall short. Textbook-based instruction usually focuses on the linguistic dimension but gives far less attention to sociocultural relevance, and it tends to assume motivation rather than actively cultivating it. Thus, for many students, especially those whose backgrounds are not reflected in standard materials, the sociocultural dimension stays inactive. As a result, their motivation decreases and their cognitive engagement is much more limited. In contrast, this chapter shows that well-designed and thoughtfully implemented contextualized AI narratives can activate all dimensions at the same time, creating richer and more meaningful learning experiences.

Storytelling as Transaction: Beyond Passive Reception

For many centuries, oral storytelling has been a primary way for humans to share knowledge, values, and cultural identity. In today's classrooms, storytelling remains powerful because it taps into fundamental human capacities for narrative thinking and emotional engagement (Egan, 1986). Young children naturally make sense of the world through stories, using narrative to organize experiences and build understanding. This makes storytelling especially valuable in primary language education, where it can create affective connections that support meaningful cognitive and linguistic development (Chavous, 2024).

However, storytelling's pedagogical value is not automatic. To understand how narratives contribute to literacy development, we must move beyond the idea that teachers tell and students simply receive. Rosenblatt's (1978, 1994) transactional theory of reading provides essential insight here. She argues that meaning does not reside solely in the text or solely in the reader. Meaning emerges through the interaction between them. Students bring personal experiences, emotions, cultural knowledge, and prior understandings to the story, making each reading or listening event unique. In this view, a story becomes a “lived-through experience” where meaning is actively constructed rather than passively absorbed.

This perspective is particularly useful for understanding how young EAL learners engage with AI-generated stories. When a first grader listens to a narrative about Pikachu shopping at the Torrefiel Market for arepas and couscous, they are doing far more than processing vocabulary. They draw on multiple sources of knowledge: their interest in Pokémon, their familiarity or curiosity about the local market, their recognition of foods linked to their own or classmates' cultures, and their emerging grasp of English. The story becomes meaningful because it invites this kind of transactional work. By activating personal and cultural resources, it transforms unfamiliar language input into something recognizable and emotionally relevant.

Research consistently shows that storytelling in EAL contexts reduces anxiety, increases motivation, and promotes deeper linguistic engagement than traditional textbook instruction (Rahmawati et al., 2025). When language is embedded in stories that are emotionally engaging and culturally meaningful, learners experience what Krashen (1985) calls low affective filter conditions, that is, contexts where they feel comfortable taking risks and experimenting with new language. Moreover, stories also provide multimodal support through text, images, and sound, helping young learners build meaning through multiple channels (Bort Caballero & Gil-Mediavilla, 2023). Digital storytelling extends these benefits by offering interactive elements and opportunities for creative expression, which can be especially helpful for students with learning challenges.

Yet it must be highlighted that storytelling is effective only when designed with clear pedagogical intent. Not all stories serve educational goals equally well. Narratives that support literacy development must follow clear learning objectives, use backward design principles (Wiggins & McTighe, 2005), and balance interest with cognitive appropriateness. Content should be engaging enough to spark genuine curiosity, a condition Mayer (2008) identifies as essential for meaningful learning, and at the same time, it should avoid unnecessary details that distract learners and add cognitive load (Paas, Renkl, & Sweller, 2003). Achieving this balance requires professional judgment. Teachers must know what makes content compelling and how to structure it for optimal processing.

Finally, the transactional nature of storytelling also highlights the importance of personalization. If meaning depends on the interaction between the learner and the narrative, then stories that reflect students' experiences, cultural backgrounds, and interests create richer opportunities for engagement. A generic story with unfamiliar characters and settings offers few or no entry points at all for meaning-making. On the contrary, a story that includes familiar characters and neighborhoods, and culturally resonant elements gives learners more ways to connect with the content. This is where AI's potential for scalable personalization becomes educationally valuable. They key lies in how teachers use it and how they guide these transactional processes.

AI, Personalization, and the Mediating Work of Teachers

Generative AI represents a major technological shift with potential to transform for educational practice. Unlike earlier tools that that delivered pre-programmed content, generative systems such as ChatGPT can produce contextually adapted outputs in response to user prompts. This capability enables what was previously logistically impossible: creating personalized learning materials tailored to specific groups of learners at scale. Teachers can generate narratives that incorporate students' interests, cultural references, familiar settings, and linguistically appropriate structures, in other words, tasks that once required extensive preparation time.

However, technical capacity alone does not ensure meaningful learning. AI systems, sophisticated as they are, lack developmental insight, cultural awareness, and pedagogical purpose. They can reproduce biases, generate culturally insensitive narratives, or produce texts that entertain without supporting learning goals (UNESCO, 2023). Because AI operates through pattern prediction rather than understanding, its outputs require careful human guidance to become educationally valuable.

This is where teacher mediation becomes indispensable. Teachers shape the entire process: from designing prompts that reflect learning objectives, linguistic needs, and cultural relevance; guiding the delivery of narratives in ways that foster engagement and comprehension; to evaluating the effectiveness of AI-generated materials. Their role involves interpreting students' reactions, adjusting pacing, and facilitating the connections that enable deeper understanding. In essence, teachers play the role of clarifier, challenger and mediator at the same time. Certainly, one of their most important goals is to guide students to think by themselves, make connection between ideas and gradually acquire the tools that allow them to begin constructing their own meaning (Reyes-Torres & García-Perera, 2022).

UNESCO's (2023) framework for teacher AI competence underscores this mediating function. It identifies five areas of preparation: adopting human-centered approaches, addressing ethical implications, understanding how AI works, applying pedagogically sound practices, and engaging in ongoing development. For early language education, this means ensuring that AI enriches cultural diversity, strengthens relationships, and amplifies rather than replaces teacher judgment.

A central concept in this work is contextualization. AI can generate coherent stories, but coherence alone does not guarantee relevance. Generic outputs lack the personal and cultural resonance that makes learning meaningful for young learners. Contextualization bridges this gap by grounding AI outputs in students' lived experiences: their interests, linguistic repertoires, home practices, and daily routines. This process transforms standard content into material that feels familiar, engaging, and cognitively accessible.

Such contextualization is only possible when teachers know their students well. A teacher who understands what characters her class admires, what foods they eat at home, what local places they visit, and what vocabulary they are currently learning holds the information needed to design effective prompts. AI provides the mechanism for rapid production, but teachers contribute the human insight that gives the material educational weight.

This chapter explores what happens when these principles are enacted in real classrooms. It examines how a teacher designs contextualized AI-generated narratives, how she mediates their delivery, and how students respond to them. The qualitative findings that follow illuminate not just outcomes but processes: how contextualized narratives activate multiple dimensions of literacy, the moments when students' engagement becomes visible, the ways different learners respond to personalized content, and the ongoing pedagogical decisions teachers must make to harness AI's potential while managing its limitations.

These theoretical perspectives shaped both the design of the intervention and the analytical approach taken in this study. The following section describes how these principles were implemented in the classroom context.

CONTEXTUALIZATION IN ACTION: A QUALITATIVE CASE STUDY

This study employed a qualitative case study approach (Cochran-Smith & Lytle, 1993) as the most appropriate methodology for examining classroom-level processes and exploring literacy development in context. Unlike quantitative designs that prioritize generalizability and outcome measurement, this case study allows us to understand how pedagogical innovations function within authentic educational settings. This approach is particularly well-suited for practitioner research that seeks to understand the complex interplay between teacher decisions, student responses and learning processes as they unfold in real time. While findings are not directly generalizable in the statistical sense, they offer transferable insights that can inform pedagogical practice in similar contexts.

This research draws on a study conducted during Spring 2025 in a public primary school in Valencia. The aim is to develop a detailed and context-sensitive understanding of how contextualized AI-generated narratives influenced literacy development in a diverse first-grade classroom. Rather than pursuing broad generalization, the methodological approach seeks close, situated insight into classroom dynamics and learner responses. This focus aligns with the study's core concern: not whether AI-generated stories "work" in an abstract or universal way, but how they function in real classrooms with real students when they are intentionally designed and skillfully mediated by an experienced teacher.

This study met all protocols of the Ethics Committee for Experimental Research at the University of Valencia, adhering to the Helsinki Declaration and Spanish and European legislation governing research with human subjects. All student names are pseudonyms, and informed consent was obtained from families. Students provided ongoing assent, with their wellbeing prioritized throughout. The use of AI-generated materials followed UNESCO's (2024) ethical guidelines for AI in education

The Context: A Classroom Marked by Diversity and Challenge

The school is located in an urban area of the city characterized by significant unemployment rates, job insecurity, and constrained access to cultural and educational resources. These material conditions profoundly shape family life and parental involvement patterns, with many families navigating multiple stressors that leave limited time or energy for supporting children's schoolwork at home. The student population reflects Spain's contemporary migration patterns, incorporating families from Morocco, Pakistan, and various South American countries alongside native Spanish-speaking households, creating extraordinary linguistic and cultural diversity within a single school building.

The first-grade classroom that became the focus of this study comprised eleven students aged six to seven years. This small number might suggest homogeneity, but the reality proved strikingly opposite. The group exhibited what teachers often describe as *extreme heterogeneity*: dramatic variation in academic readiness, linguistic competence, prior educational experience, and learning needs. One student was under evaluation for high intellectual abilities (HA), consistently performing well beyond grade-level expectations across all subjects. Two others demonstrated strong academic performance (HP), working comfortably at or slightly above expected first-grade benchmarks. Seven students progressed at rates considered typical for their age and grade level (TD), though with the normal variation found in any group of young learners. Finally, one student had been identified with Special Educational Needs (SEN), having recently entered the Spanish educational system with minimal prior formal schooling and very limited Spanish proficiency, let alone English.

This internal diversity was compounded by the classroom's plurilingual reality. Students navigated three languages daily: Spanish as the dominant language of the broader community (L1 for most students), Valencian as the co-official regional language and medium of instruction for several subjects (L2), and English as the foreign language being studied (L3). Some students spoke languages other than Spanish at home (Arabic, Urdu, or indigenous South American languages) adding further complexity to an already intricate linguistic landscape. English proficiency levels ranged from students who could engage with age-appropriate conversations and produce simple sentences to those who struggled to recognize basic vocabulary or respond to simple questions.

For a teacher working in such contexts, the challenge is profound: How do you design learning experiences that challenge high-ability students without overwhelming struggling learners? How do you make English meaningful for children whose primary concern may be mastering Spanish for school survival? How do you create a sense of belonging and engagement when students' cultural backgrounds span three continents and their home languages represent multiple language families?

Traditional one-size-fits-all materials, generally textbooks designed for mythical "average" students in comfortable middle-class contexts, prove inadequate in such settings.

The Teacher-Researcher's Role at the Intersection

The study was conducted from a dual position as both classroom teacher and educational researcher, a positionality that shaped every aspect of the design, implementation, and analysis. The role involved not observing another practitioner from a distance, but examining one's own pedagogical practice to understand how a teacher-designed innovation influenced students' learning and engagement.

This dual positioning offered several advantages. As the classroom teacher, the researcher held the type of long-term knowledge of the students that an external investigator could not develop within the timeframe of a short study. Familiarity with students' personalities, interests, family contexts, social dynamics, learning strengths, and daily emotional fluctuations proved essential for crafting contextualized narratives and for noticing subtle but meaningful classroom moments that an unfamiliar observer might overlook. Established relationships also fostered natural classroom interaction, reducing performative behavior, and enabled students to speak openly during focus group interviews with a trusted adult rather than an unknown researcher.

At the same time, this positioning carried risks that required continuous reflexive attention. The most salient concern was potential bias: as both designer and implementer of the intervention, the teacher-researcher had an inherent investment in its success, which could influence interpretation of evidence. Students' responses might have reflected their rapport with the teacher rather than the effectiveness of the narratives themselves. Power dynamics within teacher-student relationships also had the potential to shape what students felt comfortable sharing, especially regarding criticisms or negative experiences.

Several strategies were employed to mitigate these risks. A detailed research journal was maintained throughout the process, explicitly documenting assumptions, expectations, emotional reactions, and moments of uncertainty. This reflexive record helped surface instances where interpretations might have been influenced by prior hopes instead of empirical evidence. Triangulation across multiple data sources such as observations, student work, focus group discussions, and self-assessments provided a way to look for patterns of convergence and divergence rather than relying on isolated indicators. In addition, the second researcher reviewed selected field notes and student work samples to identify alternative interpretations or overlooked patterns. Finally, the analytic process was approached with openness and curiosity, allowing space for evidence of challenges, tensions, or unexpected outcomes rather than assuming a predetermined trajectory of success.

It is important to acknowledge explicitly how this dual role may have shaped student responses in specific ways. Students' familiarity with the researcher as their regular teacher likely increased their comfort level and willingness to participate authentically during both the intervention and data collection, but this familiarity may also have oriented their responses toward what they perceived as desirable or expected. The researcher's teaching responsibilities necessarily limited the extent and nature of data collection possible, and the insider perspective, while providing valuable contextual knowledge, required constant reflexive attention to avoid over-interpretation or confirmatory bias. To maintain analytic rigor despite these constraints, systematic triangulation was employed across multiple data sources —classroom observations, detailed field notes, focus group interviews, and student-generated artifacts— ensuring that emerging patterns were corroborated across different types of evidence rather than relying on any single source. Additionally, a reflexive journal was maintained throughout the study to document assumptions, emotional reactions, and interpretive choices, creating an audit trail that supported critical self-examination of how my dual role influenced both classroom dynamics and subsequent analysis.

Overall, the teacher-researcher stance is understood not as a methodological weakness but as an epistemologically valuable position. Practitioner research offers access to layers of insight unavailable in external studies: the lived complexity of daily classroom decision-making, the moment-to-moment adjustments that determine whether an intervention succeeds, and the emotional and relational dimensions of teaching that often disappear in sanitized accounts. The goal was not detached objectivity, but what Cochran-Smith and Lytle (1993) term "systematic intentionality": bringing rigor and critical reflection to the study of one's own teaching while honoring the practice-based knowledge embedded in that work.

The Intervention: Designing and Delivering Contextualized Narratives

The intervention was carried out across six sessions distributed over three weeks in April 2025. This timing was strategic: by late spring, the teacher-researcher had worked with these students for seven months and possessed deep understanding of their interests, relationships, capabilities, and needs.

Work began with two consecutive sessions (Thursday-Friday) dedicated to gathering baseline data and student input. The first session included a brief diagnostic assessment of English vocabulary and listening comprehension to determine each student's starting point so that the narratives could be appropriately calibrated. The second session introduced a child-friendly interest questionnaire supported by images, minimal writing demands, and topics grounded in students' daily lives (favorite characters, foods, activities, places). Students completed the questionnaire with enthusiasm, clearly motivated by the sense that their preferences genuinely mattered.

The weekend that followed served as the analytical foundation for narrative design. Questionnaire responses were examined to identify collective patterns and meaningful individual preferences. Pikachu, Ladybug, Messi, Bluey, and Elsa emerged as the most popular characters. Foods reflected both Spanish staples (tomatoes, apples, sandwiches) and the classroom's cultural diversity (arepas, couscous, baozi, chapati). Local references such as the Torrefiel Park and the neighborhood market appeared repeatedly. Grounded in this information, the teacher-researcher began crafting detailed prompts for ChatGPT, prompts intended to integrate learning objectives with personal and cultural elements drawn from the students' real contexts.

Prompt design required balancing several pedagogical considerations. The stories needed to target specific curricular content (Unit 6 vocabulary on healthy eating, basic structures for expressing preferences, and phonological awareness of the initial /t/ sound) while also supporting broader goals such as intercultural understanding, healthy habits, and cooperative problem-solving. They had to incorporate beloved characters in authentic ways, integrate culturally diverse foods respectfully, and situate events in familiar neighborhood settings to strengthen relevance. Linguistically, the narratives needed to offer comprehensible yet challenging input and provide opportunities for meaningful interaction.

After testing different prompts across several AI tools, the teacher-researcher selected the ChatGPT-generated stories that best satisfied these requirements. Three narratives were finalized, each presenting familiar characters navigating relatable childhood challenges: organizing a healthy picnic in Torrefiel Park, preparing for Ladybug's birthday celebration, and welcoming a new friend to their class. Target vocabulary appeared in purposeful contexts, cultural elements were embedded respectfully, and each story concluded with prompts encouraging prediction, reflection, and personal connection.

During the three consecutive delivery sessions (April 14–16), the teacher-researcher shifted from designer to facilitator. Stories were read aloud using expressive intonation, gestures, and facial cues to support comprehension. Strategic pauses allowed for checking understanding, prompting predictions, and inviting comments. Pacing was adjusted in response to attention levels, elaboration was provided when misunderstandings arose, and brief exchanges helped connect story content to students' experiences. The sessions became interactive events rather than passive listening experiences: students called out character names, helped peers with vocabulary, related events to their own lives, and raised questions that extended the narrative.

Following the Easter break, the final phase focused on reflection and assessment. Students compiled portfolios of work created during and after the storytelling sessions (drawings of key moments, simple written responses, and sequencing tasks that demonstrated comprehension). A group reflection invited students to discuss what they enjoyed, what supported their understanding, and how they felt hearing their favorite characters or familiar places in the stories. Each student then completed a parallel post-test and a simple self-assessment using a traffic-light system to express their confidence and enjoyment.

Data Collection: Capturing Complexity through Multiple Lenses

The qualitative data corpus for this study includes four primary sources, each offering distinct insights into how students experienced and responded to contextualized narratives.

Field notes and research journal: Throughout the intervention, detailed observational records were kept to document students' verbal and nonverbal reactions, moments of engagement or distraction, spontaneous comments, peer interactions, and the instructional decisions made during each session. These notes aimed to describe classroom events rather than evaluate them, capturing small but meaningful moments, such as a child repeatedly pointing at the screen when Pikachu appeared, another whispering translations to a classmate, or the shared gasp when a character faced a dilemma. The research journal complemented these observations with reflective entries written after sessions, where interpretations were reconsidered and implications for upcoming activities were explored.

Student work artifacts: The portfolios students compiled provided concrete evidence of engagement and understanding. These included drawings of story scenes or favorite characters, with some students adding captions in Spanish, English, or creative hybrid forms; written responses to comprehension questions, revealing not just accuracy but effort and confidence; sequencing activities where students arranged story events in order, demonstrating narrative understanding; and self-assessment sheets where students expressed their feelings about different aspects of the experience.

Focus group interview: At the end of the narrative sessions, a semi-structured focus group was carried out with all eleven students. Using an age-appropriate, conversational format, students were invited to talk about the stories they remembered, the parts they enjoyed most, elements that surprised them, and whether the stories helped them learn English. The discussion was audio-recorded and later transcribed, preserving the students' exact words, including their frequent code-switching between Spanish and English, their enthusiastic interruptions, and the way they built on each other's ideas.

Researcher reflections: In addition to immediate field notes, longer reflective entries were written during and after the intervention. These reflections made it possible to step back from daily classroom activity, consider broader patterns, identify unresolved questions, and connect emerging insights to the wider goals of the study.

Analysis: From Data to Insight through Thematic Coding

The qualitative corpus was examined using Braun and Clarke's (2006) approach to thematic analysis, a flexible method suitable for identifying patterns across multiple forms of data. The analysis proceeded through six recursive phases.

Phase 1: Familiarization. The analysis began with repeated engagement with all data sources: reading and rereading field notes, reviewing student work portfolios, and listening to the focus group recording while following the transcript. This immersion made it possible to develop a deep understanding of the corpus and to begin noticing early patterns and points of interest.
Phase 2: Generating initial codes. The next step involved working through the corpus and identifying meaningful features. Coding occurred at both a semantic level (capturing explicit meanings) and a latent level (capturing underlying ideas and implications). For instance, a student's enthusiastic exclamation upon recognizing a favorite character was coded semantically as excitement and recognition, while also being coded latently as evidence of personalization and emotional engagement. Coding remained intentionally inclusive at this stage, allowing for later refinement.
Phase 3: Searching for themes. Related codes were then grouped into preliminary themes. To support this process, all codes were printed and sorted manually, testing different groupings and examining how they related to each other. Some clusters emerged clearly, for example, codes relating to cultural recognition and familiarity, while others required more exploration to determine whether they belonged together.
Phase 4: Reviewing themes. Potential themes were evaluated for internal coherence (whether the coded data within each theme fit together meaningfully) and external coherence (whether themes aligned with one another and with the dataset as a whole). During this stage, some themes were merged due to overlap, others were separated to capture distinct ideas, and some were set aside when supporting evidence was insufficient.
Phase 5: Defining and naming themes. Once refined, themes were clearly defined and named to reflect their central ideas. Final themes were organized using the multidimensional literacy framework that guided the study, linking

patterns in the data to linguistic, cognitive, sociocultural, and motivational dimensions of literacy development. This theoretical alignment ensured that findings were both grounded in evidence and connected to the study's broader conceptual goals.

Phase 6: Writing. The final phase involved selecting illustrative extracts for each theme and weaving them together with analytic commentary. This narrative presentation highlighted not only what occurred in the classroom but also what these moments reveal about students' engagement with contextualized, AI-generated narratives.

Throughout all phases, close attention was paid to disconfirming or contrasting cases, that is, instances that challenged or complicated emerging interpretations. For example, while personalization generally supported high engagement, at least one student showed greater interest in plot events than in the presence of familiar characters. Such variations underscored that contextualization does not operate uniformly; rather, its effectiveness depends on individual learner characteristics and preferences. The findings that follow represent the interpretive fruits of this analytical labor.

Drawing on these methodological approaches, the analysis revealed patterns across multiple interconnected dimensions of literacy development, which are presented in the following section.

FINDINGS. WHAT MAKES AI NARRATIVES WORK? THE THREE PILLARS OF EFFECTIVE CONTEXTUALIZATION

The first major finding to emerge from this study concerns the conditions under which AI-generated narratives become pedagogically powerful. Analysis across all data sources revealed that contextualization operated through three interconnected factors: personalization based on students' interests, linguistic adaptation to their developmental capabilities, and integration of sociocultural elements reflecting their lived experiences. These were not separate variables but interwoven dimensions that worked synergistically, each amplifying the others' effects. This section examines each pillar in detail, showing how it manifested in students' responses and why it mattered for engagement and learning.

The Influence of Personal Interest

The most immediately visible effect of contextualization came through the incorporation of characters students loved. When the first narrative opened with "Once upon a time, Pikachu, Ladybug, Messi, Bluey, and Elsa were walking to Torrefiel Park…," the classroom response shifted dramatically. Students who moments earlier had been playing, whispering to neighbors, or looking out the window suddenly snapped to attention. Several even jumped in their seats. One boy pointed at the projected image and exclaimed: "¡Mira, mira, es Pikachu, mi favorito, qué guay!" Others joined in almost simultaneously: "¡Ladybug!" "¡Messi está ahí!" The atmosphere moved instantly from the polite, somewhat restrained attentiveness typical of story time to a visibly heightened level of genuine excitement.

This immediate recognition created what can be understood as an emotional hook: a point of entry into the narrative world grounded in personal relevance. Conventional textbook stories often rely on generic characters, such as Sam or Emma, functioning primarily as pedagogical tools. Students attend to these stories because they are expected to, not because the characters hold any particular meaning for them. In contrast, when a familiar and beloved character such as Pikachu appears, attention is driven by intrinsic interest. The character carries associations with pleasure and enjoyment from outside school and represents something chosen rather than imposed.

The impact of this personalization extended beyond the initial moment of engagement. Across the three narrative sessions, students demonstrated sustained focus. Field notes document consistent attention even from students who typically struggled to remain engaged. One observation from April 15 notes that a student with SEN needs remained focused for the entire 20-minute session, an uncommon occurrence during textbook-based story activities. He leaned toward the screen, smiled when Messi appeared, and exhibited none of the usual avoidance behaviors (looking around, playing with objects, requesting to leave the classroom). In Krashen's terms, the affective filter appeared significantly reduced, allowing for more productive participation in English.

Additional insight emerged during the focus group interview. When asked what they liked most about the stories, students overwhelmingly referenced characters:

Researcher: What did you like most about the stories? Student A: ¡Que sale Pikachu! Student B: Me gustó cuando Messi jugaba al fútbol. Student C: Ladybug es mi favorita. Student D: Bluey también estaba y es muy divertida.

Students did not mention vocabulary learning or language practice, which were the instructional goals behind the design. Instead, they highlighted characters, indicating that affective connection served as the pathway through which linguistic engagement occurred. Caring about what happened to Pikachu or Messi motivated close attention to the English descriptions of their actions, fostering a willingness to engage with challenging language.

Personalization also appeared to influence students' activity beyond the classroom. In the days following each narrative, students were observed referencing the stories during break, incorporating characters into their play, and drawing scenes from the narratives during free time. One child created an elaborate drawing of the five characters sharing a picnic, adding Spanish labels and including English food words from the story ("apple," "tomato," "sandwich"). Such spontaneous extensions suggested that the stories had entered students' imaginative lives, something rarely achieved by narratives in textbooks.

It was also clear, however, that personalization did not operate uniformly for all students. One high-performing student expressed relative indifference to the character choices, stating during the focus group: "Para mí me da igual los personajes. Me gustó más la historia de qué pasaba." This response highlights the need to consider individual variation even within approaches designed to maximize personal relevance.

Linguistic Bridges to Comprehension and Production

The second pillar of effective contextualization concerned linguistic design, this is, how narratives were crafted to provide comprehensible input while encouraging productive output. This required careful calibration: language needed to be challenging enough to promote growth but accessible enough to maintain engagement and understanding.

The narratives incorporated several linguistic features that supported comprehension. First, they used high-frequency vocabulary that students had encountered previously in classroom instruction, providing familiarity that aided recognition: words like "park," "friends," "food," "happy," "play." Second, they employed simplified syntactic structures typical of A1-level English, primarily simple present and present continuous tenses, basic sentence patterns, limited subordination. Third, they included significant repetition, with key vocabulary and phrases recurring across the narrative: "Do you like...?" "Yes, I do / No, I don't." "I like..." This repetition reinforced learning without becoming monotonous because it occurred within an engaging storyline.

Fourth, and perhaps most importantly, the narratives incorporated what emerged as "linguistic bridges": moments in which Spanish and English mixed strategically. While the stories were primarily in English, they occasionally included Spanish words or phrases, particularly for complex concepts or emotional expressions. For instance, when a character felt excited, the narrative might say: "Pikachu was very emocionado - very happy and excited!" This code-switching served multiple functions: it ensured comprehension for students still building English vocabulary, validated the translanguaging practices many students naturally employ, and reduced anxiety by acknowledging that mixing languages is normal rather than a failure.

Evidence of the narratives' linguistic accessibility appeared in students' comprehension during storytelling sessions. When the teacher-researcher paused to ask basic comprehension questions such as "Where are the friends going?" and "What food does Messi like?", most students could respond correctly, either in English or Spanish. Likewise, other spontaneous comments and predictions further demonstrated active meaning-making rather than passive reception.

The most compelling evidence of appropriate linguistic design came from what Swain and Lapkin (1995) call "pushed output", moments when students attempted to produce language beyond their current comfort zone. Several striking instances occurred not during formal lessons but in informal contexts afterward, particularly during break and transitions. The teacher-researcher recorded one particular memorable moment in her journal:

Research journal, April 16: "During bathroom transition after Story 3, Student TD4 came to ask permission to wash hands before snack. Instead of asking in Spanish as usual, he said: 'Teacher, me puedo wash the hands?' Mixed the Spanish request structure ('me puedo') with the English vocabulary from the story. Huge smile on his face when he said it. He was clearly proud of using English. I responded in English ('Yes, you can wash your hands') and he skipped off happily. This exact phrase was not taught directly; he constructed it by combining Spanish structures he knew with English he had heard in the story. Beautiful evidence of creative language use."

This hybrid utterance, "me puedo wash the hands?", beautifully illustrates how accessible linguistic input can encourage learners to take risks with production. The student felt confident enough with "wash the hands" (a phrase repeated multiple times in the hygiene-focused narrative) to incorporate it into his own authentic communicative act. The mixing of Spanish syntax and English vocabulary, far from representing confusion or deficit, demonstrated exactly the kind of creative, experimental language use that characterizes successful early foreign language acquisition.

Similar instances of spontaneous English production occurred with other students. During recess one day, two children were heard saying "I like apples" and "I like tomatos," adapting the preference expressions from the story to their own contexts. Another student distributing snacks commented: "Here, sandwich para ti," fluidly combining English vocabulary with Spanish grammar. These spontaneous uses of English outside the instructional frame suggested that linguistic input from the narratives had become internalized to the point of voluntary retrieval.

The focus group provided additional insight into students' perceptions of the stories as linguistic supports:

Researcher: Did the stories help you learn English words? Student TD2: Sí, porque repetías las palabras y así me acuerdo mejor. (Yes, because the words were repeated and I remember them better.) Student HP1: Había palabras fáciles que ya sabíamos pero también algunas nuevas. (There were easy words we already knew, but also new ones.) Student TD6: Me gustó que a veces decías en español cuando no entendíamos. (I liked that sometimes you said things in Spanish when we didn't understand.)

These reflections reveal emerging metalinguistic awareness. Students identified repetition as a memory aid, recognized the balance between familiar and novel vocabulary, and understood the role of Spanish as a scaffold for comprehension.

Cultural Mirrors and Windows

The third pillar of effective contextualization involved integrating sociocultural elements that reflected students' lived experiences and cultural backgrounds. This dimension proved particularly powerful, generating some of the study's most emotionally resonant moments and revealing how language learning and identity formation intertwine for young bilingual/multilingual learners.

The narratives deliberately incorporated foods representing the classroom's cultural diversity: arepas (Venezuela/Colombia), couscous (Morocco), baozi (China), chapati (Pakistan), alongside more universally familiar items like apples, tomatoes, and sandwiches. They also referenced places students knew intimately such as Torrefiel Park and the local market, grounding fantasy characters in real geography that students navigated weekly. These design choices aimed to create what Rudine Sims Bishop (1990) memorably termed "mirrors and windows": mirrors in which students could see themselves reflected, and windows through which they could look into others' experiences.

The "mirror effect", students seeing their own cultures reflected, generated profound reactions. During the second narrative, when characters discussed preparing food for Ladybug's birthday and Pikachu mentioned bringing arepas, a Colombian student's face lit up with surprise and delight. After the story concluded, she said with emotion in her voice: "Teacher, él ha dicho que también come arepas, aunque son de mi país. ¿Pikachu ha estado en Colombia?" (Teacher, he said he also eats arepas, even though they're from my country. Has Pikachu been to Colombia?)

This moment captures something profound about what representation means for children navigating multiple cultural worlds. For this student, hearing arepas mentioned in an English story at her Spanish school validated a part of her identity often invisible in educational contexts. Food, as anthropologists remind us, carries deep cultural significance; it connects to home, family, memory, belonging. When Pikachu ate arepas, he symbolically entered this student's cultural world, and she experienced recognition: her background mattered enough to be included in a story, alongside the more dominant Spanish and international cultural references that typically populate school materials.

The geographic contextualization produced similar effects. Setting stories in Torrefiel Park and mentioning the local market grounded fantasy characters in students' actual lived geography. During one narrative, when characters walked past “the big tree near the playground,” several students recognized the specific landmark and called out “¡El árbol grande!” This recognition seemed to delight them, the boundary between story world and real world became permeable, with their familiar neighborhood transformed into a stage where beloved characters enacted adventures. One student's drawing from her portfolio depicted Pikachu and Messi at the park, with careful attention to specific playground equipment she knew from weekly visits.

Yet the sociocultural dimension extended beyond providing mirrors. The narratives also functioned as “windows,” offering students glimpses into cultural practices different from their own and fostering intercultural curiosity. After hearing about diverse foods, students began asking questions that revealed emerging intercultural awareness. During the focus group, one Spanish student asked: “Teacher, ¿hay baozi en España? ¿Dónde se puede comprar?” (Teacher, are there baozi in Spain? Where can you buy them?) This question demonstrated not just recognition of unfamiliar food but genuine curiosity about accessing it, a desire to try something from another culture.

Another student, after hearing about multiple foods in the stories, commented thoughtfully: “Cada persona come cosas diferentes de su país pero todos comemos algo rico” (Each person eats different things from their country but we all eat something delicious). This observation, remarkably sophisticated for a six-year-old, showed developing understanding that cultural diversity doesn't mean hierarchy, different doesn't mean better or worse, just different. The narratives, by presenting cultural elements matter-of-factly alongside each other (arepas, couscous, baozi, chapati, apples), modeled respect for diversity without exoticizing or othering any particular culture.

Cognitive and Motivational Dimensions in Action

While personalization, linguistic accessibility, and cultural relevance created conditions for engagement, the narratives also needed to support actual literacy development. In this sense, it was important to observe the cognitive work of meaning-making and the motivational dispositions that sustain learning effort.

One clear indicator of cognitive engagement was students' ability to make inferences and predictions beyond explicit textual information. During storytelling sessions, the teacher-researcher deliberately paused at strategic moments to invite predictions: “What do you think will happen next?” “How do you think Ladybug feels?” Rather than simply guessing randomly, students frequently offered predictions grounded in narrative logic and character understanding.

For instance, during the picnic story, after hearing that friends were gathering food but before the resolution, she asked what they thought would happen next.

One high-ability student immediately responded: “Van a jugar después de recoger porque si no las cosas salen volando” (They're going to play after picking up because otherwise things will fly away). This prediction demonstrated several cognitive operations simultaneously: understanding cause-effect relationships (wind scatters unpacked items), anticipating character actions based on logical consequences, and applying real-world knowledge about outdoor activities to narrative interpretation.

Another student, during Ladybug's birthday story, predicted emotional outcomes: “Le va a gustar la sorpresa porque le gusta mucho la cake” (She's going to like the surprise because she really likes cake). This inference connected explicit information (Ladybug likes cake) to an anticipated emotional response (surprise will please her), demonstrating understanding of how characters' preferences influence their reactions—a foundational aspect of social cognition.

Student work artifacts provided additional evidence of cognitive processing. The sequencing activities, in which students arranged story events in order, were successfully completed by all students, including those who typically struggled with such tasks. One student's portfolio included a sequencing worksheet with careful attention to temporal logic: shopping for food, preparing ingredients, setting up the picnic, eating together, playing games. His work showed not just memory of events but understanding of necessary sequence, you must prepare before eating, clean up before playing.

Several students' drawings revealed inferential elaboration beyond what the narratives explicitly stated. One drawing depicted characters playing football after the picnic, with a caption (written with assistance): “After eating, they play.” The narrative had ended with friends eating together; this student inferred a logical continuation based on typical childhood activity patterns. Another student drew Messi kicking a ball toward a goal, adding details (goalposts, other players) not mentioned in the story but consistent with football contexts. These elaborations showed students were not passively absorbing narratives but actively constructing enriched mental models.

Furthermore, it is worth noting that the most striking finding concerned the motivational dimension, with students showing enthusiasm, voluntary participation, and growing confidence. This manifested in observable behaviors during sessions, in portfolio reflections, and in focus group comments about their experience.

During storytelling sessions, students made spontaneous comments and asked questions voluntarily rather than only responding when called upon. They sustained attention throughout 15-20-minute sessions, which is significantly longer than for six-year-olds. When sessions concluded, several students regularly asked “¿Hay más?” (Is there more?) or “¿Cuándo es el próximo cuento?” (When is the next story?)—expressions of desire for continuation rarely heard after textbook activities.

The most powerful evidence of motivational impact came from comparing engagement patterns across different instructional contexts. The SEN student's transformation was particularly notable. During typical English lessons using textbook materials, he exhibited what educational psychologists' term "avoidance behaviors": frequent requests for bathroom breaks, claims of not understanding, physical restlessness, and emotional withdrawal. These behaviors signal high anxiety and low self-efficacy—a student who has internalized the belief that "I can't do this" and thus protects himself by avoiding engagement rather than risking failure.

Yet during the AI-generated narrative sessions, these avoidance behaviors virtually disappeared. The field notes that the teacher-researcher recorded document his sustained attention, his smiles (rare during English instruction), his voluntary pointing to images when asked questions, and even one moment where he attempted a one-word English response unprompted. While his linguistic production remained minimal, his behavioral engagement represented dramatic change. In the portfolio self-assessment using a traffic light system (green = I liked it and felt good, yellow = it was okay, red = I didn't like it or felt bad), he colored the circle bright green and drew a large smiley face. This visual evidence of a positive emotional experience felt profoundly significant to a student who typically found English instruction threatening rather than enjoyable.

Portfolio reflections revealed students' awareness of their own emotional responses. Several students drew pictures showing themselves smiling during story time. One wrote (with spelling assistance): "Me gusta cuando Teacher cuenta los cuentos de Pikachu" (I like when Teacher tells the Pikachu stories). Another student's reflection included: "Los cuentos son divertidos y aprendo inglés" (The stories are fun and I learn English)—a statement that beautifully captures the integration of enjoyment and learning that motivated engagement produces.

The focus group conversation provided rich qualitative evidence of motivational impact. When they were asked how they felt during the stories, responses consistently emphasized positive emotion:

Researcher: How did you feel when we listened to the stories? Student TD3: ¡Muy bien! Me gustaba mucho. (Very good! I liked it a lot.) Student HP2: Emocionada porque era Ladybug y Pikachu. (Excited because it was Ladybug and Pikachu.) Student TD5: Contento porque entendía. (Happy because I understood.) Student TD7: Yo quería saber qué pasaba después. (I wanted to know what happened next.)

These responses reveal different facets of motivation: pleasure (me gustaba), excitement (emocionada), satisfaction from comprehension (entendía), and curiosity driving continued engagement (quería saber qué pasaba). Together, they paint a picture of students experiencing English instruction as enjoyable and accessible rather than frustrating and threatening.

This inclusive motivational effect matters profoundly for educational equity. In many classrooms, struggling learners experience repeated failure that gradually erodes motivation and self-efficacy, creating downward spirals where lowered confidence further impedes learning. Interventions that can break this cycle, creating positive emotional experiences of engagement and success even for students who typically struggle, offer potential pathways toward more equitable outcomes. While three narrative sessions obviously cannot transform longstanding patterns, the visible shift in the SEN student's engagement suggested that contextualized, personalized content might offer one tool for creating more inclusive literacy learning environments.

These findings reveal that effective contextualization operates holistically rather than through isolated factors. Personal interest hooks students initially but requires linguistic accessibility to sustain engagement and cultural relevance to deepen emotional connection. Together, these elements create conditions where students feel both motivated to engage and capable of engaging, a combination that enables the cognitive work of meaning-making to proceed productively.

These findings demonstrate AI's potential to support multidimensional literacy development when carefully contextualized and thoughtfully mediated. The following section explores the broader implications of these patterns for educational practice, policy, and research.

TEACHER MEDIATION AS THE BRIDGE BETWEEN TECHNOLOGY AND LEARNING

The findings presented in this chapter illuminate a deceptively simple but profoundly important insight: AI-generated narratives become pedagogically powerful not through technological sophistication alone, but through contextualization and the deliberate human work of grounding AI outputs in students' lived realities. This contextualization operated across three interconnected dimensions: personal interests that activated engagement, linguistic design that enabled comprehension and production, and sociocultural elements that validated identities while fostering intercultural awareness. Together, these factors created conditions where all students, regardless of initial competence or background, could participate meaningfully in literacy development.

Consequently, this finding carries significant implications for understanding AI's role in early language education. It suggests that the technology functions most powerfully as what Vygotsky might have termed a "cultural tool": an instrument that amplifies human capability when skillfully wielded but remains inert without expert mediation. Generic AI outputs, generated without specific knowledge of the learner, lack the personal and cultural resonance that makes narratives meaningful.

The transformation from generic to contextual required getting acquainted with the students: their favorite characters, their cultural backgrounds, their linguistic capabilities, their neighborhood geography. This knowledge emerged from seven months of daily interaction, careful observation, and relationship-building. No AI system, regardless of sophistication, possesses or can develop this situated understanding. Teacher expertise thus becomes not supplementary but constitutive of effective AI integration.

The study also reveals how contextualized narratives can support more equitable literacy development in diverse classrooms. Traditional one-size-fits-all materials systematically disadvantage students whose experiences, cultures, and languages differ from dominant norms, creating engagement gaps that compound over time. The SEN student's transformation from avoidance to active participation exemplifies how personalized, culturally responsive content can create alternative pathways to engagement. While three sessions cannot overcome longstanding disparities, the visible shifts in motivation and participation suggest that contextualization offers one tool for making literacy instruction more inclusive and accessible.

However, this promise comes with important limitations. Contextualization requires substantial teacher effort in terms of gathering interest data, analyzing patterns, crafting detailed prompts, evaluating outputs, and orchestrating delivery. It cannot be automated or scaled without teacher involvement, meaning it demands time and expertise that overburdened educators may struggle to provide. Additionally, the approach risks superficiality if cultural representation stops at naming foods or featuring characters, without deeper engagement with students' lived experiences and identities. Effective contextualization requires ongoing critical reflection about what we choose to represent, how, and why. These questions demand pedagogical wisdom AI cannot provide.

CONCLUSION

This study began with questions about whether and how AI-generated narratives could support literacy development in diverse early language classrooms. The evidence presented here offers a clear answer: when carefully contextualized by knowledgeable teachers, AI-generated narratives can activate multidimensional literacy development, creating conditions for engagement, comprehension, and meaningful learning across diverse learner profiles. The Colombian student's delight at hearing about arepas, the SEN student's sustained attention and visible enjoyment, and the spontaneous code-mixing that showed confident language experimentation; all these moments reveal AI's potential when harnessed through pedagogical expertise.

However, this potential remains precisely that, a promising pathway that requires realization through human judgment, cultural sensitivity, and ongoing critical reflection. AI does not replace teachers; it requires them more than ever. Technology provides capability, the ability to generate personalized content at scale, but teachers provide wisdom: knowing students deeply enough to contextualize meaningfully, orchestrating delivery to maximize engagement, recognizing moments of confusion or insight, and reflecting critically on what representation means and requires.

As AI tools become increasingly prevalent in education, the question is not whether to use them but how to use them responsibly, ethically, and effectively. This study suggests that the answer lies in keeping human relationships, cultural understanding, and pedagogical intentionality at the center. Technology can amplify good teaching, but it cannot substitute for the irreplaceable work of knowing students, building relationships, and making countless contextual judgments that transform generic content into meaningful learning experiences. In the age of AI, human teaching matters more than ever.

ACKNOWLEDGMENT

This research is part of a project developed within the framework of the University of Valencia's Vice-Rectorate for Research internal program, Special Actions call, reference number: UV-INV_AE 4225665

REFERENCES

Bishop, R. S. (1990). Mirrors, windows, and sliding glass doors. *Perspectives: Choosing and Using Books for the Classroom, 6*(3), ix–xi.

Bort Caballero, M. L., & Gil-Mediavilla, M. (2023). Intervención educativa con narrativas digitales en lengua y literatura española del grado universitario en educación primaria: Una perspectiva en femenino. *Formación Universitaria, 16*(4), 43–52. DOI: 10.4067/s0718-50062023000400043

Braun, V., & Clarke, V. (2006). Using thematic analysis in psychology. *Qualitative Research in Psychology, 3*(2), 77–101. DOI: 10.1191/1478088706qp063oa

Chavous, K. P. (Host). (2024, May 22). Why is storytelling important for children? [Podcast episode No. 155]. In *WIWTK Podcast*. https://youtu.be/e82LWWhX4OQ?si=fbDywXTJMwGJkKc9

Cochran-Smith, M., & Lytle, S. (1993). *Inside/outside: Teacher research and knowledge*. Teachers College Press.

Cope, B., & Kalantzis, M. (2009). Multiliteracies: New literacies, new learning. *Pedagogies, 4*(3), 164–195. DOI: 10.1080/15544800903076044

Cope, B., & Kalantzis, M. (2015). *A Pedagogy of Multiliteracies: Learning by design*. Palgrave and Macmillan. DOI: 10.1057/9781137539724

Deci, E. L., & Ryan, R. M. (1985). *Intrinsic motivation and self-determination in human behavior*. Springer., DOI: 10.1007/978-1-4899-2271-7

Dewey, J. (1913). *Interest and effort in education*. Houghton Mifflin., DOI: 10.1037/14633-000

Dupuy, B., & Hashemi, T. (2025). Infographics by Design: Beginning French Learners' Multimodal Composition and Authorial Agency. In Reyes Torres, A., Brisk, M. E., & Lacorte, M. (Eds.), *Multiliteracies, Multimodality, and Learning by Design in Second Language Learning and Teacher Education* (pp. 67–85). Routledge. DOI: 10.4324/9781032620497-7

Egan, K. (1986). *Teaching as storytelling: An alternative approach to teaching and curriculum in the elementary school.* University of Chicago Press.

Kalantzis, M., & Cope, B. (2025). Multiliteracies Since Social Media and Artificial Intelligence. *Harvard Educational Review*, *95*(1), 135–151. DOI: 10.17763/1943-5045-95.1.135

Kern, R. (2000). *Literacy and Language Teaching*. Oxford University Press.

Krashen, S. D. (1985). *The input hypothesis: Issues and implications*. Pergamon Press.

Kucer, S. B. (2014). *Dimensions of literacy: A conceptual base for teaching reading and writing in school settings* (4th ed.). Routledge. DOI: 10.4324/9780203428405

Lave, J., & Wenger, E. (1991). *Situated learning: Legitimate peripheral participation.* Cambridge University Press. DOI: 10.1017/CBO9780511815355

Mayer, R. E. (2008). *Learning and Instruction.* Prentice Hall.

New London Group. (1996). A Pedagogy of multiliteracies: Designing social futures. *Harvard Educational Review*, *66*(1), 60–93. DOI: 10.17763/haer.66.1.17370n67v-22j160u

Paas, F., Renkl, A., & Sweller, J. (2003). Cognitive load theory and instructional design: Recent developments. *Educational Psychologist*, *38*(1), 1–4. DOI: 10.1207/S15326985EP3801_1

Paesani, K., & Menke, M. (2023). *Literacies in language education: A guide for teachers and teacher educators.* Georgetown University Press. DOI: 10.2307/j.ctv31jm8v4

Rahmawati, A., Suhatmady, B., Sucahyo, D., & Hermagustiana, I. (2025). Storytelling in English language learning: Boosting confidence and discourse in EFL contexts. *Borju*, *7*(1), 1–13. DOI: 10.24903/bej.v7i1.1895

Reyes-Torres, A., Brisk, M. E., & Lacorte, M. (2025). *Multiliteracies, multimodality and learning by design in second language learning and teacher education.* Routledge., DOI: 10.4324/9781032620497

Reyes-Torres, A., & García-Perera, A. (2022). Influence of positive student-teacher interaction on the meaning-making process in virtual learning: A study in the primary English class. In Giannikas, C. (Ed.), *Transferring language learning and teaching from face-to-face to online settings* (pp. 165–188). IGI Global Scientific Publishing., DOI: 10.4018/978-1-7998-8717-1.ch009

Rosenblatt, L. M. (1994). *The reader, the text, the poem: The transactional theory of the literary work*. Southern Illinois University Press.

Swain, M., & Lapkin, S. (1995). Problems in output and the cognitive processes they generate: A step towards second language learning. *Applied Linguistics*, *16*(3), 371–391. DOI: 10.1093/applin/16.3.371

Tavares, V. (2024). *Social justice through pedagogies of multiliteracies. Developing and strengthening L2 learner agency and identity*. Routledge. DOI: 10.4324/9781003438847

Vygotsky, L. S. (1978). *Mind in Society: The Development of Higher Psychological Processes*. Harvard University Press.

Wiggins, G., & McTighe, J. (2005). Backward design. In G. Wiggins & J. McTighe, *Understanding by design* (2nd expanded ed., pp. 13–23). Association for Supervision and Curriculum Development.

Zapata, G. (2022). *Learning by design and second language teaching: Theory, research, and practice*. Taylor and Francis., DOI: 10.4324/9781003106258

KEY TERMS AND DEFINITIONS

AI-Generated Narratives: Stories or texts produced by artificial intelligence systems in response to human prompts and shaped through pedagogical mediation to create contextualized and meaningful learning content.

Artificial Intelligence: Technology that enables computer systems to perform tasks commonly associated with human thinking, such as generating content, recognizing patterns, and responding to input.

Contextualization: The process of adapting content to learners' specific interests, linguistic needs, and sociocultural backgrounds so that it becomes more meaningful and accessible.

English As an Additional Language: The learning and use of English by students who already speak one or more other languages in their home or community.

Generative AI: A type of artificial intelligence that produces new content, such as stories, text, or images, in response to prompts provided by users.

Literacy Development: The gradual growth of learners' ability to understand, interpret, and use language meaningfully across reading, listening, speaking, and writing.

Mediation: The act of facilitating understanding or communication by interpreting, adapting, or bridging between different sources, participants, or forms of information.

Motivation: The set of internal and external influences that drive learners to engage with, sustain, and invest effort in language learning activities.

Multidimensional Literacy: An approach to literacy that sees learning as the interaction of linguistic, cognitive, sociocultural and developmental dimensions.

Prompt Design: The process of crafting instructions or inputs that guide artificial intelligence systems to generate specific outputs.

Section 2
Policy: AI Policy and Ethical Concerns

Chapter 8

AI Policy in Blended Intensive Programmes (BIPs) in Europe:
Insights From ENHANCE Alliance

Alexia Larchen Costuchen
http://orcid.org/0000-0001-8260-4059
Universitat Politècnica de València, Spain

Oksana Polyakova-Nesterenko
http://orcid.org/0000-0003-0575-2386
Universitat Politècnica de València, Spain

Paula Villalba Perez
http://orcid.org/0000-0002-8708-4272
Universitat Jaume I, Spain

ABSTRACT

The increased integration of artificial intelligence (AI) into hybrid mobility within the ENHANCE Alliance in Europe raises a number of pedagogical, organisational, and regulatory questions. This chapter examines the AI policy in Blended Intensive Programmes (BIPs), by analysing its implementation, such as AI administrative chatbots, AI-supported collaboration in group tasks, AI as a reflective teammate, and LLM-enabled co-creation. The study adopts a qualitative, document-based analysis supported by institutional evidence and the EU legal frameworks, particularly the AI Act and the General Data Protection Regulation (GDPR). Additionally, UNESCO's Guidance for Generative AI in Education and Research provides a global perspective. Our findings reveal that the discussed AI cases require careful

DOI: 10.4018/979-8-3373-6420-9.ch008

alignment with the Data Protection Impact Assessment (DPIA) and human-centred (international and institutional) governance to ensure responsible and inclusive educational innovation in BIPs.

INTRODUCTION

Student mobility in Europe has progressively evolved from a geographically anchored model towards hybrid participation, digital collaboration, and multilingual inclusion (European Students' Union, 2019; Kavasakalis & Gkiza, 2022; Antal-Berbecaru et al., 2024). Erasmus+ and similar European initiatives have intended to formalise collaboration beyond just bilateral exchange (European Commission, 2025), especially after the Lisbon Recognition Convention and the Bologna Process, which laid foundations of the European Higher Education Area (EHEA) through the introduction of common degree structures, credit systems, and recognition procedures (Council of Europe & UNESCO, 1997; Eurydice, 2025). It made the European higher education system more embedded in global knowledge economies, with a conceptual shift from mobility-as-movement to mobility-as-participation (Knight, 2019; Veletsianos & Houlden, 2019).

The ENHANCE Alliance, founded in 2019, is one of the European Commission's agreements, which brought together ten universities of technology (all of them focusing on engineering, sustainability and innovation) to pursue an integrated European campus via multilingual learning and intercultural collaboration (ENHANCE Alliance, 2019; 2024; European Commission; 2024, March 26; European Parliament Research Service, 2025). It includes approximately 293,000 students and 63,000 employees, which increases both opportunities and risks of educational technology and generative AI in Blended Intensive Programmes or BIPs (Polyakova et al. 2024; Polyakova, 2024). BIPs, formalised under Erasmus+ 2021–2027, combine a short physical mobility period with a virtual component that is flexible in duration and design, and enable universities to compress the in-person phase by teaching the rest of the syllabus through online collaboration (European Commission, 2025; CIVIS Alliance, 2026). This structure is important for AI policy because it shifts its pedagogical value toward the virtual phase, in which the in-person period is short; therefore, the effectiveness of a BIP preparatory stage, shared framing, and multilingual coordination becomes decisive (O'Dowd, 2021; SEPIE, 2022; Cress & Kimmerle, 2023; OECD, 2026).

Likewise, the ENHANCE Alliance's strategy is often understood through the axes of Innovative Organisation, Future Knowledge, and One Campus (ENHANCE Alliance, 2023). This structure offers a multi-layered context in which AI can be integrated not merely as a tool but also as a sociotechnical teammate across institutional systems, languages, and cultures (European University Association, 2026; CIVIS Alliance, 2026). On the one hand, the AI component transforms alliances into powerful innovation platforms; on the other hand, it intensifies challenges related to interoperability, equal opportunities, and alignment with competence-oriented training in the European education systems (Polyakova & Gaslyan-Sargsyan, 2019). AI has been increasingly giving a response to such constraints in mobility as language barriers, time-zone asynchrony, access to institutional information, and difficulties in coordinating student teams in compressed timeframes (Nguyen et al., 2024; Li et al., 2025). In this context, conversational systems and LLM-based tools can help students work across languages, provide quick feedback, and support collaboration in challenge-based environments, including those related to the United Nations Sustainable Development Goals, SDGs (Leal Filho et al., 2024; Aditya, 2026).

Furthermore, the integration of AI in the EU higher education goes beyond purely pedagogical dimensions. It is governed by the General Data Protection Regulation (GDPR), which structures lawful data minimisation, transparency, and accountability (European Union, 2016), together with the EU Artificial Intelligence Act (AI Act), which establishes risk-based obligations that include transparency and human oversight for certain educational contexts (European Union, 2024). The AI Act's timeline has accelerated institutional work across 2025 and 2026, as early provisions came into practice in 2025 while its full implementation approaches around 2026 (European Union, 2024; European Commission, 2025). In parallel, global policy has framed generative AI in education demanding AI skills development among students, teachers, and administrative staff (UNESCO, 2023; OECD, 2023; OECD, 2026).

BACKGROUND

Today, Human-AI interaction is often understood as cognitive, social, and cultural processes through which students interact with AI systems as teammates (Zheng et al., 2024). Early research in Human-Computer Interaction (HCI) focused mainly on usability and interface design (Norman, 2013). However, recent Human-AI interaction (HAI) studies show that AI systems can influence how users think, perceive, and behave (Kaate et al., 2025). In this context, the media equation (Reeves & Nass, 1996) and the social presence theory (Short et al., 1976) suggest that people may assign social qualities to computer systems, which can affect their trust in them and their reliance on them (Biocca et al., 2003; Larchen, 2020; Klein, 2025). Similarly, research on trust calibration in automation highlights the importance of appropriate transparency when people interact with intelligent systems (Mitchell, 2025), including the participants of the ENHANCE Alliance.

Beyond cognitive and usability perspectives, sociocultural theories offer other ways to understand the AI use in higher education and in BIPs collaboration. Distributed cognition (Hutchins, 1995) explains knowledge as something that develops through interaction among people, tools, and environments. Similarly, sociometrical approaches point out that human actions and technologies are closely connected and shape practices together (Bayne, 2015; Antal-Berbecaru et al., 2024). More research argues that technologies are not just tools that support work and learning, but active team players that aid organisational and educational processes (Maack, 2024; Romero, 2025). These ideas support current views on AI as part of networks that include both human and nonhuman teammates. They connect with relational and posthuman approaches in educational technology (Wang & Wang, 2025) where hybrid intelligence emerges as a result of joint human and AI capabilities (Kong et al., 2025).

Multilingual and multicultural contexts, in this regard, introduce further complexity in the use of language technologies such as machine translation, automated transcription, and large language models (LLMs). They mediate communication across linguistic boundaries and influence epistemic authority, participation, and inclusion (Sangkawong et al., 2025; Chan, 2025) among the BIP exchange participants. Cultural dimensions such as distance, individualism versus collectivism, and uncertainty shape how users interpret technological authority and risk (Komatsu et al, 2026). Studies in intercultural communication suggest that rights and rules surrounding collaboration and academic integrity vary across cultures (Hall, 1976; Wang, 2025; Cannavale et al., 2025), which may influence how BIP students perceive AI-generated content and co-authorship with intelligent systems. Meanwhile, international policy frameworks shape how artificial intelligence can be integrated into education. Among them, UNESCO's Guidance for Generative AI in Education and Research provides a global legal perspective (UNESCO, 2023) through a human-centred approach, emphasizing on the aspect that artificial intelligence should enhance and not narrow human capabilities.

Students from the ENHANCE Alliance are an important target group to study these issues. They come from different universities, language backgrounds, and fields of study. Because of this diversity, they need to develop not only technical skills but also AI literacy, ethical awareness, and the ability to work well with others (Pan et al., 2025), especially in multicultural and multilingual contexts (Larchen Costuchen et al., 2025). In hybrid and virtual projects, which reflect wider changes in global work structures (Swartz et al., 2025), students perform in teams, communicate asynchronously, and use AI-supported tools in their workflows. Theories of computer-supported cooperative work (CSCW) and sociotechnical systems help to explain how this shared knowledge and collective intelligence develop through interaction between humans and the AI systems (Al-Abdullatif, 2025).

MAIN FOCUS OF THE CHAPTER

The main objective of this chapter is to analyse AI policy in the ENHANCE mobility context through four practical cases that address the following use of AI in Blended Intensive Programmes (BIPs): AI chatbots for administrative guidance (AI Use 1), AI-support in collaborative tasks (AI Use 2), AI as a reflective teammate (AI Use 3), and LLM-supported co-creation in the virtual phase (AI Use 4).

In relation to AI Use 1, BIP formats require formal documentation, recognition of learning outcomes, and close cooperation between the partner institutions. As student mobility involves cross-border data exchange (European Parliament & Council, 2016), the integration of AI tools must comply with the General Data Protection Regulation, GDPR (European Data Protection Board, 2020; 2024) and, increasingly, the EU Artificial Intelligence Act (European Parliament & Council, 2024). The AI use in BIPs is therefore both a pedagogical and a regulatory matter (Smuha, 2021; Veale & Borgesius, 2021) because administrative chatbots can improve access to information in multilingual and multicultural mobility settings and provide real-time guidance. However, they may process personal data, which requires identification of controller responsibilities. This component needs the lawful basis to ensure transparency and appropriate safeguards under the GDPR (European Data Protection Board, 2020; 2024). While typically it is not high-risk under the AI Act when such chatbots are limited to information provision, their classification may change if they influence eligibility or administrative decisions.

Regarding AI Use 2, AI-supported challenge-based collaboration provides the core model of intercultural teamwork in BIPs. AI tools can support coordination and knowledge creation (Järvelä et al., 2023; Ouyang et al., 2023), but they may also shape evaluation and participation (Usher, 2025¸; AlGhamdi et al., 2026). If the AI outputs influence grading or significant academic decisions, GDPR provisions on profiling and automated decision-making become relevant, and high-risk classification under the AI Act may arise (European Data Protection Board, 2020; 2024). Legal risk thus depends on how the tool is functionally integrated into assessment in BIPs (European Parliament and Council of the European Union, 2024).

With respect to AI Use 3, reflective AI teammates support metacognition and intercultural learning (Auer, 2025), yet reflective content may include sensitive personal data (European Data Protection Board, 2020; 2024). This triggers strict data protection safeguards and careful consideration of legal bases, especially where reflection is linked to credit recognition. If AI-generated feedback affects grading, requirements concerning fairness, transparency, and human oversight become central (European Parliament and Council of the European Union, 2024).

Finally, in correspondence with AI Use 4, which covers LLM-supported co-creation in the virtual phase, it transforms the online component of BIPs into space for active knowledge production (Maier et al., 2025). At the same time, generative AI raises questions about data transfer, authorship, and accountability. Under the AI Act, universities act as deployers of general-purpose AI systems and must ensure transparency and effective human supervision, particularly in task assessment (European Parliament & Council, 2024).

METHOD AND DATA SYNTHESIS

This study uses a qualitative, document-based analysis to examine four AI-enabled BIP functions, from AI Use 1 to AI Use 4 (Table 1). The empirical base combines the ENHANCE Alliance documentation and the BIP-related institutional data (ENHANCE Alliance, 2023). As some BIP details are not publicly described (e.g., specific tools, datasets, or data retention policies), our analysis relies on open data, allowing readers to verify and replicate findings.

To explore BIP chatbot regulation, this chapter uses materials from RWTH Aachen University describing their data protection framework for chatbot services and the implementation of an institutionally managed LLM system (RWTH Aachen University, 2024a, July 16; RWTH Aachen University, 2024b, December 11; RWTH Aachen University IT Center, n.d.). We also consider guidance from KTH Royal Institute of Technology on the use of generative AI in teaching contexts (KTH Royal Institute of Technology, 2026, January 8; January 28). In addition, this report draws cross-alliance pedagogical evidence from a documented BIP on science communication and generative AI delivered by the Arqus Alliance (Arqus Alliance, 2025, May 15).

At the European level, the AI Act (European Parliament & Council of the European Union, 2024) plays an important role in protecting democratic values while UNESCO's (2023) Guidance for Generative AI in Education and Research provides a global perspective. The legal analysis follows a doctrinal approach and focuses on the main principles of the GDPR (European Data Protection Board, 2020; 2024). It also examines the situations that require stronger obligations, especially when a Data Protection Impact Assessment (DPIA) is required under Article 35, as well as the risk-based framework and implementation timeline of the AI Act (European Union, 2016; 2024).

Because DPIAs are often used as internal compliance tools and are not always publicly available, this study compares the GDPR threshold in Article 35 with official guidance from EU institutions and regulators (Regulation EU 2016/679, Article 35). The analysis includes explanations from the European Commission on when a DPIA is required and guidance from the European Data Protection Board (EDPB) on AI-related data protection and DPIA practices (European Commission, 2024; European Data Protection Board, 2024).

We organised our findings into a comparative matrix (Table 1) that summarises the data and links each AI case to legal obligations in the BIP context.

Table 1. Synthesis of AI-enabled BIP Functions

Governance Dimension	AI Use 1: Administrative Chatbot	AI Use 2: AI-Supported Collaboration	AI Use 3: Reflective AI Teammate	AI Use 4: LLM Co-Creation in the Virtual Phase
Primary Function	Multilingual onboarding and administrative guidance	Team coordination, idea generation, collaborative synthesis	Metacognitive scaffolding and formative feedback	Collaborative writing, design and knowledge production
Pedagogical Role	Reduces administrative burden; gives indirect support for mobility learning	Supports intercultural teamwork and hybrid intelligence	Enhances reflection and intercultural learning	Transforms the virtual phase into active collaborative learning
Legal Basis (GDPR)	Art. 6(1)(e) Public task	Art. 6(1)(e); possibly 6(1)(f) for analytics	Art. 6(1)(e); Art. 9 if sensitive data is disclosed	Art. 6(1)(e); additional lawful basis if personal data is included in prompts
Key GDPR Risks	Transparency; data minimisation; cross-border transfers	Profiling; monitoring; automated decision-making	Sensitive personal data processing	International transfers; reuse of prompts; authorship accountability
Article 22 Risk	Low unless when influences eligibility	Moderate-High if it influences grading	Moderate if AI feedback affects assessment	High if AI outputs directly shape graded submissions
DPIA Trigger Likelihood	Low-Moderate (monitoring threshold dependent)	Moderate-High (profiling or assessment use)	Moderate (systematic sensitive data processing)	Moderate-High (integration into formal evaluation)
AI Act Risk Level (Likely)	Generally non-high risk	Potential high-risk if used in educational assessment	Context-dependent	Increased scrutiny if AI contributes to student evaluation
Required Safeguards	Transparency notice; defined retention; Article 28 contract; human escalation	Human oversight in grading; limits on profiling; assessment transparency	Strict access control; purpose limitation; sensitive data safeguards	Human supervision; clear AI-use policy; disclosure in assessed work
Controller / Processor Complexity	University controller; vendor processor; possible joint controllership	Often joint controllership between partner institutions	Elevated controller responsibility due to sensitive data	Complex vendor relationships; deployer duties under AI Act

continued on following page

Table 1. Continued

Governance Dimension	AI Use 1: Administrative Chatbot	AI Use 2: AI-Supported Collaboration	AI Use 3: Reflective AI Teammate	AI Use 4: LLM Co-Creation in the Virtual Phase
International Transfer Risk	Medium (cloud chatbot providers)	Medium-High (collaboration tools + AI APIs)	Medium	High (LLM APIs often hosted outside EU unless institutional entity used)
Retention Sensitivity	Short onboarding period	Limited to project duration	Very limited; long-term storage should be avoided	Prompt storage should be avoided unless it is strictly necessary
Empirical Case Evidence	RWTH Aachen University chatbot data protection framing (RWTH Aachen University, 2024a)	ENHANCE BIP collaboration structures; AI-supported teamwork practices (ENHANCE Alliance, 2023)	KTH Royal Institute of Technology guidance on GenAI use in teaching (KTH Royal Institute of Technology, 2026)	Arqus Alliance BIP on science communication & generative AI (Arqus Alliance, 2025)

Source: Own elaboration

Although UNESCO (2023) does not classify AI in the same way as the four categories mentioned in this study, those practices can still be examined. Table 2 summarises how the four AI uses in BIPs align with UNESCO's regulation.

Table 2. Aligning AI in BIPs with UNESCO's AI guidance

AI Use Case	ENHANCE BIPs (2023-2026)	UNESCO Guidance (2023)
Use 1: Administrative Chatbot	AI supports logistical communication, onboarding information, and administrative guidance during the virtual phase	Data protection, transparency, and human oversight are required in AI-supported services
Use 2: AI-Supported Collaboration	AI supports group coordination, idea generation, and collaborative learning among international student teams	Ethical pedagogical use of AI and protection of collaborative and inclusive learning environments are necessary
Use 3: Reflective AI Teammate	AI supports student reflection by providing feedback and guidance during learning activities	Development of critical AI literacy and preservation of human agency in AI-mediated learning are highly recommended
Use 4: LLM-Supported Co-Creation	Generative AI supports brainstorming, drafting, and co-creation of academic outputs	Responsible use of generative AI, transparency in authorship, and validation of AI tools in education are essential

Source: Own elaboration

We can observe that the AI uses in BIPs (2023–2026) support learning and collaboration while, in line with UNESCO guidance, they require transparency, data protection, human oversight, and responsible use of generative AI.

DISCUSSION OF RESULTS

The first case (AI Use 1: Administrative Chatbot) focuses on chatbots for administrative orientation and onboarding in ENHANCE. RWTH Aachen University provides an example of how such services can be legally managed. Its IT Center published a data protection statement explaining that chatbot data processing is part of the university's public service and falls under Article 6(1)(e) of the GDPR (European Data Protection Board, 2020; 2024), together with related transparency information (RWTH Aachen University, 2024a; European Parliament & Council of the European Union, 2024). This approach fits the BIPs model because onboarding often involves multilingual communication, tight schedules, and repeated questions. Chatbots can provide scalable support and improve BIP mobility access. However, they must follow key GDPR principles (European Data Protection Board, 2023; 2024). Although the pedagogical role of AI in this case is indirect, onboarding chatbots can reduce administrative workload and cognitive pressure, allowing students to focus more on collaboration and intercultural exchange during the short on-site phase. At the same time, their use raises policy considerations highlighted by UNESCO (2023), particularly in the need for privacy safeguards and age-appropriate access policies. These measures help to ensure that conversational AI systems function as support tools rather than administrative decision-makers.

Another related issue appears in RWTH's description of RWTHgpt, which presents an institutional LLM tool which stores data locally on university servers (RWTH Aachen University IT Center, n.d.). The system also restricts the reuse of chat content for external training (RWTH Aachen University, 2024b, December 11). Although RWTHgpt is not designed specifically for BIPs, it shows an example of regulation that is relevant for university alliances. In multi-institution programmes, concerns about data sovereignty increase because students come from different countries and institutions. Commercial AI services may also create uncertainty about data reuse and cross-border data processing. In this context, institutionally managed infrastructure can support innovation while still complying with GDPR requirements (European Data Protection Board, 2023, 2024). For administrative AI tools, the need for a Data Protection Impact Assessment (DPIA) depends on whether the system involves systematic monitoring, profiling, or other high-risk processing. EU guidance explains that this threshold depends on the specific context and on the possible risks to individuals' rights and freedoms (European Commission, 2024;

European Data Protection Board, 2024a). Although neither the European AI Act nor UNESCO directly regulate administrative chatbots, they emphasize on the importance of transparency and data protection when AI systems interact with users.

The second case (AI Use 2: AI-Supported Collaboration) focuses on the use of AI in challenge-based learning linked to Sustainable Development Goals (SDGs), which is a common teaching format in BIPs (European Commission, 2024). In this context, the value of AI is not in answering administrative questions but in supporting learning processes. AI can help students to explore ideas, to work across languages, and to collaborate more efficiently during the virtual phase. From this perspective, AI is useful when it supports higher-level thinking under human supervision. This approach is consistent with learning theories such as connectivism (Siemens, 2005) and boundary object theory (Star & Griesemer, 1989), which describe learning as a networked process supported by shared tools and resources.

In BIP mobility settings, AI can act as a shared tool that helps students from different linguistic and disciplinary backgrounds work together. However, UNESCO's human-centred approach draws attention to the aspect that authentic human interaction should remain central. AI can support collaboration through tasks (e.g. information summary, content translation, suggesting project ideas, or proofreading, etc.), however, it should not replace any social and cognitive processes that take place within student teams (Cress & Kimmerle, 2023). From a legal perspective, the AI Act (Regulation EU 2024/1689) becomes applicable when AI tools influence task assessment or course grading (European Parliament & Council of the European Union, 2024). Regulation classifies such educational uses of AI as high-risk and therefore requires stricter safeguards, including risk management procedures, technical documentation, transparency, and human oversight (European Union, 2024, Annex III). For this reason, more institutions are developing AI literacy frameworks and internal AI responsibility guidelines that reflect principles from international policy documents (OECD, 2023; UNESCO, 2023; European Commission, 2025; OECD, 2026).

The third case (AI Use 3: Reflective AI Teammate) involves AI assistants designed to support self-regulated learning, intercultural reflection, and learning outcomes. This role is particularly valuable in BIP mobility, where students may find it challenging to transform their experiences into learning reflections. However, such systems also raise important data protection concerns. Reflective texts may contain personal information and may reveal behavioural patterns. Under the GDPR, this may require a Data Protection Impact Assessment (DPIA), particularly when data processing poses a high risk to individuals' rights or involves systematic monitoring (European Union, 2016; European Commission, 2024). The European Data Protection Board emphasises on the importance of establishing a lawful basis when AI systems process personal data in educational contexts (European Data Protection Board, 2024b). UNESCO (2023) notes that generative AI although provides rapid feedback and suggestions for self-directed learning, it requires continuous human supervision, as AI outputs may contain inaccuracies. In learning contexts that foster critical thinking, AI can function as a cognitive partner by prompting students to reconsider arguments or to identify gaps in their reasoning. At the same time, UNESCO warns that excessive reliance on AI may weaken the learners' ability to evaluate information independently. Therefore, AI should be used to support metacognitive awareness rather than to replace human reflection.

An important policy signal in the ENHANCE context comes from guidance by KTH Royal Institute of Technology, which states that teachers cannot require students to use generative AI tools due to unresolved legal issues, including those related to GDPR and copyright (KTH Royal Institute of Technology, 2026). It effectively sets a regulatory boundary for the use of reflective AI. Such tools may be offered as optional support, but making their use mandatory could place students in situations involving unclear data-processing conditions. Therefore, institutions should implement opt-in systems, ensure transparency, apply strict data minimisation and data retention policies, and provide human alternatives for students who prefer not to use AI-based reflection tools (European Union, 2016; European Commission, 2024).

The fourth case (AI Use 4: LLM Co-Creation in Virtual Phases) addresses LLM-enabled co-creation in the virtual phase and the broader generative turn in BIP pedagogy observed in 2025 and 2026 (OECD, 2023; UNESCO, 2023). While early BIP virtual phases were often experienced as preambles, generative AI now makes it possible to structure the virtual phase as a process of continuous work with multilingual synthesis, rapid drafting and asynchronous collaboration across time zones. This transformation is not only theoretical; it is also evidenced by documented GenAI-focused BIP activities within the European university alliance ecosystem. For example, the Arqus Alliance reported a BIP focused on science communication and generative AI, involving 22 students from three countries and designed around multilingual and multimodal narrative production (Arqus Alliance, 2025). Such programmes demonstrate how generative AI can be positioned not as a hidden productivity tool but as an object of critical practice. Students can be assessed on their ability to critique, refine, and transparently document AI-generated outputs rather than focusing on the output production alone. UNESCO (2023) also notes that AI can support creative tasks such as writing, coding, and artistic production by offering suggestions or assisting with problem-solving. Nevertheless, creative learning should remain human-centred, as excessive reliance on AI may limit the development of original thinking.

Across the four use cases analysed, a broader policy pattern emerges. UNESCO guidance suggests that institutions integrating AI into teaching and administrative practices should establish internal policies aligned with international standards. These should address data protection, risk management, AI literacy training, and human oversight. When implemented responsibly, AI can enhance learning environments; however, without such governance, institutions risk weakening both data protection and the quality of teaching and learning. At the alliance level, the ENHANCE's institutionalisation of BIPs through coordinated calls suggests that AI-related policy decisions will be made at scale (Figure 1), increasing the need for shared AI literacy frameworks (ENHANCE Alliance, 2023). In this context, not only must EU AI policies be implemented, but learners, educators, and staff must also be prepared to operate within AI-informed educational environments.

CONCLUSION

Our analysis reveals that the AI policy in ENHANCE-context mobility is best understood as an intersection of pedagogical transformation and legal governance. Administrative onboarding chatbots can be viewed as public-service infrastructure under the GDPR lawful bases, while institutionally governed LLM services illustrate new approaches to data sovereignty and transparency. Challenge-based learning shows that AI can function as a cognitive partner that accelerates inquiry and supports multilingual collaboration, but only within the governance boundaries that preserve human oversight and avoid AI-driven evaluation roles. Reflective AI assistants display why the most pedagogically valuable uses can also be the most legally sensitive, because reflection data heightens the DPIA relevance and raises questions about voluntary participation and power asymmetry in educational contexts. Finally, the LLM-enabled reconfiguration of the virtual phase is supported by documented GenAI BIP activity in the European alliance ecosystem, and it is reinforced by policy pressures created by the AI Act's timeline, which has pushed institutions toward formalised governance and literacy frameworks.

Overall, the facts shift the view of the BIPs virtual phase from an administrative barrier to a collaborative space that shapes the success of the compressed physical mobility period. In this model, the real BIP mobility starts before travel with multilingual teamwork, and reaches its peak on-site through negotiation, prototyping, and intercultural exchange.

Within the AI policy framework discussed in this study, the ongoing Blended Intensive Programme "Enhancing Sustainable Communication, Professional Competences and AI" illustrates an AI-friendly learning ecosystem. It represents collaboration among three EU technical universities (Universitat Politècnica de València, Warsaw University of Technology, and Technische Universität Berlin), the ENHANCE associate partners, and two Ukrainian Technical Universities from

Kyiv and Lviv. The programme focuses on sustainability and integrates two AI uses: supported collaboration (AI Use 2) and co-creation (AI Use 4).

As ENHANCE continues to expand BIPs across different institutions, the main challenge will be to build shared AI literacy and strong data practices that protect fairness and trust. For future AI-supported BIPs, several key questions will shape how learning develops: How do legal risks differ between individual chatbot use and collaborative human-AI work? Which AI uses carry the highest risk under the AI Act? What safeguards are needed when AI is used in student assessment? By tackling these questions, the ENHANCE partnership will maintain a delicate human-AI balance in BIPs and will shape future policies.

ACKNOWLEDGMENT

We sincerely thank students and educators from all the participating institutions for their engagement, valuable insights, and diverse perspectives. Brought together through collaboration within the ENHANCE Alliance, the ENHANCEPLUS project and the ENHANCE UPV team were fundamental to this applied study. Additionally, we express our gratitude to the Institute of Education Sciences at the Universitat Politècnica de València (UPV) for its support through the Didactic Innovation Programme PIME/25-26/580, "IncludED: Virtual Collaboration for Global and Diverse STEM Learners." Moreover, we extend our appreciation to the UPV EICE team "Innovation, PLurilingualism, Universities and Sustainability" (i-PLUS), for their contribution and commitment to promote educational quality. Their support was essential for successful implementation of this initiative.

REFERENCES

Aditya, D. (2026). Leveraging conversational AI for enhanced educational experiences: A systematic review and framework. *Cogent Education*, *10*(1), 2611649. DOI: 10.1080/2331186X.2025.2611649

Al-Abdullatif, A. M. (2025). Auditing AI literacy competency in K–12 education: The role of awareness, ethics, evaluation, and use in human–machine cooperation. *Systems*, *13*(6), 490. DOI: 10.3390/systems13060490

AlGhamdi, E. M., Li, Y., Gašević, D., & Chen, G. (2026). Leveraging prompt-based LLMs for automated scoring and feedback generation in higher education. *Computers & Education*, *243*, 105511. DOI: 10.1016/j.compedu.2025.105511

Antal-Berbecaru, A., Larchen Costuchen, A., & Dev, S. (2024). Survey Gamification: Engaging Generation Z. *Computers in the Schools*, *41*(4), 448–472. DOI: 10.1080/07380569.2023.2271486

Arqus Alliance. (2025, May 15). *The University of Minho holds the in-person phase of BIP "Generative Artificial Intelligence to create multilingual and multimodal narratives from scientific open data"*. https://arqus-alliance.eu/news/in-person-bip-generative-artificial-intelligence-uminho/

Auer, M. E. (2025). Artificial intelligence–supported reflective learning in higher education: Implications for intercultural competence and metacognition. *International Journal of Emerging Technologies in Learning*, *20*(2), xx–xx. https://doi.org/xxxxx

Bayne, S. (2015). Teacherbot: Interventions in automated teaching. *Teaching in Higher Education, 20*(4), 455–467. DOI: 10.1080/13562517.2015.1020783

Biocca, F., Harms, C., & Burgoon, J. K. (2003). Towards a more robust theory and measure of social presence. *Proceedings of the 36th Annual Hawaii International Conference on System Sciences*, 1–10. DOI: 10.1109/HICSS.2003.1174289

Cannavale, C., Claudio, L., & Koroleva, D. (2025). Digitalisation and artificial intelligence development: A cross-country analysis. *European Journal of Innovation Management, 28*(11), 112–130. DOI: 10.1108/EJIM-07-2024-0828

Chan, C. K. Y. (2025). Students' perceptions of "AI-giarism": Investigating changes in understandings of academic misconduct. *Education and Information Technologies, 30*(6), 8087–8108. DOI: 10.1007/s10639-024-13151-7

CIVIS Alliance. (2026). *Blended Intensive Programmes (BIPs) strategic guide and implementation outcomes 2024-2025*. CIVIS Alliance.

Council of Europe, & UNESCO (1997). *Convention on the recognition of qualifications concerning higher education in the European region (Lisbon Recognition Convention)*. Council of Europe Publishing.

Cress, U., & Kimmerle, J. (2023). Collective knowledge construction in computer-supported collaborative learning. *International Journal of Computer-Supported Collaborative Learning, 18*(1), 1–10. DOI: 10.1007/s11412-023-09409-w

Cress, U., & Kimmerle, J. (2023). Co-constructing knowledge with generative AI tools: Reflections from a CSCL perspective. *International Journal of Computer-Supported Collaborative Learning, 18*(4), 607–614. DOI: 10.1007/s11412-023-09409-w

ENHANCE Alliance. (2019). *ENHANCE alliance mission and vision*. https://enhanceuniversity.eu

ENHANCE Alliance. (2023). *ENHANCE Alliance documentation and institutional data on Blended Intensive Programmes (BIPs)*. https://enhanceuniversity.eu/resources

ENHANCE Alliance. (2023). *ENHANCE annual report 2023*. https://enhanceuniversity.eu

ENHANCE Alliance. (2024). *ENHANCE alliance strategy and achievements report*. https://enhanceuniversity.eu

European Commission. (2024). *When is a data protection impact assessment (DPIA) required?* https://commission.europa.eu/law/law-topic/data-protection/rules-business-and-organisations/obligations/when-data-protection-impact-assessment-dpia-required_en

European Commission. (2024, March 26). *European universities initiative: Facts and figures*. https://education.ec.europa.eu

European Commission. (2025). *Artificial Intelligence Act: Timeline and phased implementation overview*. European Commission, Directorate-General for Communications Networks, Content and Technology. https://digital-strategy.ec.europa.eu

European Commission. (2025). *Erasmus+ annual report 2025*. Publications Office of the European Union.

European Commission. (2025). *Ethical guidelines on the use of artificial intelligence and data in teaching and learning for educators*. Publications Office of the European Union.

European Commission. (2025). *Implementation timeline and compliance guidance for the Artificial Intelligence Act*. Publications Office of the European Union.

European Data Protection Board. (2020). *Guidelines 05/2020 on consent under Regulation 2016/679 (Version 1.1)*. https://www.edpb.europa.eu

European Data Protection Board. (2020). *Guidelines 07/2020 on the concepts of controller and processor in the GDPR (Version 2.0)*. https://edpb.europa.eu

European Data Protection Board. (2020). *Guidelines on the concepts of controller and processor in the GDPR (Version 2.0)*. https://edpb.europa.eu/our-work-tools/our-documents/guidelines/guidelines-072020-concepts-controller-processor-gdpr-version-20_en

European Data Protection Board. (2023). *Guidelines 01/2023 on data protection impact assessment (DPIA) and determining whether processing is "likely to result in a high risk" for the purposes of Regulation (EU) 2016/679*. https://www.edpb.europa.eu

European Data Protection Board. (2023). *Guidelines 01/2023 on processing of personal data in the context of administrative public services* (Version 1.0). https://edpb.europa.eu

European Data Protection Board. (2023). *Guidelines on data protection by design and by default (Article 25 GDPR)*. https://www.edpb.europa.eu

European Data Protection Board. (2024). *Opinion 28/2024 on certain data protection aspects related to the processing of personal data in the context of AI models*. https://www.edpb.europa.eu/our-work-tools/our-documents/opinion-board-art-64/opinion-282024-certain-data-protection-aspects_en

European Data Protection Board. (2024b). *Opinion 28/2024 on certain data protection aspects related to the processing of personal data in the context of AI models*. https://www.edpb.europa.eu

European Data Protection Board. (2024b). *Guidelines on the processing of personal data in the context of AI systems* (latest version). https://www.edpb.europa.eu

European Parliament. (2024, March 8). *Artificial Intelligence Act: MEPs adopt landmark law*. European Parliament News. https://www.europarl.europa.eu/news/en/press-room/20240308IPR19015/artificial-intelligence-act-meps-adopt-landmark-law

European Parliament & Council of the European Union. (2016). Regulation (EU) 2016/679 of the European Parliament and of the Council of 27 April 2016 on the protection of natural persons with regard to the processing of personal data and on the free movement of such data (General Data Protection Regulation). *Official Journal of the European Union, L, 119*, 1–88. https://eur-lex.europa.eu

European Parliament & Council of the European Union. (2024). *Regulation (EU) 2024/1689 of the European Parliament and of the Council laying down harmonised rules on artificial intelligence (Artificial Intelligence Act). Official Journal of the European Union*. https://eur-lex.europa.eu

European Parliament and Council of the European Union. (2016). Regulation (EU) 2016/679 of the European Parliament and of the Council of 27 April 2016 on the protection of natural persons with regard to the processing of personal data and on the free movement of such data (General Data Protection Regulation). *Official Journal of the European Union, L, 119*, 1–88. https://eur-lex.europa.eu/eli/reg/2016/679/oj/eng

European Parliament and Council of the European Union. (2024). *Regulation (EU) 2024/1689 of 13 June 2024 laying down harmonised rules on artificial intelligence (Artificial Intelligence Act). Official Journal of the European Union*. https://eur-lex.europa.eu/eli/reg/2024/1689/oj

European Parliament Research Service. (2025). *European universities alliances: State of play and future perspectives*. European Parliament.

European Students' Union. (2019). *Bologna with student eyes 2018*. European Students' Union.

European Union (2016). *Regulation (EU) 2016/679 of the European Parliament and of the Council of 27 April 2016 on the protection of natural persons with regard to the processing of personal data and on the free movement of such data (General Data Protection Regulation).* Official Journal of the European Union, L119, 1–88. https://eur-lex.europa.eu/eli/reg/2016/679/oj

European Union (2024). *Annex III to Regulation (EU) 2024/1689: High-risk AI systems referred to in Article 6(2).* In *Artificial Intelligence Act.* Official Journal of the European Union.

European Union (2024). *Regulation (EU) 2024/1689 of the European Parliament and of the Council laying down harmonised rules on artificial intelligence (Artificial Intelligence Act).* Official Journal of the European Union. https://eur-lex.europa.eu

European University Association. (2026). *Artificial intelligence in European universities: Governance, strategy and responsible implementation.* European University Association.

Eurydice (2025). *The European higher education area in 2025: Bologna process implementation report.* Publications Office of the European Union.

Hall, E. T. (1976). *Beyond culture.* Anchor Press/Doubleday.

Hutchins, E. (1995). *Cognition in the wild.* MIT Press. DOI: 10.7551/mitpress/1881.001.0001

Järvelä, S., Nguyen, A., & Hadwin, A. (2023). Human and artificial intelligence collaboration for socially shared regulation in learning. *British Journal of Educational Technology, 54*(5), 1057–1076. DOI: 10.1111/bjet.13325

Kaate, I., Salminen, J., Jung, S. G., Santos, J. M., Häyhänen, E., Xuan, T., Azem, J. Y., & Jansen, B. (2025). The 'fourth wall' and other usability issues in AI-generated personas: Comparing chat-based and profile personas. *Behaviour & Information Technology, 44*(16), 4136–4152. DOI: 10.1080/0144929X.2025.2469659

Kavasakalis, A., & Gkiza, T. (2022). European higher education area, internationalization and students' mobility in 21st century. *Advances in Social Sciences Research Journal, 9*(2), 60–74. DOI: 10.14738/assrj.92.11582

Klein, S. H. (2025). The effects of human-like social cues on social responses towards text-based conversational agents: A meta-analysis. *Humanities & Social Sciences Communications, 12*(1), 1322. DOI: 10.1057/s41599-025-05618-w

Knight, J. (2019). Internationalization of higher education: Past and future. *International Higher Education, 95*, 2–4. DOI: 10.6017/ihe.2019.95.10715

Komatsu, K., Ždanovič, N., Yamabe, M., Iwata, H., Iwamoto, M., & Takeda, S. (2026). The association between national culture and AI readiness: A cross-national study. *Frontiers in Artificial Intelligence*, *9*, 1727606. DOI: 10.3389/frai.2026.1727606 PMID: 41755913

Kong, X., Fang, H., Chen, W., & Zhang, M. (2025). Examining human–AI collaboration in hybrid intelligence learning environments: Human–AI synergy model and classroom evidence. *Humanities & Social Sciences Communications*, *12*, 821. Advance online publication. DOI: 10.1057/s41599-025-05097-z

KTH Royal Institute of Technology. (2026, January 8). *FAQ generative AI* (see "Can I require students to use generative AI in my course?"). https://intra.kth.se/en/utbildning/e-larande/faqs/faq-generativ-ai-1.1417039

KTH Royal Institute of Technology. (2026, January 27). *Considerations for using generative AI* [Guidelines for teachers on ethical and legal use of generative AI]. https://intra.kth.se/en/utbildning/systemstod/generativ-ai/riktlinjer-1.1405092

KTH Royal Institute of Technology. (2026, January 27). *Legal aspects of generative AI* [Overview of GDPR, copyright and AI Act considerations for teachers]. https://intra.kth.se/en/utbildning/systemstod/generativ-ai/legal-aspects-1.1253707

Larchen, A. (2020). From generation gap to generation lap: Gen Z subcultures. In Carrió Pastor, M. L., Periñán-Pascual, C., Romero Forteza, F., & Olmo Cazevieille, F. (Eds.), *Estudios de lingüística aplicada IV* (pp. 113–130). Editorial Universitat Politècnica de València.

Larchen Costuchen, A., Reyes-Torres, A., & Tordera Yllescas, J. C. (2025). Analysis of movie trailers based on a WSH game prototype: Developing critical literacy in L2 students. In Gabonada Gatcho, A. R., Titar-Improgo, C. M., & Papadopoulos, I. (Eds.), *Literacy policies for equity and inclusion* (pp. 1–23). IGI Global., DOI: 10.4018/979-8-3693-8427-5.ch001

Leal Filho, W., Ribeiro, P. C. C., Mazutti, J., Lange Salvia, A., Bonato Marcolin, C., Lima Silva Borsatto, J. M., Sharifi, A., Sierra, J., Luetz, J., Pretorius, R., & Viera Trevisan, L. (2024). Using artificial intelligence to implement the UN sustainable development goals at higher education institutions. *International Journal of Sustainable Development and World Ecology*, *31*(6), 726–745. DOI: 10.1080/13504509.2024.2327584

Li, H., Xu, J., Cui, G., Guan, C., Mo, F., & Huang, K. (2025). Multilingual collaborative defense for large language models. In *Findings of the Association for Computational Linguistics: EMNLP 2025* (pp. 3735–3755). Association for Computational Linguistics. DOI: 10.18653/v1/2025.findings-emnlp.200

Maack, L. (2024). Redefining organizational digitality: A relational-ontological approach inspired by new materialism. *Frontiers in Sociology*, *9*, 1426930. Advance online publication. DOI: 10.3389/fsoc.2024.1426930 PMID: 39525273

Maier, S., Schneider, M., & Feuerriegel, S. (2025). *Partnering with generative AI: Experimental evaluation of human-led and model-led interaction in human-AI co-creation. arXiv*. https://doi.org//arXiv.2510.23324DOI: 10.48550

Mitchell, T. (2025). Trust and transparency in artificial intelligence. *Philosophy & Technology*, *38*(3), 87–106. DOI: 10.1007/s13347-025-00916-2

Nguyen, A., Hong, Y., Dang, B., & Huang, X. (2024). Human-AI collaboration patterns in AI-assisted academic writing. *Studies in Higher Education*, *49*(5), 847–864. DOI: 10.1080/03075079.2024.2323593

Norman, D. A. (2013). *The design of everyday things* (Revised and expanded ed.). Basic Books

O'Dowd, R. (2021). Virtual exchange: Moving forward into the next decade. *Computer Assisted Language Learning*, *34*(3), 209–224. DOI: 10.1080/09588221.2021.1902201

OECD. (2023). *Generative AI in education: Emerging trends and policy implications*. OECD Publishing.

OECD. (2023). *OECD framework for the classification of AI systems and policy implications*. OECD Publishing., DOI: 10.1787/9a87c0b7-

OECD. (2023). *OECD framework for the classification of AI systems: A tool for effective AI policies*. OECD Publishing., DOI: 10.1787/cb6d9eca-

OECD. (2026). *Artificial intelligence in education: Governance, policy and institutional transformation*. OECD Publishing.

Ouyang, F., Wu, M., Zhang, L., Xu, W., Zheng, L., & Cukurova, M. (2023). Making strides towards AI-supported regulation of learning in collaborative knowledge construction. *Computers in Human Behavior, 142*, 107650. DOI: 10.1016/j.chb.2023.107650

Pan, Z., Moore, O. A., Papadimitriou, A., & Zhu, J. (2025). AI literacy and trust: A multi-method study of human-GAI team collaboration. *Cognition and Behavior*, *8*, 100162. DOI: 10.1016/j.chbah.2025.100162

Polyakova, O. (2024). Enhancing staff weeks organisations through service action research. In *Proceedings of the 18th International Technology, Education and Development Conference (INTED2024)* (pp. 2067–2071). IATED. DOI: 10.21125/inted.2024.0576

Polyakova, O., Chrominska, D., & Zarajczyk, I. (2024). Developing professional communication skills and competences around sustainability goals. In *Proceedings of the X Congreso Nacional de Innovación Educativa y Docencia en Red (IN-RED 2024)* (pp. 1165–1177). Editorial Universitat Politècnica de València. DOI: 10.4995/INRED2024.2024.18357

Polyakova, O., & Galstyan-Sargsyan, R. (2019). Communicative competences in non-linguistic university degrees. *Language*, *11*(1), 45–70.

Reeves, B., & Nass, C. (1996). *The media equation: How people treat computers, television, and new media like real people and places*. Cambridge University Press.

Romero, M. (2025). From consumption to co-creation: A systematic review of six levels of AI-enhanced creative engagement in education. *Multimodal Technologies and Interaction*, *9*(10), 110. DOI: 10.3390/mti9100110

RWTH Aachen University. (2024a, July 16). *RWTH launches its own AI tool*. https://www.rwth-aachen.de/cms/root/wir/aktuell/pressemitteilungen/juli-2024/~bipvlz/rwth-setzt-auf-eigenes-ki-tool/?lidx=1

RWTH Aachen University. (2024b) *Implementation of RWTHgpt: Institutionally governed large language model service*. https://www.rwth-aachen.de

RWTH Aachen University. (2024b, December 11). *RWTH rolls out custom AI chatbot for students*. https://www.rwth-aachen.de/cms/root/wir/aktuell/pressemitteilungen/dezember/~blajft/ki-tool-fuer-studierende-rwthgpt-ist-am/?lidx=1

RWTH Aachen University. (2024b, December 11). *RWTH rolls out custom AI chatbot for students (RWTHgpt)*. https://www.rwth-aachen.de

RWTH Aachen University IT Center. (2024). *RWTHgpt: Data protection, hosting infrastructure, and governance framework*. https://www.itc.rwth-aachen.de

RWTH Aachen University IT Center. (2024a) *Data protection statement for chatbot services (RWTHgpt)*. https://www.itc.rwth-aachen.de

RWTH Aachen University IT Center. (n.d.). *Privacy policy* (includes chatbot service data protection information). https://www.itc.rwth-aachen.de/cms/it-center/footer/service/~myfc/datenschutzerklaerung/?lidx=1

Sangkawong, N., Bucol, J. L., & Luciano, R. (2025). Bridging language gaps in real-time: Investigating university students' self-initiated use of speech-to-text translation in English language classrooms. *Teaching English with Technology*, *25*(2), 5–28. DOI: 10.56297/vaca6841/ZDDD4208/KTKA2748

SEPIE. (2022). Blended intensive programmes (BIPs) under [*Implementation guidelines*. Servicio Español para la Internacionalización de la Educación.]. *Erasmus*, •••, 2021–2027.

Short, J., Williams, E., & Christie, B. (1976). *The social psychology of telecommunications*. Wile.

Siemens, G. (2005). Connectivism: Learning as network-creation. *ASTD Learning News*, *10*(1), 1–28.

Smuha, N. A. (2021). From a "race to AI" to a "race to AI regulation": Regulatory competition for artificial intelligence. *Law, Innovation and Technology*, *13*(1), 57–84. DOI: 10.1080/17579961.2021.1898300

Star, S. L., & Griesemer, J. R. (1989). Institutional ecology,translations' and boundary objects: Amateurs and professionals in Berkeley's Museum of Vertebrate Zoology, 1907-39. *Social Studies of Science*, *19*(3), 387–420. DOI: 10.1177/030631289019003001

Swartz, S., Luck, S., & Sharma, S. (2025). Global virtual teams projects and developing AI literacy: A mixed-methods study on preparing students for the international technology-infused workplace. *Higher Education. Skills and Work-Based Learning*, *15*(3), 690–702. DOI: 10.1108/HESWBL-09-2024-0266

UNESCO. (2023). *Guidance for generative AI in education and research*. UNESCO. https://unesdoc.unesco.org/ark:/48223/pf0000386693

UNESCO. (2023). *Guidance for generative AI in education and research*. United Nations Educational, Scientific and Cultural Organization., DOI: 10.54675/EWZM9535

Usher, M. (2025). Generative AI vs. instructor vs. peer assessments: A comparison of grading and feedback in higher education. *Assessment & Evaluation in Higher Education*, *50*(6), 912–927. DOI: 10.1080/02602938.2025.2487495

Veale, M., & Borgesius, F. Z. (2021). Demystifying the draft EU Artificial Intelligence Act. *Computer Law Review International*, *22*(4), 97–112. DOI: 10.9785/cri-2021-220402

Veletsianos, G., & Houlden, S. (2019). An analysis of flexible learning and flexibility over the last 40 years of *Distance Education*. *Distance Education*, *40*(4), 454–468. DOI: 10.1080/01587919.2019.1681893

Wang, S. (2025). Public perceptions of artificial intelligence in 20 countries: Cultural variations in acceptance and risk evaluations. *Journal of Cross-Cultural Psychology*, *56*(7), 891–910. DOI: 10.1177/10693971251336803

Wang, Z., & Wang, C. (2025). A posthumanist approach to AI literacy. *Computers and Composition*, *76*, 102933. Advance online publication. DOI: 10.1016/j.compcom.2025.102933

Zhang, M. (2025). Optimizing academic engagement and mental health through AI: An experimental study on LLM integration in higher education. *Frontiers in Psychology*, *16*, 1641212. DOI: 10.3389/fpsyg.2025.1641212 PMID: 41104404

Zheng, H., Park, S., & Kim, J. (2024). Student perceptions of generative AI as collaborative partner in higher education. *Computers & Education: Artificial Intelligence*, *6*, 100210. DOI: 10.1016/j.caeai.2024.100210

KEY TERMS AND DEFINITIONS

AI Act: The European Union's regulatory framework for artificial intelligence, which adopts a risk-based approach to classify AI systems and establish obligations to ensure safety, transparency, and protection of fundamental rights.

AI literacy: A set of competencies that enable individuals to understand, critically evaluate, and responsibly use artificial intelligence technologies, including awareness of their capabilities, limitations, ethical implications, and potential societal impacts.

AI Policy: A structured set of principles, regulating the use of artificial intelligence to make sure it is ethical, follows the law, and manages risks.

Blended Intensive Programmes (BIPs): Short EU Erasmus+ learning activities that combine online collaboration with a short period of travel to support interdisciplinary and intercultural learning.

Data Protection Impact Assessment (DPIA): Process required by the General Data Protection Regulation (GDPR) and must be carried out by data controllers, organisations or institutions that decide how and why personal data is processed.

ENHANCE Alliance: Part of the European initiative that brings together 10 universities of technology to promote innovation, inclusion and a shared global campus.

Erasmus+: An EU programme that supports education, vocational training, youth activities, and sport via intercultural exchange, skills development, and inclusive participation.

General Data Protection Regulation (GDPR): A data protection law in the European Union that governs how organizations collect, use, store, and protect personal data. It creates a set of rules across the EU and applies to any organization that handles data of the EU residents.

Human-AI Interaction (HAI): An interdisciplinary field that studies how humans and artificial intelligence systems interact, focusing on usability, trust, cognition, and broader socio-technical implications.

UNESCO: A specialised agency of the United Nations that promotes international collaboration in education, science, and culture, developing global policy frameworks in these areas.

Chapter 9
Ethical Implications on Co-Authorship in AI-Assisted Creative Writing

Raúl Gisbert
http://orcid.org/0000-0001-8302-7396
University of Valencia, Spain

ABSTRACT

This article investigates the complex role that generative AI systems play in creative writing tasks or activities conducted in Spanish, with a particular focus on co-authorship dynamics, perceptions of creativity and notions of authorship in the educational context of using AI. The study employs an experimental design based on the students' performance in writing activities, as they have created texts under two conditions: the first one entails writing independently, without technological help; then, they co-create another text of the same type with the assistance of a generative AI tool (ChatGPT). The outputs are subject to comparative textual analysis, focusing on aspects such as originality, stylistic distinctiveness and narrative coherence. This research not only promotes awareness on the use of AI Bots and authorship, but also makes students' reflect on the educational models based on the use of AI tools, preparing them to use creative digital tools with intentionality and self-awareness.

INTRODUCTION

In recent years, generative artificial intelligence (AI) has increasingly been considered from only technological investigation to a common aspect of educational practices and methodologies. AI tools such as ChatGPT and Gemini now generate a wide range of texts with a fluency and adaptability that was difficult to imagine

DOI: 10.4018/979-8-3373-6420-9.ch009

only a few years ago. These new advances have become tools for specific purposes on education, which include text translation, theoretical reviews and even artistic production. Within applied linguistics, researchers have investigated the use of AI in several fields, such as phonetics, syntax, morphology and semantics with findings that highlight promising applications but, at the same time, unavoidable challenges. Yet, despite this growing number of research, one aspect remains quite underexplored: the use of AI in creative writing tasks, especially in contexts where students experiment with literary genres such as poetry and short fiction.

The increasing accessibility of generative AI may raise important questions about creativity, authorship and ownership in this digital and audiovisual age. Even though traditional word processors were helpful to check aspects like spelling, grammar, use of words, etc., these new digital tools can generate content, suggest changes in style and even deliver and create narrative structures that may influence the writer's own choices. In this sense, an important question arises: when students use AI to create a text, are they still the unique authors, or does authorship change into a co-creation between human and machine? In this case, what does such a co-creation mean for originality, authenticity and the development of our students' voice? These questions appear at the core centre of creative writing pedagogy, where critical thinking, authorship and representation of students' own ideas and thoughts are traditionally seen as central to the writer's ability to create a text.

The urgency of addressing these questions has been emphasized by scholars that examine the social and ethical implications of using generative AI to create a text. Draxler et al. (2023), for instance, identify the "AI ghostwriter effect," where users often declare themselves as authors of AI-generated text despite not perceiving full ownership of it. This effect can be understood as proof on how notions of authorship are already being discussed and rethought in practice, even outside academic contexts. Similarly, Ryan et al. (2025) have documented how undergraduate students deal with questions of authorship and self-integrity when using AI in writing courses, highlighting the importance of introducing critical reflection into pedagogy. They state that "significant contribution to an article should not be the only indicator of authorship because it ignores the collaborative process of writing, but we also found that current theories of collaboration are insufficient for thinking about collaborating with non-humans" (2025: 54). In addition, some other studies, such as Hwang et al. (2025), reveal similar opinions on the use of AI in writing and authorship: while writers, teachers and students appreciate the brainstorming and stylistic support AI provides, they remain deeply concerned about preserving authenticity and control over their creative work.

This article, then, aims to shed some light into this current debate, with a specific focus on creative writing activities conducted in Spanish with high school students in the linguistic subject called Castellano: Lengua y Literatura. Designing several creative writing tasks offer a solid basis for examining AI's role because it emphasizes areas such as imaginative expression, experimentation with language and develops a subjective way of expressing ideas and thoughts. Unlike a more rigid way of understanding writing, literary texts help reflect on qualities, such as originality, cohesion and coherence, which are often taken as key points of human creativity. Thus, investigating how AI interacts with these qualities makes it possible to question the boundaries of the collaboration between human and machine in one of the most human domains of language use and meaning conveying.

In this sense, one of the key aspects of this research lies in its potential contribution to pedagogy and theories based on the use of AI. From a pedagogical point of view, the investigation highlights the importance of preparing reflective practices in the classroom for undergraduate students. When students critically reflect on their own use of AI, including the consideration on how and why they accept, modify or reject AI given texts, they develop a more conscious understanding of their perception as authors of a new text. This reflective procedure relies on current needs for critical AI literacy, which emphasize not just a proficient ability to write, but also ethical considerations in digital practices. Theoretically, this study places AI as a neutral tool to be manipulated and we try to argue whether AI tools should be understood as co-participants in writing that actively shapes the way our students create a text. Thus, the questions raised by this investigation may not be limited to the classroom, as AI tools are quickly becoming integrated into publishing, journalism and audiovisual industries, among many others, so we consider that the boundaries of authorship and originality are being redefined at a social level. We could think that several professional writers, such as poets, novelists, journalists and academics are experimenting with AI as a collaborative partner, while publishers and critics debate, and accept to some extent, the legitimacy of AI-generated literature. This cultural debate may serve as the basis of the use of AI's pedagogical role in creative writing. By studying how students reflect on authorship and ownership in AI-assisted tasks, we could form an opinion not only into educational practice but also into the evolving cultural development of creativity in the current digital age.

In sum, this chapter introduces a pedagogical point of view into the ethical and creative implications of using AI-assisted writing in the context of a Spanish language and literature class. By focusing on students' reflective thinking on the use of AI, it aims to shed light on how notions of creativity, authorship and originality are being considered in a society where the technologies are no longer an external tool; they are a central instrument to human expression and the basis to some artistic piece. This introduction may help to set the stage for an in-depth exploration of how educators and students consider using AI's potential tools while highlighting, at the same time, the values of critical reflection, authenticity, originality and responsibility that define a creative act such as writing in a pedagogical context.

THEORETICAL FRAMEWORK

Sociocultural Theory of Mediation

The sociocultural implications of using artificial intelligence to complete writing tasks in educational environments are diverse and always evolving. From a sociocultural learning perspective, AI writing tools function not only as a mechanical support, but as mediation instruments that consider how students reflect on the writing process itself, on the collaboration with a machine and on authorship (Deep and Chen, 2025). Thus, their application to the educational field can develop a renewed traditional understanding of writing as an individual and, at the same time, intellectual activity and raise important questions about the cultural consideration of creating a piece of writing.

First, integrating generative AI writing tools in classrooms may improve the social dynamics of writing, as it allows the adaptation of each task to each student. Blake (2024) highlights the ability of AI to adapt to individual learning styles and needs, offering personalized content and feedback that make it a valuable tool for learners. In contexts where students are learning a second language or exploring new aspects of writing in their own language, as it is Spanish in our research, AI can help structure and organise writing processes and compensate students' knowledge that may be based on limited linguistic and lexical resources. For example, Wang (2024) explores a wide range of perspectives when using AI in EFL contexts and found that AI and machine-translation tools enhance both cognitive and sociocultural dimensions of writing: learners use the AI in different writing stages, sometimes in collaboration with other students or instructors. This illustrates that AI can act as a socially adapted tool, enabling learners to develop and create more advanced writing practices through the guided use of the teacher. In addition, this sociocultural mediation may trigger the reflection on inclusivity and equity in the classroom, as students may use AI's capacity for multilingual support and structural guides to lower barriers to create academic pieces of writing. There are several studies on the matter, but we would like to mention the one provided by Zhao (2025), which indicates that AI-assisted writing tools improve writing proficiency, content structuring, creative writing facilitation and benefits particularly learners who might struggle with conventional instruction methods. In this way, we consider that AI has the potential to grant access to high-quality writing support, reducing structural inequalities in language proficiency or resource availability.

On the other hand, there are sociocultural implications related to academic norms, authorship and the ethical use of these tools. The adoption of AI elements may challenge traditional conceptions of authorship, so it could reflect a two-faced aspect: both teachers and students commonly appreciate AI's efficiency and its capacity to improve writing quality. However, there is also a consideration of this kind of tools as a way that simultaneously express, to some extent, a diminished originality and the doubt of ethical integrity (Lund et al., 2025). This ambivalence reveals a new consideration to be taken into account in the educational environment: teachers, students and institutions must reflect on the expectations about originality, attribution of creativity and the purpose of writing assignments with the use of AI tools.

We could state, then, that the sociocultural dimension of AI-assisted writing in education is characterized by an interplay of critical thinking and self-perception. On the one hand, AI can strengthen a deep reflection on authorship when writing; on the other hand, it may delimit the key aspects of using these tools and the expression of the student's own ideas to fulfil a writing task. Analysing these two aspects requires, among some other features, culturally sensitive pedagogies and continuous critical reflection by teachers and students alike.

Rethinking human and non-human procedures in a pedagogical environment

While sociocultural theory highlights mediation among teachers and students when developing a writing task, we need to consider how the use of AI may be thought as human, partly human or non-human. This perspective poses the analysis of moving the human aspect from the core centre to recognize authorism as a shared task between human and non-human actors. We could argue that using these technological tools at school does not simply grant our student's action but actively participates in shaping specific practices and helps develop author identity.

From this point, we must consider generative AI not only as a neutral instrument but a co-actor in the creative process. Its outputs when creating a piece of writing influences the material effects on the resulting text and on the writer's decision-making. When a student accepts or rejects AI-generated suggestions, they are creating a situation where there is a negotiation of authorship with a non-human tool. Creativity, in this case, emerges not just from the human imagination, but from the dialogue between human intention of writing and a machine-generated text. The statement of this procedure goes far beyond the binary opposition between the use of an AI tool (that is, the student, as an author, gives instructions to the machine) versus the implication of a co-author (which involves assuming that the student is not the only author). Instead, authorship can be seen as a hybrid practice, where the agency of the text is shared between the student and machine contributions. As Bayne (2015) suggests, posthuman pedagogy requires educators to embrace the entanglement of human and technological actors rather than maintaining rigid boundaries. In the pedagogical context of creating a piece of writing, this means acknowledging that AI has an active role in delivering textual outcomes, while still guiding students to critically reflect on their responsibility as human writers.

We could state, then, that the integration of AI into the pedagogy of written tasks has generated a substantial debate among educators. Some professional educators argue that AI offers valuable opportunities for language and stylistic experimentation. In this sense, we consider that, during a creative writing class, AI can provide prompts that expand students' imaginative lines of thought or help them overcome what is known as writer's block. This helps to develop a sociocultural perspective on scaffolding, as we have previously discussed, which can be adapted to each situation and to each student. On the other hand, some others consider the use of this kind of tools inappropriate for pedagogical tasks, such as writing a piece of text. In this case, the general opinion, along with research on this matter, as Al Kaabi's work (2025), shows that reliance on AI may weaken the development of independent ideas and critical thinking. The danger lies in treating AI as a perfect authority rather than as a collaborator requiring a debate about the outcomes provided. Students may adopt AI-generated suggestions uncritically, so it makes them feel distant to their own authorial agency. In this sense, we have already mentioned that pedagogical interventions are necessary to cultivate critical AI literacy, which involves not only AI technical proficiency, but also ethical and critical reflection. (Ryan et al., 2025). As a result, we consider that more research is needed to analyse AI-assisted creative writing, as it is not merely a technical or ethical issue, but as a cultural practice that redefines the authorship and creativity of our students in the current digital age.

Authorship and ownership in the creative digital age

The first application of AI in the field of creative digital arts positioned generative tools as experimental collaborators rather than common tools to be used by most of the population. Veale and Pérez (2020) discussed computational creativity as an effort to develop artistic production through algorithms, raising questions about whether machines could produce original works. With the evolution of generative AI tools, such as ChatGPT or Gemini, it is proven that they can generate cohesive narratives, stylistically adaptive texts and even outcomes that refer to important literary authors. Recent investigations have examined these capabilities in literary and educational contexts. As an example, Lee et al. (2024) explored how writers use AI as a creative assistant, finding that they mainly used the tool to generate new ideas and stylistic variation but expressed a dilemma about authorship. Similarly, Nafees et al. (2025) studied AI-generated English works and found that while readers often recognized some limitations, they struggled to distinguish between human and machine texts in blind evaluations. These findings suggest that AI can efficiently originate literary forms, raising both aesthetic and ethical questions about originality.

Scholars in digital humanities have begun to theorize AI as a new participant in literary and educational contexts. We would like to highlight the idea that while AI introduces new technical possibilities, a discussion, or even a dilemma, between the use of these tools and creativity has been increasingly developed in literary culture.

Theories of authorship have always been presented as an equilibrium between the creativity of an individual actor and collaborative production. Roland Barthes (1967) introduced a famous concept called "death of the author", which challenged the idea of the author as the unique originator of meaning, emphasizing the role of readers and cultural intertextuality. Thus, the implications of authorship have long been studied even before the appearance of AI. In this sense, the appearance of generative AI tools complicates this matter by introducing a non-human actor into the writing process so, unlike collaborative writing between humans, AI makes it necessary to deeply reflect on the ethical and pedagogical aspects of authorship. As Draxler et al. (2024) show, users often self-declare authorship of AI-generated texts even while recognizing that their sense of ownership is diminished. This ambiguity suggests that authorship is increasingly a shared identity to be rethought rather than a fixed combination of actors.

Contemporary researchers, as we could observe, offer different perspectives on this matter, as some of them view AI as an extension of the writer's agency, like, for example, a sophisticated spell-checker (Lee, 2024), which offers a clear view on the writer's obvious role as a sole author. Others argue that AI constitutes a form of co-authorship, since it contributes to the development of content that shapes meaning and style, as we could read in Ryan et al. work (2025). So, as we can observe, there is not an easy outcome from this debate. In this case, the implications of these opinions are more important than it may seem, as several questions may arise when thinking about the use of AI in an educational context: If students rely on AI for narrative invention, how should educators assess creativity and originality? Should assignments explicitly require banning the use of AI or should they prioritize a reflective use instead of just prohibition? These questions show, again, the need for pedagogical frameworks to promote ethical awareness among students on authorship when using this kind of tools.

One of the most cited challenges is the blurred line between tool and co-author. As we have mentioned above, Draxler et al. (2024) coined the term "AI ghostwriter effect" to describe how users often declare themselves as authors of AI-assisted writings while, at the same time, distancing themselves from full ownership. This situation illustrates the instability of authorship within the combination of human practices and AI text generation. At the same time, as we advanced in the Introduction of this research, scholars such as Hwang et al. (2024) studied to what extent students considered themselves as authors when using AI tools to generate a text. They found that participants experienced both empowerment and uneasiness: while

AI facilitated brainstorming and stylistic experimentation, students feared the loss of authenticity and the notoriety of AI being used in their pieces of writing. In educational contexts, which is our case, Ryan et al. (2025) also studied undergraduate writing courses where students used AI to draft assignments. They reported that students struggled with questions of credit, disclosure and originality, often oscillating between viewing AI as an effective writing tool and as a partner and co-author in their writing. Consequently, this ambiguity highlights the importance of teaching students to critically reflect on authorship and creativity in AI-monitored writing tasks.

METHODOLOGY

Research context and participants

The study has been conducted in the context of a Spanish-language literature subject called Castellano: Lengua y Literatura at a mid-sized high school. The subject includes creative writing activities where students experiment with multiple genres, including poetry, short fiction and prose narratives. Approximately 90 students from 3rd of ESO (Educación Secundaria Obligatoria) are the participants and all of them have prior experience in creative writing, ensuring familiarity with literary conventions.

Participation is completely compulsory and the participants are briefed on the purpose of the study, the procedures involved and their duty to complete the tasks proposed. To preserve anonymity, pseudonyms are used in all data reporting.

Experimental Design

The research design involves two writing conditions for each participant:

- Independent Writing Task: Students are asked to compose a literary text (a short narrative between 500-600 words about a topic of their interest) without the use of any technological assistance, only their background knowledge and their level of proficiency in Spanish language. This condition forms the basic stage of the students' creative production.
- AI-Assisted Writing Task: Students are asked to produce a text of similar length and genre using a generative AI system (e.g., ChatGPT or Gemini). They are encouraged to interact with the AI in ways they find useful, so they can generate prompts, request any stylistic suggestion they consider appropriate or co-develop all narrative and linguistic structures. Students are in-

structed to document the interactions and decisions they make during the co-writing process.

Each condition is completed within a fixed timeframe (60 minutes per task) to ensure comparability. The order of conditions is counterbalanced across participants to reduce ordering effects (half of the group beginning with AI-assisted writing and the other half beginning independently). There is also a pause of about 10-15 minutes to change places and adapt the material to complete both tasks.

Data collection

This study has employed three data collection instruments: First, the textual corpus, as all texts produced in both conditions are collected and compiled into a corpus for comparative analysis. This corpus has served as the basis for examining differences in originality, style and coherence. The Appendix 2 and 3 include two examples of writing from the same student, which we will call Student1. The Appendix 2 presents the piece of writing made by the student without any help and the Appendix 3 offers the writing task made with the help of ChatGPT. As we have described, both texts are made in the same context and with the same conditions.

Then, we have prepared a survey that must be completed by the participants. The items measure perceptions of creativity, authenticity and authorship, as well as attitudes toward AI as a tool or co-author. This allows for quantitative analysis of trends and correlations. Lastly, we have carried out a series of interviews. Participants are invited to participate in structured interviews, which provides deeper insights into individual experiences and allows for elaboration on themes emerging from surveys and reflections.

Analytical framework

The textual corpus has been analysed using both qualitative and quantitative approaches: on the one hand, teachers must carefully read the selected texts, which have been analysed in detail focusing on originality, stylistic features and narrative coherence. After that, educators have used automated digital tools to compare linguistic features such as lexical diversity, sentence complexity, and language use in context across the two writing conditions. This use of automated writing evaluation (AWE) and natural language processing (NLP) tools is grounded in a substantial body of research showing that such systems can systematically identify linguistic patterns that correlate with writing quality (McNamara, Crossley and McCarthy, 2010). Tools like Coh-Metrix have been widely used to extract metrics related to cohesion, syntactic complexity, and lexical sophistication, enabling researchers to quantify aspects of writing that are otherwise difficult to analyse reliably by hand. Likewise, studies in the automated assessment literature highlight that NLP-derived features, such as sentence structure, noun phrase complexity and lexical diversity, can serve as valuable proxies for human judgments, especially when combined with machine learning models trained on human-rated corpora (Goldshtein, Alhashim and Roscoe, 2024)

The reflective journals are coded thematically, and categories include perceptions of authorship, authenticity, reliance on AI and ethical considerations. This analysis sheds some light on how students articulate their sense of authorship and collaboration in relation to AI. Then, the data obtained through surveys have been analysed using descriptive elements to compare responses between the independent and AI-assisted conditions. A correlation has appeared between student's attitude toward AI and the textual outcomes from the writing tasks. To present that, a table from the UNESCO AI Competency Framework constitutes the material used, as it offers a description of the specific competencies that students must acquire to be competent and proficient in the use of AI tools (Appendix 1).

At the end of the moment when each tool is applied, findings from textual analysis, journals and surveys are triangulated to provide a comprehensive picture of AI-assisted creative writing. Thus, the observed stylistic, lexical and grammar similarities between AI-assisted texts have been cross-referenced with participants' own pieces of writings.

Ethical considerations and limitations

Several ethical challenges arise in AI-assisted writing research and must be considered when designing this kind of writing tasks. First, issues of authorship and ownership must be presented explicitly, so the students are informed that while they are the specific authors of the texts produced, AI-generated contributions are part of an experimental context nd not independently authorial actors. Second, transparency is emphasized, as participants are asked to use AI tools the way they consider necessary and, after that, to reflect on ethical issues such as co-authorship. Finally, confidentiality is maintained, with pseudonyms used in reporting and during data analysis.

The study also recognizes the risk of over-reliance on AI. To mitigate this issue, it is capital allowing students to discuss their experiences critically and to reflect on the implications of using AI for their future writing practices. We are aware of the limitations of this methodology, such as the sample size. It may be sufficient for exploratory analysis, but it may limit generalizability. The experimental setting may also influence students' natural writing practices, as the time constraints and structured conditions differ from everyday creative processes. Additionally, the choice of a specific AI system may affect outcomes, since different tools vary in stylistic capabilities and range of response. These limitations will be addressed in the discussion section, with suggestions for future research.

RESULTS

Textual differences

Once the comparative analysis of both the student's (Student1) texts is completed, we have discovered that the results reveal both improvements and limitations associated with the assistance of AI tools. As it has been mentioned before, both texts are located in Appendix 2 and Appendix 3 respectively.

First, it is necessary to clarify the concepts of originality and creativity as they are understood within the context of writing pedagogy. Originality in student writing is not limited to the production of entirely new ideas, but rather refers to the ability to combine language, imagery, and narrative choices in ways that reflect personal interpretation and authorial intention. Creativity, in turn, involves experimentation, risk-taking and the capacity to move beyond predictable linguistic or structural patterns to generate meaning in novel or expressive ways. In the tasks provided, both concepts are closely connected to the development of our students' ideas, which helps them build their identity as writers.

In this sense, regarding these two concepts of originality and creativity, AI-assisted texts tend to display greater lexical variety and more polished sentence construction, reflecting the tool's capacity to generate a wide range of expressions in Spanish based on large linguistic sets. These texts often exhibit syntactic balance, grammatical accuracy and stylistic coherence, which can give the impression of high-quality writing. However, this form of originality emerges from the recombination of existing linguistic patterns rather than from lived experience or intentional meaning-making. As a result, originality in terms of inventiveness, appears more frequently in independently written texts produced without AI assistance. In this sense, our analysis suggests that AI tends to generate well-structured and internally consistent sentence patterns, privileging clarity and formal correctness over experimentation. Our students, by contrast, often introduced unconventional elements that disrupted standard structures. These deviations commonly include syntactic irregularities that would typically be smoothed out by an AI system trained to optimise coherence. While such features may be perceived as flaws from a purely technical perspective, they frequently serve as markers of creative risk and personal expression in the student' writing.

Moreover, the tendency of AI to standardise stylistic outputs has a result in texts that are coherent and readable but less distinctive when compared to one another. As generative texts are based on patterns, AI-assisted creations often converge stylistically, leading to a degree of homogeneity across different student texts. In contrast, students' independently written texts, although sometimes inconsistent, demonstrate greater variation in tone, structure and expressive strategies. These irregularities reflect individual cognitive processes and creative decision-making, even when the final product appears less polished.

Our analysis further supports this distinction by revealing higher levels of internal similarity among AI-assisted texts than among independently written ones. This suggests that while AI can enhance linguistic quality, it may simultaneously constrain the range of stylistic possibilities available to students. Consequently, originality and creativity in AI-assisted writing should be understood not only in terms of linguistic sophistication, but also in relation to the degree of authorial recognition and divergence from conventional patterns that characterise human creative expression.

Regarding the narrative coherence, AI-assisted narratives may benefit from improved structural organization, as language models often propose linear and conventional structures to narrate a literary story. On the other hand, texts made by the participants without the help of the AI tools are, in general, less coherent, which allows greater experimentation with non-linear storytelling, even though sometimes the sense and the pace of the narration is blurred or even lost. These different results reflect the dual nature of writing, as we neglect, on some occasions, coherence to provide a grammatical and lexical rich text. So, in this case, AI appears to enhance fluency and aesthetic aspects regarding structure and coherence but may minimize stylistic risk-taking and originality.

Students' perceptions of authorship

By implementing surveys as a methodological tool, we have obtained results describing our student's attitude toward authorship in AI-assisted contexts. Many students (32%) have reported a sort of ambivalence about authorship, as some of them declare themselves authors but recognizing the AI's significant role in creating and modifying the writing content, which are directly related to what we have explained about the "AI ghostwriter effect" (Draxler et al., 2024). Other participants (68%) may resist assigning any authorship to AI, defining it as a complementary tool rather than a partner. The diversity of responses highlights the undefined nature of authorship in this kind of hybrid writing tasks.

In this case, students seem to struggle to define where creativity really is, whether in their prompts, their linguistic choices or in the AI's generated outputs. Some reflections reveal that creativity is increasingly seen as a collaborative process distributed between the student and the selected AI tool. At the same time, some students (19%) feel that AI diminishes their personal style, producing texts that sound unnatural or not at the same level as a Secondary Education student. However, most of the participants (81%) appreciate the AI's capacity to expand their stylistic range. Authenticity, in this case, becomes a subjective concept rather than a specific attribute to be considered in this kind of task.

At the same time, students' emotional engagement with AI-assisted writing is mixed. While some of them find AI inspiring or liberating (77%), especially in overcoming blocks, others experience discomfort or even guilt about the key role of their work (23%), but their number is quite low in comparison to the other group. We consider this aspect capital, as these affective responses would provide an important insight into the pedagogical implications of AI use.

Ethical and Pedagogical Reflections

This study also provides reflections on the ethical and pedagogical dimensions of the use of AI in writing tasks. On the one hand, most students had asked questions about authorship and property, and we would like to offer three examples to evidence these dilemmas: "When I use AI, the ideas I wrote are still mine?", "Do I have to admit that all the text is made by AI?" and "How can I separate the parts made by AI and the parts made by me?". As we could observe, students are still not confident about when and how to use AI properly and some of the implications it may have in an educational context. In this sense, these questions reveal the need we have previously discussed for explicit guidelines on AI acknowledgment and transparency in writing tasks.

Furthermore, for many participants, the contrast between independent and AI-assisted writing helps them understand their own creative processes and the difficulties they have when they are asked to write a piece of writing (92%). By reflecting on this comparison, students have articulated how AI serves as a complementary tool for their decision-making and authorial choices. This suggests that AI, when integrated critically and in a structured way, may function as a pedagogical instrument for linguistic awareness. It is also important to highlight our students' preferences and their previous writing experience. For example, some students are more comfortable with experimental writing, so they have resisted AI's conventionality; on the contrary, those who struggle with coherence have found its patterned influence quite useful. Recognizing this diversity is key to design flexible and individualised, if needed, pedagogical strategies.

A group of students have expressed concern that too much reliance on AI affects their ability to generate original ideas (81%). Reflective journals have helped students to include admissions, thoughts and suggestions such as, "I have used ChatGPT because it was easier than thinking on my own." This kind of statement remarks the pedagogical risk of over-reliance, which could negatively affect creative growth in an educational environment.

Final remarks on the analysis

Taken together, the obtained results clearly show that AI-assisted writing could be seen as a complementary tool or as a completely own entity. In this sense, texts may become more fluent and coherent but less stylistically unique. Moreover, students may feel empowered by AI's suggestions but simultaneously question their own authorship. In this sense, from a pedagogical point of view, AI may both trigger reflective learning and critical thinking on authorship but may involve the risk of dependency.

This synthesis supports the statement that AI in creative writing should not be understood in binary terms (tool vs. co-author) but as a combined practice that redistributes creativity, authorship and responsibility across students and AI systems. Ultimately, the findings provide a clear picture of the advantages and challenges of AI-assisted creative writing, giving a space to increase and develop theoretical debates in this kind of classroom practices.

DISCUSSION OF RESULTS

After the analysis and the findings exposed in the previous section, there are some aspects that need attention and that could be the basis for further research on this matter. On the one hand, generative AI may improve significantly fluency and coherence, as it has been stated; on the other hand, it risks originality and stylistic experimentation, as students tend to follow the patterns offered by this kind of tools. Students' reflections on authorship also help to understand the intrinsic aspects of working with AI, which entail authorship, creativity and critical thinking. In this part, we want to offer an interpretation of the outcomes described above through three interconnected sections: authorship and the role of AI as a writing agent, pedagogical implications for creative writing education and ethical considerations in using AI to complete a writing task.

To begin with, the research supports the idea that authorship in AI-assisted writing cannot be reduced to a simple dichotomy of "human versus machine." In this case, creative agency becomes distributed between human and non-human participants in the task. Students' wide range of answers to the proposed tasks sometimes frame AI as a co-author and others as a tool. As a result, this perception of AI tools illustrates the instability of authorship degrees in educational environments which use digital methodologies.

It is also important to highlight that the participants in this research generally consider that the ultimate responsibility of completing both tasks is theirs, although there is a consideration of AI as a co-author in some cases. The reflective journals also serve as a summary of this section, as they indicate that authorship is increasingly understood as a process of decision-making rather than as a way of originating content to complete the tasks.

Pedagogically, the use of AI has two different implications on the educational system. On one side, AI can act as a basis that helps students overcome blocks, experiment with a wide range of writing types and develop more coherent structures. For non-proficient writers, AI may provide models of any genre conventions (in this case, narrative) that can accelerate the process of learning how to write a specific linguistic task. However, the risk of dependence is equally important, as students who rely excessively on AI's outputs usually limit their creative growth. After the analysis of the reflective journals, we could infer that there is a danger of reducing writing to a process of selection of given information rather than promoting invention. To mitigate this issue, we consider that educators must develop critical AI literacy by teaching students not only how to use AI but how to critically analyse its outputs, recognize its limitations and reflect on the author's voice in this creative process.

One pedagogical strategy emerging from this study, and that we consider capital, is the use of the reflective practice. By asking students to document their processes, perceptions and ethical concerns, educators can guide the students through the role of AI in writing tasks. This reflection transforms AI into a debatable tool, encouraging students to express their opinion toward co-authorship. In this sense, such practices position AI not as a threat to creativity but as an element that can create a debate about what creativity and authorship mean in the educational context. Furthermore, diversity of responses suggests that AI's role in writing education should not be static, as some students thrive with AI as a brainstorming partner, while others resist its conventionality and structured patterns. Therefore, there should be revolution in education leading to the use of flexible methodologies that allow experimentation and critical engagement rather than impose a uniform adoption of the immediate AI outputs.

From the previous analysis, we can confirm that the ethical dimension of AI-assisted writing occupies an important place in students' reflections on authorship and their uncertainty about whether to acknowledge AI participation highlights the urgent need for clearer guidelines in our educational system. One of the main concerns is the risk of deleting or minimising the students' own work. According to the study carried out, if AI-generated texts are perceived as equally authored, the student's contribution is undervalued. What is more, from this study, there seems to be a clear tendency to attribute all authorship to the human writer, and this fact makes invisible the AI agency that finally shapes and develops the text in the writing task. Educators have the role to balance these positions, but this fact requires a reconceptualization of authorship, where the human remains accountable, but the machine's influence is acknowledged and even cited. In this sense, teachers must approach AI critically, not only as a writing aid but as a tool that helps them understand author values and digital limitations.

In sum, these findings and reflections suggest that AI will continue to reshape the field of creative writing in Secondary Education, not by replacing students' ideas, but by transforming the conditions and conceptions of authorship in the classroom. AI functions simultaneously as a tool, a collaborator and a reliable aid. For literary studies, the challenge is to expand traditional notions of authorship to include distributed and non-human forms of agency. And for ethics, the challenge is to design frameworks that acknowledge both the human voice and the machine influence acknowledging their attributions to the writing tasks.

CONCLUSION AND FURTHER RESEARCH

The emergence of generative AI tools has fundamentally reshaped the way our students may face creative writing and what was once considered a uniquely human task, has now developed into a machine capable of producing fluent and coherent texts. This study has explored the implications of these changes in the context of the subject Castellano: Lengua y Literatura in high school, developed through the presentation of two creative writing tasks. We have used an experimental design that combined independent students' own writing with AI-assisted production (Appendix 2 and 3). After that, we have implemented a reflective journal and a survey to know in depth our students' perceptions.

The results obtained shed light on matters on the use of AI in the creation of writing texts, and one of the key aspects to be highlighted is that AI-assisted creative writing is neither an exclusive labour of human creativity nor a simple threat to originality. Instead, it constitutes a practice in which co-authorship and originality are at stake. Students' texts demonstrated that AI could enrich fluency and, at the same time, provide a wide range of grammar and lexical structures, while key stylistic aspects play an important role as one of the main qualities that define a writer's voice. Likewise, students' reflections revealed a relief for AI's supportive role and tranquility about the authenticity and ownership of AI-provided texts. It is also noticeable that, while students remained the primary agents responsible for decisions, their role changed from unique originators to collaborators and co-authors managing the advantages and disadvantages of AI tools. This new perspective asks for a deeper cultural and educational research on what it means to be an author, nowadays and specifically in an educational environment, in creative writing.

Besides, for creative writing pedagogy, it has been observed that the integration of AI in an educational context could implement both opportunities and challenges. On the one hand, as it has been stated, AI can function as a tool that helps students overcome blocks, experiment with new ways of expressing themselves and develop greater confidence in their fluency and linguistic structures. On the other hand, it presents the risk of over-reliance, where students may leave all the imaginative work to the AI and lose the opportunity to critically think and reflect upon the ideas they want to convey. Additionally, by documenting their processes and perceptions, students had the opportunity to reflect on how AI shaped and, in a way, guided their decisions. Such reflection transforms AI from an invisible assistant into a visible subject of study, encouraging critical literacy rather than passive adoption of its initial outputs. One of the pedagogical results from this research is that AI should be introduced not merely as a writing aid but as an object of reflection and ethical awareness, which will allow students to be sensitive users through the wide range of digital AI tools.

The ethical dilemmas raised by students mainly concerned ownership and authenticity and results show that there is no clear consensus on whether AI is a tool or a co-author. This dilemma creates uncertainty that can generate discomfort among the participants from this research. As we have posed before, this issue highlights the urgent need for guidelines and frameworks that clarify the condition of authorship in this kind of writing tasks, mainly in an educational context such as a high school. In this sense, pedagogical practices should foster open dialogue about not only what can be allowed when using these tools, but also what is legitimate, making students feel confident to interact with the current complexities of AI-mediated creativity.

Future research on creative writing using AI should consider these findings by expanding the scope of investigation. Larger samples across institutions and educational and cultural contexts would help to achieve more general results, which could track how the use of AI tools influences creative growth, the development of critical thinking and a variety of perceptions about authorship. Also, we consider that comparative studies might explore distinctions across different genres (not only narrative, but poetry or theatre), different languages (with a varied range of alphabets) and types of AI tools (there is a growing number each day). Finally, further research is needed on how to design AI tools that actively promote, rather than constrain, our students' stylistic risk-taking and originality.

Ultimately, the evidence obtained from the results suggests that AI is both a collaborator that shapes and structures the text while lacking intentionality and a tool that assists students while promoting stylistic influence. In this sense, rather than resolving the debate, this study accepts the ambiguity of using AI in writing tasks. For educators, scholars and writers in general, the challenge is not to decide what exactly the role of AI is, but to continue asking critical questions about how it functions, what values it embodies and how it can be integrated into creative practices responsibly and reflectively. In doing so, we may arrive at a richer and even more interesting understanding of creativity in writing, which would be later applied to educational contexts, such as high schools or universities.

The future of creative writing, then, is not a question of replacement and prohibition of AI tools, but of reconfiguration and rethinking their possibilities. Undeniably, AI will not eliminate the human voice; rather, it may change the way we understand and consider its aid. If we approach AI with critical curiosity rather than fear or uncritical acceptance, we may find that it expands not only our expressive possibilities but also our understanding of what it means to create a piece of writing.

REFERENCES

Al Kaabi, S. (2025). “Reliance on Ai and its Effects on Critical Thinking and Graduate Readiness: Evidence from UAE Higher Education”. In *International Journal of Learning, Teaching and Educational Research*, Vol. 24, No. 8, pp. 398-417. DOI: 10.26803/ijlter.24.8.17

Barthes, R. (1967). *Le mort de l’auteur* (Vol. 5). Manteia.

Bayne, S. (2015). Teacherbot: Interventions in automated teaching. *Teaching in Higher Education*, *20*(4), 455–467. DOI: 10.1080/13562517.2015.1020783

Blake, J. (2024). Unleashing the potential: Positive impacts of generative AI on learning and teaching. In Hai-Jew, S. (Ed.), *Generative AI in teaching and learning* (pp. 31–45). IGI Global., DOI: 10.4018/979-8-3693-0074-9.ch002

Deep, P. D., & Chen, Y. (2025). The Role of AI in Academic Writing: Impacts on Writing Skills, Critical Thinking, and Integrity in Higher Education. *Societies (Basel, Switzerland)*, *15*(9), 247. DOI: 10.3390/soc15090247

Draxler, F., Werner, A., Lehmann, F., Hoppe, M., Schmidt, A., Buschek, D., & Welsch, R. (2024). The AI ghostwriter effect: When users do not perceive ownership of AI-generated text but self-declare as authors. *ACM Transactions on Computer-Human Interaction*, *31*(2), 1–40. DOI: 10.1145/3637875

Goldshtein, M., Alhashim, A. G., & Roscoe, R. D. (2024). An NLP-Based Exploration of Variance in Student Writing and Syntax: Implications for Automated Writing Evaluation. *Computers*, *13*(7), 160. DOI: 10.3390/computers13070160

Hwang, H.-C., A., Vera Liao, Q., Blodgett S. L., Olteanu, A., Trischler, A. (2025). “*“It was 80% me, 20% AI”: Seeking Authenticity in Co-Writing with Large Language Models”*. In *Proceedings of the ACM on Human-Computer Interaction*, Vol. 9, issue 2, pp. 1-41. DOI: 10.1145/3711020

Hwang, Y., & Lee, J. H. (2025). “Exploring student’s experiences and perceptions of human-AI collaboration in digital content making”. In *International Journal of Educational Technology in Higher Education. https://doi.org/*DOI: 10.1186/s41239-025-00542-

Lee, E. (2024). Prompting Progress: Authorship in the Age of AI. *SSRN*, *76*, 1–85. DOI: 10.2139/ssrn.4609687

Lund, B., Mannuru, N. R., Teel, Z. A., Lee, T. H., Ortega, N. J., Simmons, S., & Ward, E. (2025). "Student Perceptions of AI-Assisted Writing and Academic Integrity: Ethical Concerns, Academic Misconduct, and Use of Generative AI in Higher Education". In *AI in Education*, 1(1), 2. DOI: 10.3390/aieduc1010002

McNamara, D. S., Crossley, S. A., & McCarthy, P. M. (2010). Linguistic features of writing quality. *Written Communication*, *27*(1), 57–86. DOI: 10.1177/0741088309351547

Nafees, H., Kaif, M., Afnan Khan, M., Haseeb, A., & Ali Khan, P. K. (2025). *The Poetry of Error: Analyzing Mistakes in AI-Generated English Works*. In *IJIRT*, Vol. 11, Issue 12. ISSN: 2349-6002

Ryan, H., Abramov, D., Acker, S., & Elkins, S. (2025). "Can AI Be a Co-Author?: How Generative AI Challenges the Boundaries of Authorship in a General Education Writing Class". In Academy for Educational Studies, Vol. 48, Issue 1, pp. 40-56.

Veale, T., & Pérez, R. (2020). Leaps and Bounds: An Introduction to the Field of Computational Creativity. *New Generation Computing*, *38*(4), 551–563. DOI: 10.1007/s00354-020-00116-w

Wang, Y. (2024). "Cognitive and sociocultural dynamics of self-regulated use of machine translation and generative AI tools in academic EFL writing". In *System Journal*, Issue 106. DOI: 10.1016/j.system.2024.103505

Zhao, D. (2025). The impact of AI-enhanced natural language processing tools on writing proficiency: An analysis of language precision, content summarization, and creative writing facilitation. *Education and Information Technologies*, *30*(6), 8055–8086. DOI: 10.1007/s10639-024-13145-5

KEY TERMS AND DEFINITIONS

Artificial Intelligence: the capacity of a computer to perform similar functions to human abilities.

Authorship: the fact of being the source of an artistic work.

Creative: resulting from an original thought.

Critical: involving or requiring skillful judgement.

Ethical: being in accordance with the rules or standards for right conduct or practice.

Mediation: action in interfering between parties, as to reach an agreement or reconciliation.

Pedagogy: the art or science of teaching.

Writing: the act of a person or thing that writes.

APPENDIX 1

This table is a concise summary of the UNESCO AI Competency Framework for Students, designed to define the essential capabilities that secondary school students must acquire to become responsible and competent citizens in the AI era. The framework is structured around four dimensions, which represents human-centred thinking, AI ethics, AI techniques and applications and AI systems design It also includes three levels of progression (Understand, Apply and Create). These levels indicate the expected growth in mastery, ranging from foundational literacy and basic concepts (Understand) to the critical and practical use of tools for meaningful purposes (Apply), and finally, to participation in the design, adaptation and leadership of future AI technologies (Create).

Table 1.

Dimension (Domain)	Level 1: Understand (Foundational Literacy)	Level 2: Apply (Critical and Practical Use)	Level 3: Create (Design and Leadership)
I. Human-Centered Thinking	Gain an understanding that the design and use of AI must contribute to the development of human capabilities and protect people's dignity and agency.	Apply an ethical perspective to critically examine the proportionality of AI in different social contexts and the environment.	Develop an identity as co-creators of AI and future leaders who contribute to the definition and design of the next generations of AI technologies.
II. AI Ethics	Develop human-centered values, knowledge, and skills for daily interaction with AI. Internalize ethical principles and become familiar with related regulations.	Evaluate the social, economic, and environmental impacts of AI, and become conscious decision-makers about when an AI system should or should not be used.	Contribute, at an appropriate level, to the adaptation of AI norms and regulations, thus helping to shape society's relationship with technology.
III. AI Techniques and Applications	Acquire an understanding of what AI is and the technical concepts, processes, and methods underlying its tools and uses. This level is known as "AI Literacy".	Use AI tools to serve specific meaningful purposes or to address real-world challenges and promote sustainable development.	Develop interdisciplinary skills to leverage datasets, programming tools, and computing resources to create a prototype AI system.
IV. Design of AI Systems	Understand the advantages and limitations of current AI capabilities and the impact the data cycle can have on privacy and lives in general.	Acquire the ability to evaluate the suitability of different AI techniques, define data needs, and design testing and feedback metrics.	Acquire knowledge to configure a scalable, maintainable, and reusable architecture for an AI system. Improve the quality of datasets or reconfigure algorithms in response to feedback.

(UNESCO AI Competency Framework)

APPENDIX 2

El tema de las redes sociales es muy importante para nosotros los jóvenes y el uso del móvil todo el tiempo. Yo creo que todo el mundo de mi clase y de otros institutos que conozco estamos todo el rato con el móvil, es que es un hecho. Y no es solo para ver Youtube y jugar a muchos juegos, es que es la forma de estar en contacto con la mis amigos y mi familia. Por ejemplo, mi mejor amigo Javi, se fue a vivir a las islas canarias que están muy lejos y si no fuera por Tiktok y por los grupos de Whatsapp no sabríamos nada de él. Y es que es de mis mejores amigos. Mis padres siempre me dicen que estoy enganchado, que estoy perdiendo el tiempo o algo así, pero lo que pasa es que ellos no lo entienden. Para ellos el móvil es para llamar pero para mí, el móvil es un parte importantisima de mi vida social. Yo me levanto y lo primero que hago es mirar si tengo mensajes y entro a Tiktok y Instagram. Y luego en el recreo pues mis amigos y yo hablamos de todas las cosas lo que hemos visto en TikTok o el último chisme que ha salido en las redes sociales. Lo malo es que a veces si que es verdad que se me va el tiempo con el móvil y no aprovecho lo suficiente para estudiar y hacer otras cosas más importantes del instituto. Por ejemplo me pongo a mirar vídeos sobre unos dibujos animados y cuando me doy cuanta ya ha pasado más de una hora. Eso si que es algo negativo para mi porque luego mis padres se enfadan mucho comigo y me dicen que no tengo buenas notas porque estoy enganchado todo el dia. Y los profesores también nos lo dicen mucho, que siempre nos pillan con el móvil debajo de la mesa, en el patio y enseguida que salimos a la calle. Todos nos dicen que las redes sociales nos están volviendo tontos, que nos distraemos enseguida y que ya no tenemos capacidad para atender más de diez minutos seguidos una clase. Yo no creo que sea para tanto porque mis amigos y yo sabemos también cuando estudiar y dejamos el móvil para centrarnos en lo nuestro. Tambien quiero hablar de que las redes también nos pueden enseñar cosas. El otro día vi un tutorial en Youtube de como arreglar la bici, y luego otro sobre técnicas para estudiar mejor y más rápido, lo hice y me funciona porque se trata de dejar el móvil a ratos de 30 minutos. Y luego hay gente que pone cosas útiles, como cuando hay huelga de buses o si el examen de biología es el martes o el miércoles. Es información importante para todos los que estamos estudiando. Luego sobre lo de las fotos subir una *story* de lo que estoy haciendo es muy interesante para mis amigos, porque podemos estar comentando todo el rato, pero si no subes nada, es como si no estuvieras haciendo nada. Y además, a veces me doy cuenta de que paso mucho tiempo también pensando en lo que voy a subir o las fotos que poner y se que ese tiempo lo podría gastar en estudiar o estar mas con mi familia. Otro tema sobre esto de las redes sociales es el bullying. En el colegio nos han dado ya charlas sobre eso y los profesores nos cuentan lo peligroso que es. Yo nunca he visto algo muy de acoso, pero sí que hay gente que se mete con otros por lo que ponen en sus redes y luego todo eso se comenta en el aptio. Yo creo que eso es muy tóxico y en el colegio deberían tener más control con eso. Eso de meterse ocn la gente es de personas que no tienen personalidad y se aburren en sus casas. Para acabar con esta redacción yo pienso que si lo usamos con cabeza puede ser una cosa muy útil y buena para los adolescentes de hoy en dia. Yo ceo que es la mejor forma de relacionarnos ahora y el problema es más si no tienes móvil, porque te pueden tratar de *marginado* o algo así y nadie te habla y así no puedes hablar y relacionarte. Si lo usas con cabeza, no pasa nada. En conclusión opino que las redes son necesarias, aunque a veces perdemos mucho tiempo usando las aplicaciones.

(Text 1 – Title: Sobre los jóvenes y las redes sociales en la actualidad)

APPENDIX 3

La integración de las redes sociales en la vida del adolescente contemporáneo constituye un fenómeno sociodigital de profunda relevancia. El tiempo invertido en estas plataformas, lejos de ser un mero ocio, representa una faceta central de la construcción identitaria y las interacciones sociales de la juventud. Este ensayo se propone analizar las implicaciones duales de este uso intensivo, abordando tanto su funcionalidad inherente como los desafíos que plantea para el desarrollo personal y el rendimiento académico.

En primer lugar, es innegable que las plataformas digitales han redefinido la conectividad interpersonal. Para la generación actual, estas herramientas son el principal vehículo para la preservación de los lazos afectivos, superando las barreras geográficas impuestas por la movilidad. La comunicación continua, ejemplificada por la mensajería instantánea y las publicaciones efímeras, garantiza una pertenencia al grupo social que es vital durante la etapa adolescente. Este acceso ininterrumpido a la esfera social es percibido no como un lujo, sino como un requisito funcional para evitar el aislamiento social en la era de la conectividad total.

Además de su función social, estas plataformas operan como repositorios dinámicos de información y recursos. A través de canales específicos (como plataformas de vídeo y foros especializados), los jóvenes acceden a contenido educativo complementario, tutoriales prácticos para el desarrollo de habilidades técnicas y datos relevantes sobre la coordinación de eventos cotidianos o académicos. Este acceso inmediato y personalizado subraya su rol como herramientas de consulta, si bien la gestión de esta información requiere un discernimiento crítico para evitar la proliferación de desinformación o contenido de baja calidad.

Sin embargo, la permeabilidad constante de las redes sociales introduce retos significativos, principalmente en el ámbito de la gestión del tiempo y la focalización cognitiva, elementos cruciales para el éxito en Bachillerato. La naturaleza algorítmica de estas aplicaciones está intrínsecamente diseñada para maximizar la permanencia del usuario, lo que a menudo conduce a un consumo inadvertido y prolongado, fenómeno conocido como la "espiral de *scroll* infinito". Esta distracción crónica compromete directamente la concentración necesaria para tareas cognitivas complejas, mermando la productividad y el tiempo dedicado a la consolidación del aprendizaje. La dificultad para establecer límites claros entre el tiempo de ocio digital y las responsabilidades curriculares exige la implementación de rigurosas estrategias de autorregulación digital.

Adicionalmente, el impacto socio-emocional del uso constante de las redes es notoriamente complejo. La exposición a narrativas de vida altamente curadas y estéticas idealizadas fomenta ineludiblemente la comparación social, lo que puede exacerbar problemas de autoestima e inseguridad. La búsqueda de validación externa, canalizada mediante indicadores cuantitativos como los "me gusta" o las reacciones, corre el riesgo de distorsionar la percepción del propio valor personal, vinculándolo a la aceptación digital en lugar de a logros o cualidades intrínsecas.

Desde una perspectiva ética, estas plataformas son también un vector para la toxicidad digital, destacando el fenómeno del ciberacoso. La sensación de anonimato y la distancia física facilitan conductas agresivas que no se manifestarían en interacciones presenciales. Es imperativo que la comunidad educativa promueva una cultura de responsabilidad digital activa que priorice el respeto, la empatía y la rendición de cuentas por el comportamiento en línea. La implementación de mecanismos de denuncia y control debe complementarse con una formación ética sólida.

En conclusión, la presencia ubicua del teléfono móvil y las redes sociales en la vida juvenil es un hecho socioeconómico ineludible. Aunque estas herramientas proporcionan beneficios claros en términos de conexión social y acceso a la información, sus riesgos inherentes a la distracción, la ética y la salud mental demandan una respuesta formativa proactiva. Es imperativo que la educación formal integre la alfabetización mediática y digital como un componente transversal y troncal. Esto capacitará al alumnado no solo para utilizar la tecnología eficientemente, sino para gestionarla de manera consciente, estratégica y crítica, asegurando que la tecnología sirva al desarrollo humano y no se convierta en una fuente de detrimento académico o personal. La moderación consciente se erige, por tanto, como la clave para un aprovechamiento integral.

(Text 2 – Title: Sobre los jóvenes y las redes sociales en la actualidad)

Chapter 10
Beyond the Algorithm:
Navigating Ethics, Quality, and Accountability in AI-Powered Translation

Mohammed H. Alaqad
http://orcid.org/0000-0002-9953-5763
Universiti Malaya, Malaysia

Amin Amirdabbaghian
http://orcid.org/0000-0001-6503-8446
Universiti Malaya, Malaysia

Hani Alhasani
http://orcid.org/0000-0002-2468-2216
International University of Science and Technology in Kuwait, Kuwait

ABSTRACT

This chapter examines the rapid integration of artificial intelligence (AI) into translation and interpreting practices and evaluates its implications for ethics, quality, and professional accountability. Recent developments in neural machine translation and large language models have significantly expanded translation capabilities, enabling interactive and context-aware multilingual communication. However, the increasing reliance on AI-powered tools raises critical concerns regarding accuracy, bias, privacy, and the shifting role of human translators. Drawing on insights from applied linguistics, translation studies, and interpreting research, this chapter analyzes how AI reshapes translation workflows, professional competencies, and quality assessment practices. It further explores emerging governance frameworks, professional standards, and hybrid human–AI models designed to mitigate risk while preserving linguistic and cultural integrity. Ultimately, the chapter argues that

DOI: 10.4018/979-8-3373-6420-9.ch010

responsible AI integration in translation requires interdisciplinary collaboration, ethical oversight, and human-centered accountability mechanisms to ensure that technological innovation supports rather than undermines communicative trust and social responsibility.

INTRODUCTION

Artificial intelligence (AI) has moved from the margins of translation practice to its operational core. What began as experimental automation is now everyday infrastructure: neural machine translation (NMT) powers public-facing platforms, translation-memory environments increasingly pair with adaptive MT, and large language models (LLMs) are embedded in drafting, revision, terminology work, and multilingual content management. The result is not merely faster translation, but a reconfiguration of what counts as translation expertise, how quality is defined, and how responsibility is distributed across humans, tools, and institutions (Asrifan & Alaqad, 2025). In contemporary translation environments, AI systems are no longer peripheral aids but integral components of multilingual communication workflows, shaping how texts are produced, evaluated, and circulated across global contexts.

Historically, machine translation has evolved through recognizable paradigms. Rule-based approaches attempted to encode linguistic knowledge explicitly, while later generations expanded the role of data and optimization in translation modelling (Hutchins, 1995). Statistical machine translation (SMT), including phrase-based approaches, leveraged bilingual corpora to model probabilistic correspondences and became a dominant paradigm for many years (Koehn et al., 2003). Neural machine translation (NMT) then shifted the field toward end-to-end learning, and Transformer architectures accelerated this change by improving long-range dependency modelling and enabling scalable training regimes (Vaswani et al., 2017). Production-grade NMT systems further shaped industry expectations by demonstrating substantial quality gains relative to earlier phrase-based models (Wu et al., 2016). Today's LLM-driven translation workflows extend beyond sentence-level rendering into tasks such as summarization, style transfer, controlled rewriting, and interactive negotiation of meaning capabilities that increasingly position translators as meaning and risk managers rather than sole text producers.

These developments have significant implications for translation studies, interpreting studies, and applied linguistics more broadly. Translation is not merely a process of linguistic substitution; it is a situated communicative activity shaped by purpose, institutional norms, genre conventions, audience expectations, time pressure, and the ethical consequences of error. Research in interpreting studies has long demonstrated that translation and interpreting quality is socially experienced and evaluated by users and institutions, rather than measured solely through formal accuracy metrics, particularly in contexts where communicative trust and effectiveness are central (Pöchhacker, 2001). Similarly, translation scholarship conceptualizes quality as multidimensional and context-sensitive, reflecting linguistic accuracy, pragmatic adequacy, cultural appropriateness, and user expectations. In response to increasingly technology-mediated workflows, professional standards and regulatory frameworks have also emerged to formalize competence, process, and accountability, including post-editing guidelines for machine translation outputs (BS ISO 18587:2017).

Beyond its technical contributions, AI also prompts broader theoretical and epistemological questions within applied linguistics. The integration of AI into language-related research and professional practice invites reconsideration of how knowledge, expertise, and authority are constructed in technologically mediated environments. Recent scholarship argues that applied linguistics must critically interrogate the epistemological, ontological, and ethical assumptions embedded in AI and generative AI systems, as these technologies encode implicit values and forms of knowledge that may not always align with human-centered research traditions and professional norms (Curry et al., 2025). Consequently, AI-driven translation should be viewed not only as an engineering achievement capable of producing fluent multilingual output, but also as a methodological and ethical challenge concerning how translation knowledge is generated, validated, and contextualized particularly when AI systems become part of the research process, the professional workflow, and the institutional decision-making chain (Révész et al., 2025).

Against this background, the integration of AI into translation practice raises critical questions regarding ethics, quality, and professional accountability. While AI-powered tools offer significant advantages in efficiency, scalability, and accessibility, they also introduce risks related to bias, privacy, transparency, and the potential erosion of human expertise. These tensions highlight the need for critical engagement with AI translation technologies within an interdisciplinary framework that brings together insights from linguistics, translation studies, ethics, and technology policy.

Given these contexts, this chapter has four objectives. First, it maps current trends in AI translation, including neural and generative models, the proliferation of AI-assisted tools such as terminology management, speech-to-text systems, subtitling technologies, and quality estimation, as well as the integration of AI into hybrid human–machine translation workflows. Second, it surveys applications across professional domains such as healthcare, law, diplomacy, education, and literary translation, highlighting how AI reshapes practice and training (Asrifan & Alaqad, 2025). Third, it analyzes challenges and limitations, focusing on quality risks, ethical dilemmas including issues of privacy, bias, and professional deskilling and the need for ecological validity in research on AI-mediated translation practices (Cadwell et al., 2016; Ragni et al., 2022). Finally, it explores the implications of AI translation for applied linguistics, arguing that AI-powered translation is best understood as an interdisciplinary enterprise linking linguistics with cognitive science, sociolinguistics, ethics, and policy, thereby ensuring that rapid technological development does not outpace accountability and social responsibility (Alaqad et al., 2026).

TRANSLATION, INTERPRETING, AND APPLIED LINGUISTICS: A SHARED CONCERN WITH SITUATED MEANING

Translation and interpreting scholarship particularly within applied linguistics conceptualizes language mediation as purposeful communicative action performed under practical, cognitive, and institutional constraints. Rather than viewing translation simply as the transfer of words between languages, research in these fields emphasizes the complex processes through which meaning is reconstructed across linguistic and cultural boundaries. Interpreting studies, for example, foreground the cognitive demands of real-time language mediation, highlighting issues such as cognitive load, time pressure, and the need to preserve communicative intent while processing input and producing output almost simultaneously (Gile, 2009; Seeber, 2011). These constraints shape how interpreters allocate attention and memory resources during the interpreting process, often requiring rapid decision-making under conditions of uncertainty.

Translation studies, while sharing similar concerns about meaning transfer, typically place greater emphasis on the textual and contextual dimensions of language mediation. Scholars in this field examine how translators negotiate genre conventions, discourse structures, pragmatic meaning, and cultural positioning when producing texts for new audiences. From this perspective, translation is understood as a communicative and interpretive activity rather than a purely mechanical substitution of linguistic forms. Interpreting studies and translation studies are therefore best viewed as complementary traditions rather than competing ones. Both fields recognize that translation involves reconstructing meaning in contexts where perfect equivalence between languages is rarely attainable under real communicative conditions.

Two enduring contributions from this scholarship are particularly relevant for understanding translation in the age of artificial intelligence. The first concerns cognitive models of translation and interpreting, especially effort-based frameworks that describe language mediation as the management of limited cognitive resources. According to these models, translators and interpreters must strategically allocate attention, memory, and processing capacity across multiple tasks, including comprehension, reformulation, monitoring, and coordination (Gile, 2009; Seeber, 2011). When task demands exceed available cognitive resources due to time pressure, complexity, or information overload performance may degrade, leading to omissions, simplifications, or errors. These insights highlight that translation quality is closely tied to the interaction between human cognitive capacities and the constraints of specific communicative contexts.

A second important contribution concerns the evaluation of translation and interpreting quality. Research in interpreting studies demonstrates that quality is not determined solely by linguistic accuracy but is also shaped by the expectations of users, institutional contexts, and the communicative goals of the interaction. Studies have shown that audiences often evaluate interpreting performance through a broader set of criteria, including coherence, sense consistency, clarity, professional conduct, and overall communicative effectiveness (Moser, 1996; Pöchhacker, 2001). In many real-world settings such as diplomatic meetings, healthcare encounters, or legal proceedings the success of language mediation depends as much on pragmatic adequacy and trust as it does on lexical precision.

These theoretical insights are particularly significant when considering the role of artificial intelligence in translation. AI-powered translation systems are frequently evaluated using automated metrics or surface indicators of linguistic fluency. However, the perspectives developed within translation and interpreting studies suggest that such measures capture only a limited dimension of translation quality. AI systems may generate grammatically fluent output while failing at deeper levels of communication, including pragmatic interpretation (such as implicature, politeness strategies, or register), cultural appropriateness (such as humor, taboo expressions, or culturally specific references), or institutional accuracy (such as the precise terminology required in legal or medical communication).

From an applied linguistics perspective, translation quality must therefore be understood as ecological rather than purely technical. Effective translation depends on the interaction between linguistic form, communicative purpose, social context, and user expectations. This ecological view implies that evaluating AI-generated translations requires attention not only to textual fluency but also to the broader communicative environments in which translations are used. While AI systems can assist in generating multilingual content at unprecedented speed and scale, accountability for translation quality remains anchored in human oversight and professional judgment. Human translators, interpreters, and institutions continue to play a crucial role in assessing contextual appropriateness, managing risk, and ensuring that translation practices remain aligned with ethical, cultural, and communicative standards.

The Technological Turn: From CAT and MT to AI-Saturated Translation Environments

The technological transformation of translation has unfolded gradually over several decades. Earlier computer-assisted translation (CAT) environments focused primarily on tools such as translation memories, concordance systems, and terminology databases, which supported translators in maintaining consistency and efficiency when dealing with repetitive or highly specialized content. In these early workflows, machine translation often remained external to the translator's primary working environment: practitioners might consult machine output selectively, use it as a reference, or disregard it entirely depending on perceived reliability (Asrifan & Alaqad, 2025).

The development of neural machine translation (NMT) significantly altered this relationship between human translators and machine systems. By producing more fluent and contextually coherent output than earlier statistical models, NMT enabled the large-scale integration of machine translation into professional workflows. As a result, translation practice increasingly shifted toward post-editing, risk evaluation, and domain-specific adaptation of machine-generated content. Research examining the experiences of professional translators suggests that the adoption of MT technologies is strongly influenced by human and organizational factors, including ergonomics, perceived control over the translation process, task suitability, and institutional expectations (Cadwell et al., 2016; Cadwell et al., 2018). These findings highlight that technological integration is not purely technical but also shaped by workplace ecology and professional culture.

Alongside technological development, standardization initiatives have emerged to stabilize expectations regarding translation quality and professional responsibility in MT-assisted workflows. One prominent example is ISO 18587:2017, which establishes requirements for full post-editing processes and defines the competences required of post-editors. The standard recognizes that machine translation output should not automatically be treated as a final product in professional settings. Instead, quality assurance is achieved through structured post-editing procedures carried out by qualified professionals (British Standards Institution, 2017).

Intersections of AI, Translation, and Interpreting: Technology, Standards, and Professional Risk

As artificial intelligence technologies become more deeply embedded in translation and interpreting practices, they are increasingly viewed not only as productivity tools but also as potential sources of professional and institutional risk. Translator and interpreter associations have raised concerns regarding the unsupervised use of automated translation and interpreting systems in high-stakes contexts. Because AI-generated outputs can appear fluent and convincing, errors may be difficult for non-experts to detect, and responsibility for those errors may become difficult to assign. The International Federation of Translators has therefore cautioned against replacing human interpreters with unrevised machine solutions, emphasizing that such practices can introduce unacceptable risks and may contribute to the deskilling of language professionals (International Federation of Translators [FIT], 2024).

Similar concerns are reflected in evolving professional standards for interpreting services. For example, ISO 23155:2022 outlines requirements and recommendations for conference interpreting services, emphasizing that quality is shaped not only by the interpreter's individual performance but also by broader systemic conditions, including preparation, working environments, and service organization (International Organization for Standardization [ISO], 2022). This systemic view of quality becomes particularly important when AI-supported technologies such as automated transcription, glossary prompting, or live captioning are introduced into interpreting and translation workflows. In such contexts, institutions must clearly define responsibility boundaries, including who is accountable for verifying output and under what conditions human intervention is required.

More broadly, professional and international standards increasingly function as a governance framework for AI integration in language services. In translation, ISO 17100 conceptualizes quality primarily through managed processes, qualified personnel, and documented workflows an approach that becomes especially relevant when machine translation and large language models are incorporated into production pipelines (British Standards Institution, 2017). Similarly, ISO 23155:2022 treats interpreting quality as a systemic outcome, linking performance to preparation, confidentiality, professional conduct, and service-provider responsibilities (ISO, 2022). This shift toward process-based accountability reflects a growing recognition that technological tools alone cannot guarantee quality outcomes.

At the professional level, these developments have encouraged a stronger risk-management perspective toward AI-assisted language services. Organizations increasingly evaluate AI-supported translation and interpreting in terms of due diligence, contractual safeguards, and clearly defined responsibility structures. In healthcare contexts, for instance, the National Council on Interpreting in Health Care has proposed a question-based framework to guide organizations considering AI-generated interpreting, emphasizing the need to assess system limitations, safety considerations, privacy protections, and escalation procedures when accuracy is critical (National Council on Interpreting in Health Care [NCIHC], 2024). Similarly, guidelines for distance interpreting developed by the International Association of Conference Interpreters highlight how technological mediation alters interactional conditions and interpreter workload, requiring minimum technical standards and mitigation strategies to protect both working conditions and communication quality (International Association of Conference Interpreters [AIIC], 2025).

Taken together, these developments illustrate that the integration of AI into translation and interpreting cannot be understood solely in terms of technological innovation. Instead, it must also be examined through the lenses of professional standards, institutional governance, and risk management. These perspectives underscore the importance of maintaining human-centered accountability structures as AI technologies continue to reshape language mediation practices.

CURRENT TRENDS IN AI TRANSLATION

Neural and Generative AI Translation: From "Output" to "Interaction"

Neural machine translation (NMT) remains the technical backbone of most large-scale translation services, largely because it offers a stable balance of speed, cost, and quality at industrial scale. The modern NMT era built on attention-based sequence-to-sequence modeling, which reduced the "fixed-length bottleneck" of early encoder–decoder systems and enabled more context-sensitive renderings of meaning (Bahdanau et al., 2014). Industrial implementations then operationalized these ideas with production constraints in mind: Google's GNMT work is often cited as a milestone not simply because it improved fluency, but because it explicitly tackled real-world deployment problems such as inference speed, rare-word handling, and coverage issues that can cause under-translation or omissions (Wu et al., 2016). Soon after, Transformer architectures replaced recurrence with attention-only modeling, improving parallelization and scalability changes that mattered directly for both training efficiency and measurable MT quality in common benchmarks (Vaswani et al., 2017). Together, these developments helped normalize "MT-in-the-loop" as a default condition rather than an exceptional workflow.

What is changing most rapidly now is not that NMT disappeared, but that translation is increasingly packaged as a *dialogic service* rather than a one-shot output. Instruction-following large language models (LLMs) reframe translation as an interactive process in which the user can specify a translation brief ("for patients," "for a visa application," "for a journal submission"), impose constraints ("plain language," "keep legal modality," "preserve hedging"), and iteratively refine alternatives with explanations. In practice, this makes "translation" converge with revision, localization, controlled rewriting, and audience design. Research on prompting LLMs for MT shows that outcomes are highly sensitive to prompt design and in-context examples: the *number*, *quality*, and *relevance* of demonstrations can materially shift adequacy and style, and "suboptimal" exemplars can degrade translation rather than improve it (Zhang et al., 2023). This sensitivity is one reason the field is moving toward prompt literacy and workflow engineering (templates, approved briefs, constrained formats) as professional skills alongside bilingual competence.

A related trend is the growing visibility of "LLM-style upgrades" in mainstream translation products an important market signal because consumer platforms often set user expectations about what translation *should* look like. In a December 12, 2025 product update, Google stated that it was bringing Gemini-powered translation capabilities to Google Translate for text and also rolling out a beta live "speech-to-speech" translation experience (via headphones), explicitly framing the improvement as a next-generation model capability rather than incremental tuning (Yao, 2025). This matters for research and practice because it pushes translation further into interactional, multimodal contexts (live speech, turn-taking, prosody/stance cues), where "good translation" includes discourse coherence, speaker attribution, tone management, and conversational timing not just sentence-level semantic match (Asrifan & Alaqad, 2025).

However, the interaction paradigm also sharpens a core applied-linguistics concern: LLM translations can be persuasive and fluent while remaining pragmatically or factually risky. Empirical work comparing ChatGPT-based translation with human translation in literary text, for example, reports a pattern that many practitioners recognize: strong fluency and readability paired with weaknesses that matter for fidelity-sensitive tasks (e.g., subtle meaning shifts, added material, or culturally loaded choices) (Al Rousan et al., 2025). Large-scale evaluations of LLMs for multilingual MT similarly suggest rapid improvement, but also persistent gaps especially for low-resource languages and for directions where commercial MT systems remain stronger (Zhu et al., 2024). The current "state of the trend," then, is not simply *better models*, but a redefinition of professional value: translators increasingly operate as interactive meaning designers and risk managers, deciding when to accept, constrain, verify, or override AI output based on genre, stakes, users, and accountability.

AI-Assisted Translation Tooling: Beyond MT Toward Workflow Automation

A second trend is the growth of AI *around* translation rather than only *for* translation i.e., systems that automate the "edges" of multilingual work: discovery (terms, entities, inconsistencies), orchestration (routing, versioning, approvals), and risk detection (where humans must look first). This matters because, in real production settings, time and error risk are often driven less by the act of drafting a target sentence than by upstream and downstream tasks: preparing reference materials, managing terminology drift across teams, aligning parallel documents, and documenting what was checked and by whom.

Terminology extraction and consistency checking is a clear example. Automatic term extraction (ATE) has long supported domain translation by identifying candidate terms and multiword expressions from corpora and aligning them with domain knowledge (Heylen & De Hertog, 2015). In AI-saturated environments, ATE increasingly combines statistical termhood measures, embeddings, and LLM-supported suggestions to: (a) propose glossary entries, (b) flag term-variant inconsistency across chapters or product lines, and (c) surface "high-impact" lexical choices (e.g., contraindications in medical texts, legal definitions in contracts) (Fantinuoli, 2018). Yet the same automation creates new failure modes: hallucinated "terms," overconfident synonym proposals, or subtle register mismatches that can spread quickly when a glossary is reused at scale hence the growing emphasis on term governance (ownership, approval, version control) rather than term lists alone (Wissik, 2025).

Speech-to-text and subtitle pipelines illustrate how AI now supports multimodal translation work rather than only written text. Semi-automatized subtitling often chains ASR transcription, segmentation, time-coding suggestions, and draft translation creating speed gains but also shifting effort into *error localization* (finding where ASR errors distort meaning) and *temporal editing* (line breaks, reading speed, synchronization) (Tardel, 2020). In interpreting-adjacent settings, ASR-generated live subtitles/captions can function as cognitive scaffolding especially for names, numbers, and dense informational segments. Experimental evidence suggests that real-time automatic subtitles can improve interpreting accuracy and reduce cognitive load under certain conditions (Li & Chmiel, 2024). The applied implication is not that "captions solve quality," but that audio-visual assistance changes *where* interpreters spend attention and therefore requires careful configuration (accuracy thresholds, latency tolerance, and clear policies for when the human overrides the tool).

Quality estimation and error detection increasingly operationalize a "triage" model: the goal is not to *replace* review, but to allocate scarce expert attention to the segments most likely to be wrong or most costly if wrong. Early QE research already argued that predicting translation quality without reference translations could support filtering, routing, and selective post-editing (Specia et al., 2010). More recent practice-oriented syntheses emphasize QE's value in production decisions such as "send to full post-edit," "light post-edit," "human translate," or "do not use MT here" (Specia & Shah, 2018). Importantly, QE and error detection also reshape accountability: when an organization *chooses* to rely on automated risk scores, it must decide who owns the threshold settings, how false negatives are handled, and how these decisions are documented for auditability especially in regulated domains.

These developments align with translation-process research: tools are most helpful when they reduce low-level burden and preserve capacity for higher-order decisions (cohesion, register, cultural framing). But "help" becomes "friction" when tools undermine agency or increase cognitive switching costs one reason adoption varies by task, interface design, and workplace ecology (Cadwell et al., 2016).

Integration into Professional Workflows: Human–AI Hybrid Models as the Default

In many organizations, the practical question is no longer "human or AI?" but how to design a controlled pipeline where AI contributes speed *without* collapsing quality assurance or accountability. This is why hybrid workflows increasingly look like *systems engineering* for language work: content is categorized by risk, routed through different levels of review, and logged with evidence of checks (revision history, QA metrics, sign-offs). The central design challenge is that AI adds a powerful new production component while also expanding the surface area for failure (privacy leakage, wrong register, biased outputs, brittle terminology, or silent factual drift). Consequently, integration decisions are moving "up" from individual translators to organizational governance.

A useful way to describe contemporary hybrid practice is to map four recurring decision points (often embedded in procurement and SOPs):

1. **Suitability**: Which genres and content types can be safely drafted by MT/LLMs (e.g., marketing localization vs. legal clauses)?
2. **Verification depth**: What level of checking is required given the consequences of error (sampling vs. full review; bilingual review vs. monolingual revision)?
3. **Data governance**: What rules apply to confidentiality, storage, and reuse (especially if prompts contain sensitive client data)?
4. **Accountability**: Who is responsible for final meaning tool vendor, LSP, translator/post-editor, reviewer, or institution and how is that responsibility evidenced?

Here, standards are doing real work: they function as a governance layer that separates what a tool *can output* from what a service is *responsible to deliver*. ISO 18587:2017, for example, frames post-editing as a competence-based professional service with specified process requirements and post-editor competences signaling that MT output becomes publishable through controlled human intervention rather than by default (ISO, 2017). A related industry signal is that language service stakeholders increasingly describe post-editors as a distinct profile with specific competence expectations, reflecting professionalization rather than "informal cleanup" (Ginovart Cid et al., 2020). Meanwhile, professional associations emphasize risk boundaries: FIT's position paper on AI in interpreting cautions against unsupervised AI use in high-stakes contexts and foregrounds issues of harm, accountability, and deskilling (FIT, 2024).

Finally, human factors remain decisive for whether hybrid workflows actually work day-to-day. Even when an organization mandates MT/LLMs, sustained adoption depends on whether translators experience control, task fit, and ergonomic stability because poorly designed automation can increase cognitive effort through constant monitoring, patching, and interface switching (Cadwell et al., 2016). In other words, hybrid workflows are becoming the default but *good* hybrid workflows are those that treat AI as a managed component inside a human-accountable service design, not a substitute for it.

APPLICATIONS OF AI IN TRANSLATION

Professional Practice: Regulated Risk, Not Just Productivity

AI-enabled translation is now routine in business localization, customer support, technical documentation, and internal corporate communication domains where content is often repetitive, terminology can be controlled, and consequences of minor infelicities are usually limited. In these low-to-moderate risk settings, common "productive" configurations include: (a) MT/LLM drafting, (b) targeted human revision focused on terminology, numbers, and consistency, and (c) selective QA driven by quality estimation or automated checks (e.g., untranslatable, formatting, compliance strings). The practical gain is not only faster drafting, but smoother pipeline management: faster turnaround, better reuse, and more consistent multilingual content across product cycles.

In high-stakes contexts (healthcare, legal proceedings, asylum, safeguarding, diplomacy), the dominant issue is harm rather than speed. Here, professional bodies explicitly warn that unrevised or unsupervised AI interpreting/translation can create unacceptable risk especially when vulnerable users depend on accurate language mediation and when accountability for errors is legally or ethically consequential (International Federation of Translators [FIT], 2024). In parallel, interpreting standards such as ISO 23155:2022 reflect a service model in which quality depends on process, conditions, competence, confidentiality, and professional conduct not merely on a tool's apparent fluency (International Organization for Standardization [ISO], 2022). The applied-linguistics implication is that AI's "best use" in regulated settings is typically bounded support (e.g., glossary prompts, transcripts for names/numbers, structured documentation), embedded in human-accountable workflows with clear escalation rules and sign-off.

A concrete application area where these issues surface daily is video-mediated and remote interpreting. Remote configurations can improve access and coverage, but they also reconfigure turn-taking, gaze/attention cues, rapport-building, and how interpreters manage interactional trouble (e.g., interruptions, repair, overlaps). Research on video-mediated interpreting in legal settings shows that interpreters perceive technology as reshaping interactional dynamics and working conditions, which in turn affects performance, stress, and perceptions of quality making "mediation conditions" a first-order variable, not a background detail (Braun, 2018).

Education and Training: AI Literacy as Translator/Interpreter Competence

Translator and interpreter education increasingly treats AI literacy as a professional competence rather than an optional technical add-on. In practice, this means training students to (1) prompt responsibly and specify briefs (audience, genre, register, purpose), (2) evaluate outputs beyond fluency (pragmatics, implicature, stance, politeness, legal/medical precision), (3) document revision decisions and quality rationale, and (4) protect confidentiality and manage data governance (e.g., what can/cannot be pasted into third-party systems). A key pedagogical goal is to prevent "fluency bias" the tendency to accept well-formed text as correct by building habits of verification, triangulation (sources, glossaries, parallel texts), and risk-based checking.

UNESCO's AI competency frameworks reinforce this direction by explicitly centering human agency, ethics, and responsible use not only operational skill. UNESCO's AI competency framework for teachers and the parallel AI competency framework for students both foreground human-centred values, ethical judgement, and critical evaluation as core competencies for AI-saturated educational environments (UNESCO, 2024a, 2024b). For translator/interpreter curricula, these frameworks support course designs that deliberately integrate:

- **Tool competence** (CAT/MT/LLM workflows; speech-to-text/subtitling toolchains; terminology systems)
- **Evaluation competence** (error typologies; adequacy vs. acceptability; risk segmentation and verification protocols)
- **Ethical competence** (privacy/confidentiality, bias awareness, accountability, disclosure practices)

Evidence also suggests that attitudes toward MT/AI are shaped by trust, framing, and professional identity, not only by measured output quality. Experimental work with translator trainees indicates that simply telling participants a target text is "human translation" versus "MT output" can change how they approach revision and post-editing highlighting the need to teach metacognitive awareness (e.g., when confidence is inflated or reduced by labels) alongside technique (Scansani, 2019). Complementary empirical work shows that perceptions such as self-efficacy and perceived MT quality relate to cognitive effort and post-editing behavior, reinforcing that training must address the psychology of human–machine collaboration, not just the mechanics (Peng et al., 2024).

Creative and Literary Translation: AI as Draft Generator, Humans as Cultural Authors

Creative and literary translation tends to expose the *specific* limits of AI that are easy to hide in technical or repetitive genres. Long-form works demand interpretive consistency across hundreds of pages (character idiolects, recurring motifs, shifting focalization, intertextual echoes, and controlled ambiguity). By contrast, many MT/LLM systems still behave "locally": they can produce fluent segments while drifting in voice, flattening stylistic markedness, or silently normalizing the very oddities that signal an author's craft. The most damaging errors are often not obvious mis-translations but mis-calibrations of tone and stance a sarcastic line made sincere, a culturally weighted metaphor made generic, or a deliberately ambiguous phrase resolved too early (and sometimes incorrectly) by a system that prefers certainty over indeterminacy.

Humor translation is a particularly revealing stress test because it depends on layered meaning: linguistic ambiguity, culture-specific allusion, timing, taboo boundaries, and audience positioning. In multimedia contexts, humor is also distributed across multiple semiotic channels (image, prosody, editing, gesture, soundtrack), so the "meaning" is not fully recoverable from text alone. Chiaro's work on humor translation in the digital/multimedia era illustrates how these layered cues structure interpretation and why purely text-based automation can misfire while still sounding confident (Chiaro, 2020). Recent empirical work comparing NMT with GPT-style systems likewise shows that humor retention is uneven across joke mechanisms (e.g., wordplay vs. cultural reference) and that prompt strategies can help but do not eliminate the underlying fragility of humor translation under automation (Pituxcoosuvarn & Murakami, 2025). In short: creative translation is the domain where "fluent output" is most likely to be misleading evidence of adequacy.

None of this makes AI irrelevant to literary practice. In many projects, AI can be useful as a draft generator and variation engine: it can propose multiple renderings of a tricky metaphor, brainstorm dialogue registers for different characters, suggest alternatives for culture-bound items, or help maintain internal consistency via quick searches over a style sheet (names, honorifics, leitmotifs). It can also support exploratory work testing how different degrees of domestication/foreignization feel to a target readership *as long as* the translator treats outputs as provisional. Evidence from literary post-editing studies suggests that MT/LLM outputs can reduce time in some cases, but the gains are tightly coupled to the translator's ability to preserve style and narrative voice through substantial human intervention (Toral et al., 2018).

The ethical and aesthetic stakes, however, remain fundamentally human: voice ownership and cultural accountability cannot be outsourced to a tool. In Venuti's terms, the translation field's longstanding debates about fluency, domestication, and the "invisibility" of the translator become more urgent in an era where machines reliably produce smooth prose (Venuti, 2017). If machine-generated smoothness systematically nudges translations toward a neutralized "platform style," then the translator's authorship is at risk of being erased twice: first by the traditional expectation of fluent transparency, and second by algorithmic normalization. That is precisely why many literary translators increasingly frame their role not as polishing sentences, but as cultural authorship: selecting an interpretive stance, preserving deliberate ambiguity, and making ethically accountable choices about representation.

> **Practical implication for literary workflows:** AI can be integrated, but best practice is to embed it inside *translator-controlled* governance e.g., (a) a project style sheet and character bible that the human maintains, (b) explicit "do-not-invent" constraints and verification rules for culturally specific references, and (c) documentation of key interpretive decisions (especially when ambiguity is preserved intentionally). In creative translation, the highest-value human work is not correcting grammar it is protecting interpretive integrity.

CHALLENGES AND LIMITATIONS

Quality Risks: Fluency Can Hide Failure

AI systems often produce highly fluent target texts, which can mask errors that are pragmatically catastrophic (e.g., wrong negation, incorrect quantities, invented constraints, altered stance). Interpreting quality research is useful here because it reminds us that quality is not reducible to propositional accuracy; users also evaluate coherence, trustworthiness, and communicative effectiveness dimensions that can be undermined even when a message "sounds right" (Pöchhacker, 2001). Put differently, fluency can create an *illusion of reliability*: the smoother the output, the less likely non-experts are to detect subtle distortions, and the more likely organizations are to underestimate risk.

In professional translation workflows, managing this "fluency risk" requires risk-based quality design, not just stronger models. Three ingredients are especially important:

- **Explicit error taxonomies** that distinguish error *types* (e.g., meaning shift vs. terminology vs. register) and link them to severity and downstream impact.
- **Human verification protocols proportionate to stakes**, including targeted checks for known high-impact error classes (numbers, negation, modality, named entities, legal/medical terms, and culturally loaded expressions).
- **Documentation mechanisms for accountability**, such as revision history, QA logs, severity thresholds, and reviewer sign-off so that organizations can demonstrate due diligence and learn from failure cases.

Framework-based evaluation is a practical response because it converts "quality" from a vague impression into a structured analytic activity. MQM-style approaches (Multidimensional Quality Metrics) operationalize this by organizing quality into hierarchies of issue types and severity levels, enabling systematic annotation, calibration, and comparisons beyond simple "good/bad" judgments (Mariana et al., 2015; Freitag et al., 2021). This matters because MQM-like frameworks support *specification-driven quality*: a translation can be evaluated against the needs of a context (e.g., legal precision vs. marketing tone), and stakeholders can agree on what counts as critical vs. minor errors. Large-scale evidence also suggests that expert MQM annotation is especially valuable for uncovering error patterns that automatic metrics miss precisely because it captures adequacy and meaning-related failures that fluent surface forms can disguise (Freitag et al., 2021).

A final implication is methodological: when organizations rely on AI outputs, "quality control" must shift from an end-stage activity (spot-checking after delivery) to a continuous risk-control loop where model outputs trigger targeted human attention, issue patterns feed into updated style guides/glossaries, and documentation becomes part of the quality product itself. This aligns with broader findings from post-editing research: the costs of MT/AI are not only linguistic corrections but also cognitive monitoring, error detection, and decision-making under uncertainty costs that rise sharply when failures are subtle and high-stakes (Daems et al., 2017).

Ethical and Professional Issues: Privacy, Bias, Deskilling, and Liability

Ethical concerns around AI in translation/interpreting are increasingly institutional rather than hypothetical. Once LLMs and MT are embedded in production pipelines, the key questions become governance questions: *What data is processed where? Who can access it? What risks are acceptable? Who is accountable when something goes wrong?*

1. Privacy and data governance

Many LLM services require users to input raw source text sometimes containing personal data, trade secrets, privileged legal material, or protected client information. Data-protection regulators therefore frame GenAI adoption as a compliance and procurement issue, not merely an IT choice (Alvarez-Vidal, 2023). In its updated GenAI guidance, the European Data Protection Supervisor emphasizes that organizations should ensure a lawful basis for processing, apply data minimization, manage vendor/processor arrangements, conduct risk assessment (including DPIAs where relevant), and maintain clear controls over retention, security, and onward use of data (European Data Protection Supervisor [EDPS], 2025).

A core technical reason these safeguards matter is that language models can memorize and later reproduce parts of their training data. Classic evidence shows that attackers can extract verbatim or near-verbatim training sequences including sensitive strings by querying large language models, highlighting confidentiality risk if protected text is used in training or logging pipelines (Carlini et al., 2020). This is why "don't paste client text into public tools" is not merely conservative advice; it is a defensible risk-control principle in many regulated workflows.

2. Deskilling and professional displacement

Professional associations increasingly treat deskilling as a standards and safety issue, not only a labor-market concern. FIT cautions that substituting professionals with unsupervised AI especially in high-stakes contexts can erode competence capacity, weaken professional standards, and introduce harms that are difficult to detect until after the fact (International Federation of Translators [FIT], 2024).

The practical mechanism is subtle: when translators/interpreters are repositioned as "post-editors" or "output checkers" without adequate authority, time, or training, their work can shift toward high-vigilance monitoring under speed pressure. Translation-process research suggests that this can increase cognitive effort in ways that are not obvious to management (e.g., constant error detection and repair), which can undermine sustainable expertise development if the role is framed as low-skill cleanup rather than professional judgement (O'Brien, 2006). In organizational settings, adoption also depends heavily on whether tools preserve agency and reduce friction because poorly designed automation can increase switching costs and monitoring burden (Cadwell et al., 2016).

3. Bias and representational harm

Bias in AI translation is not limited to "wrong words." Even when output is semantically plausible, models can systematically shift gender marking, politeness, formality, or culturally sensitive references creating representational harm (e.g., misgendering) or institutional harm (e.g., inappropriate deference in an asylum interview record). A substantial body of work documents gender bias in MT, including challenge-set evaluations that reveal systematic stereotypical behavior (Stanovsky et al., 2019) and evidence that engineering choices (e.g., speed–quality optimization) can amplify gender bias (Renduchintala et al., 2021). A recent synthesis of the field underscores that bias has proven resistant to simple "one-shot" technical fixes and requires ongoing measurement, dataset scrutiny, and governance (Savoldi et al., 2025).

4. Liability and accountability

As AI becomes a component within language services, liability concerns push organizations toward documented accountability rather than informal "best efforts." In practice, this means: selecting secure tools, specifying contractual transparency (data use, retention, training on prompts), setting human review requirements by risk tier, and defining who signs off on final meaning. In responsible AI practice more broadly, documentation frameworks such as model cards and datasheets for datasets are often used to operationalize transparency about intended use, limitations, evaluation coverage, and known risks materials that can support procurement, auditability, and defensible deployment decisions (Gebru et al., 2021; Mitchell et al., 2019). The applied translation implication is straightforward: when institutions rely on AI-mediated multilingual communication, governance artifacts (policies, logs, review records) become part of the quality product.

Ecological Validity: Controlled Benchmarks vs. Real Communicative Life

A persistent research gap concerns ecological validity: what AI translation systems do in curated benchmarks versus what they do amid real-world ambiguity, irony, emotional stance, and multimodal context. Benchmarking traditions in MT have often relied on sentence-level comparisons and corpus-based scoring (e.g., BLEU), which are useful for engineering iteration but limited as proxies for real communicative success (Papineni et al., 2002). The core problem is not that benchmarks are "wrong," but that they typically under-represent the conditions that dominate professional communication: long-range discourse dependence, mixed registers, vague or underspecified source text, institutional constraints (time pressure, confidentiality, liability), and interactional negotiation (clarification, repair, turn-taking).

Interpreting and applied-linguistics research have long demonstrated that performance is shaped by situational constraints and interactional complexity; the same speaker, message, and interpreter can yield different outcomes when the communicative ecology changes. Video-mediated interpreting is a clear example: once interaction is mediated by a screen, participants' coordination, attention, and repair patterns shift, and the interpreter's role in managing the shared "virtual space" becomes part of what quality *is* (Braun, 2013). This is directly relevant to AI translation because current deployments increasingly live inside mediated environments (remote hearings, telehealth, hybrid conferences) where "equivalence" includes interactional timing, stance management, and the handling of uncertainty not only lexical-semantic matching.

For these reasons, evaluating AI translation requires more than BLEU-like scores or isolated sentence judgments. It calls for situated evaluation designs that connect outputs to users, purposes, and consequences:

- **Genre-aware test sets:** Build evaluations that reflect real document ecologies (legal bundles, discharge summaries, asylum narratives, tender documents, subtitled dialogue), including long-context dependencies and domain-specific conventions.
- **User-centered quality research:** Combine expert assessment with user/task outcomes (e.g., can clinicians safely act on a translated instruction; can a lawyer rely on a clause; can a viewer follow plot and humor in subtitles).
- **Consequence-based error analysis:** Classify errors by *impact*, not just frequency prioritizing failures involving negation, modality, quantities, named entities, safety instructions, and identity/stance markers.

Methodologically, this shift also aligns with where MT evaluation research is moving: toward metrics and protocols that improve correlation with human judgments and make quality assessment more transparent and diagnostic in real use (e.g., learned evaluators such as COMET variants), while still recognizing that "good" evaluation ultimately depends on matching the test to the communicative task and stakes (Guerreiro et al., 2024).

FUTURE DIRECTIONS

Human–AI Collaboration: From Replacement Anxiety to Design Principles

The most productive future is not "more automation" as a blanket goal, but better collaboration design hybrid workflows that deliver *cognitive support* rather than *cognitive replacement.* Workplace studies suggest that successful MT/AI adoption depends heavily on translator agency, ergonomic fit, and task appropriateness, not simply on output quality (Cadwell et al., 2016; Cadwell et al., 2018).

A practical way forward is to treat AI-enabled translation/interpreting as a human-centered system with explicit design principles (Alaqad, et. al., 2026). Human-centered AI scholarship argues for designs that preserve meaningful human control, clarify responsibility, and prevent "over-automation" failure modes (Shneiderman, 2020). In translation practice, professionals' views increasingly converge on "control" and "autonomy" as core requirements: the ability to *switch off*, *override*, *reject*, and *negotiate* tool behavior and job conditions (Jiménez-Crespo, 2025).

Design principles for hybrid translation/ interpreting systems (actionable):

- **Risk reminds the workflow:** route content by stakes (low-risk drafts vs. high-risk "human-first" segments); the UI should *signal* risk, not hide it.
- **Controllability by default:** simple controls to constrain style/register, lock terminology, request alternatives, and enforce "don't guess ask/flag" behavior.
- **Provenance + audit trails:** capture prompts, model/version, glossary constraints, and revision history so accountability is traceable (especially for regulated domains).
- **Cognitive ergonomics:** minimize mode-switching, reduce interruptive alerts, and prioritize smooth attention flow because "helpful" features can become friction when they increase cognitive switching costs (Cadwell et al., 2016).
- **Human agency protection:** interface design should support a stable sense of "I am in charge of the outcome," which matters for responsibility and trust in human–AI work (Legaspi et al., 2024).
- **Experience as a quality factor:** measure not only accuracy and speed but also "Machine Translation User Experience (MTUX)" fatigue, perceived effort, and workflow burden because these shape sustainable professional use (Briva-Iglesias et al., 2023).

Policy and Regulation: AI Acts, Standards, and Sector-Specific Guidance

Regulatory landscapes increasingly shape translation technology decisions especially where language mediation touches fundamental rights, safety, or legal consequences. The EU AI Act (Regulation (EU) 2024/1689) adopts a risk-based framework and provides staged applicability timelines; EU-facing providers/deployers must plan for transparency obligations and governance requirements that scale with risk (European Union, 2024; European Commission, n.d.). EU guidance also clarifies timeline and expectations for general-purpose AI (GPAI) obligations (European Commission, 2025).

For translation/interpreting organizations, the regulatory future tends to translate into operational demands such as:

- **Transparency about AI use:** disclosure and documentation of where AI was used (drafting, summarization, transcription, post-editing).
- **Human-oversight evidence:** who reviewed what, using which criteria, with recorded sign-off for high-stakes deliverables.
- **Data governance:** clear rules on confidentiality, storage, retention, and whether inputs/outputs may be used for training.
- **Auditability:** reproducible logs, model/version control, and defensible QA procedures (particularly for regulated or contested communications).

A useful way to connect regulation to everyday workflow is to treat standards and compliance as "quality engineering": design the pipeline so that procurement, training, and tools collectively enforce safe practice (rather than relying on individual heroics).

Research Implications: What Translation Studies and Applied Linguistics Should Measure Next

If AI is becoming infrastructure, research needs to track how people and institutions adapt over time, not just how models score on benchmarks.

(1) Longitudinal adaptation studies

We need evidence on how translators' competence, identity, and decision strategies evolve under AI-saturated workflows especially how revision attention changes, when people over-trust fluent output, and which "risk heuristics" professionals develop. Longitudinal process research offers a workable template for tracking stable vs. shifting decision styles over time (Lehka-Paul, 2020).

Related work on translation work satisfaction and digitalization also supports measuring quality of working life as part of the AI impact picture (Sakamoto et al., 2024).

(2) Comparative regional studies (language/resource/ecology differences)

Adoption patterns are not universal: they vary by language resources, client markets, institutional risk tolerance, and tool access. Comparative studies should examine (a) low-resource and diglossic contexts, (b) regulatory/organizational culture, and (c) domain specialization, because these factors shape what "effective" human–AI collaboration looks like in practice.

(3) Interdisciplinary evaluation as the new default

The next phase of evaluation should combine:

- **Applied linguistics:** pragmatics, stance, discourse coherence, genre conventions;
- **HCI/ergonomics:** usability, fatigue, agency, cognitive load (van Egdom et al., 2020);
- **Ethics/law:** privacy, accountability, liability allocation;
- **Translation-process outcomes:** productivity *and* MTUX (Briva-Iglesias et al., 2023).

The payoff is methodological: instead of asking whether AI is "good," research can ask what configuration is safe and effective for which task, for which users, under which constraints and then test those claims empirically.

CONCLUSION

AI is transforming translation into a multidimensional socio-technical practice that integrates computational systems, human cognition, and institutional governance. Neural machine translation and Transformer-based architectures reshaped baseline expectations for speed and fluency (Vaswani et al., 2017; Wu et al., 2016), while generative AI has extended translation into interactive drafting, rewriting, and style negotiation across a widening range of genres and settings.

Yet the chapter's central argument remains: AI's value is maximized when it functions as a partner within human-accountable workflows. Quality is not guaranteed by fluency; it must be established through professional responsibility, transparent processes, and risk-proportionate verification. Insights from interpreting research reinforce that quality is socially evaluated (e.g., coherence, trustworthiness, communicative effectiveness), not reducible to surface well-formedness (Pöchhacker, 2001).

Likewise, the professionalization of MT post-editing through standards signals that machine output becomes publishable through controlled processes and qualified intervention rather than by default (British Standards Institution, 2017). Ethical and professional concerns privacy, bias, deskilling, and liability cannot be treated as secondary; professional bodies warn explicitly against unsupervised replacement models in high-stakes contexts where harm and accountability are central (Asian Federation for Translators and Interpreters [AFTI], 2024).

For applied linguistics, the implication is clear: the key task is not simply to ask whether AI can translate, but to determine under what conditions AI-mediated translation supports valid communication, protects users, and sustains professional competence. The future of translation is therefore best understood not as automation replacing expertise, but as expertise redefining how automation is evaluated, constrained, and governed.

A final practical implication is that the field should move from "model-centered" debates to workflow-centered accountability. As AI tools become embedded in everyday translation and interpreting, the key question becomes how institutions design pipelines that make quality and ethics observable: clear disclosure of AI involvement, documented post-editing and review decisions, secure handling of sensitive data, and systematic monitoring of bias and high-impact error types. This also reframes competence development: future translators and interpreters will increasingly be assessed not only on bilingual performance, but on their ability to specify briefs, constrain tools, verify outputs proportionate to risk, and justify decisions transparently skills that align closely with applied linguistics' emphasis on situated meaning, pragmatic appropriateness, and socially responsible communication.

REFERENCES

AIIC. (2025). AIIC Guidelines on Distance Interpreting.

Al Rousan, R. M., Jaradat, R. S., & Malkawi, M. (2025). ChatGPT translation vs. human translation: An examination of a literary text. *Cogent Social Sciences*, *11*(1), 2472916. Advance online publication. DOI: 10.1080/23311886.2025.2472916

Alaqad, M. H., Al-Saggaf, M. A., & Ingilan, S. S. (2026). The Future of AI in English Language Education: Opportunities, Challenges, and Ethical Pathways. The Sociology of English Language Teaching and Learning in the Age of AI, 241-264. DOI:DOI: 10.4018/979-8-3373-3755-5.ch010

Alvarez-Vidal, S., & Oliver, A. (2023). Assessing machine translation with measures of post-editing effort: A productivity perspective. *Ampersand (Oxford, UK)*, *11*, 100125. DOI: 10.1016/j.amper.2023.100125

Asrifan, A., & Alaqad, M. H. (2025). Evolution of AI in Interpretation: From Traditional Approaches to Real-Time Solution. In Role of AI in Translation and Interpretation (pp. 63-94). IGI Global Scientific Publishing. DOI:DOI: 10.4018/979-8-3373-0060-3.ch003

Bahdanau, D., Cho, K., & Bengio, Y. (2014). Neural machine translation by jointly learning to align and translate (arXiv:1409.0473). /arXiv.1409.0473DOI: 10.48550

Braun, S. (2013). Keep your distance? Remote interpreting in legal proceedings: A critical assessment of a growing practice. *Interpreting*, *15*(2), 200–228. DOI: 10.1075/intp.15.2.03bra

Braun, S. (2018). Video-mediated interpreting in legal settings in England: Interpreters' perceptions in their sociopolitical context. *Translation and Interpreting Studies*, *13*(3), 393–420. DOI: 10.1075/tis.00022.bra

British Standards Institution. (2015). BS EN ISO 17100:2015 Translation services Requirements for translation services. DOI: 10.3403/30246895U

British Standards Institution. (2017). *BS ISO 18587:2017 Translation services Post-editing of machine translation output Requirements*. DOI: 10.3403/30279909U

Briva-Iglesias, V., O'Brien, S., & Cowan, B. R. (2023). *The impact of traditional and interactive post-editing on machine translation user experience, quality, and productivity*. Translation, Cognition & Behavior., DOI: 10.1075/tcb.00077.bri

Cadwell, P., Castilho, S., O'Brien, S., & Mitchell, L. (2016). Human factors in machine translation and post-editing among institutional translators. *Translation Spaces*, *5*(2), 222–243. DOI: 10.1075/ts.5.2.04cad

Cadwell, P., O'Brien, S., & Teixeira, C. S. C. (2018). Resistance and accommodation: Factors for the (non-) adoption of machine translation among professional translators. Perspectives. *Studies in Translation Theory and Practice*, *26*(3), 301–321. DOI: 10.1080/0907676X.2017.1337210

Carlini, N., Tramèr, F., Wallace, E., Jagielski, M., Herbert-Voss, A., Lee, K., Roberts, A., Brown, T., Song, D., Erlingsson, Ú., Oprea, A., & Raffel, C. (2020). Extracting training data from large language models (arXiv:2012.07805). /arXiv.2012.07805DOI: 10.48550

Chiaro, D. (2020). Humour translation in the digital age. In Dore, M. (Ed.), *Humour Translation in the Age of Multimedia* (pp. 10–30). Routledge., DOI: 10.4324/9780429316081-2

Curry, N., Cushing-Leubner, J., Gray, J., & McNamara, T. (2025). A question of alignment AI, GenAI and applied linguistics. *Annual Review of Applied Linguistics*, *45*, 315–336. DOI: 10.1017/S0267190525000017

Daems, J., Vandepitte, S., Hartsuiker, R. J., & Macken, L. (2017). Identifying the machine translation error types with the greatest impact on post-editing effort. *Frontiers in Psychology*, *8*, 1282. DOI: 10.3389/fpsyg.2017.01282 PMID: 28824482

Egdom, G. W. (2020). A turn to ergonomics in translator and interpreter training. *The Interpreter and Translator Trainer*, *14*(4), 363–368. Advance online publication. DOI: 10.1080/1750399X.2020.1846930

European Commission. (2025). *Guidelines for providers of general-purpose AI models*. GPAI.

European Union. (2024). Regulation (EU) 2024/1689 (Artificial Intelligence Act). EUR-Lex (ELI: https://data.europa.eu/eli/reg/2024/1689/oj

Fantinuoli, C. (2018). Interpreting and technology: The upcoming technological turn. In Fantinuoli, C. (Ed.), *Interpreting and technology* (pp. 1–12). Language Science Press., DOI: 10.5281/zenodo.1493289

FIT. (2024). *Position paper on the use of AI in interpreting. AFTI. (2025).* Conference Interpreting in the Age of AI.

Freitag, M., Foster, G., Grangier, D., Ratnakar, V., Tan, Q., & Macherey, W. (2021). Experts, errors, and context: A large-scale study of human evaluation for machine translation. *Transactions of the Association for Computational Linguistics*, *9*, 1460–1474. DOI: 10.1162/tacl_a_00437

Gebru, T., Morgenstern, J., Vecchione, B., Vaughan, J. W., Wallach, H., Iii, H. D., & Crawford, K. (2021). Datasheets for datasets. *Communications of the ACM*, *64*(12), 86–92. DOI: 10.1145/3458723

Gile, D. (2009). *Basic concepts and models for interpreter and translator training* (Rev. ed.). John Benjamins. JBE PlatformDOI: 10.1075/btl.8

Ginovart Cid, C., Colominas, C., & Oliver, A. (2020). *Language industry views on the profile of the post-editor*. Translation Spaces., DOI: 10.1075/ts.19010.cid

Google. (2025, December). Gemini-powered improvements for Google Translate (announcement). (Taylor & Francis Online)

Guerreiro, N. M., Karpinska, M., Song, H., Freitag, M., Rei, R., & Martins, A. F. T. (2024). xCOMET: Transparent machine translation evaluation through fine-grained error detection. *Transactions of the Association for Computational Linguistics*, *12*, 979–995. Advance online publication. DOI: 10.1162/tacl_a_00683

Heylen, K., & De Hertog, D. (2015). Automatic term extraction. In Kockaert, H. J., & Steurs, F. (Eds.), *Handbook of Terminology* (Vol. 1). John Benjamins., DOI: 10.1075/hot.1.aut1

Hutchins, W. J. (1995). Machine translation: A brief history. In Koerner, E. F. K., & Asher, R. E. (Eds.), *Concise history of the language sciences* (pp. 431–445). Pergamon., DOI: 10.1016/B978-0-08-042580-1.50066-0

International Federation of Translators (FIT). (2024, August). Position paper on the use of AI in interpreting.

International Organization for Standardization. (2017). *ISO 18587:2017 Translation servicesPost-editing of machine translation outputRequirements*. https://www.iso.org/standard/62970.html (ISO)

International Organization for Standardization (ISO). (2022). ISO 23155:2022 Interpreting services Conference interpreting Requirements and recommendations. https://www.iso.org/standard/74749.html (ISO)

Jiménez-Crespo, M. A. (2025). Human-centered AI and the future of translation technologies: What professionals think about control and autonomy in the AI era. *Information (Basel)*, *16*(5), 387. DOI: 10.3390/info16050387

Koehn, P., Och, F. J., & Marcu, D. (2003). Statistical phrase-based translation. In Proceedings of NAACL-HLT (pp. 127–133). Association for Computational Linguistics. https://doi:DOI: 10.3115/1073445.1073462

Legaspi, R., Xu, W., Konishi, T., Wada, S., Kobayashi, N., Naruse, Y., & Ishikawa, Y. (2024). The sense of agency in human–AI interactions. *Knowledge-Based Systems, 295*, 111298. DOI: 10.1016/j.knosys.2023.111298

Lehka-Paul, O. (2020). Behavioural indicators of translators' decisional styles in a translation task: A longitudinal study. Yearbook of the Poznań Linguistic Meeting, 6, 81–111. DOI: 10.2478/yplm-2020-0007

Li, T., & Chmiel, A. (2024). Automatic subtitles increase accuracy and decrease cognitive load in simultaneous interpreting. *Interpreting, 26*(2), 253–281. DOI: 10.1075/intp.00111.li

Mariana, V., Cox, T., & Melby, A. (2015). The Multidimensional Quality Metrics (MQM) framework: A new framework for translation quality assessment. *The Journal of Specialised Translation, 23*(23), 137–161. DOI: 10.26034/cm.jostrans.2015.343

Mitchell, M., Wu, S., Zaldivar, A., Barnes, P., Vasserman, L., Hutchinson, B., Spitzer, E., Raji, I. D., & Gebru, T. (2019). Model cards for model reporting. In Proceedings of the Conference on Fairness, Accountability, and Transparency (FAT* '19) (pp. 220–229). DOI: 10.1145/3287560.3287596

Moser, P. (1996). Expectations of users of conference interpretation. [JBE Platform]. *Interpreting, 1*(2), 145–178. DOI: 10.1075/intp.1.2.01mos

NCIHC. (2024). NCIHC guidance for contracting AI-generated interpreting (July 15, 2024).

O'Brien, S. (2006). Pauses as indicators of cognitive effort in machine translation post-editing. *Across Languages and Cultures, 7*(1), 1–21. DOI: 10.1556/Acr.7.2006.1.1

Papineni, K., Roukos, S., Ward, T., & Zhu, W.-J. (2002). BLEU: A method for automatic evaluation of machine translation. In *Proceedings of the 40th Annual Meeting of the Association for Computational Linguistics* (pp. 311–318). Association for Computational Linguistics. DOI: 10.3115/1073083.1073135

Peng, X., Wang, Z., Liu, J., & Zhang, Y. (2024). The impacts of machine translation quality and perceived self-efficacy on student translators' cognitive effort and post-editing behavior. *SAGE Open, 14*(4). Advance online publication. DOI: 10.1177/21582440241291624

Pituxcoosuvarn, M., & Murakami, Y. (2025). Jokes or gibberish? Humor retention in translation with neural machine translation vs. large language model. *Digital, 5*(4), 49. DOI: 10.3390/digital5040049

Pöchhacker, F. (2001). Quality assessment in conference and community interpreting. *Meta: Translators'. Journal, 46*(2), 410–425. DOI: 10.7202/003847ar

Ragni, V., Kobi, S., & O'Brien, S. (2022). What has changed with neural machine translation? A review of the NMT landscape. *Perspectives, 30*(1), 1–25. DOI: 10.1080/0907676X.2021.1889005

Renduchintala, A., Stanovsky, G., & Madhyastha, P. (2021). Gender bias amplification during speed–quality optimization in neural machine translation. In *Proceedings of ACL-IJCNLP 2021* (pp. 99–109). DOI: 10.18653/v1/2021.acl-short.15

Révész, A., Suzuki, S., & Jung, Y. (2025). Artificial intelligence in applied linguistics: Applications, promises, and challenges. *Annual Review of Applied Linguistics, 45*, 1–9. DOI: 10.1017/S0267190525100172

Sakamoto, A.. (2024). *Measuring translators' quality of working life and their career sustainability in the context of digitalisation and automation*. Translation Spaces., DOI: 10.1075/ts.23026.sak

Savoldi, B., Gaido, M., Bentivogli, L., Negri, M., & Turchi, M. (2025). A decade of gender bias in machine translation. *Patterns (New York, N.Y.), 6*(6), 101257. DOI: 10.1016/j.patter.2025.101257 PMID: 40575128

Scansani, R. (2019). *Do translator trainees trust machine translation? An experiment on the influence of information about authorship on post-editing performance. Proceedings (ACL anthology)*. ACL Anthology.

Seeber, K. G. (2011). Cognitive load in simultaneous interpreting: Existing theories New models. *Interpreting, 13*(2), 176–204. DOI: 10.1075/intp.13.2.02see

Shneiderman, B. (2020). Human-centered artificial intelligence: Reliable, safe & trustworthy. *International Journal of Human-Computer Interaction, 36*(6), 495–504. DOI: 10.1080/10447318.2020.1741118

Specia, L., Raj, D., & Turchi, M. (2010). Machine translation evaluation versus quality estimation. *Machine Translation, 24*(1), 39–50. DOI: 10.1007/s10590-010-9077-2

Specia, L., & Shah, K. (2018). Machine translation quality estimation: Applications and future perspectives. In Moorkens, J., Castilho, S., Gaspari, F., & Doherty, S. (Eds.), *Translation Quality Assessment: From Principles to Practice* (pp. 201–235). Springer., DOI: 10.1007/978-3-319-91241-7_10

Stanovsky, G., Smith, N. A., & Zettlemoyer, L. (2019). Evaluating gender bias in machine translation. In *Proceedings of the 57th Annual Meeting of the Association for Computational Linguistics* (pp. 1679–1684). DOI: 10.18653/v1/P19-1164

Tardel, A. (2020). Effort in semi-automatized subtitling processes: Speech recognition and experience during transcription. *Journal of Audiovisual Translation, 3*(2), 79–102. DOI: 10.47476/jat.v3i2.2020.131

Toral, A., Wieling, M., & Way, A. (2018). Post-editing effort of a novel with statistical and neural machine translation. *Frontiers in Digital Humanities, 5*, 9. DOI: 10.3389/fdigh.2018.00009

UNESCO. (2024a). *AI competency framework for teachers*. UNESCO., DOI: 10.54675/ZJTE2084

UNESCO. (2024b). *AI competency framework for students*. UNESCO., DOI: 10.54675/JKJB9835

UNESCO. (2025). *AI competency framework for students*. UNESCO.

UNESCO. (2025). *AI competency framework for teachers*. UNESCO.

Vaswani, A., Shazeer, N., Parmar, N., Uszkoreit, J., Jones, L., Gomez, A. N., Kaiser, Ł., & Polosukhin, I. (2017). *Attention is all you need* (arXiv:1706.03762). /arXiv.1706.03762DOI: 10.48550

Venuti, L. (2017). *The translator's invisibility: A history of translation* (3rd ed.). Routledge., DOI: 10.4324/9781315098746

Wissik, T. (2025). The impact of automatic term extraction on terminology work: Evidence from professional practice. *Terminology, 31*(1), 110–135. Advance online publication. DOI: 10.1075/term.00085.wis

Wu, Y., Schuster, M., Chen, Z., Le, Q. V., Norouzi, M., Macherey, W., Krikun, M., Cao, Y., Gao, Q., Macherey, K., Klingner, J., Shah, A., Johnson, M., Liu, X., Kaiser, Ł., Gouws, S., Kato, Y., Kudo, T., Kazawa, H., . . . Dean, J. (2016). Google's neural machine translation system: Bridging the gap between human and machine translation (arXiv:1609.08144). /arXiv.1609.08144DOI: 10.48550

Yao, R. (2025, December 12). Bringing state-of-the-art Gemini translation capabilities to Google Translate. Google (The Keyword)

Zhang, B., Haddow, B., & Birch, A. (2023). Prompting large language model for machine translation: A case study (arXiv:2301.07069). /arXiv.2301.07069DOI: 10.48550

Zhu, W., Liu, H., Dong, Q., Xu, J., Huang, S., Kong, L., Chen, J., & Li, L. (2024). Multilingual machine translation with large language models: Empirical results and analysis (arXiv:2304.04675). /arXiv.2304.04675DOI: 10.18653/v1/2024.findings-naacl.176

KEY TERMS AND DEFINITIONS

Artificial Intelligence: Computer systems designed to perform tasks that typically require human intelligence, including language processing, translation, and decision-making.

Human–AI Collaboration: A translation workflow in which artificial intelligence tools support human translators while humans maintain responsibility for interpretation, contextual judgment, and final quality assurance.

Large Language Models: Advanced artificial intelligence systems trained on large-scale textual datasets to generate, interpret, and manipulate natural language across multiple tasks, including translation.

Machine Translation: The automated process of translating text or speech from one language into another using computational algorithms and linguistic data.

Neural Machine Translation: A machine translation approach based on deep neural networks that learn patterns across entire sentences or texts to produce more fluent and contextually coherent translations.

Post-Editing: The process of reviewing and revising machine-generated translations to improve accuracy, clarity, and suitability for a specific communicative context.

Translation Quality: The degree to which a translation accurately conveys meaning, maintains coherence, and meets the linguistic, cultural, and functional expectations of its intended audience.

Translation Workflow: The structured sequence of processes, tools, and human interventions used to produce, review, and deliver translated content.

Translation Ethics: Principles and professional standards that guide responsible translation practices, including accuracy, confidentiality, transparency, and accountability.

Section 3

Creativity: AI in Translating Sociocultural Discourse and Assessing Specialized Writing

Chapter 11
Lost in Translation?
AI Recognition and Misinterpretation of Culturally Embedded Symbolic Language

Banan Assiri
http://orcid.org/0009-0007-8744-5748
King Khalid University, Saudi Arabia

ABSTRACT

Artificial intelligence (AI) systems, particularly large language models (LLMs), have transformed applied linguistics, enabling advances in machine translation and intercultural communication. However, these systems encounter significant challenges when processing symbolic language, idioms, proverbs, metaphors, and satirical expressions, whose interpretation depends on shared cultural knowledge. This chapter investigates the capacity of contemporary AI systems (GPT-4, Claude 3.5, Gemini Pro) to recognise, interpret, and translate culturally embedded symbolic expressions from Gulf Arabic varieties. Employing a corpus-assisted discourse analysis (CADS) methodology combined with systematic AI output evaluation, the study analysed 666 symbolic expressions across four categories (proverbs, metaphors, idioms, satire) drawn from authentic Gulf Arabic discourse. Results reveal systematic patterns of literal misinterpretation (42% of errors), inappropriate cultural mapping (28%), over-generalisation (33%), and loss of pragmatic force (58%). Statistical analysis demonstrated significant variation across expression types ($F(3,662) = 18.7, p < .001$) and thematic domains ($F(5,660) = 12.4, p < .001$), with contextual information significantly improving performance (mean improvement = 0.43, $p < .001$). These findings illuminate fundamental limitations in current NLP

DOI: 10.4018/979-8-3373-6420-9.ch011

architectures and contribute design principles for culturally aware AI systems. The chapter addresses emerging considerations including AI ethics and cultural bias, human–AI collaboration models, and policy implications for multilingual regions.

INTRODUCTION

Background and Context

The integration of artificial intelligence into linguistic practice represents one of the most significant technological shifts in the history of human communication. Large language models (LLMs) such as OpenAI's GPT-4, Anthropic's Claude, and Google's Gemini now mediate countless daily interactions across linguistic boundaries, from automated customer service to real-time translation applications used by millions worldwide. These systems have demonstrated remarkable capabilities in processing natural language, generating coherent text, and even producing creative content that can be difficult to distinguish from human authorship. Yet beneath this impressive surface lies a fundamental tension: while AI systems excel at pattern recognition and statistical prediction, they lack the embodied experience and cultural immersion that enables humans to navigate the complex terrain of symbolic language (Bender & Koller, 2020; Alhakimi et al., 2025).

Symbolic language, encompassing idioms, proverbs, metaphors, satire, and other forms of figurative expression, constitutes a significant portion of everyday human communication (Gibbs, 1994; Kövecses, 2010). These expressions derive their meaning not from the literal denotation of their component words but from shared cultural knowledge, historical associations, and contextual factors that resist straightforward algorithmic capture (Lakoff & Johnson, 1980; Sperber & Wilson, 1995). When a speaker of Gulf Arabic invokes the proverb *(alli ma yaerif alsaqr yashwyh)*, literally 'He who does not know the falcon, grills it', they invoke not merely these words but an entire cultural framework encompassing Bedouin heritage, the valued status of falconry in Gulf societies, and the broader principle that ignorance leads to the destruction of valuable things. This layered meaning, so readily apparent to cultural insiders, presents formidable challenges for AI systems trained primarily on textual patterns.

The stakes of this challenge extend far beyond academic interest. As AI-mediated communication becomes increasingly prevalent in diplomacy, international business, journalism, and everyday intercultural exchange, the capacity of these systems to preserve cultural meaning becomes a matter of practical urgency. Misinterpretation of symbolic language can lead to misunderstanding at best and offence or conflict at worst. Consider the diplomatic implications when an AI translation system renders a culturally expression of hospitality as a mere literal description, or when satirical political commentary is flattened into neutral reportage, stripping away its critical edge. In an era of increasing global connectivity, such failures of cultural transmission carry real consequences for international relations, business negotiations, and cross-cultural understanding.

Research Objectives and Questions

This chapter addresses these concerns through a systematic investigation of AI performance in recognising and interpreting culturally embedded symbolic language, with particular focus on Gulf Arabic expressions and their translation into English. The Gulf region, comprising the United Arab Emirates, Saudi Arabia, Qatar, Kuwait, Bahrain, and Oman, possesses a distinctive linguistic heritage shaped by Bedouin traditions, maritime trade, pearl-diving culture, and more recent encounters with globalisation and technological modernisation (Holes, 2011; Khalaf, 2025).

This study pursues four interrelated objectives. The first is to evaluate the extent to which contemporary AI systems, specifically GPT-4, Claude 3.5, and Gemini Pro, accurately recognise symbolic language in authentic Gulf Arabic discourse contexts. Building on this, the second objective is to identify and categorise the systematic patterns of error that emerge when these systems interpret and translate culturally embedded expressions. The third objective moves beyond description to ask whether the observed errors are specific to Gulf Arabic or reflective of broader limitations in AI figurative language processing more generally. The fourth and most applied objective is to translate these empirical findings into evidence-based design principles for culturally aware NLP systems. Together, these objectives give rise to three guiding research questions:

> RQ1: To what extent can contemporary AI systems accurately recognise symbolic language when it appears in authentic Gulf Arabic discourse contexts?
> RQ2: What patterns of error emerge when these systems attempt to interpret and translate culturally embedded expressions from Gulf Arabic, and which patterns are Gulf-specific versus general AI limitations?
> RQ3: What design principles might guide the development of more culturally aware NLP systems?

By addressing these questions through empirical analysis, this chapter contributes both to theoretical understanding of AI limitations and to practical efforts to improve these systems. The investigation is particularly timely given the rapid deployment of AI translation tools across the Gulf region and the growing recognition that linguistic technology must be evaluated not only for technical accuracy but for cultural fidelity.

THEORETICAL FRAMEWORK

This study integrates three theoretical perspectives: classical Arabic rhetoric and conceptual metaphor theory from cognitive linguistics, cultural semiotics (particularly Lotman's semiosphere concept), and contemporary approaches to NLP evaluation. This integration is not merely additive; rather, each framework addresses distinct aspects of the research problem while their intersection generates the study's analytical power. The following sections explicate each framework and demonstrate how they collectively inform the methodology and evaluation criteria.

Symbolic Language in Applied Linguistics

The Arabic linguistic tradition offers particularly rich resources for understanding symbolic language. Classical Arabic rhetoric (balāgha) developed sophisticated taxonomies of figurative expression over more than a millennium of scholarly analysis, distinguishing between majāz (figurative language), istiʿāra (metaphor), kināya (metonymy), and tashbīh (simile). These categories, refined through centuries of engagement with Quranic exegesis, poetry, and rhetorical practice, reveal the centrality of figurative expression to Arabic communicative practice and the inadequacy of simple literal-figurative dichotomies. Contemporary scholarship has sought to integrate these classical insights with modern cognitive linguistic frameworks, revealing both convergences and distinctive features of Arabic conceptual metaphor systems (Maalej, 2004).

Conceptual Metaphor Theory (CMT), as developed by Lakoff and Johnson (1980) and extended by Kövecses (2005, 2010), provides the cognitive foundation for understanding how figurative meaning operates. CMT posits that metaphor is primarily a cognitive phenomenon, systematic mappings between conceptual domains that structure thought and experience. This framework directly informs the study's evaluation criteria in two ways. First, it predicts that AI systems should perform better on metaphors grounded in universal embodied experience (spatial orientation, physical interaction) than on culturally specific metaphors, a hypothesis testable through the study's domain-based analysis. Second, it suggests that errors will not be random but systematic, reflecting AI systems' implicit reliance on English-dominant conceptual mappings. The evaluation criterion of 'semantic accuracy' operationalises CMT's concept of cross-domain mapping preservation, while 'cultural relevance' assesses whether culturally specific elaborations of mappings are maintained.

Cultural Semiotics and the Semiosphere

While cognitive linguistics illuminates the conceptual foundations of figurative language, a complete theoretical framework must also account for the cultural dimensions of symbolic meaning. Lotman's concept of the 'semiosphere' (2005) provides essential resources for this purpose. Lotman conceives of culture as a semiotic space, a bounded domain within which signs circulate, interact, and acquire meaning through their relationships with other signs and with the broader cultural context. Crucially, the semiosphere is not merely a container for pre-existing meanings but an active generative mechanism: meaning emerges through the dynamic interplay of cultural texts, codes, and interpretive practices.

This framework has particular relevance for understanding Gulf Arabic symbolic language. The Gulf semiosphere encompasses not merely linguistic signs but a complex ecology of cultural references such as Bedouin heritage and desert ecology, the historical importance of pearl diving and maritime trade, the falcon as a symbol of nobility and skill, coffee and hospitality rituals, and the transformative encounter with oil wealth and rapid modernisation. Each of these cultural domains provides source material for symbolic expression, and the meanings of specific expressions are shaped by their position within this broader semiotic network.

The semiosphere concept directly motivates this study's evaluation criteria of 'over-generalisation' and 'cultural relevance'. When AI systems substitute Gulf Arabic expressions with English 'equivalents', they effectively translate across semiospheric boundaries without preserving the original expression's position within Gulf Arabic cultural networks. The 'over-generalisation' criterion specifically captures this phenomenon: scoring whether the AI has inappropriately mapped a Gulf-specific expression onto a culturally distinct English equivalent, thereby erasing its particular semiotic positioning. The 'cultural relevance' criterion assesses whether the broader cultural resonances, namely the expression's connections to other signs within the semiosphere, are preserved in translation.

The implications for AI-mediated translation are substantial. Contemporary AI translation systems operate largely through statistical modelling of textual co-occurrence patterns and lack direct access to the semiosphere within which symbolic expressions are produced and interpreted. Meaning is thus processed primarily as a relation between linguistic forms rather than as an outcome of participation in a culturally bounded semiotic space. This text-centric mode of operation constrains AI systems' capacity to reconstruct the intertextual, historical, and pragmatic relations that give symbolic expressions their communicative force (Bender & Koller, 2020; Pym, 2025).

Recent empirical studies demonstrate that while AI systems may generate fluent and idiomatic-looking translations, they frequently fail to account for the culturally situated knowledge required to interpret symbolic language appropriately, particularly in cases involving proverbs, metaphors, and culturally dense expressions (Hendy et al., 2023; Liu et al., 2022). The boundary dynamics of the semiosphere also illuminate cross-cultural translation challenges. Lotman emphasises that the boundary of the semiosphere is a site of active translation, where meanings from external semiotic spaces are assimilated and transformed. This process is never neutral; it involves interpretation, selection, and often distortion. When Gulf Arabic expressions are translated into English, they cross not merely a linguistic boundary but a semiotic one, and the receiving semiosphere, Anglophone culture, imposes its own interpretive frameworks.

Gulf Arabic: Linguistic, Cultural, and Dialectal Context

Understanding AI performance on Gulf Arabic symbolic language requires attention to the specific linguistic and cultural characteristics of this variety. Gulf Arabic encompasses the spoken dialects of the Arabian Peninsula's eastern coast, including distinctive varieties in Saudi Arabia, Kuwait, Bahrain, Qatar, the United Arab Emirates, and Oman (Holes, 2011; Versteegh, 2014). While these varieties share common features that distinguish them from other Arabic dialects, including characteristic phonological patterns, lexical items, and grammatical structures, they also exhibit significant internal variation reflecting local histories, tribal affiliations, and degrees of contact with other languages (Watson, 2002).

This internal variation has important methodological implications for the present study. Kuwaiti Arabic, for instance, has historically been influenced by Iraqi Arabic due to geographic proximity, while Emirati varieties show substantial Persian and Baluchi influence from historical trade patterns. Omani Arabic varieties demonstrate features distinguishing them from other Gulf dialects, including retention of archaic forms and influence from South Arabian languages. Bahraini Arabic reflects the island's role as a historical trading hub. These dialectal differences affect figurative language in several ways: certain proverbs may be shared across the region while others are locally specific; metaphorical source domains may vary based on local ecology and history (e.g., pearl-diving expressions more prominent in Bahraini and Emirati contexts); and pragmatic conventions governing expression use may differ across communities.

The figurative language of Gulf Arabic draws on several distinctive cultural domains. Bedouin heritage provides a rich source of symbolic expressions relating to desert life, tribal organisation, hospitality codes, and the values of honour, generosity, patience, and endurance (Holes, 2011; Abu-Lughod, 2016). Proverbs such as (**Transliteration:** *man alab al- ulā sahira al-layālī*, **Literal English meaning:** 'He who seeks heights stays up nights') encode culturally salient values of perseverance and ambition historically grounded in the material and environmental challenges of desert existence (Hamdi, 2018).

Maritime culture, particularly the pearl-diving economy that dominated Gulf societies prior to the discovery of oil, constitutes another important source domain. Expressions derived from seafaring and trade invoke themes of patience, risk, collective labour, and delayed reward, reflecting embodied experiences of underwater work and long-distance commerce (Holes, 2004). Coffee (gahwa) occupies a particularly significant symbolic position in Gulf culture, functioning not merely as a beverage but as a metonym for hospitality, social hierarchy, negotiation, and communal interaction (Buscemi & Kaposi, 2020). The elaborate rituals surrounding Arabic coffee preparation and service, including serving order, gesture, and timing, encode social relations and pragmatic meanings that extend beyond literal reference (Algamedi, 2025). Expressions involving coffee thus frequently activate culturally embedded meanings, creating specific challenges for AI translation systems that must distinguish literal from figurative usage while preserving culturally appropriate pragmatic force.

The contemporary Gulf context introduces additional layers of complexity. Rapid modernisation, economic transformation driven by oil wealth, and intensified globalisation have produced a dynamic communicative environment in which traditional expressions coexist with new coinages and hybrid forms (Holes, 2011; Watson, 2002). Code-switching between Gulf Arabic, Modern Standard Arabic, and English is widespread, particularly in digital and professional domains (Albirini, 2016). Social media has become a particularly active site of linguistic innovation, where users creatively adapt traditional proverbs, generate satirical expressions, and negotiate shifting social and political realities (Alayba, 2025).

AI and Figurative Language Processing: Current State and Emerging Trends

The computational processing of figurative language has been a persistent challenge for natural language processing since the field's inception. Early rule-based systems struggled with the context-dependence and productivity of figurative expressions, while statistical approaches faced difficulties with the relatively low frequency and high variability of many idiomatic forms. The advent of neural network architectures, particularly transformer-based models such as BERT (Devlin et al., 2019) and GPT (Brown et al., 2020), has enabled significant advances in figurative language processing.

Contemporary large language models demonstrate impressive capabilities in certain domains of figurative language. GPT-4 can often correctly interpret English idioms, generate contextually appropriate metaphors, and explain unfamiliar expressions. However, research has consistently identified limitations, particularly when expressions are culturally specific, context-dependent, or involve subtle pragmatic functions (Liu et al., 2022). Studies examining metaphor understanding have found that while models can learn associations between expressions and interpretations, they often fail to demonstrate systematic cross-domain reasoning that characterises human comprehension (Lai & Nissim, 2024).

Recent benchmark studies (2024–2025) have begun addressing Arabic figurative language more systematically. Attia et al. (2025) found significant performance disparities in LLM processing of figurative language across languages, with Arabic proverbs yielding 4.29% lower accuracy than English equivalents, and Egyptian idioms performing 10.28% below Arabic proverbs. Their analysis revealed that pragmatic application tasks posed greater challenges than comprehension tasks, with a 14.07% accuracy decline, though contextual sentence provision partially mitigated this gap (10.66% improvement). Hamdi et al. (2023) employed machine learning techniques to investigate cross-linguistic equivalence in Arabic and English proverbs, analysing five proverbial pairs through topic modelling applied to authentic language use corpora. Their findings revealed that ostensibly equivalent proverbs across the two languages exhibited subtle semantic variations attributable to religious, cultural, and social factors. These studies underscore the need for evaluation approaches that attend specifically to dialectal and cultural variation.

However, emerging trends offer grounds for cautious optimism. Recent work on contextual sensitivity in LLMs demonstrates that chain-of-thought prompting and explicit cultural context provision can significantly improve figurative language performance (Chen et al., 2025). This aligns with growing recognition that hybrid human-AI approaches may address persistent MT limitations. Al Maaytah (2026), examining English-Arabic machine translation through mixed-methods analysis, found that while MT handles technical and literal content competently, idiomatic and culturally embedded expressions remain problematic, particularly morphologically complex Arabic structures. The study advocates integrating computational efficiency with human linguistic expertise. Similarly, Awashreh and Aboeisheh (2025) call for collaborative human-AI models, arguing that post-editing workflows combining AI translation with expert review can preserve cultural sensitivity while maintaining efficiency. These developments directly inform the present study's dual-condition design (decontextualised vs. contextualised) and its multi-dimensional evaluation framework, testing whether contextual scaffolding improves AI performance on Gulf Arabic figurative language.

The specific challenges of Arabic figurative language processing include the morphological complexity of the language, significant variation between Modern Standard Arabic and regional dialects, and relative scarcity of training data compared to English (Alayba, 2025). Studies of Arabic idiom processing have found high error rates even for common expressions, with models frequently defaulting to literal interpretations or substituting culturally inappropriate equivalents (Abdul-Mageed & Elmadany, 2021).

The evaluation of AI figurative language processing faces methodological challenges. Automated metrics such as BLEU scores correlate poorly with human judgements of translation quality for figurative content (Chatzikoumi, 2020). Human evaluation, while more reliable, introduces issues of subjectivity and scalability. Recent work has proposed specialised benchmarks for figurative language understanding, but these have predominantly focused on English and have rarely incorporated culturally specific expressions or pragmatic evaluation criteria. This methodological gap motivates the present study's use of expert human evaluation guided by a structured framework that attends specifically to cultural and pragmatic dimensions of meaning.

Positioning This Study Within Existing Scholarship

This study contributes to existing scholarship in several distinct ways. While previous work has examined AI processing of Arabic figurative language, studies have predominantly focused on Modern Standard Arabic or Egyptian Arabic, leaving Gulf varieties underexplored. The few studies addressing Gulf Arabic have typically used decontextualised expression lists rather than authentic discourse data, limiting ecological validity. Moreover, existing evaluation frameworks have rarely incorporated cultural semiotics perspectives, instead relying on semantic accuracy alone.

The present study's novelty lies in three areas: (1) its focus on Gulf Arabic varieties with explicit attention to internal dialectal variation; (2) its integration of corpus linguistics methods with AI evaluation, ensuring findings reflect real-world usage patterns rather than artificial test conditions; and (3) its theoretically grounded evaluation framework that operationalises insights from CMT and cultural semiotics into measurable criteria. By connecting theoretical frameworks explicitly to methodological choices and evaluation criteria, the study offers a replicable model for culturally informed AI assessment that can be extended to other language varieties and cultural contexts.

METHODOLOGY

Research Design and Justification

This study adopts a mixed-methods research design integrating corpus-assisted discourse analysis (CADS) with systematic evaluation of AI-generated translations.

The choice of this design reflects both theoretical and practical considerations that connect directly to the research questions.

The CADS approach, developed within the Birmingham tradition of corpus linguistics (Partington et al., 2013), was selected because it combines quantitative rigour with interpretive depth, essential for this study's objectives. RQ1 (recognition accuracy) requires systematic quantification across a large dataset, which corpus methods enable. However, RQ2 (error patterns) requires interpretive analysis of how and why errors occur, necessitating discourse-analytical attention to individual instances. CADS provides established procedures for moving between these analytical scales.

Within this framework, figurative language is explored indirectly as a discursive phenomenon emerging through recurrent collocational patterns, semantic preferences, and evaluative framings in context. This methodological choice reflects established practice in CADS, which prioritises identification of meaning-making tendencies over mechanical detection of rhetorical devices (Partington et al., 2013; Taylor, 2021). As metaphorical meaning is often implicit, context-dependent, and culturally embedded, especially in Arabic discourse, keyword-based or rule-driven metaphor identification risks oversimplification and interpretive error.

The AI evaluation component employs expert human evaluation rather than automated metrics. This choice reflects evidence that automated metrics such as BLEU correlate poorly with human judgements of translation quality for figurative language (Läubli et al., 2020), where semantically equivalent translations may differ substantially in surface form. The structured coding framework enables assessment of semantic, cultural, and pragmatic dimensions that automated metrics cannot capture.

Ecological validity serves as a core design principle. Rather than relying on constructed examples or decontextualised lists, the corpus comprises authentic texts from real-world Gulf Arabic discourse. By incorporating multiple text types, social media and public speeches, the design captures variation across registers and communicative settings, ensuring findings reflect AI performance under real-world conditions.

Corpus Design and Compilation

The study corpus comprises authentic Gulf Arabic texts containing culturally embedded symbolic language, drawn from two primary source types designed to capture register variation. The corpus totals approximately 250,000 words, with symbolic expressions identified and coded throughout. Table 1 presents the corpus composition.

Table 1. Corpus Composition

Source Type	Texts	Words	Expressions	%
Social Media Posts	500	75,000	245	36.8%
Public Speeches	50	50,000	109	16.4%
Additional Sources	,	125,000	312	46.8%
TOTAL	550+	250,000	666	100%

Social media discourse: A sample of 500 posts from X (formerly Twitter) and Instagram accounts based in Gulf countries, selected to represent everyday figurative expression in informal digital communication. Social media data provides access to colloquial Gulf Arabic usage and reveals how younger speakers adapt traditional expressions to contemporary contexts. Posts were selected using keyword searches for common Gulf Arabic expressions and through purposive sampling of accounts known for culturally embedded commentary.

Public speeches and interviews: Transcripts of 50 public speeches by Gulf political and cultural figures, along with interviews from television programmes and podcasts. These texts illustrate the rhetorical deployment of symbolic language in formal public discourse and demonstrate how speakers use proverbs and metaphors to invoke cultural authority.

Regional distribution: To address internal dialectal variation, sources were distributed across Gulf states: Saudi Arabia (Riyadh and Eastern Province) 25%, UAE 25%, Kuwait 20%, Qatar 15%, Bahrain 10%, Oman 5%. This distribution reflects population sizes while ensuring representation of each major variety. Expressions were coded for regional specificity (pan-Gulf vs. locally specific) to enable analysis of whether AI performance varies with dialectal representation in training data.

Expression Identification and Coding

Within this corpus, instances of symbolic language were initially identified through corpus-assisted techniques using AntConc (Anthony, 2022). Keyword searches targeted established Gulf Arabic proverbs and common figurative expressions documented in regional lexicographic sources, while concordance analysis enabled systematic examination of surrounding co-text to detect additional figurative uses. This corpus-driven identification was complemented by manual annotation from two native-speaker coders with expertise in Gulf Arabic linguistics. Both annotators hold advanced degrees in Arabic linguistics and have extensive experience with Gulf dialectal varieties, one specialising in Kuwaiti/Saudi varieties, the other in Emirati/Omani varieties. This pairing ensured coverage of regional variation.

Inter-annotator agreement was calculated using Cohen's kappa, achieving $\kappa = 0.84$, indicating substantial agreement. Agreement was highest for proverbs ($\kappa = 0.91$) and lowest for satire/irony ($\kappa = 0.76$), reflecting the greater interpretive complexity of ironic expressions. Disagreements were resolved through discussion and consultation with a third expert annotator specialising in Gulf Arabic proverbs and folklore.

The coding scheme distinguished four primary categories of symbolic expression, with each category operationalised according to the theoretical framework:

Table 2. Expression Type Distribution

Type	Count	%	Theoretical Connection
Proverbs (amthāl)	187	28.1%	Fixed forms; semiotic positioning
Metaphors	234	35.1%	CMT cross-domain mappings
Idioms	156	23.4%	Non-compositional meaning
Satire/Irony	89	13.4%	Pragmatic/rhetorical function

Each coded expression was additionally classified by thematic domain, enabling analysis of whether AI performance varies across different cultural domains:

Table 3. Thematic Domain Distribution

Domain	Count	%
Political Discourse	178	26.7%
Social Relations & Hospitality	142	21.3%
Resilience & Perseverance	124	18.6%
Nature & Environment	98	14.7%
Economic Activity	67	10.1%
Religion & Spirituality	57	8.6%

AI Models and Evaluation Procedure

Three leading commercial LLMs were selected for evaluation based on their prominence in real-world applications and their representation of different architectural approaches: GPT-4 (OpenAI, gpt-4-turbo-2024-04-09), representing the state of the art in general-purpose language modelling; Claude 3.5 Sonnet (Anthropic, claude-3-5-sonnet-20241022), known for reasoning and cultural sensitivity; and Gemini Pro 1.5 (Google), representing Google's multimodal approach with strong multilingual capabilities.

Each symbolic expression was input to the three models in two conditions designed to test the role of contextual information, directly testing predictions from CMT and semiosphere theory that context should improve interpretation:

> Decontextualised condition: The expression was presented in isolation with the prompt: 'Please translate the following Gulf Arabic expression into English and explain its meaning: [expression].'
> Contextualised condition: The expression was presented within its original discourse context with the prompt: 'Please translate the following Gulf Arabic text into English, paying particular attention to preserving the meaning of any figurative expressions: [full text].'

All API calls were made between September and November 2024 to ensure model version consistency.

Evaluation Framework

Model outputs were evaluated by a panel of three expert evaluators: two bilingual Arabic–English linguists with specialisation in Gulf Arabic, and one translation studies scholar with expertise in figurative language translation. The evaluation criteria were designed to operationalise the theoretical framework's key constructs:

Table 4. Evaluation Criteria and Theoretical Grounding

Criterion	Scale	Operationalises
Semantic Accuracy	0–3	CMT: cross-domain mapping preservation
Cultural Relevance	0–2	Semiosphere: cultural positioning
Over-generalisation	0–1	Semiosphere: inappropriate substitution
Pragmatic Preservation	0–2	Speech act and rhetorical function

> **Semantic Accuracy (0–3):** Assesses whether the AI output captures the intended meaning of the expression. This criterion operationalises CMT's concept of cross-domain mapping, does the translation preserve the conceptual mapping from source to target domain? Scores: 0 = meaning entirely missed or reversed; 1 = partial meaning but significant elements lost; 2 = core meaning captured with some inaccuracies; 3 = meaning fully and accurately conveyed.

Cultural Relevance (0–2): Assesses whether culturally specific framing is preserved. This criterion operationalises the semiosphere concept, does the translation maintain the expression's position within Gulf Arabic cultural networks? Scores: 0 = cultural meaning erased or distorted; 1 = cultural elements partially preserved; 2 = cultural framing appropriately maintained.

Over-generalisation (0–1): Binary coding assessing whether the output substitutes an inappropriate cultural equivalent. Directly operationalises semiosphere boundary dynamics. Scores: 0 = inappropriate substitution present; 1 = no inappropriate substitution.

Pragmatic Preservation (0–2): Assesses whether the output maintains pragmatic or rhetorical function. Particularly relevant for satirical expressions where communicative intent may diverge from literal content. Scores: 0 = pragmatic function entirely lost; 1 = pragmatic function partially preserved; 2 = pragmatic function fully maintained.

Validity and Reliability

The study addresses multiple forms of validity:

Content validity: The evaluation criteria were derived from established theoretical frameworks (CMT, cultural semiotics) and refined through pilot testing with Gulf Arabic language experts. Each criterion was reviewed by three experts for alignment with underlying constructs.

Construct validity: The multi-dimensional evaluation framework captures distinct aspects of translation quality (semantic, cultural, pragmatic), enabling discriminant analysis. The pattern of results, high semantic accuracy combined with lower cultural/pragmatic scores, provides evidence of construct validity by demonstrating predicted distinctions.

Ecological validity: Use of authentic corpus data rather than constructed examples ensures findings reflect real-world AI performance. The inclusion of multiple text types and regional varieties enhances generalisability within the Gulf Arabic context.

Reliability was assessed through multiple mechanisms. Inter-rater reliability was calculated using intraclass correlation coefficients (ICC), with two-way random effects models assessing absolute agreement:

Table 5. Inter-rater Reliability (ICC values)

Criterion	ICC	95% CI	Interpretation
Semantic Accuracy	0.86	[0.83, 0.89]	Good
Cultural Relevance	0.82	[0.78, 0.85]	Good
Over-generalisation	0.89	[0.86, 0.91]	Excellent
Pragmatic Preservation	0.78	[0.74, 0.82]	Good

ICC values ranging from 0.78 to 0.89 indicate good to excellent reliability according to established guidelines (Koo & Li, 2016). Final scores were calculated as the mean of the three evaluators' ratings.

Ethical Considerations

This study raises several ethical considerations addressed in the research design. Data collection from social media followed platform terms of service and focused on public accounts producing commentary for public audiences. No private communications were collected. Individual users are not identified in reporting; examples are presented without attribution to protect privacy.

The evaluation of AI systems for cultural competence raises broader ethical questions about AI's role in cross-cultural communication. This study does not advocate replacing human translators with AI for culturally sensitive content; rather, findings inform appropriate use cases and identify areas requiring human oversight. The documented limitations serve as cautions against over-reliance on AI translation where cultural fidelity is essential.

The study also engages with questions of cultural bias in AI systems. Findings documenting over-generalisation toward English cultural frameworks contribute to ongoing discussions about ensuring diverse cultural representation in AI training. The design principles proposed in the Discussion section explicitly address these concerns.

FINDINGS AND ANALYSIS

Overall Performance Patterns

Analysis of the evaluation data (N = 666 expressions × 3 models × 2 conditions = 3,996 evaluations) reveals significant variation in AI performance across expression types, thematic domains, and contextual conditions. Table 6 presents overall descriptive statistics.

Table 6. Overall Performance Across all Models

Metric	N	Mean	SD	Min	Max
Semantic Accuracy (0–3)	666	1.87	0.76	0	3
Cultural Relevance (0–2)	666	0.94	0.62	0	2
Over-generalisation (0–1)	666	0.67	0.47	0	1
Pragmatic Preservation (0–2)	666	0.78	0.58	0	2

These aggregate findings reveal that while contemporary LLMs can often approximate the core meaning of symbolic expressions (semantic accuracy approaching 2 on a 0–3 scale), they frequently fail to preserve cultural (M = 0.94 on 0–2 scale) and pragmatic (M = 0.78 on 0–2 scale) dimensions. This pattern, semantic adequacy combined with cultural and pragmatic deficiency, confirms theoretical predictions about the distinction between propositional content and culturally embedded meaning.

Table 7. Performance by AI Model

Model	Sem. Acc. (M)	SD	Cult. Rel. (M)	SD	Prag. Pres. (M)	SD
GPT-4	1.90	0.68	0.85	0.58	0.72	0.54
Claude 3.5	2.10	0.71	1.24	0.54	0.96	0.51
Gemini Pro	1.75	0.89	0.78	0.67	0.68	0.55

Comparison across models revealed notable differences. One-way ANOVA confirmed significant variation across models for all criteria (Table 8). Claude 3.5 Sonnet achieved the highest mean scores across all four criteria, with particularly strong performance on cultural relevance (M = 1.24, SD = 0.54) and pragmatic preservation (M = 0.96, SD = 0.51). GPT-4 demonstrated the most consistent performance (smaller variance) but showed a tendency toward literal interpretation. Gemini Pro showed the greatest variability (semantic accuracy SD = 0.89).

Table 8. ANOVA Results, Comparison Across AI Models

Metric	F	df	p	η^2
Semantic Accuracy	12.45	(2, 663)	<.001	.036
Cultural Relevance	28.67	(2, 663)	<.001	.079
Over-generalisation	8.92	(2, 663)	<.001	.026
Pragmatic Preservation	15.34	(2, 663)	<.001	.044

The contextualised condition yielded significantly higher scores than the de-contextualised condition across all models and evaluation criteria. Paired t-tests confirmed these differences (Table 9). The improvement was most pronounced for semantic accuracy (mean improvement = 0.43) and pragmatic preservation (mean improvement = 0.31), suggesting that contextual information particularly aids meaning interpretation and function recognition. However, even with full contextual information, performance remained substantially below ceiling.

Table 9. Paired T-Tests, Decontextualised vs. Contextualised Condition

Metric	Mean Diff.	t	df	p
Semantic Accuracy	0.43	8.72	665	<.001
Cultural Relevance	0.24	5.89	665	<.001
Pragmatic Preservation	0.31	7.14	665	<.001

Error Typology

Qualitative analysis of model outputs enabled identification of four primary error types. Notably, these error types are not mutually exclusive, a single output could exhibit multiple error types simultaneously.

Table 10. Distribution of Error Types

Error Type	Frequency	%	Primary Characteristic
Literal Misinterpretation	142	42%	Figurativity unrecognised
Incorrect Cultural Mapping	95	28%	Wrong cultural meaning assigned
Over-generalisation	112	33%	Inappropriate English equivalent
Loss of Pragmatic Force	196	58%	Rhetorical function lost

Literal Misinterpretation

The most frequent error type (42% of low-scoring outputs) involved treating figurative expressions as literal statements. Consider the Gulf Arabic proverb (**Transliteration:** *allī yibī al- asal ya bir alā qar al-na l,* **Literal English meaning:** 'He who wants honey must endure bee stings'). This proverb conveys the cultural value that worthwhile achievements require willingness to endure difficulty. When presented in the decontextualised condition, GPT-4 produced:

‘This Arabic saying translates to: “Whoever wants honey must tolerate bee stings.” It refers to the process of collecting honey from beehives, which historically involved exposure to bee stings. The proverb may be used to describe beekeeping practices or the literal effort required to harvest honey in traditional settings.’

While linguistically accurate, this interpretation entirely misses the figurative meaning, treating the expression as literal agricultural advice rather than a statement about human perseverance. This pattern was particularly common for proverbs involving concrete imagery.

Incorrect Cultural Mapping

A second error type (28%) involved recognising figurativity but mapping to an incorrect meaning due to lack of cultural knowledge. The expression (**Transliteration:** *yā awīl al- umr*, **Literal English meaning:** 'O long of life') functions as a respectful form of address toward elders or authority figures. Gemini Pro interpreted this as:

‘A blessing wishing someone longevity, similar to “May you live long” in English birthday greetings.’

This interpretation captures the life-wishing element but misses the crucial pragmatic function as an honorific address term, closer in function to ‘Your Honour’ than to birthday wishes.

Over-Generalisation and Cultural Substitution

A particularly problematic error type involved replacing Gulf Arabic expressions with superficially similar but culturally distinct English equivalents. The proverb (**Transliteration:** *al-jār qabl al-dār*, **Literal English meaning:** 'The neighbour before the house') encapsulates a profound cultural value: that the quality of neighbours is more important than the quality of one’s dwelling, reflecting the primacy of community bonds. GPT-4 translated this as ‘Good fences make good neighbours’, an English proverb with nearly opposite meaning, emphasising boundaries rather than community integration.

Such over-generalisation represents cultural erasure, replacing specific Gulf Arabic concepts with dominant English-language equivalents. This pattern was particularly pronounced for expressions related to hospitality, social obligation, and family relations.

Loss of Pragmatic and Rhetorical Force

The fourth and most prevalent error type (58%) involved outputs that captured semantic meaning but stripped away pragmatic functions. A social media post commenting on slow governmental processes used (**Transliteration:** *qahwatunā mā tabrud*, **Literal English meaning:** 'Our coffee does not get cold'). In Gulf culture, Arabic coffee is traditionally served hot and drunk quickly; saying 'our coffee doesn't get cold' sarcastically implies endless meetings. The expression functions as political satire.

All three models translated this with reference to hospitality, GPT-4 offered 'Our coffee is always fresh and ready for guests,' while Gemini produced 'We maintain warm hospitality.' These translations entirely miss the satirical intent, transforming political criticism into praise of hospitality.

Performance by Expression Type

Analysis by expression type revealed significant variation (ANOVA, $F(3, 662) = 18.7$, $p < .001$, $\eta^2 = .078$):

Table 11. Performance by Expression Type

Type	Sem. Acc. (M)	SD	Cult. Rel. (M)	SD	Prag. Pres. (M)	SD
Proverbs	2.14	0.71	0.72	0.58	0.81	0.56
Metaphors	1.94	0.74	0.98	0.61	0.83	0.54
Idioms	1.62	0.82	0.87	0.65	0.72	0.59
Satire/Irony	1.78	0.79	1.14	0.62	0.54	0.52

Proverbs achieved the highest semantic accuracy (M = 2.14) but lowest cultural relevance (M = 0.72), suggesting models can identify and translate proverbial expressions but struggle to convey their cultural significance. Idioms presented the greatest challenge (semantic accuracy M = 1.62). Satirical expressions showed the lowest pragmatic preservation (M = 0.54), confirming that detecting non-literal communicative intent remains a fundamental challenge.

Performance by Thematic Domain

Thematic domain emerged as a significant factor (ANOVA, $F(5, 660) = 12.4$, $p < .001$, $\eta^2 = .086$):

Table 12. Performance by Thematic Domain

Domain	Sem. Acc. (M)	SD	Cult. Rel. (M)	SD
Nature & Environment	2.21	0.68	1.08	0.59
Resilience & Perseverance	2.08	0.72	0.96	0.61
Religion & Spirituality	1.94	0.74	0.91	0.64
Economic Activity	1.82	0.77	0.88	0.62
Political Discourse	1.71	0.79	0.82	0.66
Social Relations & Hospitality	1.68	0.81	0.64	0.54

Expressions related to nature and environment achieved the highest scores (M = 2.21), supporting CMT predictions about cross-cultural overlap in nature-based metaphors. Expressions related to social relations and hospitality showed markedly lower performance (M = 1.68), particularly on cultural relevance (M = 0.64). Gulf hospitality culture involves elaborate codes differing significantly from Anglophone norms, and AI systems consistently failed to convey these distinctions.

Gulf-Specific vs. General AI Limitations

A key question (RQ2) concerns whether observed errors are specific to Gulf Arabic or reflect general AI limitations with figurative language. Analysis suggests both factors operate:

General AI limitations: Literal misinterpretation errors (42%) appear to reflect general challenges with figurativity recognition documented across languages. The struggle with satirical intent (58% pragmatic loss for satire) similarly reflects known limitations in irony detection that are not Arabic-specific.

Gulf-specific challenges: Over-generalisation errors (33%) were concentrated in culturally distinctive domains (hospitality, social relations, political satire), suggesting these reflect specifically Gulf Arabic knowledge gaps rather than general figurative language difficulties. The substitution of Gulf proverbs with culturally incongruent English equivalents indicates training data gaps for Gulf Arabic varieties.

Dialectal variation effects: Comparison across regional sources revealed that expressions documented in MSA corpora (more likely present in training data) performed better than locally specific Gulf expressions. Pan-Gulf expressions shared across the region performed better than highly localised Omani or Bahraini expressions, suggesting training data representation as a factor.

DISCUSSION

Theoretical Implications

The findings carry significant implications for theoretical understanding of both figurative language and AI capabilities. The consistent pattern of semantic adequacy combined with cultural and pragmatic deficiency supports the view that meaning in symbolic language is irreducible to propositional content. Contemporary LLMs, despite impressive capabilities in pattern recognition, operate fundamentally differently from human language users who bring embodied experience, cultural immersion, and pragmatic awareness to interpretation.

From the CMT perspective, results illuminate the cultural grounding of metaphorical thought. While some conceptual metaphors (those based on universal embodied experience) transferred relatively successfully, those drawing on culturally specific source domains consistently lost their resonance. This supports Kövecses's (2005) arguments about cultural variation in conceptual metaphors and suggests that AI systems require explicit cultural knowledge to handle culturally grounded figurative expressions.

The prevalence of over-generalisation errors, replacing Gulf Arabic expressions with English 'equivalents', raises important questions about implicit cultural biases in AI training. Large language models trained predominantly on English data may position English cultural frameworks as universal while marginalising alternative frameworks. Lotman's semiosphere concept helps explain this: AI systems process texts as decontextualised symbol sequences, isolated from the semiotic networks that give them meaning.

Why Satire and Irony Are Most Failure-Prone

Satirical and ironic expressions showed the lowest pragmatic preservation scores, warranting deeper analysis. Several factors contribute:

Meaning inversion: Irony involves stating the opposite of what is meant, requiring recognition that surface meaning diverges from intended meaning. While humans detect this through contextual cues, tone, and shared knowledge, AI systems trained primarily on correspondence between form and meaning struggle with systematic non-correspondence.

Cultural context dependence: Satirical expressions often target culturally specific phenomena (bureaucratic processes, social expectations, political dynamics). Without access to these cultural referents, the satirical point is lost even if individual words are correctly translated.

Positivity bias: Analysis suggests AI systems exhibit a 'positivity bias', defaulting to positive or neutral interpretations when faced with ambiguous content. This systematically transforms satirical criticism into sincere statements, as seen with the coffee expression transformed into hospitality praise.

Training data effects: Satirical content may be underrepresented in training corpora relative to sincere discourse, reducing exposure to ironic patterns during model development.

These findings have significant implications for AI-mediated political discourse. In contexts where satire serves important functions of social criticism, as it does in Gulf social media, systematic failure to preserve satirical intent may distort public discourse analysis and misrepresent community perspectives.

AI Ethics and Cultural Bias

The documented patterns raise significant ethical concerns regarding AI development and deployment. Over-generalisation errors represent not merely technical failures but a form of cultural erasure, the replacement of Gulf Arabic conceptualisations with English-dominant alternatives. When AI systems consistently substitute 'Good fences make good neighbours' for 'The neighbour before the house', they participate in what scholars have termed 'algorithmic colonialism': the imposition of dominant cultural frameworks through technological systems (Mohamed et al., 2020).

This concern extends beyond translation accuracy to questions of representation and power. Training data for LLMs is predominantly English-language, and even multilingual training often privileges English conceptual frameworks. The result is systems that may technically 'understand' Arabic text while systematically misrepresenting Arabic cultural perspectives. For Gulf Arabic specifically, the relative scarcity of dialectal Arabic in training corpora compounds this issue.

These findings contribute to growing calls for culturally responsive AI development (Sambasivan et al., 2021). Rather than treating cultural competence as an afterthought, developers must consider cultural representation at every stage of system design, from training data curation to evaluation metric selection. The evaluation framework developed in this study, with its explicit attention to cultural relevance and over-generalisation, offers one model for how cultural considerations can be operationalised in AI assessment.

Human–AI Collaboration Models

Given documented limitations, what role should AI play in cross-cultural communication? The findings suggest not wholesale rejection of AI translation but thoughtful integration within human-centred workflows:

Post-editing workflows: AI can provide first-pass translations that human experts then review and refine. This approach leverages AI efficiency for literal content while ensuring human oversight for culturally embedded material. The study's error typology can guide post-editors toward expressions most likely requiring intervention.

Flagging systems: AI systems could be designed to flag potentially figurative expressions for human review rather than attempting confident translations. The variability patterns documented (high variance for idioms, satire) could inform flagging thresholds.

Tiered confidence: Different confidence thresholds could apply to different content types, with AI granted greater autonomy for nature-based metaphors (highest performance) and mandatory human review for satirical content (lowest performance).

Collaborative explanation: Rather than providing only translations, AI systems could explain their interpretive reasoning, enabling human experts to identify and correct cultural missteps.

These models position AI as augmenting human capabilities rather than replacing human cultural expertise, an important distinction for domains where cultural fidelity is essential.

Design Principles for Culturally Aware NLP

Based on the patterns identified, several design principles emerge for developing more culturally aware NLP systems. Table 13 links each principle to the error patterns it addresses:

Table 13. Design Principles Linked to Error Patterns

Design Principle	Error Type Addressed	Recommendation
Cultural Knowledge Integration	Incorrect Mapping (28%)	Incorporate structured cultural knowledge bases
Explicit Figurativity Detection	Literal Misinterpretation (42%)	Implement dedicated detection modules
Preservation Over Substitution	Over-generalisation (33%)	Favour explanatory approaches over 'equivalents'
Uncertainty Signalling	All error types	Flag uncertainty for human verification
Diverse Training Representation	Gulf-specific gaps	Include dialectal Arabic with cultural annotations
Irony-Aware Processing	Loss of Pragmatic Force (58%)	Develop mechanisms for satirical intent detection

Policy and Regulatory Considerations

The findings have implications for policy frameworks governing AI deployment in multilingual regions. Gulf states face decisions about AI adoption in governmental, educational, and commercial contexts where cultural fidelity is important:

Transparency requirements: Regulators might require disclosure when AI translation is used in public communications, enabling citizens to understand the provenance and limitations of content.

Quality standards: Standards bodies could develop culturally specific evaluation criteria for AI translation systems, moving beyond semantic accuracy to incorporate cultural and pragmatic dimensions.

Use-case restrictions: Certain high-stakes applications (diplomatic communications, legal proceedings, medical consultations) might require human translation or mandatory human review.

Investment in regional AI: Gulf states might invest in developing AI systems trained specifically on regional data with attention to cultural competence, rather than relying solely on systems developed elsewhere.

Limitations and Future Directions

This study has several limitations suggesting directions for future research. The focus on Gulf Arabic, while enabling depth of analysis, limits generalisability to other Arabic varieties. Future research should extend this methodology to examine AI performance across diverse linguistic contexts, including comparison with Egyptian Arabic, Levantine Arabic, and Maghrebi Arabic.

The reliance on expert evaluation, while providing nuanced assessment, introduces potential subjectivity. Future studies might complement expert judgement with reception studies examining how target-language readers interpret AI-translated symbolic content. The rapid evolution of AI systems means that findings may become outdated as new models emerge. Longitudinal research tracking performance over successive model generations would illuminate whether advances address identified limitations.

Finally, this study focused on recognition and interpretation; future research should examine AI generation of symbolic language and investigate whether systems can produce culturally appropriate figurative expressions in target languages.

CONCLUSION

This chapter has investigated the capacity of contemporary AI systems to recognise, interpret, and translate culturally embedded symbolic language, with particular focus on Gulf Arabic expressions. Through systematic corpus-assisted analysis and expert evaluation of outputs from GPT-4, Claude 3.5, and Gemini Pro, the study documented patterns of literal misinterpretation (42%), incorrect cultural mapping (28%), over-generalisation (33%), and loss of pragmatic force (58%) that characterise current AI performance on figurative language.

The findings reveal a fundamental gap between semantic processing and cultural understanding. While contemporary LLMs demonstrate impressive capabilities in capturing propositional content, they consistently fail to preserve the cultural resonances, pragmatic functions, and rhetorical effects that constitute the full meaning of symbolic expressions. This gap reflects not merely insufficient training data but deeper limitations in architectures that process language as patterns of symbols rather than culturally embedded communicative practice.

Statistical analysis confirmed that performance varies significantly by expression type, with idioms presenting the greatest challenge (semantic accuracy $M = 1.62$) and satirical expressions showing the lowest pragmatic preservation ($M = 0.54$). Thematic domain emerged as a significant factor, with nature-based expressions performing best ($M = 2.21$) and hospitality-related expressions performing worst ($M = 1.68$), patterns aligning with theoretical predictions from Conceptual Metaphor Theory about universal versus culturally specific figurative language.

As AI-mediated communication becomes increasingly prevalent in global discourse, the stakes of these limitations grow correspondingly higher. The erasure or distortion of culturally specific meaning in AI translation is not merely a technical problem but a matter of cultural preservation and intercultural understanding. When Gulf Arabic proverbs are compacted into generic wisdom, when satirical commentary is transformed into neutral description, and when hospitality traditions are mapped onto Western equivalents, something valuable is lost, not just linguistic accuracy but cultural knowledge and intercultural respect. Despite these contributions, this study is not without limitations. The corpus, while carefully compiled, is necessarily selective, and findings reflect the specific Gulf Arabic varieties, text types, and time period sampled rather than the full breadth of the dialect continuum. The reliance on expert human evaluation, though methodologically appropriate for culturally specific content, introduces an element of subjectivity that automated approaches cannot entirely replicate. Addressing these limitations will require AI systems built on a fundamentally different set of priorities. Progress depends on embedding cultural knowledge at every stage of system design: integrating structured cultural knowledge bases, developing dedicated figurativity detection mechanisms, favouring meaning-preserving explanations over culturally inappropriate substitutions, signalling interpretive uncertainty for human review, and ensuring training corpora reflect the full diversity of Arabic dialectal and cultural expression. By working toward AI systems that respect and preserve cultural meaning, we can bond the transformative potential of these technologies while safeguarding the linguistic and cultural diversity that enriches human communication.

ACKNOWLEDGMENT

This research received no specific grant from any funding agency in the public, commercial, or not-for-profit sectors.

REFERENCES

Abdul-Mageed, M., & Elmadany, A. (2021, August). ARBERT & MARBERT: Deep bidirectional transformers for Arabic. In *Proceedings of the 59th Annual Meeting of the Association for Computational Linguistics and the 11th International Joint Conference on Natural Language Processing (*Volume 1*: Long Papers)* (pp. 7088–7105). DOI: 10.18653/v1/2021.acl-long.551

Abu-Lughod, L. (2016). *Veiled sentiments: Honor and poetry in a Bedouin society*. University of California Press. DOI: 10.1525/9780520965980

Al Maaytah, S. A. (2026). Evaluating three neural machine translation platforms for English-Arabic translation: A comparative study of linguistic accuracy and cultural fidelity. *World Journal of English Language*, *16*(2), 1. DOI: 10.5430/wjel.v16n2p1

Alayba, A. M. (2025). Arabic natural language processing (NLP): A comprehensive review of challenges, techniques, and emerging trends. *Computers*, *14*(11), 497. DOI: 10.3390/computers14110497

Albirini, A. (2016). *Modern Arabic sociolinguistics: Diglossia, variation, codeswitching, attitudes and identity*. Routledge. DOI: 10.4324/9781315683737

Algamedi, S. (2025). *Rhetoric of soft power and public diplomacy: A case study of Saudi Arabia* (Doctoral dissertation, Duquesne University).

Alhakimi, A., Alkholidi, A., Adar, N., Sefa, B., & Ahmed, W. M. A. (2025, May). AI versus human translators: Accuracy and context in the translation of cultural idioms and proverbs. In *International Conference on Intelligence-Based Transformations of Technology and Business Trends* (pp. 231–246). Springer Nature Switzerland.

Anthony, L. (2022). AntConc (Version 4.2.0) [Computer software]. Waseda University. https://www.laurenceanthony.net/software/antconc/

Attia, M., Muhamed, A., Alkhamissi, M., Solorio, T., & Diab, M. (2025). Beyond understanding: Evaluating the pragmatic gap in LLMs' cultural processing of figurative language. *arXiv preprint arXiv:2510.23828*.

Awashreh, R., & Aboeisheh, A. (2025). The collaborative future of translation between human-AI partnerships. In *Role of AI in Translation and Interpretation* (pp. 205–236). IGI Global Scientific Publishing. DOI: 10.4018/979-8-3373-0060-3.ch008

Bender, E. M., & Koller, A. (2020). Climbing towards NLU: On meaning, form, and understanding in the age of data. *Proceedings of the 58th Annual Meeting of the Association for Computational Linguistics*, 5185–5198. DOI: 10.18653/v1/2020.acl-main.463

Brown, T., Mann, B., Ryder, N., Subbiah, M., Kaplan, J. D., Dhariwal, P., & Amodei, D. (2020). Language models are few-shot learners. *Advances in Neural Information Processing Systems*, *33*, 1877–1901.

Buscemi, E., & Kaposi, I. (2020). *Everyday youth cultures in the Gulf Peninsula*. Routledge. DOI: 10.4324/9781003048626

Chatzikoumi, E. (2020). How to evaluate machine translation: A review of automated and human metrics. *Natural Language Engineering*, *26*(2), 137–161. DOI: 10.1017/S1351324919000469

Chen, S., Wang, W., Chen, X., Zhang, M., Lu, P., Li, X., & Du, Y. (2025). Enhancing Chinese comprehension and reasoning for large language models: An efficient LoRA fine-tuning and tree of thoughts framework. *The Journal of Supercomputing*, *81*(1), 50. DOI: 10.1007/s11227-024-06499-7

Devlin, J., Chang, M. W., Lee, K., & Toutanova, K. (2019). BERT: Pre-training of deep bidirectional transformers for language understanding. *Proceedings of NAACL-HLT*, *2019*, 4171–4186.

Gibbs, R. W. (1994). *The poetics of mind: Figurative thought, language, and understanding*. Cambridge University Press.

Hamdi, S., Hashem, R., Holbah, W., Azi, Y., & Mohammed, S. (2023). Proverbs translation for intercultural interaction: A comparative study between Arabic and English using artificial intelligence. *World Journal of English Language*, *13*(7), 282. DOI: 10.5430/wjel.v13n7p282

Hamdi, S. A. (2018). *The impact of ideology on lexical borrowing in Arabic: A synergy of corpus linguistics and CDA* (Doctoral dissertation, The University of New Mexico).

Hendy, A.. (2023). How good are GPT models at machine translation? A comprehensive evaluation. *Proceedings of the 61st Annual Meeting of the Association for Computational Linguistics*, 1910–1931.

Holes, C. (2004). *Modern Arabic: Structures, functions, and varieties* (Rev. ed.). Georgetown University Press.

Holes, C. (2011). Language and identity in the Arabian Gulf. *Journal of Arabic and Islamic Studies, 11*, 129–154.

Khalaf, M. H. (2025). Diglossia challenges in Arabic translation: Navigating linguistic duality in contemporary translation practice. *Lark, 17*(4), 1690–1663. DOI: 10.31185/lark.4478

Koo, T. K., & Li, M. Y. (2016). A guideline of selecting and reporting intraclass correlation coefficients for reliability research. *Journal of Chiropractic Medicine, 15*(2), 155–163. DOI: 10.1016/j.jcm.2016.02.012 PMID: 27330520

Kövecses, Z. (2005). *Metaphor in culture: Universality and variation*. Cambridge University Press. DOI: 10.1017/CBO9780511614408

Kövecses, Z. (2010). *Metaphor: A practical introduction* (2nd ed.). Oxford University Press.

Lai, H., & Nissim, M. (2024). A survey on automatic generation of figurative language: From rule-based systems to large language models. *ACM Computing Surveys, 56*(10), 1–34. DOI: 10.1145/3654795

Lakoff, G., & Johnson, M. (1980). *Metaphors we live by*. University of Chicago Press.

Läubli, S., Sennrich, R., & Volk, M. (2020). Has machine translation achieved human parity? A case for document-level evaluation. *Proceedings of the 2018 Conference on Empirical Methods in Natural Language Processing*, 4791–4796.

Liu, E., Cui, C., Zheng, K., & Neubig, G. (2022). Testing the ability of language models to interpret figurative language. *Proceedings of NAACL, 2022*, 4437–4452. DOI: 10.18653/v1/2022.naacl-main.330

Lotman, Y., & Clark, W. (2005). On the semiosphere. *Sign Systems Studies, 33*(1), 205–229. DOI: 10.12697/SSS.2005.33.1.09

Maalej, Z. (2004). Figurative language in anger expressions in Tunisian Arabic: An extended view of embodiment. *Metaphor and Symbol, 19*(1), 51–75. DOI: 10.1207/S15327868MS1901_3

Mohamed, S., Png, M. T., & Isaac, W. (2020). Decolonial AI: Decolonial theory as sociotechnical foresight in artificial intelligence. *Philosophy & Technology, 33*(4), 659–684. DOI: 10.1007/s13347-020-00405-8

Partington, A., Duguid, A., & Taylor, C. (2013). *Patterns and meanings in discourse: Theory and practice in corpus-assisted discourse studies*. John Benjamins. DOI: 10.1075/scl.55

Pym, A. (2025). Translation technologies as the end of translation as we know it: Empiricism as a search for a way forward. In *Confronting digital dilemmas in translator and interpreter training* (pp. 18–34). Routledge. DOI: 10.4324/9781003562535-3

Sambasivan, N., Arnesen, E., Hutchinson, B., Doshi, T., & Prabhakaran, V. (2021). Re-imagining algorithmic fairness in India and beyond. *Proceedings of the 2021 ACM Conference on Fairness, Accountability, and Transparency*, 315–328. DOI: 10.1145/3442188.3445896

Sperber, D., & Wilson, D. (1986). *Relevance: Communication and cognition*. Harvard University Press.

Taylor, C. (2021). Metaphors of migration over time. *Discourse & Society*, *32*(4), 463–481. DOI: 10.1177/0957926521992156

Versteegh, K. (2014). *The Arabic language* (2nd ed.). Edinburgh University Press. DOI: 10.1515/9780748645299

Watson, J. C. (2002). *The phonology and morphology of Arabic*. Oxford University Press. DOI: 10.1093/oso/9780199257591.001.0001

KEY TERMS AND DEFINITIONS

Corpus-Assisted Discourse Analysis (CADS): A methodological approach combining quantitative corpus linguistics techniques with qualitative discourse analysis to identify and interpret recurrent patterns of meaning in large collections of authentic texts.

Cultural Semiotics: The study of how meaning is produced, transmitted, and interpreted within culturally bounded semiotic spaces, drawing on the work of scholars such as Yuri Lotman to understand how cultural signs acquire significance through their relationships with other signs.

Figurative Language: Language whose meaning departs from its literal or compositional interpretation, including idioms, proverbs, metaphors, similes, and irony; it typically relies on shared cultural knowledge for correct interpretation.

Gulf Arabic: A cluster of Arabic dialects spoken on the Arabian Peninsula, including varieties in Saudi Arabia, UAE, Kuwait, Qatar, Bahrain, and Oman, characterised by distinctive phonological, lexical, and grammatical features and a rich tradition of figurative expression.

Large Language Model (LLM): A type of artificial intelligence system trained on vast quantities of text data using transformer-based neural network architectures, capable of generating and processing natural language across a wide range of tasks including translation, summarisation, and question answering.

Over-Generalisation: An error type in AI translation in which a culturally specific expression is replaced with a superficially similar but culturally distinct equivalent from another linguistic tradition, thereby erasing the original expression's particular cultural significance.

Pragmatic Preservation: The degree to which a translation maintains the communicative function, rhetorical intent, and social force of the original expression beyond its propositional or semantic content.

Semiosphere: A concept introduced by Yuri Lotman referring to the totality of semiotic space within a culture, the bounded domain in which signs circulate and acquire meaning through dynamic interaction with other signs, cultural texts, and interpretive practices.

Symbolic Language: Language that encodes meaning through culturally established associations beyond the literal denotations of words, encompassing proverbs, metaphors, idioms, and other forms of figurative expression whose interpretation requires cultural knowledge.

Transliteration: The systematic representation of the sounds or letters of one writing system using the letters or characters of another, used in this chapter to render Gulf Arabic expressions in Latin script for readers unfamiliar with the Arabic alphabet.

Chapter 12

AI Feedback:
A Critical Perspective From ESP Written Discourse

Asma Abdullah Alshahrani
http://orcid.org/0009-0001-4021-4455
King Khalid University, Saudi Arabia

ABSTRACT

This study examines the effectiveness of AI-generated feedback from Google Gemini and Microsoft Copilot on ESP writing tasks completed by Medical Records students. An exploratory mixed-methods design was employed, collecting data from healthcare practitioners' written tasks and ESP experts' evaluations. Feedback was analysed using Automated Writing Evaluation criteria, focusing on linguistic accuracy, vocabulary appropriateness, organization, coherence, content relevance, and effectiveness. Results indicate Gemini provided more precise, explanatory, and context-sensitive feedback than Copilot. While AI bots demonstrated potential for enhancing formative assessment and supporting learner self-regulation, limitations in comprehension of specialized ESP contexts highlight the need for human oversight. These findings support the supplementary use of AI feedback alongside traditional instructor evaluation in ESP pedagogy.

INTRODUCTION

Artificial Intelligence (AI) has been increasingly applied in learning environments, specifically in second language learning and writing evaluation (Aladini et al., 2025; Chen & Gong, 2025). Recent systematic reviews indicate that AI feedback mechanisms are being adopted in writing instruction due to their ability to provide personalized, timely, and constructive guidance to learners (Bao et al., 2025; Youn

DOI: 10.4018/979-8-3373-6420-9.ch012

& Salam, 2025). Empirical investigations also show that automated written corrective feedback can significantly improve learners' writing accuracy, lexical choice, coherence, and overall writing performance in English as a Foreign Language (EFL) and English for Specific Purposes (ESP) contexts (Rahimi et al., 2025; Torres & Kahveci, 2025). These developments have highlighted AI's capacity not only to augment traditional instructional approaches but also to foster learner autonomy, engagement, and higher-order writing skills (Xu et al., 2025).

Recently, AI-based tools such as ChatGPT, Google Gemini, and Microsoft Copilot have gained increasing interest for their capability to provide instant, explanatory, and interactive feedback, making them promising tools in English for Specific Purposes (ESP) learning (Imran et al., 2024). Among these, Google Gemini has been recognized for its multi-modal processing abilities, which allow the integration of text, images, and audio inputs, thereby enhancing the feedback experience for learners (Imran & Almusharraf, 2024). Empirical evidence also suggests that Gemini can facilitate higher-order writing abilities by providing content-related cues and suggestions for enriched vocabulary and syntactic structures (Jinowat et al., 2024). Likewise, Microsoft Copilot has been identified for its contribution to teaching efficiency, enabling educators to perform evaluations, generate summaries, and manage academic tasks more effectively (Moeis et al., 2024).

Despite these technological advances, questions remain regarding the appropriateness, depth, and contextual relevance of AI-generated feedback in ESP settings. Literature on automated writing evaluation (AWE) continues to demonstrate AI's capacity to assess grammatical accuracy, lexical choice, cohesion, organization, and discourse consistency (Burstein & Attali, 2024). However, research such as that by Kim (2025) cautions against relying exclusively on AI for writing assessment, emphasizing the complementary role of human judgment to ensure meaningful evaluation. Notably, very few studies examine the comparative effectiveness of multiple AI bots in ESP domains, particularly for specialized fields such as medical writing. In response to these gaps, the present study investigates the effectiveness of AI-enabled feedback from Google Gemini and Microsoft Copilot on the ESP writing skills of students enrolled in a Medical Records program, with a focus on empirically determined evaluation parameters for AWE software.

PREVIOUS STUDIES

ESP: English for Medical Records

English for Specific Purposes (ESP) focuses on the use of English in specific academic, professional, or workplace contexts (Basturkmen, 2025; Yan, 2025).

ESP not only equips learners with specialized linguistic skills but also functions as a strategic bridge between theoretical knowledge and practical application in academic and professional contexts (Belcher, 2006; Tan et al., 2023). This needs-driven approach emphasizes tailoring instruction to learners' specific academic or occupational requirements, thereby ensuring that language acquisition directly supports professional competence and career readiness (Ginting & Tinambunan, 2025). The evolution of ESP over the past two decades has been marked by a proliferation of programs, specialized research, and methodological sophistication, reflecting its growing relevance in applied linguistics and pedagogy (Nodoushan, 2020).

A core feature of ESP is its systematic course design, which is grounded in four interrelated pillars: needs analysis, learning objectives, methods and materials, and evaluation (Anthony, 2018). Needs analysis provides an empirical foundation for understanding learners' necessities, lacks, and goals, guiding the selection of content and skills most relevant to their target contexts (Basturkmen, 2010; Rahman, 2015). Another key pillar is learning objectives that translate these needs into measurable outcomes, aligning instruction with the genres, tasks, and communicative practices encountered in real-world professional or academic settings (Anthony, 2018; Liu et al., 2024). Furthermore, methods and materials prioritize authenticity and contextual relevance, incorporating practical exercises, specialized texts, and interactive approaches that facilitate the application of language skills (Anthony, 2018). Finally, evaluation, which encompasses both formative and summative assessments, monitors learner progress while providing evidence for continuous improvement of the curriculum (Anthony, 2018; Celik, 2018).

Within this framework, feedback emerges as a pivotal component of effective ESP instruction. Formative feedback enables instructors to adjust teaching strategies and provide timely guidance tailored to individual learners' writing and communicative development (Celik, 2018). Research demonstrates that the timing and type of feedback significantly influence learners' linguistic processing and skill acquisition. For example, Kourtali and Borges (2024) found that delayed feedback can facilitate deeper semantic processing, while Halim et al. (2021) highlighted learners' positive perceptions of corrective feedback as both motivational and instrumental in language development. These insights underscore the importance of integrating advanced feedback mechanisms, potentially leveraging technology, to complement traditional instructional methods. Consequently, ESP pedagogy not only addresses learners' current communicative needs but also provides a foundation for exploring innovative, scalable, and automated feedback systems, bridging seamlessly into the emerging field of AI-mediated assessment and formative support.

Building upon the foundational principles of ESP, particularly the pillars of needs analysis, targeted learning objectives, and contextualized methods and materials, feedback, as part of evaluation, emerges as a critical mechanism for bridging instructional goals with actual learner performance. Traditional formative feedback provides timely guidance that informs learners about linguistic accuracy, genre conventions, and task-specific expectations, thereby supporting the alignment between theoretical knowledge and practical application (Celik, 2018; Kourtali & Borges, 2024). However, the increasing complexity of ESP tasks, the diversity of learner needs, and the demand for more immediate, scalable, and individualized responses have highlighted the limitations of conventional instructor-led feedback. In this context, technological interventions, and in particular AI-powered tools, offer promising avenues for augmenting feedback delivery. By providing instant, tailored, and context-aware guidance, AI bots have the potential to complement human evaluation, enhance learner autonomy, and foster deeper engagement with disciplinary writing practices (Burner et al.,2025; Mekheimer, 2025; Mohammed et al., 2025). In contrast, teacher feedback might be more context-sensitive and pedagogically nuanced, although it may not always be as immediate as AI. However, direct evidence linking AI feedback to greater revision comfort remains limited (Tony Burner et al., 2025). Consequently, exploring the use of AI bots in ESP writing assessment represents a natural progression from traditional feedback models, aligning with ESP's overarching goal of preparing learners for authentic professional and academic communication.

The Use of AI Bots for EFL/ESP Written Feedback

The integration of AI into ESP and EFL writing instruction has gained considerable attention in recent years, particularly for its potential to provide instant, personalized, and scalable feedback. Tools such as ChatGPT, Google Gemini, and Microsoft Copilot have been employed to support learners in enhancing grammatical accuracy, lexical choice, coherence, and organization in their written tasks (Lee, 2023; Moeis et al., 2024; Imran et al., 2024). For instance, ChatGPT, developed by OpenAI, has been investigated for its role in supporting academic writing among EFL learners. A study by Al-Sofi (2024) investigated the use of ChatGPT, an AI chatbot created by OpenAI, for improving academic writing among Saudi EFL undergraduate students, revealing both the potential benefits and challenges of advanced AI tools in language education. It asserted that, while students generally reported satisfaction with ChatGPT's ability to improve their writing skills, there were concerns raised over potential plagiarism and over-reliance. It is recommended that the use of ChatGPT in academic writing should be governed by teacher guidelines to ensure that its potential benefits are realized and promote responsible usage among learners. For instance, ChatGPT should be used to assist in improving writing skills, rather than generating ideas for various writing tasks (Al-Sofi, 2024). Therefore, AI systems can provide immediate and scalable feedback, enabling students to learn independently through consistent, detailed insights into their writing.

Moreover, Google Gemini represents a recent advancement in AI-powered feedback systems. Gemini's multi-modal processing capabilities allow integration of text, images, and audio, thereby enhancing the feedback experience for learners (Imran & Almusharraf, 2024). Evidence suggests that Gemini can facilitate higher-order writing skills by providing content-related cues, vocabulary enhancement, and syntactic suggestions (Jinowat et al., 2024). Moreover, Gemini's interactive features, such as quizzes and simulations, support learner engagement and adapt to diverse learning needs.

Microsoft Copilot has also been explored in ESP/EFL contexts, mainly for its capacity to support educators and learners in writing assessment. Studies indicate that Copilot improves teaching efficiency, generates summaries, assists in content evaluation, and manages academic tasks, thereby fostering a more interactive learning environment (Chen, 2024; Moeis et al., 2024). Additionally, Copilot and other Intelligent Tutoring Systems (ITSs) can provide personalized, real-time feedback by tracking individual performance and learning patterns (Chen, 2024).

Despite the promising potential of AI bots, several limitations and ethical considerations must be acknowledged. For instance, AI hallucination, where AI generates plausible but incorrect feedback, remains a concern and may affect learners' writing accuracy and confidence (Lee, 2023; Kim, 2025). Moreover, ethical considerations, including data privacy, security, and potential algorithmic bias, are critical to ensure fair and equitable assessment (Rahimi et al., 2025; Youn & Salam, 2025).

Evaluate AI Feedback

One of the techniques that is used to assess written feedback discourse in a language learning context is the Automated Writing Evaluation (AWE) (Burstein & Attali, 2024). AWE has been under development since the 1960s, when it was designed to save time and effort in grading a large number of learners' writing (Chen & Cheng, 2008). AWE systems offer a practical framework for understanding how technology can support second language (L2) writing instruction. A study by Woodworth and Barkaoui (2020) states that AWE systems such as Criterion and MyAccess! can help learners identify and correct linguistic errors while fostering autonomy and motivation, where they provide immediate and frequent Written Corrective Feedback (WCF). These findings are particularly aligned with cognitive theories of language acquisition, which emphasize the importance of noticing errors and engaging with explicit feedback to facilitate the development of procedural knowledge (Schmidt, 2001). Another study by Feng and Chukharev-Hudilainen (2022) has shown the potential role of AWE in providing valuable feedback when it supports genre-specific writing. The study emphasizes that AWE systems may collaborate with genre conventions to ensure their relevance and usability, which can increase focus on meaning and rhetorical organization. These findings highlight the effectiveness of using AWE in enhancing the given feedback when emphasizing specific areas such as genre.

In the context of AI feedback, AWE is a technology that utilizes generative AI where computers are trained on large datasets to predict language sequences and provide the required responses according to the prompt given by humans. Grading automated writing evaluation dwells on the important criteria to be measured across the writing produced, and they are: grammatical accuracy, mechanical usage, vocabulary appropriateness, coherence, organization, and discourse consistency (Burstein & Attali, 2024). In the present study, researchers use AWE to identify criteria that assess the AI feedback on learners' compositions. The first criterion 'linguistic accuracy' is established based on Mizumoto et al. (2024) which demonstrates the precision of AI tools, such as ChatGPT, Copilot and Gemini, in automated writing assessment. Attali and Burstein (2006) confirm the importance of linguistic accuracy in addition to the criteria 'vocabulary appropriateness' and 'organization and structure'. Moreover, the work by Burstein et al. (2018) provided an exploration of the role of 'content relevance' and 'feedback quality' in AWE, as well as the rest of the criteria (i.e. accuracy, vocabulary, and structure). By synthesizing all elements, we developed a coherent set of criteria for AWE, specifically with AI bots (see Table 1).

Table 1. The Criteria for Evaluating AI-Enhanced Feedback on Learners' Compositions

Linguistic Accuracy	**• This entails the grammar, spelling errors, and sentence structure.**
Vocabulary Appropriateness	• This gauges the appropriateness of the vocabulary used in terms of the given context.
Organization and Structure	• This refers to the logical flow and cohesive writing concerning the relationship between paragraphs/sentences.
Content Relevance	• This would give an idea of how relevant the content is concerning the requirement.
Feedback Quality	• Feedback quality refers to how much an item of feedback is personalized and useful for the learner.

Nevertheless, although AI shows promise in language education, further research is required to better understand its influence on learners' language skills, especially writing, in specific contexts such as ESP. To conduct the current study, Medical Records (MR) were chosen as a specific field in ESP. Producing English for Medical Records (EMR) is one domain where teaching English is required in specific contexts. As MR continues to improve, English writing for medical records remains crucial as English is the predominant language for medical publications (Baron, 2012). That, in turn, addresses the significance of ESP in the medical field. Because of the importance of feedback in EMR (Alharbi & Alqefari, 2021), using technologies, such as AI assistance bots, can provide feedback on the learner's writing, which can improve communication and organization (Hansen et al., 2024). The present study investigates the effectiveness of using AI bots, namely Gemini and Copilot, in providing feedback on learners' compositions.

Conceptual Framework

This study is conceptually grounded in formative feedback theory and ESP-specific writing pedagogy, particularly viewing feedback as a dialogic and developmental process rather than a purely corrective mechanism (Hattie & Timperley, 2007; Shute, 2008). Effective feedback, from this perspective, extends beyond surface-level error correction to provide diagnostic, explanatory, and improvement-oriented guidance that promotes learner autonomy and self-regulation. In the context of ESP, feedback must also address domain-specific accuracy, linguistic appropriateness, and organizational clarity, aligning with the learners' professional or academic requirements (Anthony, 2018; Basturkmen, 2010). AI-mediated feedback tools, such as Google Gemini and Microsoft Copilot, can be understood as supportive instructional agents within this framework, complementing rather than replacing human judgment (Burstein & Attali, 2024; Jinowat et al., 2024). The assessment of AI feedback should therefore consider accuracy, specificity, pedagogical usefulness, and alignment with disciplinary conventions.

Consequently, the analytical criteria adopted in this study (see Table 1) are directly informed by this integrated conceptual framework. The comparison of Gemini and Copilot evaluates not only the technical correctness of feedback but also its capacity to fulfil core pedagogical functions of formative, domain-sensitive guidance (Imran et al., 2024; Kim, 2025). This approach ensures that the study situates AI feedback within both the theoretical and practical dimensions of ESP writing instruction.

Research Gap and Contribution

Although AI has demonstrated considerable potential in language education, existing research has primarily focused on general EFL contexts or on the use of a single AI tool. Limited attention has been given to the application of AI-generated feedback in specialized ESP domains such as Medical Records. Furthermore, few studies have comparatively examined the effectiveness of different AI assistance tools in improving learners' writing performance within discipline-specific contexts (e.g., Al-Sofi, 2024; Chen, 2024; Kim, 2025). To address this gap, the present study investigates the effectiveness of two AI tools, Gemini and Copilot, in providing feedback on Medical Records students' compositions. By focusing on a specific ESP field and comparing multiple AI feedback tools, this study extends current research on AI-assisted writing and offers pedagogical insights for ESP instructors in medical contexts.

Research Questions

Accordingly, the current study investigates the significant value of the ever-growing understanding of AI feedback provided by AI bots and their potential use in the advancement of ESP by addressing the following questions:

> **RQ1:** How effective is the feedback discourse provided by AI bots in improving learners' ESP writing?
> **RQ.2:** What challenges are encountered when using AI bots to deliver feedback discourse for ESP writing?

METHODOLOGY

Research Design

This study employed an exploratory mixed-methods research design (Morgan, 2007) to investigate the effectiveness of AI-generated feedback in English for Specific Purposes (ESP) writing, specifically in the medical field. The mixed-methods approach was adopted to capture both quantitative trends and qualitative insights into how two AI bots, Google Gemini and Microsoft Copilot, provide feedback on ESP writing tasks. This design allowed for triangulation of data from multiple sources, including practitioner writing samples and expert evaluations, ensuring a more comprehensive understanding of the feedback's quality, relevance, and instructional utility. The exploratory nature of the research was appropriate given the novelty of using AI in ESP writing assessment and the limited prior empirical studies in this specific domain.

Participants

The study involved two distinct groups of participants, carefully selected to reflect the expertise required for the study objectives:

Phase One: *Health Practitioners (Writers):* Eight native Arabian healthcare practitioners, both male and female, aged 24–27, participated voluntarily. Each had at least four years of English language education, and professional experience ranged from one to four years. Participants were asked to complete a written task in medical reporting, based on real-life scenarios typical of their clinical practice. The goal was to capture authentic ESP writing performance in a contextually relevant and realistic manner. Personal data were anonymized, and all writing samples were treated with strict confidentiality to comply with ethical research standards.

Phase Two: *ESP Experts (Evaluators):* Eight ESP experts with MA degrees in TEFL and at least three years of professional experience participated in evaluating AI-generated feedback. These experts assessed the quality, accuracy, and pedagogical usefulness of the AI feedback. Their involvement ensured content validity of the survey instrument and added professional judgment to the assessment of AI outputs (Creswell & Creswell, 2017; Haynes et al., 1995; Polit & Beck, 2006). Ethical considerations for this group included informing participants about the study purpose, anonymizing AI bots to prevent bias, and maintaining privacy in handling their responses. These measures ensured that both phases of data collection adhered to high ethical standards while supporting the study's validity and reliability.

Data Collection Instruments and Procedure

Phase One: Writing Task

Health practitioners were provided with a structured medical report template and asked to draft a narrative description including all necessary patient information, procedures, and outcomes. Each submission required at least six complete sentences to ensure sufficient content for AI evaluation. Participants could ask clarifying questions before starting. Handwritten reports were converted to electronic format using English writing detection software. Some submissions required manual verification to preserve the accuracy of spelling, punctuation, and structural representation. This ensured that the AI bots received an authentic and precise representation of the original writing.

Two AI bots, Google Gemini and Microsoft Copilot, anonymized as AI Bot A and AI Bot B, were prompted with the same set of evaluation criteria covering linguistic accuracy, vocabulary appropriateness, organization, content relevance, and overall feedback utility (see Table 1). Their outputs were compiled for expert evaluation.

Table 2. The Prompts Used to Trigger the AI-bots Feedback

	Assess the quality of Learner 1's writing according to the following criteria:
1	A- Linguistic Accuracy: this includes grammatical correction, correct use of punctuation, and
	B- Vocabulary Appropriateness: this means the appropriateness of the medical vocabulary used by the learner
	C- Organization and Structure: this means assessing the coherence, and cohesion of the learner's writing.
	D- Content Relevance: this means assessing the relevance of the learner's writing according to the details provided in the medical report.

Phase Two: Expert Evaluation

The second phase involved a structured survey administered via Microsoft Forms. Experts received the original practitioner submissions along with AI-generated feedback. The survey contained: Closed-ended items using a 4-point Likert scale, evaluating each AI bot on linguistic accuracy, vocabulary, organization, content relevance, and overall usefulness. Additionally, open-ended questions provide qualitative insight into perceived strengths, weaknesses, and recommendations for improvement.

Anonymization of the AI bots ensured unbiased evaluation. Experts were instructed on the survey criteria and the evaluation process and had approximately 30 minutes to complete the survey.

Data Analysis

Closed-ended survey responses were analysed using descriptive statistics, including percentages of agreement, to compare expert perceptions of Gemini and Copilot across all assessment criteria (Field, 2024; Pallant, 2020). Descriptive statistics were appropriate as the study aimed to provide a detailed mapping of expert consensus, rather than infer causality. Internal consistency of the survey instrument was confirmed (Gliem & Gliem, 2003), and alignment with research objectives ensured content validity (Creswell & Creswell, 2017).

Open-ended responses were analysed using content analysis (Lyhne et al., 2025). Similar responses were coded and organized into categories, highlighting patterns in expert feedback regarding AI strengths, limitations, and pedagogical implications. Themes were then integrated with quantitative findings to provide a holistic understanding of AI feedback effectiveness.

FINDINGS

The comparison of the two AI bots, Gemini (AI-bot A) and Copilot (AI-bot B), revealed several notable findings across the main evaluation criteria of linguistic accuracy, vocabulary appropriateness, organization and structure, content relevance, and overall usefulness. Regarding linguistic accuracy, Gemini provided a detailed evaluative assessment for grammatical errors, punctuation, and capitalization. Each type of error was addressed separately, and a single corrected example was provided for illustration. For example, the sentence "Patient Mona Abdullah Alshehri with file number 84396 admitted by dr hamad Nasser" was corrected to "Patient Mona Abdullah Alshehri with file number 84396 was admitted by Dr. Hamad Nasser." Copilot, in contrast, directly addressed grammatical errors without an evaluative framework, providing six corrected phrases but grouping punctuation and capitalization together without detailed explanation. Participants' evaluations reflected this difference: all participants agreed that Gemini provided informative feedback, with 62.5% strongly agreeing and 37.5% agreeing, whereas for Copilot, only 37.5% agreed, 50% disagreed, and 12.5% strongly disagreed (Figure 1).

Figure 1. Linguistic accuracy agreement percentages in each AI-bot

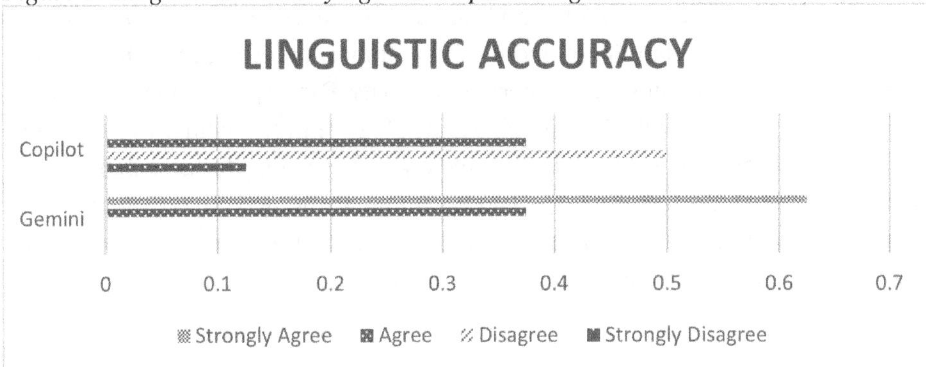

In terms of vocabulary appropriateness within the medical domain, Gemini divided feedback into two categories: Medical Terminology and Clarity and Conciseness. Under Medical Terminology, it identified the correct use of medical terms but highlighted unsuitable abbreviations with examples, while Clarity and Conciseness addressed overly long or complex sentences containing irrelevant information. Copilot provided a single category, Medical Vocabulary, commenting on two abbreviations and suggesting expansions (e.g., "'OR' → 'Operating Room'"). Participant feedback prefers Gemini, with 50% agreeing and 50% strongly agreeing on its usefulness, while Copilot received 37.5% agreement, 50% disagreement, and 12.5% strong disagreement (Figure 2).

Figure 2. Vocabulary appropriateness agreement percentages in each AI-bot

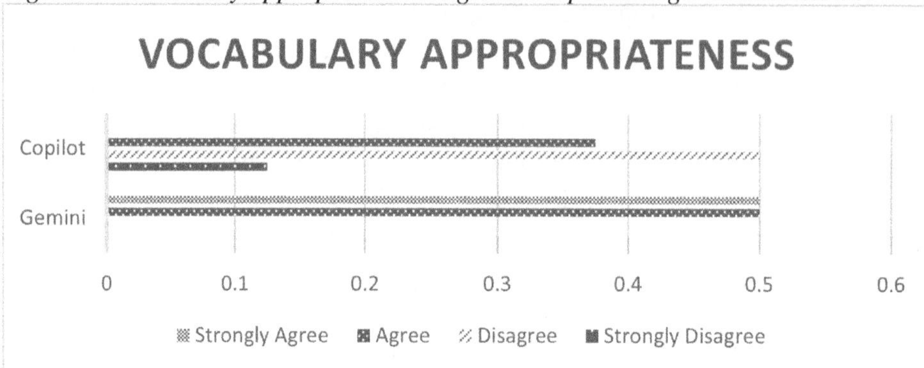

Regarding organization and structure, Gemini separated Coherence and Cohesion as distinct sub-criteria. It identified issues such as ineffective use of time stamps and abrupt transitions between sentences, providing specific guidance for improving the logical flow. Copilot combined both under Coherence and Cohesion, offering prescriptive recommendations, including chronological ordering, smoothing transitions, and using bullet points or numbering for clarity. Participant ratings indicated a preference for Gemini, with 50% agreeing and 50% strongly agreeing, while Copilot received 37.5% agreement, 37.5% disagreement, and 25% strong disagreement (Figure 3). These findings demonstrate that Gemini's diagnostic and analytical approach was considered more effective in highlighting underlying organizational problems, whereas Copilot focused on surface-level structural improvements.

Figure 3. Organization and structure agreement percentages in each AI-bot

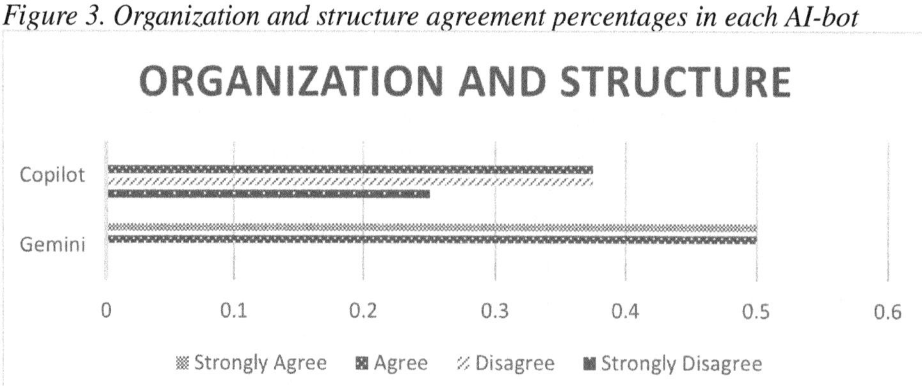

In evaluating content relevance, Gemini distinguished between Missing Information and Inaccurate Information. Missing Information included omitted patient vital signs, lab results, and post-surgery instructions, while Inaccurate Information captured errors such as incorrectly reported discharge times. This level of granularity also allowed participants to identify instances of AI hallucination. Copilot, however, provided only a single category, Relevance to Medical Report, commenting on discrepancies or non-correlated facts, for example, the unnecessary inclusion of "McBurney's test." Participant feedback prefers Gemini (75% agreement, 25% strong agreement) over Copilot (37.5% agreement, 62.5% disagreement) (Figure 4), demonstrating the value of detailed, category-based feedback in ESP contexts where accuracy is paramount.

Figure 4. Content relevance agreement percentages in each AI-bot

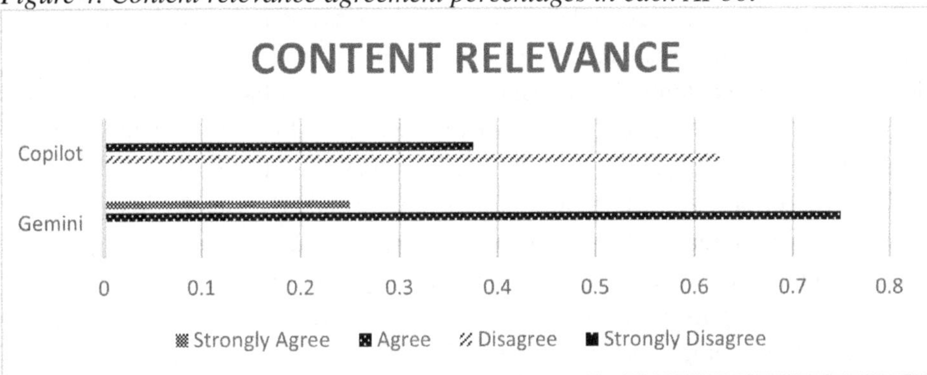

Moreover, the overall usefulness and personalization of feedback were assessed. Participants indicated that Gemini's feedback was precise, structured, and easy to follow, allowing learners to clearly identify areas for improvement, with 62.5% strongly agreeing and 37.5% agreeing. Copilot received only 25% agreement, with 37.5% each for disagreement and strong disagreement (Figure 5).

Figure 5. Effectiveness agreement percentages in each AI-bot

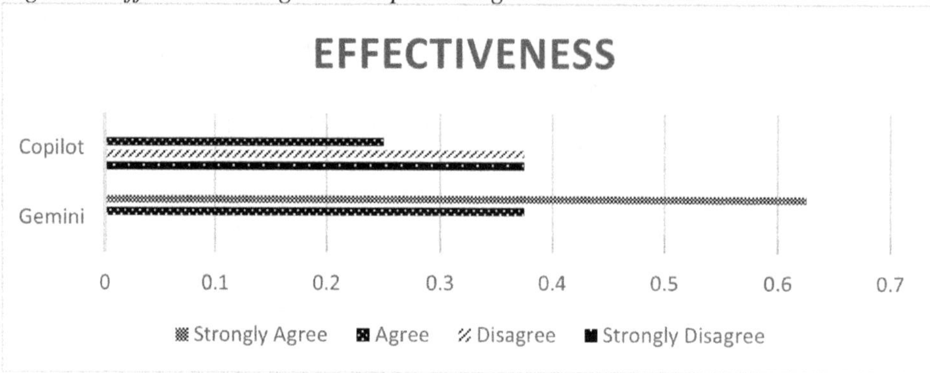

Finally, participants assessed the overall usefulness and personalization of feedback. The open-ended responses consistently highlighted Gemini as more precise, clear, and learner-centered. Participants noted that the feedback not only corrected errors but also guided learners to improve their writing, offering actionable insights for grammar, vocabulary, and organization. Copilot, while efficient in providing immediate corrections, was seen as less comprehensive and less effective in facilitating independent learning. Most participants suggested that AI bots should supplement rather than replace human assessment, particularly in complex ESP writing tasks, combining AI insights with teacher guidance for accurate and nuanced evaluation.

Overall, the findings demonstrate that Gemini consistently outperformed Copilot across all evaluated dimensions, with both quantitative agreement percentages and qualitative comments aligning to show the benefits of detailed, diagnostic, and context-aware AI feedback. The integration of open-ended responses enriched the understanding of participants' perceptions, emphasizing the pedagogical value of AI when paired with expert oversight.

DISCUSSION

The current study examined the efficacy of AI feedback in ESP writing tasks through a comparative analysis of two AI bots, namely Google Gemini and Microsoft Copilot, based on Automated Writing Evaluation criteria. Overall, participants perceived Gemini as more effective than Copilot across all domains of effectiveness, including linguistic accuracy, vocabulary choice, organizational skills, relevance of content, and feedback quality. These findings indicate that AI-based feedback tools vary in performance even within specific ESP domains such as medical writing.

Regarding linguistic accuracy, participants reported that Gemini provided more informative evaluative and explanatory feedback than Copilot. The ability of Gemini to identify grammatical mistakes, punctuation errors, and capitalization issues, and to provide explanations regarding their types and meanings, aligns with research highlighting the effectiveness of explanatory feedback for linguistic development (Burstein & Attali, 2024). In contrast, Copilot's provision of multiple corrected instances may have contributed to lower levels of participant satisfaction. In terms of domain-appropriate vocabulary, particularly within the medical context, Gemini's categorized comments about medical terms were better understood and received more positive feedback than Copilot's general suggestions. This finding suggests that ESP learners and assessors value feedback that is tailored to the specific conventions of the domain, such as the use of medical abbreviations, corroborating previous studies on contextualized AI feedback in ESP contexts (Imran et al., 2024; Jinowat et al., 2024).

Evaluation of organization, coherence, and cohesion revealed divergent feedback styles. Gemini employed a diagnostic approach, highlighting weaknesses in text flow and connections between sentences, whereas Copilot used prescriptive feedback, rearranging information and employing bullet points. Participants preferred Gemini's diagnostic style, which facilitates the recognition of deeper structural issues rather than surface-level editing. Content relevance was another domain in which Gemini outperformed Copilot. Gemini differentiated between missing and incorrect information, allowing more precise identification of problematic areas, an essential factor in ESP and medical writing where accuracy is critical. Although AI hallucinations were observed in a few instances, highlighting a limitation of AI-generated feedback in high-stakes contexts, participants still found Gemini's feedback more specific and task-related than Copilot's general suggestions (Kim, 2025).

Findings regarding personalization and general utility further confirmed Gemini's superiority. Participants found Gemini's feedback more understandable, better organized, and more supportive of learner improvement, going beyond mere error correction. These results align with previous research emphasizing the potential of AI tools as formative feedback instruments that assist learners in improving their writing (Jinowat et al., 2024; Moeis et al., 2024). Pedagogically, the study confirms that AI bots hold promise in ESP writing instruction, particularly in providing structured, vocabulary-focused, coherent, and efficient feedback. However, consistent with prior findings (Kim, 2025), AI feedback cannot replace human assessment and should serve only as a complementary tool to assist instructors in formative evaluation.

Implications

The findings of this study have important implications beyond the classroom level. The observed differences between Gemini and Copilot highlight the need for careful selection and integration of AI tools within ESP programs to ensure alignment with learning objectives, assessment standards, and overall program goals (Imran & Almusharraf, 2024; Jinowat et al., 2024). Additionally, the increasing use of AI feedback underscores the importance of faculty training and professional development, enabling instructors to interpret AI-generated feedback, manage potential inaccuracies, and guide learners in critically engaging with automated suggestions (Kim, 2025; Youn & Salam, 2025). Incorporating digital literacy components into ESP courses can further enhance students' ability to use AI tools responsibly and effectively.

Finally, ESP curricula may need to adapt learning outcomes and feedback protocols to reflect AI integration. This could include structured AI-assisted assignments, clear guidelines for responsible use, and evaluation rubrics that consider both human and AI contributions. Addressing these programmatic and institutional dimensions ensures that AI serves as a complementary resource, enhancing learning efficiency and autonomy while maintaining pedagogical quality. Despite the promising outcomes, several limitations and ethical considerations warrant attention. First, the study relied on a relatively small sample of ESP learners and expert evaluators, which may limit the generalizability of findings and the robustness of comparisons between Google Gemini and Microsoft Copilot (Kim, 2025; Rahimi et al., 2025). Second, instances of AI hallucinations were observed, underscoring the risk of providing inaccurate guidance in specialized contexts like medical writing (Lee, 2023; Kim, 2025). Finally, AI feedback should complement, not replace, human evaluation, ensuring pedagogical validity and promoting responsible and informed use of AI in ESP writing contexts (Burstein & Attali, 2024; Jinowat et al., 2024). Transparently addressing these limitations enhances the credibility of the study and informs responsible implementation of AI bots.

CONCLUSION

This study examined the efficiency of AI-generated feedback on learners' ESP writing, focusing on Google Gemini and Microsoft Copilot. Findings indicate that the constructive and explanatory nature of AI feedback can be highly effective when it is specific, contextually relevant, and finely tuned. Gemini demonstrated superior performance compared to Copilot in terms of linguistic accuracy, vocabulary appropriateness, organization, coherence, cohesion, and content relevance. Participants highlighted that Gemini's feedback helped learners understand the reasoning behind corrections and supported improvements in line with the principles of feedback discourse, which emphasizes guidance for enhancement rather than mere correction.

Despite these strengths, some limitations were observed. Copilot's feedback was generally corrective rather than explanatory, reducing its effectiveness. Both AI systems struggled with ESP-specific contexts and specialized medical vocabulary. Instances of AI "hallucination," where inaccurate feedback was generated, further underscore that AI cannot fully replace human evaluators. Participants emphasized that AI should serve as a complementary tool, enhancing instructors' ability to provide immediate and formative feedback while ensuring fairness and reliability in assessment.

From a pedagogical perspective, incorporating AI tools such as Gemini and Copilot into ESP writing processes offers several advantages. It facilitates formative assessment in large classes or repetitive writing tasks, supports learner self-regulation through reflection and revision, and raises awareness of domain-specific writing conventions. Moreover, despite being small in size and simple, the current study contributes growing evidence on the relative effectiveness of AI bots in providing ESP feedback, reinforcing the role of AI as a supportive rather than substitutive agent in language education.

FUTURE RESEARCH DIRECTIONS

Building on these results, future research should consider expanding the participant pool to include diverse professional and academic backgrounds, enhancing generalizability. Additionally, comparative studies involving additional AI tools across multiple ESP domains could provide deeper insights into tool-specific strengths and limitations. Also, longitudinal studies integrating AI feedback with human evaluation would shed light on long-term impacts on learner writing development. Finally, addressing ethical and practical concerns, such as data privacy, potential bias, and the reliability of AI-driven assessment, will be critical for responsible and effective adoption of AI-assisted feedback in ESP and specialized language learning contexts.

REFERENCES

Al-Sofi, B. B. M. A. (2024). Artificial intelligence-powered tools and academic writing: To use or not to use ChatGPT. *Saudi Journal of Language Studies*, *4*(3), 145–161. DOI: 10.1108/SJLS-06-2024-0029

Aladini, A., Ismail, S. M., Khasawneh, M. A. S., & Shakibaei, G. (2025). Self-directed writing development across computer/AI-based tasks: Unraveling the traces on L2 writing outcomes, growth mindfulness, and grammatical knowledge. *Computers in Human Behavior Reports*, *17*, 100566. DOI: 10.1016/j.chbr.2024.100566

Alharbi, M.A., & Alqefari, A.N. (2021). The Impact of Teacher Feedback Via Google Doc in L2 Learners' Writing. *International Journal of Learning, Teaching and Educational Research, 29* (11), PP. 170-194. https://doi.org/DOI: 10.26803/ijlter.20.11.10

Anthony, L. (2018). *Introducing English for specific purposes.* Routledge. DOI: 10.4324/9781351031189

Attali, Y., & Burstein, J. (2006). Automated Essay Scoring With e-rater® V.2. *The Journal of Technology, Learning, and Assessment*, *4*(3). http://www.jtla.org

Bao, W., Wang, T., Zhang, L., Yusop, F. D., & Ruan, X. (2025). A systematic review of AI in second language acquisition using the expanded SAMR model (2015–2024). *Interactive Learning Environments*, *28*(1), 292. Advance online publication. DOI: 10.1007/s10791-025-09833-6

Baron, T. H. (2012). ABC's of Writing Medical Papers in English. *Korean Journal of Radiology*, *13*(Suppl 1), S1–S11. DOI: 10.3348/kjr.2012.13.S1.S1 PMID: 22563279

Basturkmen, H. (2010). *Developing courses in English for specific purposes.* Palgrave Macmillan., DOI: 10.1057/9780230290518

Basturkmen, H. (2025). Learning a specialized register: An English for Specific Purposes research agenda. *Language Teaching*, *58*(1), 57–68. DOI: 10.1017/S0261444823000472

Belcher, D. D. (2006). English for Specific Purposes: Teaching to Perceived Needs and Imagined Futures in Worlds of Work, Study, and Everyday Life. *TESOL Quarterly*, *40*(1), 133–156. DOI: 10.2307/40264514

Burner, T., Lindvig, Y., & Wærness, J. I. (2025). "We should not be like a dinosaur"—Using AI technologies to provide formative feedback to students. *Education Sciences*, *15*(1), 58. DOI: 10.3390/educsci15010058

Burstein, J., & Attali, Y. (2024). Automated Writing Evaluation. IN, The Concise Companion to Language Assessment. *John Wiley & Sons, Inc*. pp. 661-670

Burstein, J., Elliot, N., Klebanov, B. B., Madnani, N., Napolitano, D., Schwartz, M., Houghton, P., & Molloy, H. (2018). Writing mentor: Writing progress using self-regulated writing support. *Journal of Writing Analytics, 2*, 285-313. https://wac.colostate.edu/docs/jwa/vol2/bursteinetal.pdf

Celik, H. (2018). A CLOSER LOOK INTO AN ESP COURSE THROUGH STUDENTS'END-OF-COURSE EVALUATIONS: A CASE STUDY. *Journal of Teaching English for Specific and Academic Purposes*, *6*(1), 125–139. DOI: 10.22190/JTESAP1801125C

Chen, C., & Gong, Y. (2025). The role of AI-assisted learning in academic writing: A mixed-methods study on Chinese as a second language students. *Education Sciences*, *15*(2), 141. DOI: 10.3390/educsci15020141

Chen, C. F. E., & Cheng, W. Y. E. C. (2008). Beyond the design of automated writing evaluation: Pedagogical practices and perceived learning effectiveness in EFL writing classes.

Chen, W. Y. (2024). Intelligent tutor: Leveraging chatgpt and microsoft copilot studio to deliver a generative ai student support and feedback system within teams. *arXiv preprint arXiv:2405*.13024.

Creswell, J. W., & Creswell, J. D. (2017). *Research design: Qualitative, quantitative, and mixed methods approaches*. Sage publications.

Feng, H. H., & Chukharev-Hudilainen, E. (2022). Genre-based AWE system for engineering graduate writing: Development and evaluation.

Field, A. (2024). Discovering statistics using IBM SPSS statistics. Sage publications limited.

Gliem, J. A., & Gliem, R. R. (2003). Calculating, interpreting, and reporting Cronbach's alpha reliability coefficient for Likert-type scales. Midwest research-to-Practice Conference in Adult, Continuing, and community education.

Halim, T., Wahid, R., & Halim, S. (2021). EFL students' attitudes toward corrective feedback: A study conducted at undergraduate level. *Saudi Journal of Language Studies*, *1*(1), 40–49. DOI: 10.1108/SJLS-03-2021-0004

Hansen, A., Klute, R. M., Yadav, M., Bansal, S., & Bond, W. F. (2024). How Do Learners Receive Feedback on Note Writing? A Scoping Review. *Academic Medicine*, *99*(6), 683–690. DOI: 10.1097/ACM.0000000000005653 PMID: 38306581

Hattie, J., & Timperley, H. (2007). The power of feedback. *Review of Educational Research, 77*(1), 81–112. DOI: 10.3102/003465430298487

Haynes, S. N., Richard, D., & Kubany, E. S. (1995). Content validity in psychological assessment: A functional approach to concepts and methods. *Psychological Assessment, 7*(3), 238–247. DOI: 10.1037/1040-3590.7.3.238

Imran, M., & Almusharraf, N. (2024). Google Gemini as a next generation AI educational tool: A review of emerging educational technology. *Smart Learning Environments, 11*(1), 22. DOI: 10.1186/s40561-024-00310-z

Imran, M., Almusharraf, N., Abdellatif, M. S., & Abbasova, M. Y. (2024). Artificial intelligence in higher education: Enhancing learning systems and transforming educational paradigms.

Jinowat, N., Unapang, J., Kangsawiwat, T., & Sapai, P. (2024). Fostering Critical Writing Excellence: Leveraging Google Gemini and Collaborative Online Writing with Google Docs. *International Workshop on Learning Technology for Education in Cloud*.p. 349-363. https://doi.org/DOI: 10.1007/978-3-031-61678-5_25

Kim, Y. (2025). Automated Essay Scoring With GPT-4 for a Local Placement Test: Investigating Prompting Strategies, Intra-Rater Reliability, and Alignment With Human Scores. *TESOL Quarterly, 59*(S1). Advance online publication. DOI: 10.1002/tesq.3405

Kourtali, N. E., & Borges, L. (2024). The effects of feedback timing on L2 development in written SCMC. *Computer Assisted Language Learning, 37*(8), 2291–2319. DOI: 10.1080/09588221.2023.2171066

Lee, A. V. Y. (2023). Supporting students' generation of feedback in large-scale online course with artificial intelligence-enabled evaluation. *Studies in Educational Evaluation, 77*, 101250. Advance online publication. DOI: 10.1016/j.stueduc.2023.101250

Liu, W., Jamaludin, K. A., Song, Z., & Song, Z. (2024). Implementation of technical communication pedagogy in higher education institutions: A systematic literature review. *International Journal of Learning. Teaching and Educational Research, 23*(9), 307–324.

Lyhne, C. N., Thisted, J., & Bjerrum, M. (2025). Qualitative content analysis–framing the analytical process of inductive content analysis to develop a sound study design. *Quality & Quantity, 59*(6), 1–21. DOI: 10.1007/s11135-025-02220-9

Mekheimer, M. (2025). Generative AI-assisted feedback and EFL writing: A study on proficiency, revision frequency and writing quality. *Discover Education, 4*(1), 170. DOI: 10.1007/s44217-025-00602-7

Moeis, D., Usman, N., Faisal, M., Harmin, A., Mulyadi, I., & Thamrin, M. (2024). Microsoft Copilot training for monitoring student learning: A case study vocational high school Makassar-Indonesia. *I-Com: Indonesian Community Journal*, *4*(3), 1911–1922.

Mohammed, S. J., & Khalid, M. W. (2025). Under the world of AI-generated feedback on writing: Mirroring motivation, foreign language peace of mind, trait emotional intelligence, and writing development. *Language Testing in Asia*, *15*(1), 7. DOI: 10.1186/s40468-025-00343-2

Morgan, D. L. (2007). Paradigms lost and pragmatism regained: Methodological implications of combining qualitative and quantitative methods. *Journal of Mixed Methods Research*, *1*(1), 48–76. DOI: 10.1177/2345678906292462

Pallant, J. (2020). *SPSS survival manual: A step by step guide to data analysis using IBM SPSS*. Routledge.

Polit, D. F., & Beck, C. T. (2006). The content validity index: Are you sure you know what's being reported? Critique and recommendations. *Research in Nursing & Health*, *29*(5), 489–497. DOI: 10.1002/nur.20147 PMID: 16977646

Rahimi, M., Fathi, J., & Zou, D. (2025). Exploring the impact of automated written corrective feedback on the academic writing skills of EFL learners: An activity theory perspective. *Education and Information Technologies*, *30*(3), 2691–2735. DOI: 10.1007/s10639-024-12896-5

Rahman, M. (2015). English for Specific Purposes (ESP): A Holistic Review. *Universal Journal of Educational Research*, *3*(1), 24–31. DOI: 10.13189/ujer.2015.030104

Salmani-Nodoushan, M. A. (2020). English for Specific Purposes: Traditions, Trends, Directions. *Online Submission*, *7*(1), 247–268. DOI: 10.24815/siele.v7i1.16342

Schmidt, R. (2001). Attention. In Robinson, P. (Ed.), *Cognition and second language instruction* (pp. 3–32). Cambridge University Press. DOI: 10.1017/CBO9781139524780.003

Shute, V. J. (2008). Focus on formative feedback. *Review of Educational Research*, *78*(1), 153–189. DOI: 10.3102/0034654307313795

Torres, P. J., & Kahveci, Y. E. (2025). Effectiveness of Artificial Intelligence (AI) in language teaching. *Computers and Education: Artificial Intelligence*, 100522.

Woodworth, J., & Barkaoui, K. (2020). Perspectives on using automated writing evaluation systems to provide written corrective feedback in the ESL classroom. *TESL Canada Journal*, *37*(2), 234–247. DOI: 10.18806/tesl.v37i2.1340

Xu, L., Zhang, L., Ou, L., & Wang, D. (2025). The development and validation of a scale on student AI literacy in L2 writing: A domain-specific perspective. *Journal of Second Language Writing*, *69*, 101227. DOI: 10.1016/j.jslw.2025.101227

Yan, H. (2025). Trends in empirical research in English for specific purposes: A systematic review of SSCI-indexed journal articles (2014–2023). *SAGE Open*, *15*(1), 21582440251328460. DOI: 10.1177/21582440251328460

Youn, C. H., & Salam, A. R. (2025). A Systematic Review on the Use of Artificial Intelligence in Providing Feedback in Teaching Writing. *LSP International Journal*, *12*(2), 133–142. DOI: 10.11113/lspi.v12.26003

APPENDIX 1

This appendix outlines the research task that participants in the first phase were required to complete.

Task 1: Based on the admission form provided, write a report (not less than 6 sentence paragraphs) that covers the following: Patient Details, Current Symptoms, Examination Findings, Diagnosis and Treatment Plan, and Follow-up and Physician's Signature. The report will be read by the health insurance company to pay the treatment cost.

Table 3.

<table>
<tr><td colspan="6">Admission Form</td></tr>
<tr><td>Hospital</td><td>SGH</td><td colspan="3">Ward Number</td><td>03</td></tr>
<tr><td colspan="2">MR Number</td><td>84396</td><td colspan="2">Date of Admission</td><td>25.05.2022</td></tr>
<tr><td colspan="2">Attending Physician</td><td>Dr. Hamad Nassr</td><td colspan="2">Time of Admission</td><td>10.20 am</td></tr>
<tr><td colspan="2">Patient Name in Full</td><td colspan="4">Mona Abdullah Alshehri</td></tr>
<tr><td colspan="2">Patient ID</td><td>1023345678</td><td colspan="2">Telephone Number</td><td>0538762569</td></tr>
<tr><td colspan="2">Age</td><td>28</td><td>Sex F</td><td>Date of Discharge</td><td></td></tr>
<tr><td colspan="2">Civil Condition</td><td>Married</td><td colspan="2">Time of Discharge</td><td>3.00 pm</td></tr>
<tr><td colspan="2">Final Diagnosis/ Main Condition</td><td colspan="2">ACUTE APPENDICITIS</td><td>ICD Code</td><td>K35.8</td></tr>
<tr><td colspan="2">Date</td><td colspan="4">Clinical Notes</td></tr>
<tr><td colspan="2">Symptoms</td><td colspan="4">O/e looks ill, r/s abdominal pain, C/o Fever, Vomiting</td></tr>
<tr><td colspan="2">Diagnosis at 10:50 AM</td><td colspan="4">Acute Appendicitis</td></tr>
<tr><td colspan="2">(The admitting doctor)</td><td colspan="4">Dr. Hamad Nasser</td></tr>
<tr><td colspan="2">Diagnosis and treatment 3:00 PM</td><td colspan="4">Appendicectomy done</td></tr>
<tr><td colspan="2">Prescription and follow-up treatment</td><td colspan="4">IV fluids and antibiotics (Ceftriaxone 1 g IV, Metronidazole 500 mg IV)
Paracetamol 1 g IV as needed AND Monitor vital signs every 4 hours</td></tr>
<tr><td colspan="2">3.00 pm, 30.05.22</td><td colspan="4">Dr. Basel Mahmod
Specialist Doctor</td></tr>
</table>

Compilation of References

50Languages. (n.d.). *50Languages language learning app*. Goethe Verlag. https://www.50languages.com

AbdAlgane, M., & Elmahdi, O. E. H.AbdAlgane. (2024). Preferred EFL teaching approaches to university professors: A case study of Saudi tertiary level. *International Journal of Language and Literary Studies*, *6*(4), 274–291. DOI: 10.36892/ijlls.v6i4.1940

Abdelhalim, S. M., Alsahil, A. A., Baek, C., & Warschauer, M. (2025). University EFL instructors' engagement with generative AI: A cross-cultural analysis. *System*, *135*, 103861. DOI: 10.1016/j.system.2025.103861

Abdul-Mageed, M., & Elmadany, A. (2021, August). ARBERT & MARBERT: Deep bidirectional transformers for Arabic. In *Proceedings of the 59th Annual Meeting of the Association for Computational Linguistics and the 11th International Joint Conference on Natural Language Processing (*Volume 1*: Long Papers)* (pp. 7088–7105). DOI: 10.18653/v1/2021.acl-long.551

Abu-Lughod, L. (2016). *Veiled sentiments: Honor and poetry in a Bedouin society*. University of California Press. DOI: 10.1525/9780520965980

Acton, W. (1984). Changing fossilized pronunciation. *TESOL Quarterly*, *18*(1), 71–85. DOI: 10.2307/3586336

Adelana, O. P., & Akinyemi, A. L. (2022). Artificial intelligence-based tutoring systems utilization for learning: A survey of senior secondary students' awareness and readiness in Ijebu-Ode, Ogun State. *UNIZIK Journal of Educational Research and Policy Studies*, *9*, 16–28.

Aditya, D. (2026). Leveraging conversational AI for enhanced educational experiences: A systematic review and framework. *Cogent Education*, *10*(1), 2611649. DOI: 10.1080/2331186X.2025.2611649

AIIC. (2025). AIIC Guidelines on Distance Interpreting.

Akan, M. F., Almosa, A., Siddiqui, S., Chowdhury, G., Ahamed, M. M., Mishu, A., Ahmed, J., & Sultana, S. (2023). On linguistic reviews of Arabic and Bangla: A comparative study. *Theory and Practice in Language Studies*, *13*(9), 2375–2383. DOI: 10.17507/tpls.1309.25

Akhter, E. (2025). AI In the Classroom: Evaluating the Effectiveness of Intelligent Tutoring Systems for Multilingual Learners In Secondary Education. *ASRC Procedia: Global Perspectives in Science and Scholarship*, *1*(01), 532–563. DOI: 10.63125/gcq1qr39

Aktuğ, B. (2015). *Common pronunciation errors of seventh grade EFL learners: A case from Turkey*. Middle East Technical University.

Al Fraidan, A., & Alaliwi, M. (2024). Digital transformation for sustainable English language learning: Insights from Saudi Arabia and global perspectives. *Forum for Linguistic Studies*, *6*, 439–449. DOI: 10.30564/fls.v6i6.7754

Al Kaabi, S. (2025). "Reliance on Ai and its Effects on Critical Thinking and Graduate Readiness: Evidence from UAE Higher Education". In *International Journal of Learning, Teaching and Educational Research*, Vol. 24, No. 8, pp. 398-417. DOI: 10.26803/ijlter.24.8.17

Al Maaytah, S. A. (2026). Evaluating three neural machine translation platforms for English-Arabic translation: A comparative study of linguistic accuracy and cultural fidelity. *World Journal of English Language*, *16*(2), 1. DOI: 10.5430/wjel.v16n2p1

Al Rousan, R. M., Jaradat, R. S., & Malkawi, M. (2025). ChatGPT translation vs. human translation: An examination of a literary text. *Cogent Social Sciences*, *11*(1), 2472916. Advance online publication. DOI: 10.1080/23311886.2025.2472916

Al-Abdullatif, A. M. (2025). Auditing AI literacy competency in K–12 education: The role of awareness, ethics, evaluation, and use in human–machine cooperation. *Systems*, *13*(6), 490. DOI: 10.3390/systems13060490

Aladini, A., Ismail, S. M., Khasawneh, M. A. S., & Shakibaei, G. (2025). Self-directed writing development across computer/AI-based tasks: Unraveling the traces on L2 writing outcomes, growth mindfulness, and grammatical knowledge. *Computers in Human Behavior Reports*, *17*, 100566. DOI: 10.1016/j.chbr.2024.100566

Alanazi, T. (2025). Addressing the Challenges and Complexities of Teaching English in Saudi Higher Education: Insights through a Sociocultural Lens. *Education Quarterly Eeview*, *8*(2), 95–106. DOI: 10.31014/aior.1993.08.02.582

Alaqad, M. H., Al-Saggaf, M. A., & Ingilan, S. S. (2026). The Future of AI in English Language Education: Opportunities, Challenges, and Ethical Pathways. The Sociology of English Language Teaching and Learning in the Age of AI, 241-264. DOI:DOI: 10.4018/979-8-3373-3755-5.ch010

Alayba, A. M. (2025). Arabic natural language processing (NLP): A comprehensive review of challenges, techniques, and emerging trends. *Computers*, *14*(11), 497. DOI: 10.3390/computers14110497

Albirini, A. (2016). *Modern Arabic sociolinguistics: Diglossia, variation, codeswitching, attitudes and identity*. Routledge. DOI: 10.4324/9781315683737

Algamedi, S. (2025). *Rhetoric of soft power and public diplomacy: A case study of Saudi Arabia* (Doctoral dissertation, Duquesne University).

AlGhamdi, E. M., Li, Y., Gašević, D., & Chen, G. (2026). Leveraging prompt-based LLMs for automated scoring and feedback generation in higher education. *Computers & Education*, *243*, 105511. DOI: 10.1016/j.compedu.2025.105511

Alghamdi, E., Otaif, F., & Gruba, P. (2018). Designing a video playing interface for second language learners. In *Open Oceans: Learning without borders. Proceedings ASCILITE, 2018*, 298–302. DOI: 10.14742/ascilite2018.1978

Alhakimi, A., Alkholidi, A., Adar, N., Sefa, B., & Ahmed, W. M. A. (2025, May). AI versus human translators: Accuracy and context in the translation of cultural idioms and proverbs. In *International Conference on Intelligence-Based Transformations of Technology and Business Trends* (pp. 231–246). Springer Nature Switzerland.

Alharbi, M.A., & Alqefari, A.N. (2021). The Impact of Teacher Feedback Via Google Doc in L2 Learners' Writing. *International Journal of Learning, Teaching and Educational Research, 29* (11), PP. 170-194. https://doi.org/DOI: 10.26803/ijlter.20.11.10

Alhudaithy, H. I., Mishu, A., & Chowdhury, G. (2025). Reclaiming voice and identity: Teaching creative writing as a tool for empowerment in multicultural classrooms. *Journal of Language Teaching and Research, 16*(1). Advance online publication. DOI: 10.17507/jltr.1701.29

Alhusaiyan, E. (2025). A systematic review of current trends in artificial intelligence in foreign language learning. *Saudi Journal of Language Studies*, *5*(1), 1–16. DOI: 10.1108/SJLS-07-2024-0039

Al-khresheh, M. H. (2024). Bridging technology and pedagogy from a global lens: Teachers' perspectives on integrating ChatGPT in English language teaching. *Computers and Education: Artificial Intelligence*, *6*, 100218. DOI: 10.1016/j.caeai.2024.100218

Almutairi, F. (2025). Language and AI interaction: Studying how AI language models are affecting human communication and language learning. *World Conference on Emerging Science, Innovation and Policy 2025*. Futurity Research Publishing. https://doi.org/DOI: 10.5281/zenodo.15852254

Al-Seghayer, K. (2015). Salient Key Features of Actual English Instructional Practices in Saudi Arabia. *English Language Teaching*, *8*(6), 89–99. DOI: 10.5539/elt.v8n6p89

Al-Seghayer, K. (2024). Pragmatic competence in Saudi EFL learners: Challenges, consequences, and strategies for overcoming barriers. *Journal for the Study of English Linguistics*, *12*(1), 209–235. DOI: 10.5296/jsel.v12i1.22438

Alshammari, S. R. (2020). EFL vocabulary learning strategies used by Saudi Arabian university students. *Advanced Education*, *7*(16), 28–38. DOI: 10.20535/2410-8286.202436

AlShareef, S. N. A. (2024). Applying the Communicative Approach in Assessing EFL Young Learners. *Eurasian Journal of Applied Linguistics*, *10*(1), 14–27. DOI: 10.32601/ejal.10102

Al-Sofi, B. B. M. A. (2024). Artificial intelligence-powered tools and academic writing: To use or not to use ChatGPT. *Saudi Journal of Language Studies*, *4*(3), 145–161. DOI: 10.1108/SJLS-06-2024-0029

Alvarez-Vidal, S., & Oliver, A. (2023). Assessing machine translation with measures of post-editing effort: A productivity perspective. *Ampersand (Oxford, UK)*, *11*, 100125. DOI: 10.1016/j.amper.2023.100125

Alzubi, A. A. F., Nazim, M., & Alyami, N. (2025). Do AI-generative tools kill or nurture creativity in EFL teaching and learning? *Education and Information Technologies*, *30*(11), 15147–15184. DOI: 10.1007/s10639-025-13409-8

Amin, E. A.-R. (2024). EFL students' perception of using artificial intelligence-powered text-to-speech apps in learning pronunciation. *Migration Letters : An International Journal of Migration Studies*, *21*(3), 887–903.

Ananiadou, K., & Claro, M. (2009), "21st Century Skills and Competences for New Millennium Learners in OECD Countries", *OECD Education Working Papers*, No. 41, OECD Publishing, Paris, https://doi.org/DOI: 10.1787/19939019

Antal-Berbecaru, A., Larchen Costuchen, A., & Dev, S. (2024). Survey Gamification: Engaging Generation Z. *Computers in the Schools*, *41*(4), 448–472. DOI: 10.1080/07380569.2023.2271486

Anthony, L. (2022). AntConc (Version 4.2.0) [Computer software]. Waseda University. https://www.laurenceanthony.net/software/antconc/

Anthony, L. (2018). *Introducing English for specific purposes*. Routledge. DOI: 10.4324/9781351031189

Aqueveque, F. C. (2024). Entrenamiento en Formulación de Casos en Psicoterapia a Través de Inteligencia Artificial Generativa. *Revista de Psicoterapia*, *35*(127), 97–112. DOI: 10.5944/rdp.v35i127.37798

Arqus Alliance. (2025, May 15). *The University of Minho holds the in-person phase of BIP "Generative Artificial Intelligence to create multilingual and multimodal narratives from scientific open data"*. https://arqus-alliance.eu/news/in-person-bip-generative-artificial-intelligence-uminho/

Asrifan, A., & Alaqad, M. H. (2025). Evolution of AI in Interpretation: From Traditional Approaches to Real-Time Solution. In Role of AI in Translation and Interpretation (pp. 63-94). IGI Global Scientific Publishing. DOI:DOI: 10.4018/979-8-3373-0060-3.ch003

Attali, Y., & Burstein, J. (2006). Automated Essay Scoring With e-rater® V.2. *The Journal of Technology, Learning, and Assessment*, *4*(3). http://www.jtla.org

Attia, M., Muhamed, A., Alkhamissi, M., Solorio, T., & Diab, M. (2025). Beyond understanding: Evaluating the pragmatic gap in LLMs' cultural processing of figurative language. *arXiv preprint arXiv:2510.23828.*

Auer, M. E. (2025). Artificial intelligence–supported reflective learning in higher education: Implications for intercultural competence and metacognition. *International Journal of Emerging Technologies in Learning*, *20*(2), xx–xx. https://doi.org/xxxxx

Awashreh, R., & Aboeisheh, A. (2025). The collaborative future of translation between human-AI partnerships. In *Role of AI in Translation and Interpretation* (pp. 205–236). IGI Global Scientific Publishing. DOI: 10.4018/979-8-3373-0060-3.ch008

Babanoğlu, M. P., Karataş, T. Ö., & Dündar, E. (2025). Envisioning the Future of AI-Assisted EFL Teaching and Learning: Conceptual Representations of Prospective Teachers. *SAGE Open*, *15*(2), 21582440251341590. Advance online publication. DOI: 10.1177/21582440251341590

Bahari, A., Han, F., & Strzelecki, A. (2025). Integrating CALL and AI-ALL for an interactive pedagogical model of language learning. *Education and Information Technologies, 30*(10), 14305–14333. DOI: 10.1007/s10639-025-13388-w

Baker, A., & Burri, M. (2016). Feedback on second language pronunciation: A case study of EAP teachers' beliefs and practices. *The Australian Journal of Teacher Education, 41*(6), 1–20. DOI: 10.14221/ajte.2016v41n6.1

Balla, A. A. S. (2025). AI-Driven Innovations in Adult EFL Learning: Exploring Potentials and Practicalities. *International Journal of Interactive Mobile Technologies, 19*(8), 4–26. Advance online publication. DOI: 10.3991/ijim.v19i08.52295

Bao, W., Wang, T., Zhang, L., Yusop, F. D., & Ruan, X. (2025). A systematic review of AI in second language acquisition using the expanded SAMR model (2015–2024). *Interactive Learning Environments, 28*(1), 292. Advance online publication. DOI: 10.1007/s10791-025-09833-6

Bardakçı, M. (2015). Turkish EFL pre-service teachers pronunciation problems. *Educational Research Review, 10*(16), 2370–2378. DOI: 10.5897/ERR2015.2396

Baron, T. H. (2012). ABC's of Writing Medical Papers in English. *Korean Journal of Radiology, 13*(Suppl 1), S1–S11. DOI: 10.3348/kjr.2012.13.S1.S1 PMID: 22563279

Barthes, R. (1967). *Le mort de l'auteur* (Vol. 5). Manteia.

Bartolomé, A. (2023). [Prólogo]. En Fernández-Ferrer, M. (Ed.). (2023). *Chatbots en educación. Tendencias actuales y desafíos futuros* (pp.9-13). LMI.

Basaula, A. (2025). From Challenges to Opportunities: AI in English Language Teaching Classrooms. *Kalika Journal of Multidisciplinary Studies, 7*(1), 13–37. DOI: 10.3126/kjms.v7i1.86428

Basri, W. S. (2024). Effectiveness of AI-powered Tutoring Systems in Enhancing Learning Outcomes. *Eurasian Journal of Educational Research, 110*, 33–52. DOI: 10.14689/ejer.2024.110.003

Basturkmen, H. (2010). *Developing courses in English for specific purposes*. Palgrave Macmillan., DOI: 10.1057/9780230290518

Basturkmen, H. (2025). Learning a specialized register: An English for Specific Purposes research agenda. *Language Teaching, 58*(1), 57–68. DOI: 10.1017/S0261444823000472

Bayne, S. (2015). Teacherbot: Interventions in automated teaching. *Teaching in Higher Education, 20*(4), 455–467. DOI: 10.1080/13562517.2015.1020783

Bekleyen, N. (2011). Pronunciation problems of the Turkish EFL learners. *Electronic Journal of Social Sciences, 10*(36), 94–107.

Belcher, D. D. (2006). English for Specific Purposes: Teaching to Perceived Needs and Imagined Futures in Worlds of Work, Study, and Everyday Life. *TESOL Quarterly, 40*(1), 133–156. DOI: 10.2307/40264514

Belda-Medina, J., & Calvo-Ferrer, J. R. (2022). Using Chatbots as AI Conversational Partners in Language Learning. *Applied Sciences (Basel, Switzerland), 12*(17), 8427. DOI: 10.3390/app12178427

Bender, E. M., & Koller, A. (2020). Climbing towards NLU: On meaning, form, and understanding in the age of data. *Proceedings of the 58th Annual Meeting of the Association for Computational Linguistics*, 5185–5198. DOI: 10.18653/v1/2020.acl-main.463

Benek, K. (2025). EFL learners' and teachers' perceptions of AI-powered language learning technologies: Benefits and challenges. *International Journal of Instruction, 18*(2), 103–120. DOI: 10.29333/iji.2025.1827a

Bhardwaj, V., Dhaliwal, B. K., Sarangi, S. K., Thiyagu, T. M., Patidar, A., & Pithawa, D. (2024). Conversational AI: Introduction to chatbot's security risks, their probable solutions, and the best practices to follow. In Rawat, R., Chakrawarti, R. K., Sarangi, S. K., Vyas, P., Alamanda, M. S., Srividya, K., & Sankaran, K. S. (Eds.), *Conversational AI* (pp. 435–457)., DOI: 10.1002/9781394200801.ch26

Biocca, F., Harms, C., & Burgoon, J. K. (2003). Towards a more robust theory and measure of social presence. *Proceedings of the 36th Annual Hawaii International Conference on System Sciences*, 1–10. DOI: 10.1109/HICSS.2003.1174289

Bishop, R. S. (1990). Mirrors, windows, and sliding glass doors. *Perspectives: Choosing and Using Books for the Classroom, 6*(3), ix–xi.

Bissiri, M., & Pfitzinger, H. (2009). Italian speakers learn lexical stress of German morphologically complex words. *Speech Communication, 51*(10), 933–947. DOI: 10.1016/j.specom.2009.03.001

Blake, J. (2024). Unleashing the potential: Positive impacts of generative AI on learning and teaching. In Hai-Jew, S. (Ed.), *Generative AI in teaching and learning* (pp. 31–45). IGI Global., DOI: 10.4018/979-8-3693-0074-9.ch002

Boran, G. (2005). A study on commonly mispronounced words by the EFL teacher trainees at the ELT Department of Gazi Education Faculty. *Selcuk University Institute of Social Sciences Journal, 13*, 81–90.

Bort Caballero, M. L., & Gil-Mediavilla, M. (2023). Intervención educativa con narrativas digitales en lengua y literatura española del grado universitario en educación primaria: Una perspectiva en femenino. *Formación Universitaria, 16*(4), 43–52. DOI: 10.4067/s0718-50062023000400043

Braun, S. (2013). Keep your distance? Remote interpreting in legal proceedings: A critical assessment of a growing practice. *Interpreting, 15*(2), 200–228. DOI: 10.1075/intp.15.2.03bra

Braun, S. (2018). Video-mediated interpreting in legal settings in England: Interpreters' perceptions in their sociopolitical context. *Translation and Interpreting Studies, 13*(3), 393–420. DOI: 10.1075/tis.00022.bra

Braun, V., & Clarke, V. (2006). Using thematic analysis in psychology. *Qualitative Research in Psychology, 3*(2), 77–101. DOI: 10.1191/1478088706qp063oa

Braun, V., & Clarke, V. (2021). Thematic analysis: A practical guide. *Sage (Atlanta, Ga.).*

British Standards Institution. (2015). BS EN ISO 17100:2015 Translation services Requirements for translation services. DOI: 10.3403/30246895U

British Standards Institution. (2017). *BS ISO 18587:2017 Translation services Post-editing of machine translation output Requirements*. DOI: 10.3403/30279909U

Briva-Iglesias, V., O'Brien, S., & Cowan, B. R. (2023). *The impact of traditional and interactive post-editing on machine translation user experience, quality, and productivity*. Translation, Cognition & Behavior., DOI: 10.1075/tcb.00077.bri

Browne, K., & Fulcher, G. (2017). Pronunciation and intelligibility in assessing spoken fluency. In Isaacs, T., & Trofimovich, P. (Eds.), *Second language pronunciation assessment: Interdisciplinary perspectives* (pp. 37–53). Multilingual Matters.

Brown, H. D. (2007). *Principles of Language Learning and Teaching*. Longman.

Brown, H. D., & Lee, H. (2025). *Principles of Language Learning and Teaching: A course in second language acquisition.* Taylor & Francis. DOI: 10.4324/9781003494294

Brown, S. (2011). *Listening myths: Applying second language research to classroom teaching*. University of Michigan Press. DOI: 10.3998/mpub.2132445

Brown, S. (2017). L2 Listening. In Hinkel, E. (Ed.), *Handbook of Research in Second Language Teaching and Learning* (Vol. 3, pp. 201–213). Routledge.

Brown, T., Mann, B., Ryder, N., Subbiah, M., Kaplan, J. D., Dhariwal, P., & Amodei, D. (2020). Language models are few-shot learners. *Advances in Neural Information Processing Systems, 33*, 1877–1901.

Bryfonski, L., & Ma, X. (2020). Effects of implicit versus explicit corrective feedback on Mandarin tone acquisition in a SCMC learning environment. *Studies in Second Language Acquisition, 42*(1), 61–88. DOI: 10.1017/S0272263119000317

Burner, T., Lindvig, Y., & Wærness, J. I. (2025). "We should not be like a dinosaur"—Using AI technologies to provide formative feedback to students. *Education Sciences, 15*(1), 58. DOI: 10.3390/educsci15010058

Burstein, J., & Attali, Y. (2024). Automated Writing Evaluation. IN, The Concise Companion to Language Assessment. *John Wiley & Sons, Inc*. pp. 661-670

Burstein, J., Elliot, N., Klebanov, B. B., Madnani, N., Napolitano, D., Schwartz, M., Houghton, P., & Molloy, H. (2018). Writing mentor: Writing progress using self-regulated writing support. *Journal of Writing Analytics, 2*, 285-313. https://wac.colostate.edu/docs/jwa/vol2/bursteinetal.pdf

Buscemi, E., & Kaposi, I. (2020). *Everyday youth cultures in the Gulf Peninsula*. Routledge. DOI: 10.4324/9781003048626

Busso, A., & Sanchez, B. (2024). Advancing communicative competence in the digital age: A case for AI tools in Japanese EFL education. *Technology in Language Teaching & Learning, 6*(3), 1–17. DOI: 10.29140/tltl.v6n3.1211

Butler-Pascoe, M., & Wiburg, K. (2003). *Technology and teaching English language learners*. Pearson.

Cadwell, P., Castilho, S., O'Brien, S., & Mitchell, L. (2016). Human factors in machine translation and post-editing among institutional translators. *Translation Spaces, 5*(2), 222–243. DOI: 10.1075/ts.5.2.04cad

Cadwell, P., O'Brien, S., & Teixeira, C. S. C. (2018). Resistance and accommodation: Factors for the (non-) adoption of machine translation among professional translators. Perspectives. *Studies in Translation Theory and Practice, 26*(3), 301–321. DOI: 10.1080/0907676X.2017.1337210

Canale, M., & Swain, M. (1980). Theoretical bases of communicative approaches to second language teaching and testing. *Applied Linguistics, 1*(1), 1–47. DOI: 10.1093/applin/1.1.1

Cannavale, C., Claudio, L., & Koroleva, D. (2025). Digitalisation and artificial intelligence development: A cross-country analysis. *European Journal of Innovation Management*, *28*(11), 112–130. DOI: 10.1108/EJIM-07-2024-0828

Carrasco-Sáez, J. L., Contreras-Saavedra, C., San-Martín-Quiroga, S., Contreras-Saavedra, C. E., & Viveros-Muñoz, R. (2025). Analyzing Higher Education Students' Prompting Techniques and Their Impact on *ChatGPT*'s Performance: An Exploratory Study in Spanish. *Applied Sciences (Basel, Switzerland)*, *15*(14), 7651. DOI: 10.3390/app15147651

Casañ Núñez, J. (2017). Testing audiovisual comprehension tasks with questions embedded in videos as subtitles: A pilot multimethod study. *The EUROCALL Review*, *25*(1), 36–60. DOI: 10.4995/eurocall.2017.7062

Casheekar, A., Lahiri, A., Rath, K., Prabhakar, K. S., & Srinivasan, K. (2024). A contemporary review on chatbots, AI-powered virtual conversational agents, *ChatGPT*: Applications, open challenges and future research directions. *Computer Science Review*, *52*, 100632. DOI: 10.1016/j.cosrev.2024.100632

Cecilio-Fernandes, D., & Sandars, J. (2025). The hallucination of learning with generative artificial intelligence. *Medical Teacher*, *47*(12), 2057–2058. DOI: 10.1080/0142159X.2025.2531812 PMID: 40638506

Celik, H. (2018). A CLOSER LOOK INTO AN ESP COURSE THROUGH STUDENTS'END-OF-COURSE EVALUATIONS: A CASE STUDY. *Journal of Teaching English for Specific and Academic Purposes*, *6*(1), 125–139. DOI: 10.22190/JTESAP1801125C

Chan, C. K. Y. (2025). Students' perceptions of "AI-giarism": Investigating changes in understandings of academic misconduct. *Education and Information Technologies*, *30*(6), 8087–8108. DOI: 10.1007/s10639-024-13151-7

Chapelle, C. (1998). Multimedia CALL: Lessons to be learned from research on instructed SLA. *Language Learning & Technology*, *2*(1), 22–34. DOI: 10.64152/10125/25030

Chapelle, C. (2001). *Computer applications in second language acquisition*. Cambridge University Press. DOI: 10.1017/CBO9781139524681

Chapelle, C. (2007). Technology and second language acquisition. *Annual Review of Applied Linguistics*, *27*, 98–114. DOI: 10.1017/S0267190508070050

Chapelle, C. A. (2009). The relationship between second language acquisition theory and computer-assisted language learning. *Modern Language Journal*, *93*(s1), 741–753. DOI: 10.1111/j.1540-4781.2009.00970.x

Chapelle, C. A. (2014). *English Language Learning and Technology*. John Benjamins.

Chatzikoumi, E. (2020). How to evaluate machine translation: A review of automated and human metrics. *Natural Language Engineering*, *26*(2), 137–161. DOI: 10.1017/S1351324919000469

Chavous, K. P. (Host). (2024, May 22). Why is storytelling important for children? [Podcast episode No. 155]. In *WIWTK Podcast*. https://youtu.be/e82LWWhX4OQ?si=fbDywXTJMwGJkKc9

Chen, C. F. E., & Cheng, W. Y. E. C. (2008). Beyond the design of automated writing evaluation: Pedagogical practices and perceived learning effectiveness in EFL writing classes.

Chen, H. (2017). Developing a speaking practice website by using automatic speech recognition technology. In *Emerging Technologies for Education* (pp. 671–676). DOI: 10.1007/978-3-319-52836-6_71

Chen, W. Y. (2024). Intelligent tutor: Leveraging chatgpt and microsoft copilot studio to deliver a generative ai student support and feedback system within teams. *arXiv preprint arXiv:2405*.13024.

Chen, C., & Gong, Y. (2025). The role of AI-assisted learning in academic writing: A mixed-methods study on Chinese as a second language students. *Education Sciences*, *15*(2), 141. DOI: 10.3390/educsci15020141

Chen, S., Wang, W., Chen, X., Zhang, M., Lu, P., Li, X., & Du, Y. (2025). Enhancing Chinese comprehension and reasoning for large language models: An efficient LoRA fine-tuning and tree of thoughts framework. *The Journal of Supercomputing*, *81*(1), 50. DOI: 10.1007/s11227-024-06499-7

Cheung, S. K., Kwok, L. F., Phusavat, K., & Yang, H. H. (2021). Shaping the future learning environments with smart elements: Challenges and opportunities. *International Journal of Educational Technology in Higher Education*, *18*(1), 16. DOI: 10.1186/s41239-021-00254-1 PMID: 34778521

Chiaro, D. (2020). Humour translation in the digital age. In Dore, M. (Ed.), *Humour Translation in the Age of Multimedia* (pp. 10–30). Routledge., DOI: 10.4324/9780429316081-2

Chiu, T. K. (2022). School learning support for teacher technology integration from a self-determination theory perspective. *Educational Technology Research and Development*, *70*(3), 931–949. DOI: 10.1007/s11423-022-10096-x PMID: 35228784

Chomsky, N. (1965). *Aspects of the Theory of Syntax*. M.I.T. Press.

Chowdhury, G. U. A., & Mishu, A. (2019). *Literature in EFL: A gateway to a successful teaching–learning experience by stimulating human psyche*. Arab World English Journal (Special Issue: The Dynamics of EFL in the Arab World). https://doi.org/DOI: 10.24093/awej/efl1.18

Chowdhury, G. A. J., Koka, N. A., & Mishu, A. (2025). Bridging or dividing? Chinese language integration and the resilience of ELT in Saudi higher education under Vision 2030: Policy symbolism vs. pedagogical realities. *World Journal of English Language*, *16*(2), 309–323. DOI: 10.5430/wjel.v16n2p309

CIVIS Alliance. (2026). *Blended Intensive Programmes (BIPs) strategic guide and implementation outcomes 2024-2025*. CIVIS Alliance.

Clifford, R., & Granoien, N. (2008). Applications of technology to language acquisition processes. In M. Holland & F. Fisher (Eds.), *The path of speech technologies in CALL* (pp. 25–43). Routledge.

Cochran-Smith, M., & Lytle, S. (1993). *Inside/outside: Teacher research and knowledge*. Teachers College Press.

Cope, B., & Kalantzis, M. (2009). Multiliteracies: New Literacies, New Learning. *Pedagogies*, *4*(3), 164–195. DOI: 10.1080/15544800903076044

Cope, B., & Kalantzis, M. (2015). *A Pedagogy of Multiliteracies: Learning by design*. Palgrave and Macmillan. DOI: 10.1057/9781137539724

Cope, B., & Kalantzis, M. (Eds.). (2000). *Multiliteracies: Literacy Learning and the Design of Social Futures*. Routledge.

Corder, S. (1971). The significance of learners' error. *International Journal of Applied Linguistics*, *5*(1), 161–170.

Council of Europe, & UNESCO (1997). *Convention on the recognition of qualifications concerning higher education in the European region (Lisbon Recognition Convention)*. Council of Europe Publishing.

Creely, E. (2024). Exploring the role of generative AI in enhancing language learning: Opportunities and challenges. *International Journal of Changes in Education*, *1*(3), 158–167. DOI: 10.47852/bonviewIJCE42022495

Cress, U., & Kimmerle, J. (2023). Collective knowledge construction in computer-supported collaborative learning. *International Journal of Computer-Supported Collaborative Learning*, *18*(1), 1–10. DOI: 10.1007/s11412-023-09409-w

Creswell, J. (2014). Research design : Qualitative, quantitative, and mixed methods approaches. *Sage (Atlanta, Ga.)*.

Creswell, J. W., & Creswell, J. D. (2017). *Research design: Qualitative, quantitative, and mixed methods approaches*. Sage publications.

Creswell, J. W., & Poth, C. N. (2016). *Qualitative inquiry and research design: Choosing among five approaches*. Sage Publications.

Cucchiarini, C., Neri, A., & Strik, H. (2009). Oral proficiency training in Dutch L2: The contribution of ASR-based corrective feedback. *Speech Communication*, *51*(10), 853–863. DOI: 10.1016/j.specom.2009.03.003

Curry, N., Cushing-Leubner, J., Gray, J., & McNamara, T. (2025). A question of alignment AI, GenAI and applied linguistics. *Annual Review of Applied Linguistics*, *45*, 315–336. DOI: 10.1017/S0267190525000017

Daems, J., Vandepitte, S., Hartsuiker, R. J., & Macken, L. (2017). Identifying the machine translation error types with the greatest impact on post-editing effort. *Frontiers in Psychology*, *8*, 1282. DOI: 10.3389/fpsyg.2017.01282 PMID: 28824482

Dai, D. W., Zhu, H., & Chen, G. (2025). How does interaction with LLM powered chatbots shape human understanding of culture? The need for Critical Interactional Competence. *Annual Review of Applied Linguistics*, *45*, 28–49. DOI: 10.1017/S0267190525000054

Dara, D., Soomro, A. G., Ny, S., Hong, C. K., & Elshamy, E. (2024). Exploring Communicative Competence: Definitions, Advancements, and Implementations across Disciplines. *AITU Scientific Research Journal*, *3*(2). Advance online publication. DOI: 10.63094/AITUSRJ.24.3.2.2

Darcy, I. (2018). Powerful and effective pronunciation instruction: How can we achieve it? *The CATESOL Journal*, *30*(1), 13–45. DOI: 10.5070/B5.35963

Davis, F. D. (1989). Perceived usefulness, perceived ease of use, and user acceptance of information technology. *Management Information Systems Quarterly*, *13*(3), 319–340. DOI: 10.2307/249008

Davis, N., Clemens, M., Rezwana, J., & Browne, E. (2025). Human-AI co-creation: A new interaction paradigm for human-AI interaction. In Xu, W. (Ed.), *Handbook of Human-Centered Artificial Intelligence* (pp. 1–57). Springer Nature., DOI: 10.1007/978-981-97-8440-0_76-1

de Andrés-Sánchez, J., & Gené-Albesa, J. (2024). Assessing Attitude and Behavioral Intention toward Chatbots in an Insurance Setting: A Mixed Method Approach. *International Journal of Human-Computer Interaction*, *40*(17), 4918–4933. DOI: 10.1080/10447318.2023.2227833

De Meo, A., Vitale, M., Pettorino, M., Cutugno, F., & Origlia, A. (2012). Imitation/self-imitation in computer-assisted prosody training for Chinese learners of L2 Italian. *Proceedings of the 4th Pronunciation in Second Language Learning and Teaching Conference*, 90–10.

Deci, E. L., & Ryan, R. M. (1985). *Intrinsic motivation and self-determination in human behavior*. Springer., DOI: 10.1007/978-1-4899-2271-7

Deci, E. L., & Ryan, R. M. (1985). The general causality orientations scale: Self-determination in personality. *Journal of Research in Personality*, *19*(2), 109–134. DOI: 10.1016/0092-6566(85)90023-6

Deep, P. D., & Chen, Y. (2025). The Role of AI in Academic Writing: Impacts on Writing Skills, Critical Thinking, and Integrity in Higher Education. *Societies (Basel, Switzerland)*, *15*(9), 247. DOI: 10.3390/soc15090247

Dekhakhena, A. (2025). AI-Powered Personalized Learning in EFL Acquisition: Exploring Adaptive Instruction and Feedback Systems. *Journal of Studies in Language* [JSLCS]. *Cultura e Scuola*, *8*(1), 111–131.

Despujol Zabala, I. (2024). ChatGPT Hacer chatbots con POE.COM | 16/37 | UPV Universitat Politècnica de València [Vídeo]. YouTube: https://www.youtube.com/watch?v=DB2b5mgH6CE

Devlin, J., Chang, M. W., Lee, K., & Toutanova, K. (2019). BERT: Pre-training of deep bidirectional transformers for language understanding. *Proceedings of NAACL-HLT*, *2019*, 4171–4186.

Dewey, J. (1913). *Interest and effort in education.* Houghton Mifflin., DOI: 10.1037/14633-000

Dokukina, I., & Gumanova, J. (2020). The rise of chatbots–new personal assistants in foreign language learning. *Procedia Computer Science*, *169*, 542–546. DOI: 10.1016/j.procs.2020.02.212

Dombi, J., Sydorenko, T., & Timpe-Laughlin, V. (2024). Openings and closings in human-human versus human-spoken dialogue system conversations. *Language Learning & Technology*, *28*(2), 30–58. DOI: 10.64152/10125/73571

Doughty, C., & Williams, J. (1998). Pedagogical choices in focus on form. In Doughty, C., & Williams, J. (Eds.), *Focus on form in classroom second language acquisition* (pp. 197–261). Cambridge University Press.

Draxler, F., Werner, A., Lehmann, F., Hoppe, M., Schmidt, A., Buschek, D., & Welsch, R. (2024). The AI ghostwriter effect: When users do not perceive ownership of AI-generated text but self-declare as authors. *ACM Transactions on Computer-Human Interaction, 31*(2), 1–40. DOI: 10.1145/3637875

Duolingo. (2023). *How Duolingo works.* https://www.duolingo.com

Dupuy, B., & Hashemi, T. (2025). Infographics by Design: Beginning French Learners' Multimodal Composition and Authorial Agency. In Reyes Torres, A., Brisk, M. E., & Lacorte, M. (Eds.), *Multiliteracies, Multimodality, and Learning by Design in Second Language Learning and Teacher Education* (pp. 67–85). Routledge. DOI: 10.4324/9781032620497-7

Du, Q. (2025). How artificially intelligent conversational agents influence EFL learners' self-regulated learning and retention. *Education and Information Technologies, 30*(15), 1–67. DOI: 10.1007/s10639-025-13602-9

Egan, K. (1986). *Teaching as storytelling: An alternative approach to teaching and curriculum in the elementary school.* University of Chicago Press.

Egdom, G. W. (2020). A turn to ergonomics in translator and interpreter training. *The Interpreter and Translator Trainer, 14*(4), 363–368. Advance online publication. DOI: 10.1080/1750399X.2020.1846930

Ellis, R. (2003). Designing a task-based syllabus. *RELC Journal, 34*(1), 64–81. DOI: 10.1177/003368820303400105

Ellis, R. (2009). Corrective feedback and teacher development. *Journal of Linguistics and Language Teaching, 1*(1), 3–18. DOI: 10.5070/L2.V1I1.9054

ENHANCE Alliance. (2019). *ENHANCE alliance mission and vision.* https://enhanceuniversity.eu

ENHANCE Alliance. (2023). *ENHANCE Alliance documentation and institutional data on Blended Intensive Programmes (BIPs).* https://enhanceuniversity.eu/resources

ENHANCE Alliance. (2023). *ENHANCE annual report 2023.* https://enhanceuniversity.eu

ENHANCE Alliance. (2024). *ENHANCE alliance strategy and achievements report.* https://enhanceuniversity.eu

Erdogan, N., & Christina, K. (2025). Integrating AI in language learning: Boosting pragmatic competence for young English learners. *LatIA, 3*, 115. DOI: 10.62486/latia2025115

European Commission. (2024). *When is a data protection impact assessment (DPIA) required?* https://commission.europa.eu/law/law-topic/data-protection/rules-business-and-organisations/obligations/when-data-protection-impact-assessment-dpia-required_en

European Commission. (2024, March 26). *European universities initiative: Facts and figures*. https://education.ec.europa.eu

European Commission. (2025). *Artificial Intelligence Act: Timeline and phased implementation overview*. European Commission, Directorate-General for Communications Networks, Content and Technology. https://digital-strategy.ec.europa.eu

European Commission. (2025). *Erasmus+ annual report 2025*. Publications Office of the European Union.

European Commission. (2025). *Ethical guidelines on the use of artificial intelligence and data in teaching and learning for educators*. Publications Office of the European Union.

European Commission. (2025). *Guidelines for providers of general-purpose AI models*. GPAI.

European Commission. (2025). *Implementation timeline and compliance guidance for the Artificial Intelligence Act*. Publications Office of the European Union.

European Data Protection Board. (2020). *Guidelines 05/2020 on consent under Regulation 2016/679 (Version 1.1)*. https://www.edpb.europa.eu

European Data Protection Board. (2020). *Guidelines 07/2020 on the concepts of controller and processor in the GDPR (Version 2.0)*. https://edpb.europa.eu

European Data Protection Board. (2020). *Guidelines on the concepts of controller and processor in the GDPR (Version 2.0)*. https://edpb.europa.eu/our-work-tools/our-documents/guidelines/guidelines-072020-concepts-controller-processor-gdpr-version-20_en

European Data Protection Board. (2023). *Guidelines 01/2023 on data protection impact assessment (DPIA) and determining whether processing is "likely to result in a high risk" for the purposes of Regulation (EU) 2016/679*. https://www.edpb.europa.eu

European Data Protection Board. (2023). *Guidelines 01/2023 on processing of personal data in the context of administrative public services* (Version 1.0). https://edpb.europa.eu

European Data Protection Board. (2023). *Guidelines on data protection by design and by default (Article 25 GDPR).* https://www.edpb.europa.eu

European Data Protection Board. (2024). *Opinion 28/2024 on certain data protection aspects related to the processing of personal data in the context of AI models.* https://www.edpb.europa.eu/our-work-tools/our-documents/opinion-board-art-64/opinion-282024-certain-data-protection-aspects_en

European Data Protection Board. (2024b). *Guidelines on the processing of personal data in the context of AI systems* (latest version). https://www.edpb.europa.eu

European Data Protection Board. (2024b). *Opinion 28/2024 on certain data protection aspects related to the processing of personal data in the context of AI models.* https://www.edpb.europa.eu

European Parliament & Council of the European Union. (2016). Regulation (EU) 2016/679 of the European Parliament and of the Council of 27 April 2016 on the protection of natural persons with regard to the processing of personal data and on the free movement of such data (General Data Protection Regulation). *Official Journal of the European Union, L, 119*, 1–88. https://eur-lex.europa.eu

European Parliament & Council of the European Union. (2024). *Regulation (EU) 2024/1689 of the European Parliament and of the Council laying down harmonised rules on artificial intelligence (Artificial Intelligence Act). Official Journal of the European Union.* https://eur-lex.europa.eu

European Parliament and Council of the European Union. (2024). *Regulation (EU) 2024/1689 of 13 June 2024 laying down harmonised rules on artificial intelligence (Artificial Intelligence Act). Official Journal of the European Union.* https://eur-lex.europa.eu/eli/reg/2024/1689/oj

European Parliament Research Service. (2025). *European universities alliances: State of play and future perspectives.* European Parliament.

European Parliament. (2024, March 8). *Artificial Intelligence Act: MEPs adopt landmark law.* European Parliament News. https://www.europarl.europa.eu/news/en/press-room/20240308IPR19015/artificial-intelligence-act-meps-adopt-landmark-law

European Students' Union. (2019). *Bologna with student eyes 2018.* European Students' Union.

European Union (2016). *Regulation (EU) 2016/679 of the European Parliament and of the Council of 27 April 2016 on the protection of natural persons with regard to the processing of personal data and on the free movement of such data (General Data Protection Regulation).* Official Journal of the European Union, L119, 1–88. https://eur-lex.europa.eu/eli/reg/2016/679/oj

European Union (2024). *Annex III to Regulation (EU) 2024/1689: High-risk AI systems referred to in Article 6(2).* In *Artificial Intelligence Act.* Official Journal of the European Union.

European Union (2024). *Regulation (EU) 2024/1689 of the European Parliament and of the Council laying down harmonised rules on artificial intelligence (Artificial Intelligence Act).* Official Journal of the European Union. https://eur-lex.europa.eu

European Union. (2024). Regulation (EU) 2024/1689 (Artificial Intelligence Act). EUR-Lex (ELI: https://data.europa.eu/eli/reg/2024/1689/oj

European University Association. (2026). *Artificial intelligence in European universities: Governance, strategy and responsible implementation.* European University Association.

Eurydice (2025). *The European higher education area in 2025: Bologna process implementation report.* Publications Office of the European Union.

Evers, K., & Chen, S. (2021). Effects of Automatic Speech Recognition Software on pronunciation for adults with different learning styles. *Journal of Educational Computing Research, 59*(4), 669–685. DOI: 10.1177/0735633120972011

Fantinuoli, C. (2018). Interpreting and technology: The upcoming technological turn. In Fantinuoli, C. (Ed.), *Interpreting and technology* (pp. 1–12). Language Science Press., DOI: 10.5281/zenodo.1493289

Fathi, H., Sharifi, A., & Ahmadi, H. (2025). Empowering Students with Innovative AI-Language Learning Tools and Pedagogy to Master Speaking Skills. *Iranian Journal of Applied Language Studies, 17*(1), 197–220. DOI: 10.22111/ijals.2024.48157.2432

Fathi, J., & Rahimi, M. (2024). Utilising artificial intelligence-enhanced writing mediation to develop academic writing skills in EFL learners: A qualitative study. *Computer Assisted Language Learning, 39*(1–2), 263–302. DOI: 10.1080/09588221.2024.2374772

Fathi, J., Rahimi, M., & Derakhshan, A. (2024). Improving EFL learners' speaking skills and willingness to communicate via artificial intelligence-mediated interactions. *System, 121*, 103254. DOI: 10.1016/j.system.2024.103254

Feng, H. H., & Chukharev-Hudilainen, E. (2022). Genre-based AWE system for engineering graduate writing: Development and evaluation.

Fernández-Ferrer, M. (Ed.). (2023). *Chatbots en educación. Tendencias actuales y desafíos futuros*. LMI.

Ferreiro-Santamaria, G. (2024). Exploring the role of *ChatGPT* in English teaching within higher education settings. *International Journal of Trends and Developments in Education*, *4*(1), 44–58. DOI: 10.5281/zenodo.11204781

Field, A. (2024). Discovering statistics using IBM SPSS statistics. Sage publications limited.

FIT. (2024). *Position paper on the use of AI in interpreting. AFTI. (2025).* Conference Interpreting in the Age of AI.

Flexner, S., & Hauck, L. (1988). *Random House Dictionary of the English Language*. Random House.

Foote, J., & Trofimovich, P. (2018). Second language pronunciation learning: An overview of theoretical perspectives. In Kang, O., Thomson, R. I., & Murphy, J. (Eds.), *The Routledge Handbook of Contemporary English Pronunciation* (pp. 75–90). Routledge.

Freire, P. (1970). *Pedagogy of the Oppressed.* Continuum.

Freitag, M., Foster, G., Grangier, D., Ratnakar, V., Tan, Q., & Macherey, W. (2021). Experts, errors, and context: A large-scale study of human evaluation for machine translation. *Transactions of the Association for Computational Linguistics*, *9*, 1460–1474. DOI: 10.1162/tacl_a_00437

Fryer, L. K., & Carpenter, R. (2006). Bots as language learning tools. *Language Learning & Technology*, *10*(3), 8–14. DOI: 10.64152/10125/44068

García-López, C., Tabuenca-Cuevas, M., & Navarro-Soria, I. (2025). A systematic review of the use of AI in EFL and EL classrooms for gifted students. *Trends in Higher Education*, *4*(3), 33. DOI: 10.3390/higheredu4030033

Gebru, T., Morgenstern, J., Vecchione, B., Vaughan, J. W., Wallach, H., Iii, H. D., & Crawford, K. (2021). Datasheets for datasets. *Communications of the ACM*, *64*(12), 86–92. DOI: 10.1145/3458723

Gee, J. P. (2014). *An introduction to discourse analysis: Theory and method* (4th ed.). Routledge., DOI: 10.4324/9781315819679

Gibbs, R. W. (1994). *The poetics of mind: Figurative thought, language, and understanding*. Cambridge University Press.

Gile, D. (2009). *Basic concepts and models for interpreter and translator training* (Rev. ed.). John Benjamins. JBE PlatformDOI: 10.1075/btl.8

Gilmore, A. (2007). Authentic materials and authenticity in foreign language learning. *Language Teaching, 40*(2), 97–118. DOI: 10.1017/S0261444807004144

Ginovart Cid, C., Colominas, C., & Oliver, A. (2020). *Language industry views on the profile of the post-editor*. Translation Spaces., DOI: 10.1075/ts.19010.cid

Gliem, J. A., & Gliem, R. R. (2003). Calculating, interpreting, and reporting Cronbach's alpha reliability coefficient for Likert-type scales. Midwest research-to-Practice Conference in Adult, Continuing, and community education.

Godwin-Jones, R. (2023). Emerging spaces for language learning: AI bots, ambient intelligence, and the metaverse. *Language Learning & Technology, 27*(2), 6–27. DOI: 10.64152/10125/73501

Godwin-Jones, R. (2024). Distributed agency in language learning and teaching through generative AI. *Language Learning & Technology, 28*(2), 5–30. DOI: 10.64152/10125/73570

Goldshtein, M., Alhashim, A. G., & Roscoe, R. D. (2024). An NLP-Based Exploration of Variance in Student Writing and Syntax: Implications for Automated Writing Evaluation. *Computers, 13*(7), 160. DOI: 10.3390/computers13070160

Golonka, E. M., Bowles, A. R., Frank, V. M., Richardson, D. L., & Freynik, S. (2014). Technologies for foreign language learning: A review of technology types and their effectiveness. *Computer Assisted Language Learning, 27*(1), 70–105. DOI: 10.1080/09588221.2012.700315

Google. (2025, December). Gemini-powered improvements for Google Translate (announcement). (Taylor & Francis Online)

Gruba, P. (1999). *The role of digital video in second language listening*. Unpublished PhD Thesis, University of Melbourne.

Gruba, P., & Hinkelman, D. (2012). *Blending technologies in second language classrooms*. Palgrave Macmillan. DOI: 10.1057/9780230356825

Guba, E. G., & Lincoln, Y. S. (1994). Competing paradigms in qualitative research. In K. Lincoln & Y. S. Denzin (Eds.), *Handbook of qualitative research* (pp. 105–118). Sage.

Guerreiro, N. M., Karpinska, M., Song, H., Freitag, M., Rei, R., & Martins, A. F. T. (2024). xCOMET: Transparent machine translation evaluation through fine-grained error detection. *Transactions of the Association for Computational Linguistics*, *12*, 979–995. Advance online publication. DOI: 10.1162/tacl_a_00683

Guo, K., Li, Y., Li, Y., & Chu, S. K. W. (2024). Understanding EFL students' use of self-made AI chatbots as personalized writing assistance tools: A mixed methods study. *Education and Information Technologies*, *29*, 1–20. DOI: 10.1007/s10639-023-12230-5

Gu, W., & Yu, Z. (2025). A bibliometric analysis of the application of AI chatbots in language learning contexts. *Quality & Quantity*, *59*(1), 639–661. DOI: 10.1007/s11135-024-01946-2

Habib, M. U., Sattar, A., Iqbal, M. J., & Saleem, S. (2025). AI Driven Tutoring vs. Human Teachers Examining the on Student Teacher Relationship. *Review of Applied Management and Social Sciences*, *8*(1), 363–374. Advance online publication. DOI: 10.47067/ramss.v8i1.466

Hago Elmahdi, O. E. (2024). AI's Role in EFL: Optimizing Opportunities while Mitigating Risks. *International Journal of Linguistics. Literature & Translation*, *7*(10), 21–37. Advance online publication. DOI: 10.32996/ijllt.2024.7.10.4

Halim, T., Wahid, R., & Halim, S. (2021). EFL students' attitudes toward corrective feedback: A study conducted at undergraduate level. *Saudi Journal of Language Studies*, *1*(1), 40–49. DOI: 10.1108/SJLS-03-2021-0004

Hall, E. T. (1976). *Beyond culture*. Anchor Press/Doubleday.

Hamdi, S. A. (2018). *The impact of ideology on lexical borrowing in Arabic: A synergy of corpus linguistics and CDA* (Doctoral dissertation, The University of New Mexico).

Hamdi, S., Hashem, R., Holbah, W., Azi, Y., & Mohammed, S. (2023). Proverbs translation for intercultural interaction: A comparative study between Arabic and English using artificial intelligence. *World Journal of English Language*, *13*(7), 282. DOI: 10.5430/wjel.v13n7p282

Hansen, A., Klute, R. M., Yadav, M., Bansal, S., & Bond, W. F. (2024). How Do Learners Receive Feedback on Note Writing? A Scoping Review. *Academic Medicine*, *99*(6), 683–690. DOI: 10.1097/ACM.0000000000005653 PMID: 38306581

Haristiani, N. (2019). Artificial Intelligence (AI) chatbot as language learning medium: An inquiry. *Journal of Physics: Conference Series*, *1387*(1), 012020. DOI: 10.1088/1742-6596/1387/1/012020

Harmer, J. (2001). *The practice of English language teaching*. Longman.

Hattie, J., & Timperley, H. (2007). The power of feedback. *Review of Educational Research*, *77*(1), 81–112. DOI: 10.3102/003465430298487

Hayashi, K., & Sato, T. (2024). The Effectiveness of ChatGPT in Enhancing English Language Proficiency and Reducing Second Language Anxiety (L2). *WorldCALL Official Conference Proceedings*. https://doi.org/DOI: 10.22492/issn.2759-1182.2023.23

Haynes, S. N., Richard, D., & Kubany, E. S. (1995). Content validity in psychological assessment: A functional approach to concepts and methods. *Psychological Assessment*, *7*(3), 238–247. DOI: 10.1037/1040-3590.7.3.238

Heil, C., Wu, J., Lee, J., & Schmidt, T. (2016). A review of mobile language learning applications: Trends, challenges, and opportunities. *The EuroCALL Review*, *24*(2), 32–50. DOI: 10.4995/eurocall.2016.6402

Hendy, A.. (2023). How good are GPT models at machine translation? A comprehensive evaluation. *Proceedings of the 61st Annual Meeting of the Association for Computational Linguistics*, 1910–1931.

Hew, K. F., Huang, W., Du, J., & Jia, C. (2023). Using chatbots to support student goal setting and social presence in fully online activities: Learner engagement and perceptions. *Journal of Computing in Higher Education*, *35*(1), 40–68. DOI: 10.1007/s12528-022-09338-x PMID: 36101883

Heylen, K., & De Hertog, D. (2015). Automatic term extraction. In Kockaert, H. J., & Steurs, F. (Eds.), *Handbook of Terminology* (Vol. 1). John Benjamins., DOI: 10.1075/hot.1.aut1

Hidayat-ur-Rehman, I. (2024). Examining AI competence, chatbot use and perceived autonomy as drivers of students' engagement in informal digital learning. *Journal of Research in Innovative Teaching & Learning*, *17*(2), 196–212. DOI: 10.1108/JRIT-05-2024-0136

Holes, C. (2004). *Modern Arabic: Structures, functions, and varieties* (Rev. ed.). Georgetown University Press.

Holes, C. (2011). Language and identity in the Arabian Gulf. *Journal of Arabic and Islamic Studies*, *11*, 129–154.

Horwitz, E. K. (2001). Language anxiety and achievement. *Annual Review of Applied Linguistics*, *21*, 112–126. DOI: 10.1017/S0267190501000071

Horwitz, E. K., Horwitz, M. B., & Cope, J. (1986). Foreign language classroom anxiety. *Modern Language Journal, 70*(2), 125–132. DOI: 10.1111/j.1540-4781.1986.tb05256.x

Hsieh, C.-N. (2024). Mobile-assisted language learning (MALL). In *The TESOL encyclopedia of English language teaching*. Wiley., DOI: 10.1002/9781118784235.eelt1053

Huang, W., Hew, K. F., & Fryer, L. K. (2022). Chatbots for language learning—Are they really useful? A systematic review of chatbot-supported language learning. *Journal of Computer Assisted Learning, 38*(1), 237–257. DOI: 10.1111/jcal.12610

Huang, W., Jia, C., Hew, K. F., & Guo, J. (2024). Using chatbots to support EFL listening decoding skills in a fully online environment. *Language Learning & Technology, 28*(2), 62–90. DOI: 10.64152/10125/73572

Huang, X., Zou, D., Cheng, G., Chen, X., & Xie, H. (2023). Trends, research issues and applications of artificial intelligence in language education. *Journal of Educational Technology & Society, 26*(1), 112–131. DOI: 10.30191/ETS.202301_26(1).0009

Huesca, G., Martínez-Treviño, Y., Molina-Espinosa, J. M., Sanromán-Calleros, A. R., Martínez-Román, R., Cendejas-Castro, E. A., & Bustos, R. (2024). Effectiveness of using ChatGPT as a tool to strengthen benefits of the flipped learning strategy. *Education Sciences, 14*(6), 660. DOI: 10.3390/educsci14060660

Hutchins, E. (1995). *Cognition in the wild.* MIT Press. DOI: 10.7551/mitpress/1881.001.0001

Hutchins, W. J. (1995). Machine translation: A brief history. In Koerner, E. F. K., & Asher, R. E. (Eds.), *Concise history of the language sciences* (pp. 431–445). Pergamon., DOI: 10.1016/B978-0-08-042580-1.50066-0

Hwang, H.-C., A., Vera Liao, Q., Blodgett S. L., Olteanu, A., Trischler, A. (2025). "*"It was 80% me, 20% AI": Seeking Authenticity in Co-Writing with Large Language Models"*. In *Proceedings of the ACM on Human-Computer Interaction*, Vol. 9, issue 2, pp. 1-41. DOI: 10.1145/3711020

Hwang, Y., & Lee, J. H. (2025). "Exploring student's experiences and perceptions of human-AI collaboration in digital content making". In *International Journal of Educational Technology in Higher Education. https://doi.org/*DOI: 10.1186/s41239-025-00542-

Hwang, Y., & Lee, J. H. (2025). Exploring students' experiences and perceptions of human-AI collaboration in digital content making. *International Journal of Educational Technology in Higher Education, 22*(1), 44. DOI: 10.1186/s41239-025-00542-0

Hymes, D. (1966). *Two types of linguistic relativity". Sociolinguistics*. Mouton.

Hymes, D. (1972). *On Communicative Competence. Sociolinguistics, edited by J. B. Pride and Janet Holmes, 269–93*. Penguin Books.

Imran, M., Almusharraf, N., Abdellatif, M. S., & Abbasova, M. Y. (2024). Artificial intelligence in higher education: Enhancing learning systems and transforming educational paradigms.

Imran, M., & Almusharraf, N. (2024). Google Gemini as a next generation AI educational tool: A review of emerging educational technology. *Smart Learning Environments, 11*(1), 22. DOI: 10.1186/s40561-024-00310-z

International Federation of Translators (FIT). (2024, August). Position paper on the use of AI in interpreting.

International Organization for Standardization (ISO). (2022). ISO 23155:2022 Interpreting services Conference interpreting Requirements and recommendations. https://www.iso.org/standard/74749.html (ISO)

International Organization for Standardization. (2017). *ISO 18587:2017 Translation servicesPost-editing of machine translation outputRequirements*. https://www.iso.org/standard/62970.html (ISO)

Jara Chiriboga, S. P., Troncoso Burgos, A. L., Ruiz Avila, M. M., Cosquillo Chida, J. L., Aldas Macias, K. J., Castro Morante, Y. E., & Bernal Párraga, A. P. (2025). Inteligencia Artificial y Aprendizaje Personalizado en Lenguas Extranjeras: Un Análisis de los Chatbots y los Asistentes Virtuales en Educación. *Revista Científica de Salud y Desarrollo Humano, 6*(1), 882–905. DOI: 10.61368/r.s.d.h.v6i1.515

Jarosz, A. (2023). Key aspects of pronunciation learning and teaching. In Sardegna, V. G., & Jarosz, A. (Eds.), *English pronunciation teaching: Theory, practice and research findings* (pp. 8–20). Channel View Publications.

Järvelä, S., Nguyen, A., & Hadwin, A. (2023). Human and artificial intelligence collaboration for socially shared regulation in learning. *British Journal of Educational Technology, 54*(5), 1057–1076. DOI: 10.1111/bjet.13325

Jegede, O. O. (2024). Artificial intelligence and English language learning: Exploring the roles of AI-driven tools in personalizing learning and providing instant feedback. *Universal Library of Languages and Literatures, 1*(2), 06–19. Advance online publication. DOI: 10.70315/uloap.ullli.2024.0102002

Jenkins, S. (2022). Higher Education in Saudi Arabia: A Vehicle for Global Promotion and Advancement. In *The Past, Present, and Future of Higher Education in the Arabian Gulf Region* (pp. 143-158). Routledge.

Jeya Santhi, V. (2024). Technology-enhanced language learning: Innovations and impact. In C. J. Fernandez, N. Kumar, & S. Gayathri S. (Eds.), *Bridging disciplines: Exploring multidisciplinary research frontiers* (pp. 199–208). Red Unicorn Publishing Pvt. Ltd.

Jiang, M., Jong, M., Lau, W., Chai, C., & Wu, N. (2021). Using automatic speech recognition technology to enhance EFL learners' oral language complexity in a flipped classroom. *Australasian Journal of Educational Technology*, *37*(2), 110–131. DOI: 10.14742/ajet.6798

Ji, H., Han, I., & Ko, Y. (2023). A systematic review of conversational AI in language education: Focusing on the collaboration with human teachers. *Journal of Research on Technology in Education*, *55*(1), 48–63. DOI: 10.1080/15391523.2022.2142873

Ji, H., Han, I., & Park, S. (2024). Teaching foreign language with conversational AI: Teacher-student-AI interaction. *Language Learning & Technology*, *28*(2), 91–108. DOI: 10.64152/10125/73573

Jiménez-Crespo, M. A. (2025). Human-centered AI and the future of translation technologies: What professionals think about control and autonomy in the AI era. *Information (Basel)*, *16*(5), 387. DOI: 10.3390/info16050387

Jinowat, N., Unapang, J., Kangsawiwat, T., & Sapai, P. (2024). Fostering Critical Writing Excellence: Leveraging Google Gemini and Collaborative Online Writing with Google Docs. *International Workshop on Learning Technology for Education in Cloud*.p. 349-363. https://doi.org/DOI: 10.1007/978-3-031-61678-5_25

Jusoh, S., & Kadir, R. A. (2025). Chatbot in education: Trends, personalization, and techniques. *Multimedia Tools and Applications*, *84*(30), 1–24. DOI: 10.1007/s11042-025-20659-8

Kaate, I., Salminen, J., Jung, S. G., Santos, J. M., Häyhänen, E., Xuan, T., Azem, J. Y., & Jansen, B. (2025). The 'fourth wall' and other usability issues in AI-generated personas: Comparing chat-based and profile personas. *Behaviour & Information Technology*, *44*(16), 4136–4152. DOI: 10.1080/0144929X.2025.2469659

Kahlerras, W., & Bennacer, F. (2025). AI-driven approaches to advance speaking proficiency in LMOOCS: Insights, innovations, and pedagogical implications. *Journal of Studies in Language* [JSLCS]. *Cultura e Scuola*, *8*(1), 226–251.

Kalantzis, M., & Cope, B. (2025). Multiliteracies Since Social Media and Artificial Intelligence. *Harvard Educational Review*, *95*(1), 135–151. DOI: 10.17763/1943-5045-95.1.135

Katsarou, E., Wild, F., Sougari, A., & Chatzipanagiotou, P. (2023). A Systematic Review of Voice-based Intelligent Virtual Agents in EFL Education. *International Journal of Emerging Technologies in Learning*, *18*(10), 65–85. DOI: 10.3991/ijet.v18i10.37723

Kavasakalis, A., & Gkiza, T. (2022). European higher education area, internationalization and students' mobility in 21st century. *Advances in Social Sciences Research Journal*, *9*(2), 60–74. DOI: 10.14738/assrj.92.11582

Kenworthy, J. (1987). *Teaching English pronunciation*. Longman.

Kern, R. (2000). *Literacy and Language Teaching*. Oxford University Press.

Khalaf, M. H. (2025). Diglossia challenges in Arabic translation: Navigating linguistic duality in contemporary translation practice. *Lark*, *17*(4), 1690–1663. DOI: 10.31185/lark.4478

Khine, M. S. (2024). AI in teaching and learning and intelligent tutoring systems. In *Artificial Intelligence in Education: A Machine-Generated Literature Overview* (pp. 467–570). Springer Nature Singapore. DOI: 10.1007/978-981-97-9350-1_4

Kim, Y. (2025). Automated Essay Scoring With GPT-4 for a Local Placement Test: Investigating Prompting Strategies, Intra-Rater Reliability, and Alignment With Human Scores. *TESOL Quarterly*, *59*(S1). Advance online publication. DOI: 10.1002/tesq.3405

Klein, S. H. (2025). The effects of human-like social cues on social responses towards text-based conversational agents: A meta-analysis. *Humanities & Social Sciences Communications*, *12*(1), 1322. DOI: 10.1057/s41599-025-05618-w

Knight, J. (2019). Internationalization of higher education: Past and future. *International Higher Education*, *95*, 2–4. DOI: 10.6017/ihe.2019.95.10715

Koehn, P., Och, F. J., & Marcu, D. (2003). Statistical phrase-based translation. In Proceedings of NAACL-HLT (pp. 127–133). Association for Computational Linguistics. https://doi:DOI: 10.3115/1073445.1073462

Komatsu, K., Ždanovič, N., Yamabe, M., Iwata, H., Iwamoto, M., & Takeda, S. (2026). The association between national culture and AI readiness: A cross-national study. *Frontiers in Artificial Intelligence*, *9*, 1727606. DOI: 10.3389/frai.2026.1727606 PMID: 41755913

Kong, X., Fang, H., Chen, W., & Zhang, M. (2025). Examining human–AI collaboration in hybrid intelligence learning environments: Human–AI synergy model and classroom evidence. *Humanities & Social Sciences Communications*, *12*, 821. Advance online publication. DOI: 10.1057/s41599-025-05097-z

Koo, T. K., & Li, M. Y. (2016). A guideline of selecting and reporting intraclass correlation coefficients for reliability research. *Journal of Chiropractic Medicine*, *15*(2), 155–163. DOI: 10.1016/j.jcm.2016.02.012 PMID: 27330520

Kot, S. O., & Nykyporets, S. S. (2024). *Utilization of artificial intelligence in enhancing English language proficiency in tertiary education. Science and Education in the Third Millennium: Information Technology*. Education, Law, Psychology, Social Sphere, Management.

Kourtali, N. E., & Borges, L. (2024). The effects of feedback timing on L2 development in written SCMC. *Computer Assisted Language Learning*, *37*(8), 2291–2319. DOI: 10.1080/09588221.2023.2171066

Kövecses, Z. (2005). *Metaphor in culture: Universality and variation*. Cambridge University Press. DOI: 10.1017/CBO9780511614408

Kövecses, Z. (2010). *Metaphor: A practical introduction* (2nd ed.). Oxford University Press.

Krashen, S. D. (1985). *The input hypothesis: Issues and implications*. Laredo Publishing.

KTH Royal Institute of Technology. (2026, January 27). *Considerations for using generative AI* [Guidelines for teachers on ethical and legal use of generative AI]. https://intra.kth.se/en/utbildning/systemstod/generativ-ai/riktlinjer-1.1405092

KTH Royal Institute of Technology. (2026, January 27). *Legal aspects of generative AI* [Overview of GDPR, copyright and AI Act considerations for teachers]. https://intra.kth.se/en/utbildning/systemstod/generativ-ai/legal-aspects-1.1253707

KTH Royal Institute of Technology. (2026, January 8). *FAQ generative AI* (see "Can I require students to use generative AI in my course?"). https://intra.kth.se/en/utbildning/e-larande/faqs/faq-generativ-ai-1.1417039

Kucer, S. B. (2014). *Dimensions of literacy: A conceptual base for teaching reading and writing in school settings* (4th ed.). Routledge. DOI: 10.4324/9780203428405

Kundu, A., & Bej, T. (2025). Transforming EFL teaching with AI: A systematic review of empirical studies. *International Journal of Artificial Intelligence in Education*, *35*(4), 1–34. DOI: 10.1007/s40593-025-00470-0

Lai, H., & Nissim, M. (2024). A survey on automatic generation of figurative language: From rule-based systems to large language models. *ACM Computing Surveys*, *56*(10), 1–34. DOI: 10.1145/3654795

Lakoff, G., & Johnson, M. (1980). *Metaphors we live by*. University of Chicago Press.

Lan, Y. J. (2025). Language Learning in the Metaverse: Research Trends, Opportunities, and Challenges. In Lan, Y. J., Qi, G. Y., & Chun, D. (Eds.), *AI-Mediated Language Education in the Metaverse Era. Chinese Language Learning Sciences*. Springer., DOI: 10.1007/978-981-95-0245-5_2

Larchen Costuchen, A., Reyes-Torres, A., & Tordera Yllescas, J. C. (2025). Analysis of movie trailers based on a WSH game prototype: Developing critical literacy in L2 students. In Gabonada Gatcho, A. R., Titar-Improgo, C. M., & Papadopoulos, I. (Eds.), *Literacy policies for equity and inclusion* (pp. 1–23). IGI Global., DOI: 10.4018/979-8-3693-8427-5.ch001

Larchen, A. (2020). From generation gap to generation lap: Gen Z subcultures. In Carrió Pastor, M. L., Periñán-Pascual, C., Romero Forteza, F., & Olmo Cazevieille, F. (Eds.), *Estudios de lingüística aplicada IV* (pp. 113–130). Editorial Universitat Politècnica de València.

Läubli, S., Sennrich, R., & Volk, M. (2020). Has machine translation achieved human parity? A case for document-level evaluation. *Proceedings of the 2018 Conference on Empirical Methods in Natural Language Processing*, 4791–4796.

Laurillard, D. (2002). *Rethinking University Teaching: A conversational framework*. Routledge. DOI: 10.4324/9780203160329

Lave, J., & Wenger, E. (1991). *Situated learning: Legitimate peripheral participation*. Cambridge University Press. DOI: 10.1017/CBO9780511815355

Leal Filho, W., Ribeiro, P. C. C., Mazutti, J., Lange Salvia, A., Bonato Marcolin, C., Lima Silva Borsatto, J. M., Sharifi, A., Sierra, J., Luetz, J., Pretorius, R., & Viera Trevisan, L. (2024). Using artificial intelligence to implement the UN sustainable development goals at higher education institutions. *International Journal of Sustainable Development and World Ecology*, *31*(6), 726–745. DOI: 10.1080/13504509.2024.2327584

Lee, A. V. Y. (2023). Supporting students' generation of feedback in large-scale online course with artificial intelligence-enabled evaluation. *Studies in Educational Evaluation*, *77*, 101250. Advance online publication. DOI: 10.1016/j.stueduc.2023.101250

Lee, A., & Lyster, R. (2017). Can corrective feedback on second language speech perception errors affect production accuracy? *Applied Psycholinguistics*, *38*(2), 371–393. DOI: 10.1017/S0142716416000254

Lee, D., & Palmer, E. (2025). Prompt engineering in higher education: A systematic review to help inform curricula. *International Journal of Educational Technology in Higher Education*, *22*(1), 7. DOI: 10.1186/s41239-025-00503-7

Lee, E. (2024). Prompting Progress: Authorship in the Age of AI. *SSRN*, *76*, 1–85. DOI: 10.2139/ssrn.4609687

Lee, H., & Lee, J. H. (2024). The effects of AI-guided individualized language learning: A meta-analysis. *Language Learning & Technology*, *28*(2), 134–162. DOI: 10.64152/10125/73575

Lee, J. H., Shin, D., & Hwang, Y. (2024). Investigating the capabilities of large language model-based task-oriented dialogue chatbots from a learner's perspective. *System*, *127*, 1–12. DOI: 10.1016/j.system.2024.103538

Legaspi, R., Xu, W., Konishi, T., Wada, S., Kobayashi, N., Naruse, Y., & Ishikawa, Y. (2024). The sense of agency in human–AI interactions. *Knowledge-Based Systems*, *295*, 111298. DOI: 10.1016/j.knosys.2023.111298

Lehka-Paul, O. (2020). Behavioural indicators of translators' decisional styles in a translation task: A longitudinal study. Yearbook of the Poznań Linguistic Meeting, 6, 81–111. DOI: 10.2478/yplm-2020-0007

Levy, M., & Hubbard, P. (2005). Why call CALL "CALL"? *Computer Assisted Language Learning*, *18*(3), 205–214. DOI: 10.1080/09588220500208884

Li, H., Xu, J., Cui, G., Guan, C., Mo, F., & Huang, K. (2025). Multilingual collaborative defense for large language models. In *Findings of the Association for Computational Linguistics: EMNLP 2025* (pp. 3735–3755). Association for Computational Linguistics. DOI: 10.18653/v1/2025.findings-emnlp.200

Liang, W., Yuksekgonul, M., Mao, Y., Wu, E., & Zou, J. (2023). GPT detectors are biased against non-native English writers. *Patterns (New York, N.Y.)*, *4*(7), 100779. Advance online publication. DOI: 10.1016/j.patter.2023.100779 PMID: 37521038

Lin, C. C., Huang, A. Y., & Lu, O. H. (2023). Artificial intelligence in intelligent tutoring systems toward sustainable education: a systematic review. *Smart learning environments, 10*(1), 41. https://doi.org/DOI: 10.1186/s40561-023-00260-y

Lin, C. C., Huang, A. Y., & Yang, S. J. (2023). A review of AI-driven conversational chatbots implementation methodologies and challenges (1999–2022). *Sustainability (Basel)*, *15*(5), 4012. DOI: 10.3390/su15054012

Lin, C. J., & Mubarok, H. (2021). Learning analytics for investigating the mind map-guided AI chatbot approach in an EFL flipped speaking classroom. *Journal of Educational Technology & Society*, *24*(4), 1635. 10.30191%2fETS.202110_24(4).0002

Li, T., & Chmiel, A. (2024). Automatic subtitles increase accuracy and decrease cognitive load in simultaneous interpreting. *Interpreting*, *26*(2), 253–281. DOI: 10.1075/intp.00111.li

Liu, E., Cui, C., Zheng, K., & Neubig, G. (2022). Testing the ability of language models to interpret figurative language. *Proceedings of NAACL, 2022*, 4437–4452. DOI: 10.18653/v1/2022.naacl-main.330

Liu, F., Jiang, Y., Lai, C., & Jin, T. (2024). Teacher engagement with automated text simplification for differentiated instruction. *Language Learning & Technology*, *28*(2), 1–25. DOI: 10.64152/10125/73576

Liu, G. L., Lee, J. S., & Zhao, X. (2025). Critical digital literacies, agentic practices, and AI-mediated informal digital learning of English. *System*, *103797*, 103797. Advance online publication. DOI: 10.1016/j.system.2025.103797

Liu, W., Jamaludin, K. A., Song, Z., & Song, Z. (2024). Implementation of technical communication pedagogy in higher education institutions: A systematic literature review. *International Journal of Learning. Teaching and Educational Research*, *23*(9), 307–324.

Li, Y., Shadiev, R., & Chiu, T. K. F. (2026). Applying Generative Artificial Intelligence to Task-based Language Teaching and Learning: A Systematic Review and Meta-analysis. *TechTrends*, *70*(1), 150–163. DOI: 10.1007/s11528-025-01140-7

Long, M. (1983). Native speaker/non-native speaker conversation and the negotiation of comprehensible input. *Applied Linguistics*, *4*(2), 126–141. DOI: 10.1093/applin/4.2.126

Long, M. H. (1996). The role of the linguistic environment in second language acquisition. In Ritchie, W. C., & Bhatia, T. K. (Eds.), *Handbook of second language acquisition* (pp. 413–468). Academic Press.

Lotman, Y., & Clark, W. (2005). On the semiosphere. *Sign Systems Studies*, *33*(1), 205–229. DOI: 10.12697/SSS.2005.33.1.09

Lukešová, A., & Jennings, P. J. (2025). Clue before correction: ChatGPT-enhanced strategy for promoting autonomous and reflective language learning. *Innovation in Language Learning and Teaching*, •••, 1–29. DOI: 10.1080/17501229.2025.2612532

Lund, B., Mannuru, N. R., Teel, Z. A., Lee, T. H., Ortega, N. J., Simmons, S., & Ward, E. (2025). "Student Perceptions of AI-Assisted Writing and Academic Integrity: Ethical Concerns, Academic Misconduct, and Use of Generative AI in Higher Education". In *AI in Education*, 1(1), 2. DOI: 10.3390/aieduc1010002

Lyhne, C. N., Thisted, J., & Bjerrum, M. (2025). Qualitative content analysis–framing the analytical process of inductive content analysis to develop a sound study design. *Quality & Quantity*, *59*(6), 1–21. DOI: 10.1007/s11135-025-02220-9

Maack, L. (2024). Redefining organizational digitality: A relational-ontological approach inspired by new materialism. *Frontiers in Sociology*, *9*, 1426930. Advance online publication. DOI: 10.3389/fsoc.2024.1426930 PMID: 39525273

Maalej, Z. (2004). Figurative language in anger expressions in Tunisian Arabic: An extended view of embodiment. *Metaphor and Symbol*, *19*(1), 51–75. DOI: 10.1207/S15327868MS1901_3

MacIntyre, P. D., Clément, R., Dörnyei, Z., & Noels, K. A. (1998). Conceptualizing willingness to communicate in a L2: A situational model of L2 confidence and affiliation. *Modern Language Journal*, *82*(4), 545–562. DOI: 10.1111/j.1540-4781.1998.tb05543.x

MacIntyre, P. D., & Gardner, R. C. (1994). The subtle effects of language anxiety on cognitive processing in the second language. *Language Learning*, *44*(2), 283–305. DOI: 10.1111/j.1467-1770.1994.tb01103.x

Ma, G., & Yang, X. (2025). Fostering Intercultural Competence Through AI-Driven Tools: A Case Study of Linguistic and Cultural Adaptability in Chinese EFL Education. *Digital Technologies Research and Applications*, *4*(1), 158–169. DOI: 10.54963/dtra.v4i1.1131

Mageira, K., Pittou, D., Papasalouros, A., Kotis, K., Zangogianni, P., & Daradoumis, A. (2022). Educational AI Chatbots for Content and Language Integrated Learning. *Applied Sciences (Basel, Switzerland)*, *12*(7), 3239. Advance online publication. DOI: 10.3390/app12073239

Maier, S., Schneider, M., & Feuerriegel, S. (2025). *Partnering with generative AI: Experimental evaluation of human-led and model-led interaction in human-AI co-creation. arXiv*. https://doi.org//arXiv.2510.23324DOI: 10.48550

Mariana, V., Cox, T., & Melby, A. (2015). The Multidimensional Quality Metrics (MQM) framework: A new framework for translation quality assessment. *The Journal of Specialised Translation*, *23*(23), 137–161. DOI: 10.26034/cm.jostrans.2015.343

Martin, F., & Borup, J. (2022). Online learner engagement: Conceptual definitions, research themes, and supportive practices. *Educational Psychologist*, *57*(3), 162–177. DOI: 10.1080/00461520.2022.2089147

Martins, L. (2023). Una introducción a los *chatbots* y sus aplicaciones en educación. En Fernández-Ferrer, M. (Ed.). (2023). *Chatbots en educación. Tendencias actuales y desafíos futuros* (pp.15-37). LMI.

Mayer, R. (2009). *Multimedia learning* (2nd ed.). Cambridge University Press. DOI: 10.1017/CBO9780511811678

Mayer, R. E. (2008). *Learning and Instruction*. Prentice Hall.

Mazzilli, F. (2021). Chatbots for action-oriented language learning. Using Elbot to enhance conflict-solving skills in learners of German as a foreign language. *EL.LE*, *10*(1), 95–116.

McNamara, D. S., Crossley, S. A., & McCarthy, P. M. (2010). Linguistic features of writing quality. *Written Communication*, *27*(1), 57–86. DOI: 10.1177/0741088309351547

Mekheimer, M. (2025). Generative AI-assisted feedback and EFL writing: A study on proficiency, revision frequency and writing quality. *Discover Education*, *4*(1), 170. DOI: 10.1007/s44217-025-00602-7

Memrise. (2023). *Memrise: Learn a new language with AI*. https://www.memrise.com

Mishu, A. (2025, August 3). *The role of affective filter in ELT classrooms: A study on anxiety, motivation, and comprehensible input using literature-based materials*. Paper presented at the International Conference on Arts and Humanities for Peacebuilding.

Mishu, A., Ahamed, M. M., Akan, M. F., Abdul-Rab, S. D., Chowdhury, G., Ahmad, J., & Sultana, I. (2025). How AI is ushering in a new era in ELT: Teachers' perspectives. *Theory and Practice in Language Studies*, *15*(2), 592–605. Advance online publication. DOI: 10.17507/tpls.1502.29

Mishu, A., & Jaashan, H. M. S. (2025). Effects of Transformational Generative Grammar (TGG) on writing skills of KKU EFL students. *Journal of Language Teaching and Research*, *16*(6), 1878–1888. DOI: 10.17507/jltr.1606.09

Mishu, A., Mohammed, H. A., Hakami, S. A. A., & Chowdhury, G. (2022). The impact of online presentations on reducing the introverted EFL learners' stress and anxiety. *Saudi Journal of Language Studies*, *3*(1), 32–46. DOI: 10.1108/SJLS-03-2022-0037

Mitchell, M., Wu, S., Zaldivar, A., Barnes, P., Vasserman, L., Hutchinson, B., Spitzer, E., Raji, I. D., & Gebru, T. (2019). Model cards for model reporting. In Proceedings of the Conference on Fairness, Accountability, and Transparency (FAT* '19) (pp. 220–229). DOI: 10.1145/3287560.3287596

Mitchell, T. (2025). Trust and transparency in artificial intelligence. *Philosophy & Technology*, *38*(3), 87–106. DOI: 10.1007/s13347-025-00916-2

Moeis, D., Usman, N., Faisal, M., Harmin, A., Mulyadi, I., & Thamrin, M. (2024). Microsoft Copilot training for monitoring student learning: A case study vocational high school Makassar-Indonesia. *I-Com: Indonesian Community Journal*, *4*(3), 1911–1922.

Mohamed, S., Png, M. T., & Isaac, W. (2020). Decolonial AI: Decolonial theory as sociotechnical foresight in artificial intelligence. *Philosophy & Technology*, *33*(4), 659–684. DOI: 10.1007/s13347-020-00405-8

Mohamed, Y. A., Mohamed, A. H. H., Khanan, A., Bashir, M., Adiel, M. A., & Elsadig, M. A. (2024). Navigating the ethical terrain of AI-generated text tools: A review. *IEEE Access : Practical Innovations, Open Solutions*, *12*, 197061–197120. DOI: 10.1109/ACCESS.2024.3521945

Mohammed, S. J., & Khalid, M. W. (2025). Under the world of AI-generated feedback on writing: Mirroring motivation, foreign language peace of mind, trait emotional intelligence, and writing development. *Language Testing in Asia*, *15*(1), 7. DOI: 10.1186/s40468-025-00343-2

Mohebbi, A. (2025). Enabling learner independence and self-regulation in language education using AI tools: A systematic review. *Cogent Education*, *12*(1), 2433814. DOI: 10.1080/2331186X.2024.2433814

Moorhouse, B. L., & Wong, K. M. (2025). *Generative Artificial Intelligence and Language Teaching*. Cambridge University Press., DOI: 10.1017/9781009618823

Morales, E., García, F., & Barrón, A. (2011). Quality learning objective in instructional design. In *Instructional design: Concepts, methodologies, tools, and applications* (pp. 70–79). IGI Global. DOI: 10.4018/978-1-60960-503-2.ch107

Morales, L. E., & Calla, W. H. (2025). El uso de Chatbots en el aprendizaje de idiomas: Una revisión sistemática. *Revista InveCom*, *5*(3), 1–7. DOI: 10.5281/zenodo.14532857

Morgan, D. L. (2007). Paradigms lost and pragmatism regained: Methodological implications of combining qualitative and quantitative methods. *Journal of Mixed Methods Research*, *1*(1), 48–76. DOI: 10.1177/2345678906292462

Morton, H., Gunson, N., & Jack, M. (2012). Interactive language learning through speech-enabled virtual scenarios. *Advances in Human-Computer Interaction, 2012*, 1–14. DOI: 10.1155/2012/389523

Moser, P. (1996). Expectations of users of conference interpretation. [JBE Platform]. *Interpreting, 1*(2), 145–178. DOI: 10.1075/intp.1.2.01mos

Moskovsky, C. (2018). EFL teaching and learning in Saudi Arabia: 25 years of research. In Moskovsky, C., & Picard, M. (Eds.), *English as a foreign language in Saudi Arabia: New insights into teaching and learning English* (pp. 4–69). Routledge. DOI: 10.4324/9781315688466-2

Moya, S., & Camacho, M. (2024). Leveraging AI-powered mobile learning: A pedagogically informed framework. *Computers and Education: Artificial Intelligence, 7*, 100276. DOI: 10.1016/j.caeai.2024.100276

Nafees, H., Kaif, M., Afnan Khan, M., Haseeb, A., & Ali Khan, P. K. (2025). *The Poetry of Error: Analyzing Mistakes in AI-Generated English Works*. In *IJIRT*, Vol. 11, Issue 12. ISSN: 2349-6002

Nafisah, S., Oktarina, I., Santri, D., & Suwartono, T. (2024). Teachers' perception and practices of intercultural communicative competence integration in EFL classroom: A systematic literature review. *Educalitra: English Education, Linguistics, and Literature Journal, 3*(1), 1–19. DOI: 10.5281/zenodo.10596575

Nagano, K., & Ozawa, K. (1990). English speech training using voice conversion. *Proceedings of the First International Conference on Spoken Language Processing*, 1169–1172.

Nazaretsky, T., Mejia-Domenzain, P., Swamy, V., Frej, J., & Käser, T. (2026). Who Gives Feedback Matters: Student Biases Towards Human and AI-Generated Formative Feedback. *Journal of Computer Assisted Learning, 42*(1), e70153. Advance online publication. DOI: 10.1111/jcal.70153

NCIHC. (2024). NCIHC guidance for contracting AI-generated interpreting (July 15, 2024).

Neri, A., Cucchiarini, C., & Strik, H. (2006). ASR corrective feedback on pronunciation: Does it really work? *Proceedings of Interspeech*, 1982–1985.

Neri, A., Cucchiarini, C., Strik, H., & Boves, L. (2002). The pedagogy-technology interface in computer assisted pronunciation training. *Computer Assisted Language Learning, 15*(5), 441–467. DOI: 10.1076/call.15.5.441.13473

New London Group. (1996). A Pedagogy of Multiliteracies: Designing Social Futures. *Harvard Educational Review*, *66*(1), 60–92. DOI: 10.17763/haer.66.1.17370n67v22j160u

Ng, D., Leung, J., Chu, S., & Qiao, M. (2021). Conceptualizing AI literacy: An exploratory review. *Computers & Education*, *2*, 1–11.

Nguyen, A., Hong, Y., Dang, B., & Huang, X. (2024). Human-AI collaboration patterns in AI-assisted academic writing. *Studies in Higher Education*, *49*(5), 847–864. DOI: 10.1080/03075079.2024.2323593

Nishida, T., & Fujimoto, N. (2025). Leveraging Artificial Intelligence for Self-Regulated Learning in EFL Presentation Skill Acquisition: Learner Perceptions and Practices. *Current Research Journal of Pedagogics*, *6*(06), 1–7.

Noels, K. A., Pelletier, L. G., Clément, R., & Vallerand, R. J. (2000). Why are you learning a second language? Motivational orientations and self-determination theory. *Language Learning*, *50*(1), 57–85. DOI: 10.1111/0023-8333.00111

Norman, D. A. (2013). *The design of everyday things* (Revised and expanded ed.). Basic Books

Nouzri, S., & Arisaka, R.. (2025). In Arisaka, R. (Eds.), *PRIMA 2024: Lecture Notes in Artificial Intelligence 15395* (pp. 385–401). Springer Nature Switzerland AG. [Beyond chatbots]

Noy, S., & Zhang, W. (2023). Experimental evidence on the productivity effects of generative artificial intelligence. *Science*, *381*(6654), 187–192. https://www.science.org/doi/10.1126/science.adh2586. DOI: 10.1126/science.adh2586 PMID: 37440646

Nunan, D. (2004). *Task-based language teaching*. Cambridge University Press. DOI: 10.1017/CBO9780511667336

NVivo. (2022). *NVivo (Version 14) [Computer software]*. QSR International. https://www.qsrinternational.com/nvivo-qualitative-data-analysis-software/home

O'Brien, S. (2006). Pauses as indicators of cognitive effort in machine translation post-editing. *Across Languages and Cultures*, *7*(1), 1–21. DOI: 10.1556/Acr.7.2006.1.1

O'Dowd, R. (2021). Virtual exchange: Moving forward into the next decade. *Computer Assisted Language Learning*, *34*(3), 209–224. DOI: 10.1080/09588221.2021.1902201

OECD. (2023). *Generative AI in education: Emerging trends and policy implications*. OECD Publishing.

OECD. (2023). *OECD framework for the classification of AI systems and policy implications*. OECD Publishing., DOI: 10.1787/9a87c0b7-

OECD. (2023). *OECD framework for the classification of AI systems: A tool for effective AI policies*. OECD Publishing., DOI: 10.1787/cb6d9eca-

OECD. (2026). *Artificial intelligence in education: Governance, policy and institutional transformation*. OECD Publishing.

Olesova, L., Sadaf, A., & Yan, W. (2026). *Exploring Relationships Between Undergraduate Students' Perceived Community of Inquiry, Engagement, and Shared Metacognition in Asynchronous Online Courses*. Technology Knowledge and Learning., DOI: 10.1007/s10758-026-09953-y

Oliveira, E., de Barba, P. G., & Corrin, L. (2021). Enabling adaptive, personalized, and context-aware interaction in a smart learning environment: Piloting the iCollab system. *Australasian Journal of Educational Technology*, *37*(2), 1–23. DOI: 10.14742/ajet.6792

Omidvar, S., & Meihami, H. (2025). Exploring the "What" and "How" of Opportunities and Challenges of AI in EFL Teacher Education. *Computers and Education: Artificial Intelligence*, *100443*, 100443. Advance online publication. DOI: 10.1016/j.caeai.2025.100443

Otaif, F. A. (2021). Towards evaluating interactivity in video-based task design: A perspective from computer-based L2 listening. *Saudi Journal of Language Studies*, *1*(1), 26–39. DOI: 10.1108/SJLS-03-2021-0008

Oudeyer, P. Y., Gottlieb, J., & Lopes, M. (2016). Intrinsic motivation, curiosity, and learning: Theory and applications in educational technologies. *Progress in Brain Research*, *229*, 257–284. DOI: 10.1016/bs.pbr.2016.05.005 PMID: 27926442

Ouyang, F., Wu, M., Zhang, L., Xu, W., Zheng, L., & Cukurova, M. (2023). Making strides towards AI-supported regulation of learning in collaborative knowledge construction. *Computers in Human Behavior*, *142*, 107650. DOI: 10.1016/j.chb.2023.107650

Ouyang, P., Zheng, F., & Jiao, L. (2022). Artificial intelligence in online higher education: A systematic review of empirical research from 2011 to 2020. *Education and Information Technologies*, *27*(6), 7893–7925. DOI: 10.1007/s10639-022-10925-9

Paas, F., Renkl, A., & Sweller, J. (2003). Cognitive load theory and instructional design: Recent developments. *Educational Psychologist*, *38*(1), 1–4. DOI: 10.1207/S15326985EP3801_1

Pack, A., & Maloney, J. (2023). Using generative artificial intelligence for language education research: Insights from using OpenAI's ChatGPT. *TESOL Quarterly*, *57*(4), 1571–1582. DOI: 10.1002/tesq.3253

Paesani, K., & Menke, M. (2023). *Literacies in language education: A guide for teachers and teacher educators*. Georgetown University Press. DOI: 10.2307/j.ctv31jm8v4

Pallant, J. (2020). *SPSS survival manual: A step by step guide to data analysis using IBM SPSS*. Routledge.

Pan, Z., Moore, O. A., Papadimitriou, A., & Zhu, J. (2025). AI literacy and trust: A multi-method study of human-GAI team collaboration. *Cognition and Behavior*, *8*, 100162. DOI: 10.1016/j.chbah.2025.100162

Papineni, K., Roukos, S., Ward, T., & Zhu, W.-J. (2002). BLEU: A method for automatic evaluation of machine translation. In *Proceedings of the 40th Annual Meeting of the Association for Computational Linguistics* (pp. 311–318). Association for Computational Linguistics. DOI: 10.3115/1073083.1073135

Paredes, C., & Martínez, A. (2023). Los chatbots en educación secundaria: retos y propuestas para su aplicación en el aula. En Fernández-Ferrer, M. (Ed.). (2023). *Chatbots en educación. Tendencias actuales y desafíos futuros* (pp.39-65). LMI.

Partington, A., Duguid, A., & Taylor, C. (2013). *Patterns and meanings in discourse: Theory and practice in corpus-assisted discourse studies*. John Benjamins. DOI: 10.1075/scl.55

Pawlik, L. (2025). How the choice of LLM and prompt engineering affects chatbot effectiveness. *Electronics (Basel)*, *14*(5), 888. DOI: 10.3390/electronics14050888

Pearson, V. (2011). *Test description and validation summary*. Pearson Education.

Peng, J. E., & Liang, W. (2025). Willingness to communicate with artificial intelligence (AI)? Insights from tracking EFL learners' perceived acceptance and chat output. *Computer Assisted Language Learning*, •••, 1–27. DOI: 10.1080/09588221.2025.2486147

Peng, X., Wang, Z., Liu, J., & Zhang, Y. (2024). The impacts of machine translation quality and perceived self-efficacy on student translators' cognitive effort and post-editing behavior. *SAGE Open*, *14*(4). Advance online publication. DOI: 10.1177/21582440241291624

Pennycook, A. (2010). Critical and alternative directions in applied linguistics. *Australian Review of Applied Linguistics, 33*(2), 16.1–16.16. https://doi.org/DOI: 10.2104/aral1016

Pica, T. (1994). Research on negotiation: What does it reveal about second-language learning conditions, processes, and outcomes? *Language Learning*, *44*(3), 493–527. DOI: 10.1111/j.1467-1770.1994.tb01115.x

Pirjan, A., & Petrosanu, D. M. (2024). Exploring large language models in the education process with a view towards transforming personalized learning. *Journal of Information Systems & Operations Management*, *18*(2), 125–171. https://jisom.rau.ro/Vol.18%20No.1%20-%202024/JISOM%2018.1_225-260.pdf

Pituxcoosuvarn, M., & Murakami, Y. (2025). Jokes or gibberish? Humor retention in translation with neural machine translation vs. large language model. *Digital*, *5*(4), 49. DOI: 10.3390/digital5040049

Pöchhacker, F. (2001). Quality assessment in conference and community interpreting. *Meta: Translators'. Journal*, *46*(2), 410–425. DOI: 10.7202/003847ar

Pokrivcakova, S. (2019). Preparing teachers for the application of AI-powered technologies in foreign language education. *Journal of Language and Cultural Education*, *7*(3), 135–153. DOI: 10.2478/jolace-2019-0025

Polakova, P., & Klimova, B. (2024). Implementation of AI-driven technology into education – a pilot study on the use of chatbots in foreign language learning. *Cogent Education*, *11*(1), 2355385. DOI: 10.1080/2331186X.2024.2355385

Polit, D. F., & Beck, C. T. (2006). The content validity index: Are you sure you know what's being reported? Critique and recommendations. *Research in Nursing & Health*, *29*(5), 489–497. DOI: 10.1002/nur.20147 PMID: 16977646

Polyakova, O., Chrominska, D., & Zarajczyk, I. (2024). Developing professional communication skills and competences around sustainability goals. In *Proceedings of the X Congreso Nacional de Innovación Educativa y Docencia en Red (IN-RED 2024)* (pp. 1165–1177). Editorial Universitat Politècnica de València. DOI: 10.4995/INRED2024.2024.18357

Polyakova, O. (2024). Enhancing staff weeks organisations through service action research. In *Proceedings of the 18th International Technology, Education and Development Conference (INTED2024)* (pp. 2067–2071). IATED. DOI: 10.21125/inted.2024.0576

Polyakova, O., & Galstyan-Sargsyan, R. (2019). Communicative competences in non-linguistic university degrees. *Language*, *11*(1), 45–70.

Pym, A. (2025). Translation technologies as the end of translation as we know it: Empiricism as a search for a way forward. In *Confronting digital dilemmas in translator and interpreter training* (pp. 18–34). Routledge. DOI: 10.4324/9781003562535-3

Qi, X., & Chen, Z. (2025). A Systematic Review of Technology Integration in Developing L2 Pragmatic Competence. *Education Sciences*, *15*(2), 172. Advance online publication. DOI: 10.3390/educsci15020172

Ragni, V., Kobi, S., & O'Brien, S. (2022). What has changed with neural machine translation? A review of the NMT landscape. *Perspectives*, *30*(1), 1–25. DOI: 10.1080/0907676X.2021.1889005

Rahimi, M., Fathi, J., & Zou, D. (2025). Exploring the impact of automated written corrective feedback on the academic writing skills of EFL learners: An activity theory perspective. *Education and Information Technologies*, *30*(3), 2691–2735. DOI: 10.1007/s10639-024-12896-5

Rahman, M. (2015). English for Specific Purposes (ESP): A Holistic Review. *Universal Journal of Educational Research*, *3*(1), 24–31. DOI: 10.13189/ujer.2015.030104

Rahmawati, A., Suhatmady, B., Sucahyo, D., & Hermagustiana, I. (2025). Storytelling in English language learning: Boosting confidence and discourse in EFL contexts. *Borju*, *7*(1), 1–13. DOI: 10.24903/bej.v7i1.1895

Raji, I. D., Smart, A., White, R. N., Mitchell, M., Gebru, T., Hutchinson, B., Smith-Loud, J., Theron, D., & Barnes, P. (2020). Closing the AI accountability gap: Defining an end-to-end framework for internal algorithmic auditing. *Proceedings of the 2020 Conference on Fairness, Accountability, and Transparency*, 33–44. https://doi.org/ DOI: 10.1145/3351095.3372873

Ranbom, L., & Connine, C. (2011). Silent letters are activated in spoken word recognition. *Language and Cognitive Processes*, *26*(2), 236–261. DOI: 10.1080/01690965.2010.486578

Reeves, B., & Nass, C. (1996). *The media equation: How people treat computers, television, and new media like real people and places*. Cambridge University Press.

Renduchintala, A., Stanovsky, G., & Madhyastha, P. (2021). Gender bias amplification during speed–quality optimization in neural machine translation. In *Proceedings of ACL-IJCNLP 2021* (pp. 99–109). DOI: 10.18653/v1/2021.acl-short.15

Révész, A., Suzuki, S., & Jung, Y. (2025). Artificial intelligence in applied linguistics: Applications, promises, and challenges. *Annual Review of Applied Linguistics*, *45*, 1–9. DOI: 10.1017/S0267190525100172

Reyes-Torres, A., Brisk, M. E., & Lacorte, M. (2025). *Multiliteracies, multimodality and learning by design in second language learning and teacher education*. Routledge., DOI: 10.4324/9781032620497

Reyes-Torres, A., & García-Perera, A. (2022). Influence of positive student-teacher interaction on the meaning-making process in virtual learning: A study in the primary English class. In Giannikas, C. (Ed.), *Transferring language learning and teaching from face-to-face to online settings* (pp. 165–188). IGI Global Scientific Publishing., DOI: 10.4018/978-1-7998-8717-1.ch009

Richards, J. (2015). The changing face of language learning: Learning beyond the classroom. *RELC Journal*, *46*(1), 5–22. DOI: 10.1177/0033688214561621

Riessman, C. (2008). Narrative methods for the human sciences. *Sage (Atlanta, Ga.)*.

Robinson, P. (2007). Criteria for grading and sequencing pedagogic tasks. In M. Mayo (Ed.), *Investigating tasks in formal language learning* (pp. 2-27). Multilingual Matters.

Robinson, P. (2011). *Second Language Task Complexity: Researching the Cognition Hypothesis of Language Learning and Performance*. John Benjamins. DOI: 10.1075/tblt.2

Romero, M. (2025). From consumption to co-creation: A systematic review of six levels of AI-enhanced creative engagement in education. *Multimodal Technologies and Interaction*, *9*(10), 110. DOI: 10.3390/mti9100110

Rosenblatt, L. M. (1994). *The reader, the text, the poem: The transactional theory of the literary work*. Southern Illinois University Press.

RWTH Aachen University IT Center. (2024). *RWTHgpt: Data protection, hosting infrastructure, and governance framework*. https://www.itc.rwth-aachen.de

RWTH Aachen University IT Center. (2024a) *Data protection statement for chatbot services (RWTHgpt)*. https://www.itc.rwth-aachen.de

RWTH Aachen University IT Center. (n.d.). *Privacy policy* (includes chatbot service data protection information). https://www.itc.rwth-aachen.de/cms/it-center/footer/service/~myfc/datenschutzerklaerung/?lidx=1

RWTH Aachen University. (2024a, July 16). *RWTH launches its own AI tool*. https://www.rwth-aachen.de/cms/root/wir/aktuell/pressemitteilungen/juli-2024/~bipvlz/rwth-setzt-auf-eigenes-ki-tool/?lidx=1

RWTH Aachen University. (2024b) *Implementation of RWTHgpt: Institutionally governed large language model service*. https://www.rwth-aachen.de

RWTH Aachen University. (2024b, December 11). *RWTH rolls out custom AI chatbot for students (RWTHgpt)*. https://www.rwth-aachen.de

RWTH Aachen University. (2024b, December 11). *RWTH rolls out custom AI chatbot for students*. https://www.rwth-aachen.de/cms/root/wir/aktuell/pressemitteilungen/dezember/~blajft/ki-tool-fuer-studierende-rwthgpt-ist-am/?lidx=1

Ryan, H., Abramov, D., Acker, S., & Elkins, S. (2025). "Can AI Be a Co-Author?: How Generative AI Challenges the Boundaries of Authorship in a General Education Writing Class". In Academy for Educational Studies, Vol. 48, Issue 1, pp. 40-56.

Ryan, R. M., & Deci, E. L. (2020). Intrinsic and extrinsic motivation from a self-determination theory perspective: Definitions, theory, practices, and future directions. *Contemporary Educational Psychology*, *61*, 101860. DOI: 10.1016/j.cedpsych.2020.101860

Saito, K. (2021). Effects of corrective feedback on second language pronunciation development. In Nassaji, H., & Kartchava, E. (Eds.), *The Cambridge Handbook of Corrective Feedback in Second Language Learning and Teaching* (pp. 407–428). Cambridge University Press. DOI: 10.1017/9781108589789.020

Sakamoto, A.. (2024). *Measuring translators' quality of working life and their career sustainability in the context of digitalisation and automation*. Translation Spaces., DOI: 10.1075/ts.23026.sak

Salmani-Nodoushan, M. A. (2020). English for Specific Purposes: Traditions, Trends, Directions. *Online Submission*, *7*(1), 247–268. DOI: 10.24815/siele.v7i1.16342

Salokhojaeva, F. (2025). Impact of the digital revolution on the development of students' communicative competences. *Perspectives of higher education development, 17*(1), 53-62. https://doi.org/DOI: 10.34920/phe.2024.17.04

Salvetti, F., Bertagni, B., & Contardo, I. (2025). AI Conversational Agents for Corporate Language Learning: Enhancing Engagement and Retention. *International Journal of Advanced Corporate Learning*, *18*(3), 60–69. DOI: 10.3991/ijac.v18i3.52593

Sambasivan, N., Arnesen, E., Hutchinson, B., Doshi, T., & Prabhakaran, V. (2021). Re-imagining algorithmic fairness in India and beyond. *Proceedings of the 2021 ACM Conference on Fairness, Accountability, and Transparency*, 315–328. DOI: 10.1145/3442188.3445896

Sangkala, I., & Mardonovna, N. S. (2024). Artificial Intelligence as a Personalized Tutor in Language Learning: A Systematic Review. *KLASIKAL: Journal of Education. Language Teaching And Science*, *6*(2), 565–576. DOI: 10.52208/klasikal.v6i2.1193

Sangkawong, N., Bucol, J. L., & Luciano, R. (2025). Bridging language gaps in real-time: Investigating university students' self-initiated use of speech-to-text translation in English language classrooms. *Teaching English with Technology*, *25*(2), 5–28. DOI: 10.56297/vaca6841/ZDDD4208/KTKA2748

Savoldi, B., Gaido, M., Bentivogli, L., Negri, M., & Turchi, M. (2025). A decade of gender bias in machine translation. *Patterns (New York, N.Y.)*, *6*(6), 101257. DOI: 10.1016/j.patter.2025.101257 PMID: 40575128

Scansani, R. (2019). *Do translator trainees trust machine translation? An experiment on the influence of information about authorship on post-editing performance. Proceedings (ACL anthology)*. ACL Anthology.

Schmidt, R. (1990). The role of consciousness in second language learning. *Applied Linguistics*, *11*(2), 129–158. DOI: 10.1093/applin/11.2.129

Schmidt, R. (2001). Attention. In Robinson, P. (Ed.), *Cognition and second language instruction* (pp. 3–32). Cambridge University Press. DOI: 10.1017/CBO9781139524780.003

Seeber, K. G. (2011). Cognitive load in simultaneous interpreting: Existing theories New models. *Interpreting*, *13*(2), 176–204. DOI: 10.1075/intp.13.2.02see

Seel, N., Lehmann, T., Blumschein, P., & Podolskiy, O. (2017). *Instructional design for learning: Theoretical foundations*. Sense Publishers., DOI: 10.1007/978-94-6300-941-6

Seliger, H. W., & Shohamy, E. (1989). *Second language research methods*. Oxford University Press.

SEPIE. (2022). Blended intensive programmes (BIPs) under [*Implementation guidelines*. Servicio Español para la Internacionalización de la Educación.]. *Erasmus*, •••, 2021–2027.

Sharwood-Smith, M. (1993). Input enhancement in instructed SLA: Theoretical bases. *Studies in Second Language Acquisition*, *15*(2), 165–179. DOI: 10.1017/S0272263100011943

Shneiderman, B. (2020). Human-centered artificial intelligence: Reliable, safe & trustworthy. *International Journal of Human-Computer Interaction*, *36*(6), 495–504. DOI: 10.1080/10447318.2020.1741118

Short, J., Williams, E., & Christie, B. (1976). *The social psychology of telecommunications*. Wile.

Shute, V. J. (2008). Focus on formative feedback. *Review of Educational Research, 78*(1), 153–189. DOI: 10.3102/0034654307313795

Siddiqui, S., Ahamed, M. M., Chowdhury, G., Mishu, A., & Monira, S. (2023). Teaching writing skills to EFL learners: Issues and concerns. *Journal of Language Teaching and Research, 14*(6), 1541–1550. DOI: 10.17507/jltr.1406.12

Sidgi, F., & Shaari, A. (2017). The usefulness of automatic speech recognition (ASR) Eyespeak Software in improving Iraqi EFL students' pronunciation. *Advances in Language and Literary Studies, 8*(1), 221–225. DOI: 10.7575/aiac.alls.v.8n.1p.221

Siegle, D. (2024). Using AI Prompt Engineering to Improve Gifted Students' Questioning. *Gifted Child Today, 48*(1), 68–72. DOI: 10.1177/10762175241289886

Siemens, G. (2005). Connectivism: Learning as network-creation. *ASTD Learning News, 10*(1), 1–28.

Smuha, N. A. (2021). From a "race to AI" to a "race to AI regulation": Regulatory competition for artificial intelligence. *Law, Innovation and Technology, 13*(1), 57–84. DOI: 10.1080/17579961.2021.1898300

Spagnolli, A., Cenzato, G., & Gamberini, L. (2023). Modeling the conversation with digital health assistants in adherence apps: Some considerations on the similarities and differences with familiar medical encounters. *International Journal of Environmental Research and Public Health, 20*(12), 6182. DOI: 10.3390/ijerph20126182 PMID: 37372768

Specia, L., Raj, D., & Turchi, M. (2010). Machine translation evaluation versus quality estimation. *Machine Translation, 24*(1), 39–50. DOI: 10.1007/s10590-010-9077-2

Specia, L., & Shah, K. (2018). Machine translation quality estimation: Applications and future perspectives. In Moorkens, J., Castilho, S., Gaspari, F., & Doherty, S. (Eds.), *Translation Quality Assessment: From Principles to Practice* (pp. 201–235). Springer., DOI: 10.1007/978-3-319-91241-7_10

Sperber, D., & Wilson, D. (1986). *Relevance: Communication and cognition.* Harvard University Press.

Stanovsky, G., Smith, N. A., & Zettlemoyer, L. (2019). Evaluating gender bias in machine translation. In *Proceedings of the 57th Annual Meeting of the Association for Computational Linguistics* (pp. 1679–1684). DOI: 10.18653/v1/P19-1164

Star, S. L., & Griesemer, J. R. (1989). Institutional ecology,translations' and boundary objects: Amateurs and professionals in Berkeley's Museum of Vertebrate Zoology, 1907-39. *Social Studies of Science, 19*(3), 387–420. DOI: 10.1177/030631289019003001

Stiegemeier, D., Kraus, J., Bringeland, S., & Baumann, M. (2023). Motivated to use: Beliefs and motivation influencing the acceptance and use of assistance and navigation systems. *International Journal of Human-Computer Interaction, 39*(14), 2926–2941. DOI: 10.1080/10447318.2022.2088658

Stockwell, G., & Wang, Y. (2025). Framing human-AI collaboration in language education. *Technology in Language Teaching & Learning, 7*(4), 103824. DOI: 10.29140/tltl.v7n4.103824

Sun, W. (2023). The impact of automatic speech recognition technology on second language pronunciation and speaking skills of EFL learners: A mixed methods investigation. *Frontiers in Psychology, 14*, 1210187. Advance online publication. DOI: 10.3389/fpsyg.2023.1210187

Swain, M. (1985). Communicative competence: Some roles of comprehensible input and comprehensible output in its development. *Input in second language acquisition, 15*, 165-179.

Swain, M., & Lapkin, S. (1995). Problems in output and the cognitive processes they generate: A step towards second language learning. *Applied Linguistics, 16*(3), 371–391. DOI: 10.1093/applin/16.3.371

Swartz, S., Luck, S., & Sharma, S. (2025). Global virtual teams projects and developing AI literacy: A mixed-methods study on preparing students for the international technology-infused workplace. *Higher Education. Skills and Work-Based Learning, 15*(3), 690–702. DOI: 10.1108/HESWBL-09-2024-0266

Taecharungroj, V. (2023). "What Can *ChatGPT* Do?" Analyzing Early Reactions to the Innovative AI Chatbot on Twitter. *Big Data and Cognitive Computing, 7*(2), 35. DOI: 10.3390/bdcc7010035

Taguchi, N. (2018). Pragmatic competence in foreign language education: Cultivating learner autonomy and strategic learning of pragmatics. *New perspectives on the development of communicative and related competence in foreign language education*, 53-69. https://doi.org/DOI: 10.1515/9781501505034-004

Taguchi, N. (2022). Immersive virtual reality for pragmatics task development. *TESOL Quarterly, 56*(1), 308–335. DOI: 10.1002/tesq.3070

Tai, T. Y., & Chen, H. H. J. (2023). The impact of Google Assistant on adolescent EFL learners' willingness to communicate. *Interactive Learning Environments*, *31*(3), 1485–1502. DOI: 10.1080/10494820.2020.1841801

Tardel, A. (2020). Effort in semi-automatized subtitling processes: Speech recognition and experience during transcription. *Journal of Audiovisual Translation*, *3*(2), 79–102. DOI: 10.47476/jat.v3i2.2020.131

Tavares, V. (2024). *Social justice through pedagogies of multiliteracies. Developing and strengthening L2 learner agency and identity*. Routledge. DOI: 10.4324/9781003438847

Taylor, C. (2021). Metaphors of migration over time. *Discourse & Society*, *32*(4), 463–481. DOI: 10.1177/0957926521992156

Teimouri, Y., Goetze, J., & Plonsky, L. (2019). Second language anxiety and achievement: A meta-analysis. *Studies in Second Language Acquisition*, *41*(2), 363–387. DOI: 10.1017/S0272263118000311

Thi-Nhu Ngo, T., Hao-Jan Chen, H., & Kuo-Wei Lai, K. (2024). The effectiveness of automatic speech recognition in ESL/EFL pronunciation: A meta-analysis. *ReCALL*, *36*(1), 4–21. DOI: 10.1017/S0958344023000113

Thomas, J., & Harden, A. (2008). Methods for the thematic synthesis of qualitative research in systematic reviews. *BMC Medical Research Methodology*, *8*(1), 45. DOI: 10.1186/1471-2288-8-45 PMID: 18616818

Toral, A., Wieling, M., & Way, A. (2018). Post-editing effort of a novel with statistical and neural machine translation. *Frontiers in Digital Humanities*, *5*, 9. DOI: 10.3389/fdigh.2018.00009

Torres, P. J., & Kahveci, Y. E. (2025). Effectiveness of Artificial Intelligence (AI) in language teaching. *Computers and Education: Artificial Intelligence*, 100522.

Tseng, W., & Warschauer, M. (2023). AI-writing tools in education: If you can't beat them, join them. *Journal of China Computer-Assisted Language Learning*, *3*(2), 258–262. DOI: 10.1515/jccall-2023-0008

Tutton, M., & Cohen, D. (2025). Reconceptualizing the role of the university language teacher in light of generative AI. *Education Sciences*, *15*(1), 56. DOI: 10.3390/educsci15010056

Underwood, J. (2017). Exploring AI language assistants with primary EFL students. In *CALL in a climate of change: adapting to turbulent global conditions – Short papers from EUROCALL 2017* (pp. 317–321). Research-publishing.net. DOI: 10.14705/rpnet.2017.eurocall2017.733

UNESCO. (2017). *E2030: education and skills for the 21st century.* https://unesdoc.unesco.org/ark:/48223/pf0000250117_eng

UNESCO. (2019). Draft recommendation on Open Educational Resources (OER). https://unesdoc.unesco.org/ark:/48223/pf0000370936

UNESCO. (2023). *Guidance for generative AI in education and research.* UNESCO. https://unesdoc.unesco.org/ark:/48223/pf0000386693

UNESCO. (2023). *Guidance for generative AI in education and research.* United Nations Educational, Scientific and Cultural Organization., DOI: 10.54675/EWZM9535

UNESCO. (2024a). *AI competency framework for teachers.* UNESCO., DOI: 10.54675/ZJTE2084

UNESCO. (2024b). *AI competency framework for students.* UNESCO., DOI: 10.54675/JKJB9835

Urbaite, G. (2025). Adaptive Learning with AI: How Bots Personalize Foreign Language Education. *Luminis Applied Science and Engineering*, *2*(1), 13–18. DOI: 10.69760/lumin.20250001002

Usher, M. (2025). Generative AI vs. instructor vs. peer assessments: A comparison of grading and feedback in higher education. *Assessment & Evaluation in Higher Education*, *50*(6), 912–927. DOI: 10.1080/02602938.2025.2487495

Vaira, L. A., Lechien, J. R., Abbate, V., Gabriele, G., Frosolini, A., De Vito, A., Maniaci, A., Mayo-Yáñez, M., Boscolo-Rizzo, P., Saibene, A. M., Maglitto, F., Salzano, G., Califano, G., Troise, S., Chiesa-Estomba, C. M., & De Riu, G. (2025). Enhancing AI Chatbot responses in health care: The SMART prompt structure in head and neck surgery. *OTO Open*, *9*(1), e70075. DOI: 10.1002/oto2.70075 PMID: 39822375

Van Loon, J. (2002). Improving pronunciation of adult ESL students. *TESL Canada Journal*, *20*(1), 83. DOI: 10.18806/tesl.v20i1.941

Vanjani, M., Aiken, M., & Park, M. (2020). Using a multilingual chatbot for foreign language practice. *Issues in Information Systems*, *21*(2), 85–92. DOI: 10.48009/2_iis_2020_85-92

Veale, M., & Borgesius, F. Z. (2021). Demystifying the draft EU Artificial Intelligence Act. *Computer Law Review International*, *22*(4), 97–112. DOI: 10.9785/cri-2021-220402

Veale, T., & Pérez, R. (2020). Leaps and Bounds: An Introduction to the Field of Computational Creativity. *New Generation Computing*, *38*(4), 551–563. DOI: 10.1007/s00354-020-00116-w

Veletsianos, G., & Houlden, S. (2019). An analysis of flexible learning and flexibility over the last 40 years of *Distance Education. Distance Education*, *40*(4), 454–468. DOI: 10.1080/01587919.2019.1681893

Venkatesh, V., & Davis, F. D. (2000). A Theoretical Extension of the Technology Acceptance Model: Four Longitudinal Field Studies. *Management Science*, *46*(2), 186–204. https://www.jstor.org/stable/2634758. DOI: 10.1287/mnsc.46.2.186.11926

Venuti, L. (2017). *The translator's invisibility: A history of translation* (3rd ed.). Routledge., DOI: 10.4324/9781315098746

Versteegh, K. (2014). *The Arabic language* (2nd ed.). Edinburgh University Press. DOI: 10.1515/9780748645299

Vygotsky, L. S. (1978). *Mind in society: The development of higher psychological processes* (M. Cole, V. John-Steiner, S. Scribner, & E. Souberman, Eds. & Trans.). Harvard University Press. (Original work published 1930–1934).

Vygotsky, L. S. (1978). *Mind in Society: The Development of Higher Psychological Processes*. Harvard University Press.

Vygotsky, L. S., & Cole, M. (1978). *Mind in society: Development of higher psychological processes*. Harvard university press.

Wah, J. N. K. (2025). Artificial Intelligence in Language Learning: A Systematic Review of Personalization and Learner Engagement. *Forum for Linguistic Studies*, *7*(9), 327–341. DOI: 10.30564/fls.v7i9.10336

Wang, Y. (2024). "Cognitive and sociocultural dynamics of self-regulated use of machine translation and generative AI tools in academic EFL writing". In *System Journal*, Issue 106. DOI: 10.1016/j.system.2024.103505

Wang, C., & Zou, B. (2025). AI versus teachers and peers: A comparative study on speaking performance, willingness to communicate, self-perceived communicative competence and foreign language anxiety. *International Review of Applied Linguistics in Language Teaching*. Advance online publication. DOI: 10.1515/iral-2024-0310

Wang, C., Zou, B., Du, Y., & Wang, Z. (2024). The impact of different conversational generative AI chatbots on EFL learners: An analysis of willingness to communicate, foreign language speaking anxiety, and self-perceived communicative competence. *System, 127*, 103533. DOI: 10.1016/j.system.2024.103533

Wang, Q. (2025). AI-driven autonomous interactive English learning language tutoring system. *Journal of Computational Methods in Sciences and Engineering, 25*(2), 1155–1166. DOI: 10.1177/14727978241296719

Wang, S. (2025). Public perceptions of artificial intelligence in 20 countries: Cultural variations in acceptance and risk evaluations. *Journal of Cross-Cultural Psychology, 56*(7), 891–910. DOI: 10.1177/10693971251336803

Wang, X., Liu, Q., Pang, H., Tan, S. C., Lei, J., Wallace, M. P., & Li, L. (2023). What matters in AI-supported learning: A study of human-AI interactions in language learning using cluster analysis and epistemic network analysis. *Computers & Education, 194*, 104703. DOI: 10.1016/j.compedu.2022.104703

Wang, Y. F., Hsu, M. H., Wang, M. Y. F., & Chang, Y. T. (2025). Enhancing phonetic accuracy through chatbot-assisted language learning. *Educational Technology Research and Development, 73*(3), 1723–1739. DOI: 10.1007/s11423-025-10466-1

Wang, Z., & Wang, C. (2025). A posthumanist approach to AI literacy. *Computers and Composition, 76*, 102933. Advance online publication. DOI: 10.1016/j.compcom.2025.102933

Warschauer, M., Tseng, W., Yim, S., Webster, T., Jacob, S., Du, Q., & Tate, T. (2023). The affordances and contradictions of AI-generated text for writers of English as a second or foreign language. *Journal of Second Language Writing, 62*, 101071. Advance online publication. DOI: 10.1016/j.jslw.2023.101071

Warschauer, M., & Xu, Y. (2024). Generative AI for language learning: Entering a new era. *Language Learning & Technology, 28*(2), 1–4. DOI: 10.64152/10125/73569

Watson, J. C. (2002). *The phonology and morphology of Arabic*. Oxford University Press. DOI: 10.1093/oso/9780199257591.001.0001

Wei, L. (2023). Artificial intelligence in language instruction: Impact on English learning achievement, L2 motivation, and self-regulated learning. *Frontiers in Psychology, 14*, 1261955. DOI: 10.3389/fpsyg.2023.1261955

Wiboolyasarin, W., Wiboolyasarin, K., Tiranant, P., Jinowat, N., & Boonyakitanont, P. (2025). AI-driven chatbots in second language education: A systematic review of their efficacy and pedagogical implications. *Ampersand (Oxford, UK), 14*, 100224. DOI: 10.1016/j.amper.2025.100224

Wiggins, G., & McTighe, J. (2005). Backward design. In G. Wiggins & J. McTighe, *Understanding by design* (2nd expanded ed., pp. 13–23). Association for Supervision and Curriculum Development.

Wissik, T. (2025). The impact of automatic term extraction on terminology work: Evidence from professional practice. *Terminology, 31*(1), 110–135. Advance online publication. DOI: 10.1075/term.00085.wis

Woo, D. J., Susanto, H., Yeung, C. H., Guo, K., & Fung, A. K. Y. (2024). Exploring AI-Generated text in student writing: How does AI help? *Language Learning & Technology, 28*(2), 183–209. DOI: 10.64152/10125/73577

Woodworth, J., & Barkaoui, K. (2020). Perspectives on using automated writing evaluation systems to provide written corrective feedback in the ESL classroom. *TESL Canada Journal, 37*(2), 234–247. DOI: 10.18806/tesl.v37i2.1340

Woolard, K. A., & Schieffelin, B. B. (1994). Language ideology. *Annual Review of Anthropology, 23*(1), 55–82. DOI: 10.1146/annurev.an.23.100194.000415

Xiao, W., & Park, M. (2021). Using automatic speech recognition to facilitate English pronunciation assessment and learning in an EFL context. *International Journal of Computer-Assisted Language Learning and Teaching, 11*(3), 74–91. DOI: 10.4018/IJCALLT.2021070105

Xia, Y., Shin, S. Y., & Kim, J. C. (2024). Cross-cultural intelligent language learning system (CILS): Leveraging AI to facilitate language learning strategies in cross-cultural communication. *Applied Sciences (Basel, Switzerland), 14*(13), 5651. DOI: 10.3390/app14135651

Xu, H., Wang, Y., & Ma, J. (2025). A comprehensive review of intercultural communicative competence in EFL education and global business. *Cogent Education, 12*(1), 2557608. DOI: 10.1080/2331186X.2025.2557608

Xu, L., Zhang, L., Ou, L., & Wang, D. (2025). The development and validation of a scale on student AI literacy in L2 writing: A domain-specific perspective. *Journal of Second Language Writing, 69*, 101227. DOI: 10.1016/j.jslw.2025.101227

Yang, H., Kim, H., Lee, J., & Shin, D. (2022). Implementation of an AI chatbot as an English conversation partner in EFL speaking classes. *ReCALL, 34*(3), 327–343. DOI: 10.1017/S0958344022000039

Yan, H. (2025). Trends in empirical research in English for specific purposes: A systematic review of SSCI-indexed journal articles (2014–2023). *SAGE Open, 15*(1), 21582440251328460. DOI: 10.1177/21582440251328460

Yao, R. (2025, December 12). Bringing state-of-the-art Gemini translation capabilities to Google Translate. Google (The Keyword)

Yigit, G., & Bayraktar, R. (2025). Chatbot development strategies: A review of current studies and applications. *Knowledge and Information Systems, 67*(9), 7319–7354. DOI: 10.1007/s10115-025-02462-x

Yin, R. K. (2018). *Case study research and applications: Design and methods* (6th ed.). SAGE Publications.

Youn, C. H., & Salam, A. R. (2025). A Systematic Review on the Use of Artificial Intelligence in Providing Feedback in Teaching Writing. *LSP International Journal, 12*(2), 133–142. DOI: 10.11113/lspi.v12.26003

Young, R. F. (2019). Interactional competence and L2 pragmatics. In *The Routledge Handbook of LSecond language Acquisition and Pragmatics* (pp. 93–110). Routledge.

Yuan, Y. (2024). An empirical study of the efficacy of AI chatbots for English as a foreign language learning in primary education. *Interactive Learning Environments, 32*(10), 6774–6789. DOI: 10.1080/10494820.2023.2282112

Yu, W. (2025). Reducing anxiety, promoting enjoyment and enhancing overall English proficiency: The impact of AI-assisted language learning in Chinese EFL contexts. *British Educational Research Journal*, berj.4187. Advance online publication. DOI: 10.1002/berj.4187

Zaim, M., Arsyad, S., Waluyo, B., Ardi, H., Al Hafizh, M., Zakiyah, M., Syafitri, W., Nusi, A., & Hardiah, M. (2025). Generative AI as a cognitive co-pilot in English language learning in higher education. *Education Sciences, 15*(6), 686. DOI: 10.3390/educsci15060686

Zapata, G. (2022). *Learning by design and second language teaching: Theory, research, and practice*. Taylor and Francis., DOI: 10.4324/9781003106258

Zhai, X. (2023). ChatGPT for next generation science learning. XRDS: *Crossroads. The ACM Magazine for Students, 29*(3), 42–46. DOI: 10.1145/3589649

Zhang, C., Meng, Y., & Ma, X. (2024). Artificial intelligence in EFL speaking: Impact on enjoyment, anxiety, and willingness to communicate. *System, 121*, 103259. Advance online publication. DOI: 10.1016/j.system.2024.103259

Zhang, F., Liu, X., Wu, W., & Zhu, S. (2024). Evolution of chatbots in nursing education: Narrative review. *JMIR Medical Education, 10*(1), e54987. DOI: 10.2196/54987 PMID: 38889074

Zhang, M. (2025). Optimizing academic engagement and mental health through AI: An experimental study on LLM integration in higher education. *Frontiers in Psychology*, *16*, 1641212. DOI: 10.3389/fpsyg.2025.1641212 PMID: 41104404

Zhang, X., Li, H., Yin, M., Zhang, M., Li, Z., & Chen, Z. (2025). Investigating AI chatbot dependence: Associations with Internet and smartphone dependence, mental health outcomes, and the moderating role of usage purposes. *International Journal of Human-Computer Interaction*, •••, 1–13. DOI: 10.1080/10447318.2025.2545464

Zhao, D. (2025). The impact of AI-enhanced natural language processing tools on writing proficiency: An analysis of language precision, content summarization, and creative writing facilitation. *Education and Information Technologies*, *30*(6), 8055–8086. DOI: 10.1007/s10639-024-13145-5

Zheng, C., Chen, X., Zhang, H., & Chai, C. S. (2024). Automated versus peer assessment: Effects on learners' English public speaking. *Language Learning & Technology*, *28*(2), 210–228. DOI: 10.64152/10125/73578

Zheng, H., Park, S., & Kim, J. (2024). Student perceptions of generative AI as collaborative partner in higher education. *Computers & Education: Artificial Intelligence*, *6*, 100210. DOI: 10.1016/j.caeai.2024.100210

Zhong, S., Gatti, E., Hardwick, J., Ribul, M., Cho, Y., & Obrist, M. (2025). LLM-mediated domain-specific voice agents: The case of TextileBot. *Behaviour & Information Technology*, *44*, 1–33. DOI: 10.1080/0144929X.2025.2456667

Zhou, D., & Li, Q. (2025). The role of teacher-student developmental relationships in linking communicative language teaching and communicative competence. *Frontiers in Psychology*, *16*, 1635428. DOI: 10.3389/fpsyg.2025.1635428

Zhou, R., Samad, A., & Perinpasingam, T. (2024). A systematic review of cross-cultural communicative competence in EFL teaching: Insights from China. *Humanities & Social Sciences Communications*, *11*(1), 1–11. DOI: 10.1057/s41599-024-04071-5

Zhu, W., Liu, H., Dong, Q., Xu, J., Huang, S., Kong, L., Chen, J., & Li, L. (2024). Multilingual machine translation with large language models: Empirical results and analysis (arXiv:2304.04675). /arXiv.2304.04675DOI: 10.18653/v1/2024.findings-naacl.176

Zhu, M., & Wang, C. (2025). A systematic review of AI in language education: Current status and future implications. *Language Learning & Technology*, *29*(1), 1–29. DOI: 10.64152/10125/73606

Ziegler, N., & González-Lloret, M. (Eds.). (2022). *The Routledge handbook of second language acquisition and technology*. Routledge., DOI: 10.4324/9781351117586

About the Contributors

Alexia Larchen Costuchen is a lecturer at the Universitat Politècnica de València, Spain, where she teaches English for Specific Purposes (ESP) to Computer Engineering students. Her research interests address the intersection of emerging technologies and second-language (L2) teaching with an emphasis on motivation, cognition, and creativity. During her predoctoral stage, she was an invited researcher at Malmö University and University College Dublin, where she contributed to projects on game-based learning for L2 vocabulary recall with a focus on spatial environment. Before entering academia, she taught English as L2 in multinational corporations and language schools, frequently dealing with multilingual groups and the challenges of CEFRL testing systems. She currently collaborates on topic coordination and peer-review activities with such academic publishers as Frontiers in Education, IGI Global, Taylor & Francis (Routledge), and Springer Nature.

Fahad Ahmed Otaif is an associate Professor of Linguistics with a specialization in Discourse Analysis. He is an academic researcher, writer, and creative translator of ideas who has led and devised innovative initiatives on the use of AI in linguistics and translation. He publishes and writes on topics of applied linguistics, AI technologies, discourse and translation. He is the author of: Otaif, F. A. (2023). Riwayah, a journey into literary translation, and Otaif, F. A. (2025). Last-minute Syndrome in the AI Age. His recent research is mainly focused on how generative AI, as an unprecedented technology, can be incorporated into applied linguistics. He held several positions and presented cutting-edge proposals in this regard, among them is his supervision and design of the Translation Hackathon: Translating Culture in the AI Age sponsored by the Literature, Publishing and Translation Commission at the Ministry of Culture, Saudi Arabia in October 2022. He is the Co-editor of this current volume: AI Bots in Applied Linguistics: Practice, Policy, and Creativity.

***

Mohammed H. Alaqad is a distinguished associate professor and researcher specializing in translation studies and applied linguistics, with over a decade of academic experience at MSU University, Malaysia, and Israa University, Palestine. He currently serves as an assistant professor of translation and interpreting at the Universiti Malaya. Dr. Alaqad has been an invited speaker and presenter at over 40 international conferences and events. He has published numerous scientific papers and book chapters globally and has authored several articles and a book chapter on Palestinians in the diaspora. Additionally, he serves on the editorial boards of the Cambridge Scholars of Language & Linguistics in the UK and the International Journal of Applied Linguistics and Translation (IJALT) in the USA. He is the founder and CEO of the Asian Federation of Translators and Interpreters, Malaysia. His research interests include AI applications, applied linguistics, education technology, and translation.

Hani Alhasani is a scholar and researcher with expertise in educational technology and linguistics. He is currently a lecturer at the International University of Kuwait (IUK). He graduated from Universiti Sains Malaysia (USM) in 2018 with a PhD in E-learning and Applied Linguistics. His areas of interest in research are improving student engagement in ESL contexts, computer-assisted language learning (CALL), and flipped learning.

Hana Al-Hudaithy is an Assistant Professor and academic leader specializing in Applied Linguistics. Her research focuses on Applied linguistics, technology-enhanced language learning and discourse analysis. With a Ph.D. from the University of the West of England-Bristol, UK, she has extensive experience in curriculum development, accreditation, and administrative leadership at King Khalid University. She is an ISO-certified lead auditor and a recipient of the Saudi Cultural Attaché's Award.

Abdulaziz Alshahrani is an assistant professor of Applied linguistics at the Department of English, Najran University, Saudi Arabia. He has published several articles in international journals such as Australian Journal of Applied Linguistics, Assessing Writing, and Teaching English withTechnology. His research interests includes L2 writing, corrective feedback, and CALL.

Amin Amirdabbaghian is a Senior Lecturer in Translation and Interpreting Studies at the Faculty of Languages and Linguistics, Univeriti Malaya. His main areas of research interest include socio-ideological aspects of translation, literary translation and audiovisual translation.

Banan A. Assiri is an Assistant Professor of Applied Linguistics at King Khalid University, Saudi Arabia. She holds a PhD in Language and Communication from Cardiff University. Her research explores intercultural and cross-cultural communication, corpus-assisted discourse analysis, and media communication.

Selami Aydın, a professor in the Department of English Language Teaching at Istanbul Medeniyet University, focuses on the psychological and technological dimensions of language education. His research examines affect, emotion, and technology in developing basic language skills. He teaches ELT courses in undergraduate and graduate programs, focusing on technology, psychology, research skills, and statistics.

Ricardo Casañ Pitarch is an Associate Professor in the Department of Applied Linguistics at the Universitat Politècnica de València (UPV). He holds a PhD in Applied Linguistics from Universitat Jaume I, where his doctoral thesis focused on corporate language in digital banking. His academic career is closely linked to language teaching and discourse analysis. In his teaching activity, he delivers undergraduate and master's courses related to English for Specific Purposes and second language acquisition. His research interests include professional discourse analysis, technology-based language learning, and telecollaboration in higher education contexts. Within this field, he places particular emphasis on the use of serious video games and gamification strategies as tools for language learning and the development of communicative competence. He is a member of the GALE (Group for the Analysis of Languages for Specific Purposes) and DL2 (Digital Language Learning) research groups.

Gaus Chowdhury is a lecturer in the English Language Centre at King Khalid University, Saudi Arabia. He received his B.A. and M.A. in English (Language & Literature) from Khulna University, Bangladesh. He also did a CELTA in the UAE. His research interests include CALL, CLIL, and Mobile Platform-based Language Teaching. Email: chowdhury@kku.edu.sa

Eduardo España Palop is a Professor in the field of Language and Literature Didactics at the Universitat de València. He holds a degree in Hispanic Philology and a PhD in Spanish Language. His main research focuses on the use of writing and speaking from a multimodal perspective within contemporary digital contexts. This interest in multimodality has led him to further develop his work in the areas of digital competence and critical thinking, particularly given that the digital environment is a primary space of disinformation. His engagement with digital media and literacy is reflected both in his publications, where he explores critical thinking through multimodal projects, and in his participation in research groups.

He is a member of the Multimodal and Multiliteracies Education Research Group through literature, art, foreign languages and learning technologies (Lit(T)erart) at the Universitat de València, as well as the Literary Geographies research group (GEOLIT), also at the Universitat de València.

Raúl Gisbert Cantó is an associate lecturer at the University of Valencia, with a PhD in Languages, Literatures and Cultures (UV) and a degree in English Philology. He also has a master's degree in Profesor en Educación Secundaria and a master's degree in Traducción Creativa y Humanística. For the past few years, he has been a collaborator in the cinematographical journal L'Atalante. Revista de estudios cinematográficos and in the Faculty of Medicine as a teacher of conversational English for professors and a translator of medical texts. He is also a member of the research groups CiTrans (UV) and INCOGNITO (UA). His research is focused on linguistic, translational and cultural analysis of comics, cinema and video games, as well as translation and terminology of educational, medical and scientific texts.

Héctor Hernández Gassó holds a PhD from the Universitat de València (UV), and he is an Associate Professor at the Department of Didactics (Language and Literature) at the Faculty of Teacher Training at the same university. His academic work is situated within the field of Digital Humanities. With over a decade of experience participating in national research projects, he is currently focused on Digital Competence for Teachers. He is a member of the ICT academic itinerary team within the Degree in Primary School Education, where he contributes both to the design of Teaching Guides and to teaching activities. His research interests include the development and implementation of ICT in the classroom, as well as students' digital literacy processes. He also serves as co-director and lecturer in the postgraduate course "Digital Competence for Teachers" at the Universitat de València. In addition, he has been involved in several European projects. He was a member of the Erasmus+ project "Developing ICT in Teacher Education" (2017-1-NO01-KA203-034194), and he is currently participating in the Erasmus+ project "Enhancing students´ and teachers' abilities to facilitate learners' digital competence" (2025-1-NO01-KA220-HED-000359652), both funded by the European Union.

Alexia Larchen Costuchen is a lecturer at the Universitat Politècnica de València, Spain, where she teaches English for Specific Purposes (ESP) to Computer Engineering students. Her research interests address the intersection of emerging technologies and second-language (L2) teaching with an emphasis on motivation, cognition, and creativity. During her predoctoral stage, she was an invited researcher at Malmö University and University College Dublin, where she contributed to projects on game-based learning for L2 vocabulary recall with a focus on spatial environment. Before entering academia, she taught English as L2 in multinational corporations and language schools, frequently dealing with multilingual groups and the challenges of CEFRL testing systems. She currently collaborates on topic coordination and peer-review activities with such academic publishers as Frontiers in Education, IGI Global, Taylor & Francis (Routledge), and Springer Nature.

Lola Lopez-Navas is a lecturer and researcher in English language teaching, bilingual education and CLIL in higher education, as well as in teacher training pedagogical innovations such as multiliteracies and multimodality. She holds a degree in English Philology from the Universitat de València, an MA in Applied Linguistics from the University of Sheffield, an MA in Language Testing from Lancaster University, and a PhD in English Linguistics from the Universitat Politècnica de València. She has extensive teaching experience in Spanish universities. From 2010 to 2020, she worked as a lecturer at Universidad Católica de Valencia, where she taught English language and its didactics in Early Years and Primary Education degrees, advanced English grammar and writing, oral expression and Anglo-Saxon cultures, English for non-specialists, and foreign language didactics. She later joined Universidad Internacional de Valencia, where she served as Programme Director of the Master's in Bilingual Education until June 2025, and taught modules on innovation and research in bilingual education, English didactics for secondary and upper secondary education, and planning and assessment in Spanish as a Foreign Language. Since June 2025, she holds a lecturer position at Universidad Rey Juan Carlos, where she teaches English Language and English for Tourism. Her research focuses on bilingual and plurilingual education, CLIL, multiliteracies/pluriliteracies, democratic competence, and intercultural dialogue in educational settings. Her recent work examines how dialogic pedagogies and multimodal projects foster interculturality and key competences for a plural and sustainable society, particularly in higher education and language teacher education.

Mohd Nazim earned his Ph.D. in English (Literary Stylistics) from Aligarh Muslim University, India in 2008. His master's degree in English Language Teaching, also from AMU, in 2002, and a postgraduate diploma in Linguistics enriched his academic qualifications further. He has been teaching a variety of English linguistics and literature courses for more than 15 years. He is currently an Associate Professor in the Department of English at Najran University, Saudi Arabia. His research interests include (but are not limited to) developing LSRW through technology and AI, assessment literacy, teacher training, teacher professional develoment and ethical interpretation of literature. He has rich experience in journal editorial services and currently sits on the editorial board of the English Language

Teaching journal, published by the Canadian Center of Science and Education. He can be contacted at email: nazimspeaking@yahoo.co.in.

Oksana Polyakova holds BA in Translation Studies, MA and Doctorate degree (cum laude) in Applied Linguistics. She now works as associate professor at the Applied Linguistics Department of the Universitat Politècnica de València (UPV). She is a lab Group of Analysis of Languages of Specialty (GALE) member. Her current research explores Higher Education, sustainability, applied linguistics, second language acquisition, virtual collaborations, AI and active learning methodologies. As the coordinator of the iPLUS educational innovation team, she leads various UPV didactic projects focused on transversal competences and the Sustainable Development Goals of the 2030 Agenda. Through her involvement in the ENHANCE Alliance EU Project, she supports the development of innovative learning pathways and staff training methodologies.

Agustín Reyes-Torres is an Associate Professor in the Department of Languages and Literature Education at the Universitat de València, Spain. He holds an M.A. in Comparative Literature from the University of Iowa and a Ph.D. in English Philology from the Universitat de València. He has lectured an extensive range of courses and conducted research fellowships at the University of Virginia, Boston College, Middlebury Language Schools and Columbia University. His current lines of research focus on the development of multiliteracies in the teaching of additional languages and teacher education. His publications include a significant number of journal articles on postcolonial studies, multicultural literature and the use of multimodal resources in the language classroom. He's the coeditor of Multiliteracies, Multimodality and Learning by Design in Second Language Learning and Teacher Education (Routledge, 2025). Since 2019, he directs the research group Lit(T)erart.

Katia Ruiz-Saiz holds a Bachelor's Degree in Primary Education with a specialization in English Language Teaching from the University of Valencia. She is currently pursuing her MA in Specific Didactics and working as a research assistant in the Department of Language and Literature Education at the same institution, where she contributed to the development of a multimodal corpus focused on the use of AI. Her research examines the pedagogical applications of multimodal resources and multiliteracies frameworks in English as an Additional Language teaching, with emphasis on primary education contexts and technology-mediated learning.

Paula Villalba Pérez is a Lecturer at the University of Jaume I (Castellón) and a PhD candidate at the University of Valencia, where she is writing her thesis. As part of her doctoral research, she completed a research stay at the University of Bristol. She also holds an MSc in Education (Teaching & Learning) from the

University of Bristol, where she focused her dissertation on the user-centred design of an app to support Spanish speaking skills in secondary language classrooms. In addition, she holds a PGCE in Modern Languages Teaching from the University of St Mark and St John (Plymouth). Her academic background includes a BA in English Studies from the University of Valencia, with an Erasmus year at Cardiff University. She is currently working as a Substitute Professor at the University of Jaume I (Castellon) and has previous experience working as an English Teacher at the Escuela Oficial de Idiomas, as a Lecturer at the Universitat de València and as a Spanish teacher at Bristol Grammar School and Broadlands Academy. Her research interests include British contemporary poetry, poetic reception, language education, and digital learning tools.

AbdullahYıldız completed his PhD at the University of Sheffield and is a lecturer in the Department of Foreign Language Education at Istanbul Medeniyet University, Turkiye. He teaches across undergraduate and postgraduate programs and supervises postgraduate research. His research interests focus on language teaching materials, TESOL materials development, corpus linguistics, and discourse analysis.

Index

A

C

D

E

F

G

H

I

L

M

N

P

R

S

T

W

www.ingramcontent.com/pod-product-compliance
Lightning Source LLC
LaVergne TN
LVHW080910300926
849162LV00003B/626